Energy Law in Argentina

Energy Law in Argentina

Third Edition

Pablo Ferrara
María Angela Rascovsky

This book was originally published as a monograph in the International Encyclopaedia of Laws/Energy Law.

Founding Editor: Roger Blanpain
General Editor: Frank Hendrickx
Volume Editors: Kurt Deketelaere & Bram Delvaux

Wolters Kluwer

Published by:
Kluwer Law International B.V.
PO Box 316
2400 AH Alphen aan den Rijn
The Netherlands
E-mail: international-sales@wolterskluwer.com
Website: lrus.wolterskluwer.com

Sold and distributed by:
Wolters Kluwer Legal & Regulatory U.S.
7201 McKinney Circle
Frederick, MD 21704
United States of America
Email: customer.service@wolterskluwer.com

ISBN 978-94-035-2710-9

e-Book: ISBN 978-94-035-2711-6
web-PDF: ISBN 978-94-035-2712-3

To the memory of my beloved father Alberto M. Ferrara (1943–2018)

The Authors

Pablo Ferrara was born in Buenos Aires, Argentina, in 1979. He is an arbitrator at the Permanent Court of Arbitration (UNCLOS Annex VII), a professor at the University of Petroleum and Energy (UPES) and at Universidad del Salvador (USAL), and co-director at the Institute IDEAS para una Nueva Argentina. He works as a consultant both in government and private sectors. He was Rajawali Fellow at the Ash Center for Democratic Governance and Innovation (Harvard Kennedy School of Government). He was an energy consultant at the Argentine Ministry of Energy and Mining as well as the Honourable Chamber of National Deputies (HCDN). He was also Chair of the International Bar Association Public Law Committee, and a board member at the Argentine Institute of Energy 'General Mosconi'. Previously, he was an assistant professor at the South China Sea Institute, Xiamen University (Xiamen, People's Republic of China), He was a post-doctoral researcher at the Groningen Centre of Energy Law (Groningen, The Netherlands) and a visiting fellow at the Max Planck Institute for Comparative Public Law and Public International Law (Heidelberg, Germany). He obtained his LLB at the University of Buenos Aires (Buenos Aires, Argentina), and his doctorate at the University of California at Berkeley (Berkeley, California). He worked as an associate in energy law (Brons & Salas; Baker & McKenzie) and in International Center for the Settlement of Investment Disputes arbitration (M&M Bomchil). He is recognized as a Jurist focused on public law, energy law, and dispute settlement.

María Angela Rascovsky has an LLB in English Legal Translation from the Universidad del Salvador, Argentina. She has been a professor of English and translator since 1992.

The Authors

Table of Contents

List of Abbreviations

AIPN	Association of International Petroleum Negotiators
ARN	Nuclear Regulation Authority (Autoridad Regulatoria Nacional)
BID	Inter-American Development Bank
BOO	Built, Own, Operate
BOOT	Built, Own, Operate, Transfer
BOT	Built, Operate, Transfer
CAMMESA	Compañía Administradora del Mercado Mayorista Eléctrico Sociedad Anónima (WEM Administration Corporation)
CDU	Crude Distillation Unit
CENCH	Concession of Non-conventional Hydrocarbons
CIF	Cost Insurance and Freight Sale
CNEA	National Atomic Energy Commission
COCO	Company Owned-Dealer Operated
CODO	Company Owned-Dealer Operated
CS	Continental Shelf
DBFO	Design, Build, Finance, Operate
DODO	Dealer Owned-Dealer Operated
EEFC	Electrical Energy Federal Council
EEZ	Exclusive Economic Zone
ENARGAS	National Gas Regulatory Agency
ENARSA	Energía Argentina Sociedad Anónima
ENRA	National Atomic Regulation Agency
ENRE	National Power Regulatory Agency
FOB	Free on Board Sale
FONINVEMEM	Fund for the Necessary Investments
GDP	Gross Development Product
ICSID	International Centre for the Settlement of Investment Disputes
IEA	International Energy Agency

List of Abbreviations

IMO	International Maritime Organization
IS / ISA	Interconnection System (SADI)
ISA	Interconnection System Argentina
JOA	Joint Operating Agreement
MARPOL	Convention Against Pollution
MERCOSUR	Mercado Común del Sur
NHR	National Hydroelectric Regime
NOCs	National Oil Companies
PAE	Pan American Energy
RenovAr	Programa de Energias Renovables Argentinas
UNCLOS	United Nations Convention for the Law of the Sea
VAT	Value Added Tax
WEM	Wholesale Electric Market
YPF	Yacimientos Petroliferos Fiscales Sociedad Anonima

Preface to the First Edition

The present work was born as a proposal oriented to the elaboration of an integral approach to the regulation of energy in Argentina.

Indeed, up to the moment of this publication, there was no English text devoted entirely to energy regulation in Argentina. In this sense, the present work was born to cover a vitally important space and promote the understanding of the functioning of one of the foundational and core axes of the functional structure of the South American State.

This proposal evokes most of the regulatory sectors related to energy activity, including some issues that are little or not developed academically at the local level.

The first part analyses the role of energy in contemporary society as a basic pillar of its functioning, starting from being the engine and, at the same time, the object of public policy, regulation and economy.

The second part is an elaboration of the power value chain: it begins with describing the ordering and operation of the Wholesale Electricity Market, continued by detailing the regulations and jurisprudence related to the sources of electric generation, to transport and to distribution regime.

The third part addresses meticulous shredding of the regulatory norms of conventional and unconventional hydrocarbons, including examples of daily practice and carrying out a comparative scheme by type of fuel and geographical basin in the Argentine Republic.

The fourth part refers to the new regulatory role of the State after the privatization process of the 1990s, also positioning itself at the centre of the national regulators of gas and power.

The fifth part unveils a detailed analysis of the energy tax regime.

The sixth part concludes with a review of energy financing and risk assessment.

In the future

Fortunately, this work is just a beginning. There are, undoubtedly, issues to be addressed – whether due to imprudence, disagreement, or lack of need. In any case, there is a commitment to correct any lack of this in the not too distant future.

Arlington, 10 December 2017.

General Introduction

§1. General Background: Energy and Economic-Social Development

1. We must take off from the basics: without development there will be no economic growth or social inclusion. Without a supply of safe, reliable and competitively priced energy, it will be impossible to have a competitive industry and, therefore, the creation of jobs to incorporate the population into the productive process that is now outside the formal system and does not have paid employment. In an adequate way to guarantee the social ascent and the egalitarian society to which we legitimately aspire.

2. In general terms, it is accepted that there is a positive correlation between economic growth and energy demand. Economic and social development requires ensuring a reliable energy supply; of quality and competitive. A well-managed energy sector that uses the country's significant energy resources, adds value to them and produces energy efficiently and at competitive prices will act as a catalyst for the economy, produce quality jobs and raise the level of energy. The professionals of the sector. On the contrary, a country without a quality energy supply or with an unresolved energy problem is an unreliable country with no productive future to achieve development.

§2. The Background by 2015

3. The Argentine energy sector in 2015 was in a critical situation as a result of a set of decisions adopted in previous decades, which, although warned in advance, were not corrected with criteria of reasonableness and rationality. In this context, we can affirm the following:

(a) Oil production has been decreasing year after year for seventeen years.
(b) The production of natural gas has been uninterrupted for eleven years.
(c) Proven reserves of oil are equal in magnitude to those that the country had in 1970 despite the great growth of population and Gross Development Product (GDP) for forty-five years.
(d) Natural gas reserves are now half of what the country had at the beginning of the democratic era in 1983. This process of loss of reserves was accentuated from 2003 onwards at an alarming rate.

(e) The production of electric energy is increasingly dependent on thermoelectric energy generated by fossil fuels at the expense of hydroelectric energy and other forms of renewable energy production.
(f) There is no long-term Strategic Energy Planning. The capital-intensive energy sector is trapped in the short-term.
(g) Users do not pay for the energy consumed by prices that compensate for the costs of their value chain.
(h) An onerous and unjust system of energy subsidies has been set up with budgetary resources financed by monetary emission.
(i) The country has lost self-sufficiency in energy and has become a strong importer of energy; and, as a result, this sector has become a great demand for foreign currency. From 2010 to date, 50,000 million dollars were spent on energy imports.
(j) The private sector has paralyzed the realization of genuine investments due to lack of credibility in the policies applied. The State decides high-cost investments with irrational methods.
(j) The legislation and applicable regulations are obsolete and are not adapted to the needs of Argentina.
(k) Institutionality is deficient. The regulatory bodies of the sector are intervened and degraded in their technical professionalism. The nation-producer provinces relationship is exposed to discretional intervention and political discrimination, with imprecise roles not delimited by the new oil law. Technical entities such as Compañía Administradora del Mercado Mayorista Eléctrico Sociedad Anónima (CAMMESA) have been politicized and companies such as Energía Argentina Sociedad Anónima (ENARSA) have been created whose exclusionary role has been the parasitic intermediation in purchasing processes without adequate transparency and control. Since the urgency and the asymmetry, agreements have been signed with countries such as China and Russia that, in exchange for export credits, commit millions in investments for energy infrastructure works without the proper processes of certification and competition.

§3. A Possible Role of Government Institutions in the Shaping and Administration of Energy Law and Policy

4. One way to understand public energy policy is to consider it as the set of legal systems through which a State promotes the achievement of a summation of individual objectives, which make up – at the same time – a general plan or a State plan. Of the total of legal systems, they constitute the centre of the direction of the energy policy: the production of hydrocarbons, the distribution of gas, electricity, foreign trade, economic competition, public spending and the patrimonial regime.

5. In this way, there are three aspects that define the strategy of a public energy policy: the predominance of certain regulations, such as prohibitions or incentives, the objectives of the law and the sustenance of each one of them.

6. We can point out the following spotlights of attention:

- Natural resources: Argentine resources are large and sufficient to achieve a competitive energy development and overcome the current difficulties that show us as a weak country and highly dependent on third parties. Our strengths are: the existence of non-conventional extraction resources, in particular shale gas, shale oil and tight gas; the existence of extensive sedimentary basins –continental and marine – that have not yet been explored with wide favourability for the existence of hydrocarbons; the existence of an important inventory of water resources not yet used; the wide favourability of our territory for the economic use of wind and solar energy.
- Human, institutional and technological resources: Argentina has relevant historical capacities in energy matters: it is a regional leader in the use of nuclear power; It has the most important transportation and distribution infrastructure of natural gas in the region; has the experience and knowledge to carry out large hydroelectric projects with the highest integration of the national industry; It has a pioneer oil industry in Latin America with a level of activity in the number of drilling per year that is among the most important in the world.
- Energy matrix: it is strongly dependent on hydrocarbons. In 2013, out of a total of 81 million equivalent tons of oil used in the year; natural gas represents 52.8%; 32.9% oil; and the rest of 14.3% is covered by renewable sources 9.2%, nuclear energy 2.3% and coal 1.5%.

7. On this point it is important to emphasize that from 2003 onwards the country has made a notable involution regarding the type of energy matrix. In this twelve-year period, the electric sector experienced a development that accentuates Argentina's dependence on hydrocarbons: while electricity generation increased by 60%, the fuel it used increased by 180%.

The Federal Energy Agreement

8. President Mauricio Macri headed the signing of the Federal Energy Agreement in April 2017, which commits the Nation and the provinces to generate State policies that guarantee a secure and full supply of energy for all Argentines. The Head of State argued that, based on this consensus, Argentina will be in a position to 'restore the balance we had lost' in energy matters in order to 'project the country's growth in terms of the long-term'.

9. The president delivered a message after the signing of the agreement with the provinces, through which the parties commit themselves to coordinate and implement policies to consolidate a reliable, inclusive, competitive and environmentally sustainable energy sector. Macri was accompanied on occasion by the Chief of Staff, Marcos Peña and the Minister of Energy and Mining, Juan José Aranguren. The governors of Chaco, Domingo Peppo, participated in the ceremony; of Chubut, Mario Das Neves; from Entre Ríos, Gustavo Bordet; from Jujuy, Gerardo Morales; from Neuquén, Omar Gutiérrez; from Río Negro, Alberto Weretilneck; from San Juan, Sergio Uñac; of Santa Fe, Miguel Lifschitz and Tierra del Fuego, Roxana Bertone.

10. The agreement signed establishes the basis for implementing a Strategic Energy Plan and creates a Federal Energy Council that will function as a consultative body with the participation of the Nation, the provinces and the Energy Commissions of the Congress.

11. Meanwhile, Minister Aranguren said that 'the energy policy of our country requires a broad debate and basic consensus for its development and implementation as a true State policy that transcends the different administrations'.

12. The agreement consists of ten fundamental clauses, among which stand out those that aim to diversify the energy matrix through increasing the share of clean and renewable energies, the development and use of biofuels and nuclear energy, together with their associated technologies, and the social rate. A Strategic Energy Plan will be launched with the participation of the Council and areas of consultation with other actors in the activity, within which the criteria of efficiency, diversification, regional integration, sustainable development and energy security will be included. In order for the country to achieve self-sufficiency, the government declared the electric emergency a year ago and began a process of tariff and investment adequacy to normalize the situation. The commitment signed includes the creation of the Federal Energy Council as an advisory body, which will have the necessary powers to present proposals for the development of the sector. It will be chaired by the Ministry of Energy and integrated by a representative of each province and authorities of the Energy Commissions of the Congress. The tasks of coordination in charge include the harmonization of regulatory and tariff criteria, the definition of quality levels for services and the exchange of information to improve the operation of the system. Another of the clauses refers to climate change, in which framework measures will be promoted so that the activity considers the care of the environment in line with Argentina's international commitment to the Paris COP 21 Agreement. As regards hydrocarbons, the government will coordinate and promote the national policy on exploration and exploitation, in coordination with the provinces. In addition, it will seek to generate legal security for investments through open, transparent and competitive bids and a policy of predictable and stable rates and prices will be developed to ensure quality in the provision of the service. It emphasizes that a social rate will be maintained for the most vulnerable sectors and that prices must compensate the economic costs of goods and services. Energy saving and efficiency programmes and policies will also be carried out, while promoting the use of technologies and good practices that promote savings in consumption in homes, businesses, industries and transport. The remaining clauses cover issues that have to do with roles and organization; the Federal Energy Council; the regulatory bodies and State companies; and the tax aspects.

§4. THE SOURCES OF ENERGY IN ARGENTINA BEFORE 2016

13. The Argentine energy sources are the following (Figure 1).

Figure 1 Argentine Energy Sources

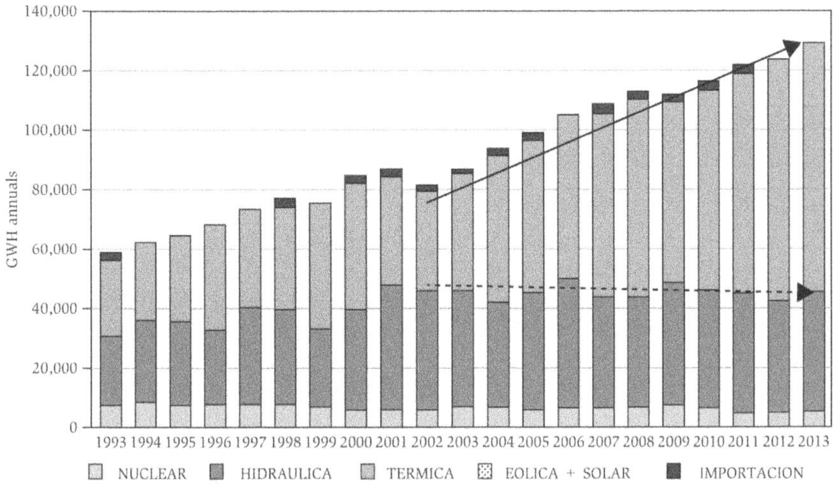

14. Now, regarding status and management of energy in Argentina, it is possible to make the following assertions:

- Management of hydrocarbon reserves. It is a true and proven fact that our country has dropped alarmingly its inventory of proven reserves of natural gas and oil. As a consequence, we operate increasingly older and lower yielding deposits. It is also the logical cause of the persistent fall of the national production of hydrocarbons that has precipitated us in the growing and uncontrolled importation (Figure 2).

Figure 2 Oil & Gas Reserves in Argentina

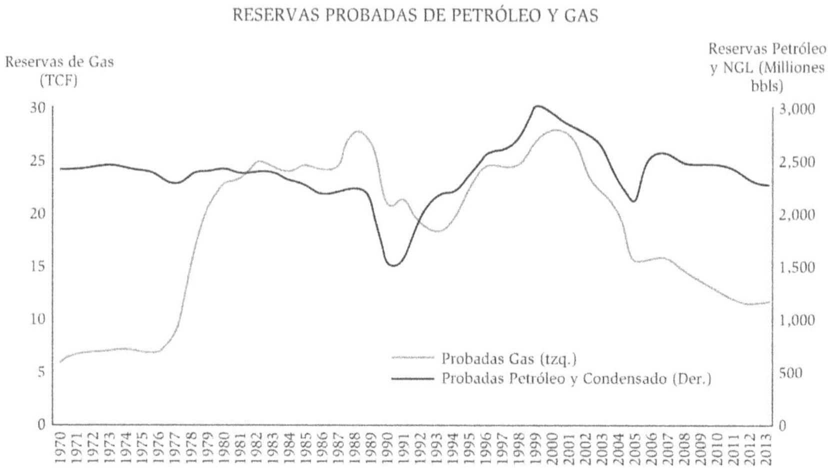

- Production of conventional oil: the total oil production of Argentina continues to decline. The declining trend has been maintained for the past seventeen years, and this is characteristic of mature basins and ancient sites that are not replaced by new discoveries. There is consensus among experts that these deposits will continue to decline production.
- Non-conventional hydrocarbons – Vaca Muerta: although they represent an opportunity for Argentina; there is consensus among experts that unconventional deposits will be a source of wealth in the medium and long term. At present, the production of unconventional hydrocarbons reaches 3% of the total production and the effective materialization of that opportunity requires large investments; of oil prices that make such investments competitive; of competitive costs in the local industry, and of a dynamic and enthusiastic investment climate today absent in our country.
- Productivity: it has been confirmed and there is a sectoral consensus on the loss of productivity in oil production in Argentina, which includes lower production per well; higher cost of drilling; greater use of drilling equipment, all of which results in higher production costs.
- Regionalization: the relative decline of our country can be clearly expressed in any comparison made at a regional or an international level; the decade lost in energy can be summarized by comparison with that of Brazil, our main MERCOSUR partner.
- Imbalances: consequences of the last decade provoke strong macroeconomic problems and disturb the entire national economy.
- Energy imports reached USD 11 billion in 2014, and this is a drain on foreign currency that complicates the entire functioning of our external sector. It is inadmissible in a country with the endowment of potential resources of Argentina.

– Subsidies: they have reached an unprecedented figure close to USD 15,000 million in 2014; they have grown exponentially in the last ten years. Its existence conspires against the functioning of the economy as a whole and against the energy economy in particular.

As the offer is subsidized, 95% of the subsidies are received by companies that improve their profits and whose income would allow them to pay the true costs of energy. Less than 5% of the total mass of subsidies is perceived by poor social sectors or extreme poverty. In turn, the mass of subsidies favours the inhabitants of the metropolitan area (AMBA) more than those of the interior of the country:

– Rates: the tariffs of the public services of electricity are facing the longest delay (2001–2015) of the last fifty years; and also the deepest with respect to the fall in real terms (73%) of the last fifty years. A relevant fact is that 80% of all electricity sales pay with their tariffs just 22% of the costs of generating the energy consumed.
– Companies: the analysis of the balance sheets and results tables of the companies supplying natural gas and electricity public services indicate asset losses and strong operating losses; and this clearly exposes an incorrect tariff policy applied in a systemic way during the last decade.
– Rationalization: In the last twelve years, the incorporation of electrical generation equipment has corresponded in 73% to thermoelectric plants whose operation is based on the intensive consumption of hydrocarbons. A large part of the power incorporations of that period consisted of high-cost machines designed to alleviate emergencies. In contrast, the incorporation of renewable energies was practically insignificant.
– Planning: sectoral policy decisions always obeyed criteria and short-term urgencies. It has also been evident that in this period decisions have been taken to promote works without the full technical, economic and environmental feasibility studies required.

§5. The Energy Balance in Argentina Between 2016 and 2019

15. The Argentine energy policy followed a radically liberal twist during Mauricio Macri's administration. First, Macri didn't follow the Federal Energy Agreement he had signed. Second, though he appointed consecutive energy ministers and secretaries, energy policy was directed from the Presidency until Gustavo Lopetegui assumed office in the late 2018.

16. Broadly, Macri's energy policy followed these milestones:[1]

– power and gas tariff's dollarization;

1. *See* http://www.energia.gob.ar/contenidos/archivos/Reorganizacion/sintesis_balance/2019-11-20_SE_Sintesis_balance_de_gestion_energia_2016-2019_dist.pdf.

- oil barrel income securitization with the 'barril criollo' policy;[2]
- offshore oil negotiation development;
- 'Vaca Muerta' negotiation development;
- renewables promotion based on weak project financial basis.

17. Regarding oil and gas production, conventional sources continued to decline, compensated by new non-conventional sources (Figures 3 and 4).[3]

Figure 3 Non-conventional Oil Production in Argentina

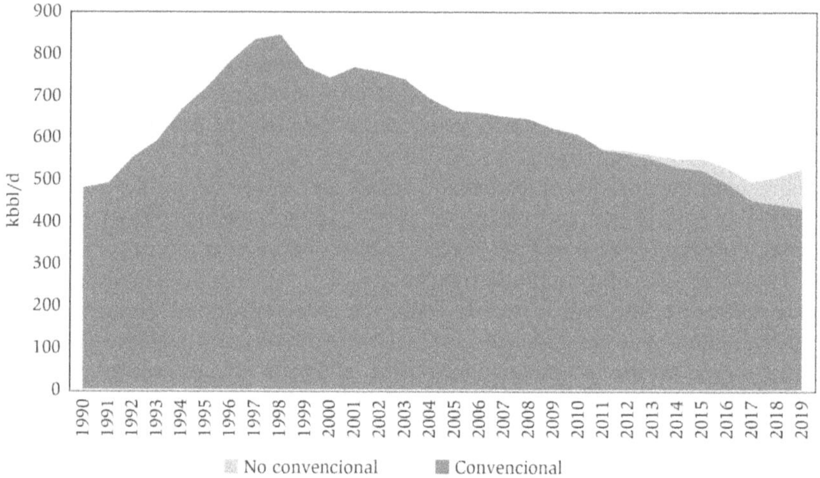

Fuente: Dirección Nacional de Información Energética -SSPE - Secretaría de Gobierno de Energía.

2. This policy set a minimum price that was higher than the international commodity value.
3. *See* '*Balance de gestion en energía 2016 2019*', available at http://www.energia.gob.ar/contenidos/archivos/Reorganizacion/sintesis_balance/2019-12-09_Balance_de_Gestion_en_Energia_2016-2019_final_y_anexo_pub_.pdf.

Figure 4 Non-conventional Gas Production in Argentina

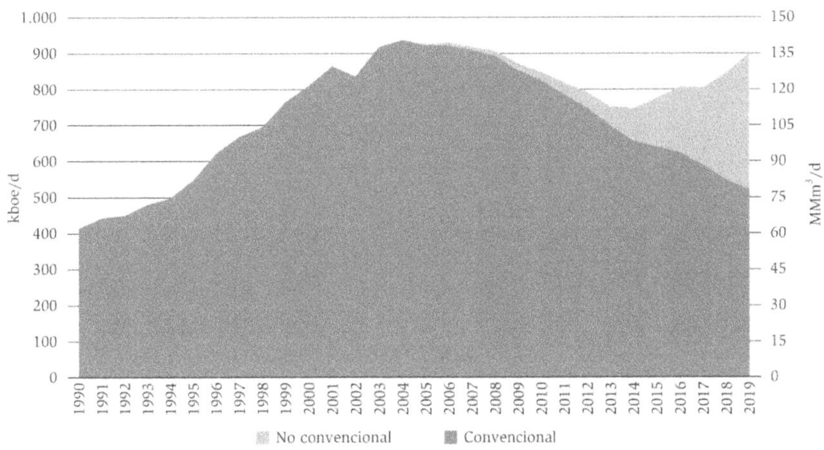

Fuente: Dirección Nacional de Información Energética – SSPE- Secretaría de Gobierno de Energía.

18. Installed power increased between 2015 and 2019 (Figure 5). The graph shows the passage of an energy park with 32.8 GW of installed power in December 2015 to a park that is expected to close the year 2019 with 41.9 GW. Thanks to the incorporation of thermal power in the framework of the emergency as well as thanks to the improvement of the availability of the equipment, the maximum power demands of the years 2017, 2018 and 2019 were supplied, without major inconveniences, with reserves that remain in line with international standards linked to the reliability of the system. The increase in the installed capacity of the thermal park was approximately 5.4 GW, while the year 2019 was expected to end with an increase in the installed capacity of renewable energy in addition to large hydroelectricity of the order of 3.7 GW (Figure 6).

19. As a consequence of this accelerated incorporation of renewable generation, while in December 2015, electricity demand was covered in just 2.3% for renewables, this coverage was expected to exceed in December 2019 by 10%. This increase was a consequence of the successful rounds of the Programa de Energias Renovables Argentinas (RenovAr) programme and the new renewables market *'MaTer'*, in whose frames there are currently 156 projects in commercial operation or delivering energy to the grid for a total of 5,012 MW and an estimated investment at 7,521 MMUSD. Likewise, in 2019 another 44 projects were awarded in the framework of the MiniRen (RenovAr 3), for a total power of 274 MW, of which 25 supply contracts for 157 MW of installed power have already been signed. Of these projects, 62 were already in commercial operation by December 2019 and 94 under construction, contributing and to contribute 1,799 MW and 3,213 MW, respectively.

Figure 5 Installed Power 2015–2019

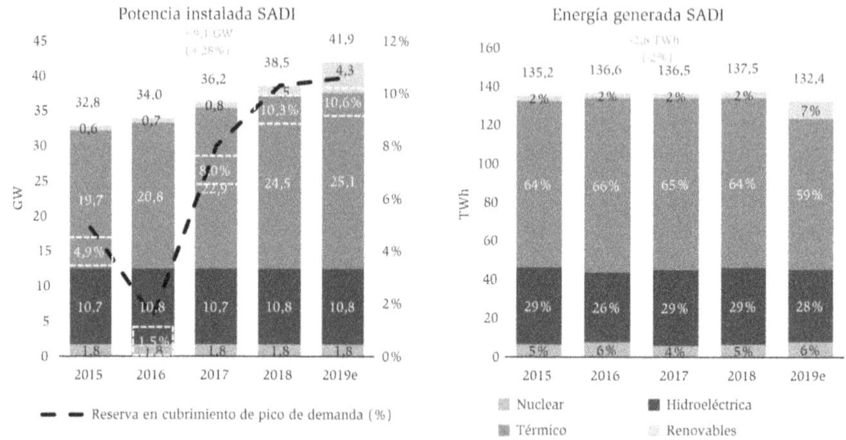

Fuente: Dirección Nacional de Escenarios y Planeamiento Energético — SSPE — Secretaría de Gobierno de Energía sobre la base de datos de CAMMESA y estimaciones propias

Figure 6 Installed Renewables Power 2015–2019

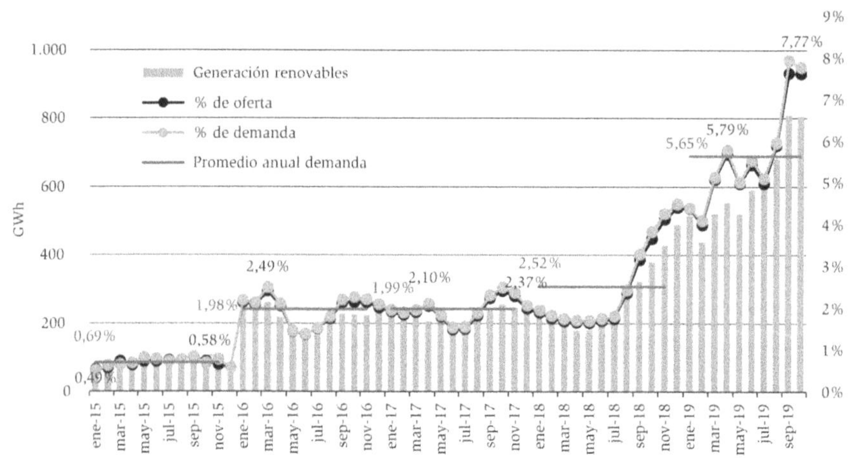

Fuente: Dirección Nacional de Escenarios y Planeamiento Ener gético — SSP E — Secretaría de Gobierno de Energía sobre la base de datos de CAMMESA.

Part I. Regulatory Framework Concerning Electricity

Chapter 1. Introduction: Precedents to Law No 24065

20. The 1960 Electric Power Act No 15336 is not only the direct precedent of the current legal power framework but also the creator of its core mindlines and its first milestone. Indeed, this law set the division between power and media usage of electricity.[4] It defined the material and commercial substance of power: 'electric energy, whatever its source and the persons of a public or private nature to which it belongs, shall be considered a legal thing susceptible of trade by the means and forms authorized by common codes and laws insofar as they do not oppose this'.[5] Also, it stated its liaison avec le droit administrative (Continental Law), defining the 'public service' and 'general interest' substance of power distribution and transportation.[6]

The second power milestone is Law No 23696: 'This law puts into practice the state's emergency police power, in order to overcome the situation of collective danger created by the serious economic and social circumstances that the Nation suffers.'[7] Pursuant to this norm, transitional regulation Decree No 634/1991 of 12 April 1990, materialized the reconversion of the power industry and public service sector through a transitional period (1991–1993).

§1. WEM: Original Conception & Structure

21. Decree No 634/1991 also set the Wholesale Electric Market (hereinafter 'WEM'). Originally, the WEM intended to create two market levels: a *supra* level composed of producers, transporters, distributors, and 'to-be-defined-by-regulation' individual users, and *a sub-distributor* level composed of distributors and final consumers (individuals). The former would work on a free-market basis, and the latter on a regulated-market basis. This mechanism was completely distorted by later administrations.[8]

4. Section 1, Law No 15336, BO 15 Sep. 1960.
5. Sections 2 and 4, Law No 15336.
6. Section 4, Law No 24065, BO 3 Jan. 1992.
7. Section 1, Law No 23697.
8. Chapter 2, Decree No 634/1991, BO 12 /04/1991.

22. Additionally, Law No 24065 – third and last power milestone – provided consumers with the capacity to build transportation lines at their own risk.

23. Law No 24065 defined WEM actors: producers, self-producers, co-producers, transport, distributors, great users, traders.[9]

§2. WEM: General Policy

24. Law No 24065 is clear about the public policy principles in relation to power:

a) Adequately protect the rights of users;
b) Promote the competitiveness of electricity production and demand markets and encourage investments to ensure long-term supply;
c) Promote the operation, reliability, equality, free access, non-discrimination and widespread use of services and installation of transportation and distribution of electricity;
d) Regulate electricity transport and distribution activities, ensuring that the rates applied to services are fair and reasonable;
e) Encourage the supply, transportation, distribution and efficient use of electricity by establishing appropriate tariff methodologies;
f) Encourage private investment in production, transportation and distribution, ensuring the competitiveness of markets where possible.

The National Electricity Regulatory Entity created in Article 54 of this law will subject its actions to the principles and provisions of this standard and must control to ensure that the activity of the electricity sector conforms to them.[10]

§3. WEM: Dispatch

25. Law No 24065 provides that the technical dispatch of the Argentine Grid or *Sistema Argentino de Interconexión (SADI)* will be in charge of a *limited corporation.*[11] This company is CAMMESA, which will be later discussed in depth.

9. Chapter 2, Decree No 634/1991.
10. Section 2, Law No 24065.
11. Chapter IX, Law No 24065.

Chapter 2. Production

§1. Preliminary Issues

26. Who is the electrical energy generator according to the National legislation?

27. To address the proposal for the study herein we will consider of importance to take into account what an electric energy generator is according to our judicial order and the characteristics of the activity of electric energy generation under the national jurisdiction.

28. We will not analyse, in the study herein, the situation or the regulatory frameworks of the provincial legislation regulating the activity of generation, as its incidence is minor especially because it is not related to a system subject to the national jurisdiction.

29. In that sense, it is important to consider the provisions under laws 24065 and 15336 that, it is worth mentioning, are in full force.

30. Section 5 of the Law No 24065 clearly establishes that: 'the generator is the one who-being the holder of a power station acquired or installed under the terms of this law, or of a concession of a service of exploitation under section 14 of the Law No 15.336, places his production partially or totally in the distribution and/or transport system subject to a national jurisdiction.'

31. Thus, it is clear from the reading of the article transcribed that a generator subject to a national jurisdiction is an individual holder or concessioner of a plant of energy production; however from the interpretation of the section, it seems that one of the most important aspects that defines the electric generator subject to a national jurisdiction is that the electric energy that is being produced should be totally or partially placed in a transport and/or distribution system subject to national jurisdiction.

32. However, it should be taken into account that the definition of electric energy generator subject to a national jurisdiction on the Law No 24065, should be completed with the one under section 6 of the Law No 15336 which defines the national jurisdiction when clearly expresses: ' … of national jurisdiction, the electric energy generation, whatever source … when: a) it is related to national defence; b) it is destined to serve the commerce of electric energy between the federal capital and one or more provinces or one province with another or with a territory of Tierra de Fuego, Antártida Argentina and islands of the South Atlantic Ocean; c) it corresponds to a place submitted to the legislation exclusive of the National Congress; d) it is about the hydroelectric or tidal power necessary to interconnect between them or with others of the same or different source, for the rational and economical utilization thereof; e) in any point of the country, they integrate the Interconnection

National Network; f) it is linked to the energy commerce of with another Nation; g) it is about electrical energy generation stations by means of the utilization or transformation of nuclear or atomic energy.'

33. As a consequence, sections 5 of the Law No 15336 and section 6 of the Law No 24065 define and precise who the electric energy generator subject to national jurisdiction is.

34. Furthermore, for the purposes of this study, it is important to elaborate on the role, from the regulatory point of view, of the electric energy generator inside the Wholesale Electric Market.

35. In that sense, item 3.1. from Annex 32 from The Procedures for the Operation Planning, Load Dispatch and the Price-Fixing ('The Procedures') expressly indicates that inside the WEM the generator's role is: 'physical, responsible for the operation of the station, auxiliary services included, which are required for the electric system operation as a whole, such as the frequency regulation and reactive control; commercial, as a seller of the spot and of the Futures Market in its production capacity of energy and power, being responsible for the payment of the debts resulting from the WEM of such commercialization, for instances the purchases made in the Spot Market to realize the hired sales in the Futures Market, transport charges and management expenses of the DA; being as well the beneficiary of the income resulting from the commercialization'.

36. Hence, the electric energy generator has a double role in the regulatory frame in the WEM: physical and commercial.

37. For the purpose of the present study, we will deal with the commercial aspects of the generation activity, mainly the way in which the generation is remunerated.

38. Another issue of importance is that, pursuant to section 4 of the Law No 15336, the purchase and sale operations of electric energy with the administrative company of the Wholesale Electric Market S.A (CAMMESA) and/or with the public service renderer of electric energy distribution[12] have to be considered as 'commercial private acts'.

39. In accordance with this provision, section 6 of the Law No 24065 seems to make emphasis on the private character of the act of purchase and sale of electric energy and the autonomy of the parties to agree upon the terms for the electric

12. Even though s. 4 of the Law No 15 336 does not make a specific reference to the public service distribution, – it is based upon a harmonic interpretation of the legal text that we say so since the other activity considered as public service and subject to concession is the electric energy transport and by application of s. 30 of the Law No 24065, the Carrier is not entitled to buy or sell energy.

energy operation when establishing that the generators can enter into contracts of supply directly with distributors and large users. Such contracts will be freely negotiated between the parties.

40. Last but not least, it is important to clarify that the generation considered as an activity of general interest[13] not as a public service, as transport and distribution of electric energy are. Even though this characterization of energy generation as of 'general interest' has no legal Precision, as it does have that of public service, that 'general interest' is evident in the strong regulation of the commercial activity due to the fact that it has a great influence on the supply for the residential and industry users.[14]

41. So, in the frame of the present study, we have defined who the electric energy generator subject to national jurisdiction is, saying that herein we will mainly concentrate on the commercial aspect of the activity of generation.

42. We have also referred to which, according to laws 15336 and 24065, are the principles ruling the activity of electric energy trade saying that the generator may freely and directly negotiate the respective supply with the distribution and large users and hence, among other things, to agree upon quantities and prices.

§2. The Context of the Electric Generation in Argentina

43. Considering the aforementioned, so as to be able to be aware of the context and to have a diagnosis of the current situation of the electric energy generation sector of the national jurisdiction, we will base the information given by the administration company of the Wholesale Electric Market ('CAMMESA') on their annual report corresponding to the year 2014.[15]

44. We seemed it was important to take as a starting point, the information of this objective point of view of, CAMMESA's, taking into consideration that in such institution participate not only agents from the electric market, that is to say generators, carriers, distributors and large users by means of the respective associations,[16] who at the same time have the majority of the capital, but also the National State who by means of the Ministry of Federal Planning, Public Investment and Services, appoints the Head of the Board of Directors and it is also the authority in the National Energy Department that passes the resolutions that influence the generation activity.

---

13. Cf. s. 1° Law No 24065 (1992).
14. Cf. Cassagne (2014) p. 78.
15. CAMMESA (2014).
16. We refer to the Association of Electric Energy Generators of Argentina (AGEERA), the Association of Electric Energy Carriers of Argentina (ATEERA), the Association of Electric Energy Distributors of Argentina (ADEERA) and, the Association of Large Users of Electric Energy of Argentina (AGUEERA). Each one of these associations has the 20% CAMMESA's social capital.

45. As follows, we will elaborate on the data arising from the referred report connected with the electric energy generation activity and based upon thereof, we will try to deeply look into what has happened in the sector lately and what to be transformed to develop its potentialities.

46. In the introduction of such report, among other things, CAMMESA indicates the following:

- The demand of energy could be supplied 'throughout the year without much difficulty'.
- 'The same as in December 2013, in January 2014, due to the high demand, the dispatch of the total park was required with a shoestring operation.'
- In relation to the new generation, it is said: 'The incoming generation during the year [in relation to 2014] was approximately of 40 MW inside of which the entrance of the wind Park Arauco with 25 MW second stage is worth mentioning.' Moreover, it is said that in the short time an entrance of a new power is expected and the entrance of '… CT Guillermo Brown with 600 MW is highlighted, the closing of the combined cycles B. López and Ensenada Barragán with additional 450 MW and the new nuclear power station Atucha II with 740 MW'.
- Regarding the prices, the report clearly states that 'The representative monomic price of the total costs of the WEM's operations, the charge of power and associated services, the surcharges due to utilization of fuels, charges for GU exceeding demand and the WEM's contracts of Supply included, reached an average of ARS 550/MWh, vis-à-vis ARS 389/MWh of the previous year.'
- After indicating the monomic price for 2014, which was for about ARS 550/MWh, it is reported that 'The annual seasonal monomic price, represented of the collection of the distributor agents was about 95, ARS 2/MWh. The same as the year before, the payments of the demanding parties did not offset the real costs, which had to be covered by the national treasure contributions.'

47. It is interesting also to analyse, the charts of 'Annual Balance Sheets of the Energy [GWh]' related to the 'Demand' and the 'Generation', on page 13 of the referred report, as from them it can be inferred that the electric energy exportation in 2014, registered the second lowest volume for a total of 6 GWh of the ones registered since CAMMESA's creation in 1992.

48. If the historical export volume have been maintained, it is possible that the generation capacity would not have been enough to meet the demand. Moreover, there is a reference to the importation of 1390 GWh, a quantity representing three times as much as the ones registered for 2012 and 2013.

49. This last piece of information, apart from the 'shoestring operation' of the generation park, it is evidencing the lack of reserves regarding power and energy self-supply in Argentina.

50. Furthermore, from the charts 'Monthly demands with/without fixed-term agreement [GWh]' and 'Monthly demands by type of WEM's agent [GWh]' added to the mentioned report, in general terms, the following important data is to be considered for the purposes of this study: (i) only 12% of the demand has a fixed-term agreement; and (ii) that distributors demand 79% of the energy and large users demand 20%.[17]

51. As it was stated at the beginning of the present study, the generation of electric energy is a link in the energy chain.

52. In Argentina, the electric energy generation strongly depends on the hydrocarbons.[18]

53. According to CAMMESA's annual report the before – cited, during 2014, 64.1% of the energy generated was of a thermal source. The 31.3% was of a hydroelectrical source, 4.1% was of a nuclear source, whereas the wind and solar energy represented only 0.5% of the total of the energy generated.

54. Moreover, it seems that the dependence of the activity of generation with fuels and thus with the hydrocarbons sector can have an influence in the mid-term, as the next power to be incorporated to the Wholesale Electric Market, according to CAMMESA's report, is especially of a thermal source.[19]

55. Thus, CAMMESA's annual report, for 2014, let us know about the current condition of the electric energy generation sector and from that it is clear that:

(1) The generation of energy, was able to meet the demand but in a 'tight' way; that is to say without having the necessary, '*expanse*' or, better said, the reserve of power needed to adequately meet the peaks of demand that could arise, in the case of an extreme weather conditions of high or low temperatures, or in the case of lack of availability in the means of transportation. On this, it is important to point out that the offer of electrical energy in 2014 included as well the importation of energy from bordering countries, without which it would have been impossible to meet the total demand of the market, considering that Argentina registered minimum levels of exportation – according to the referred report – in such period.
(2) The power incorporated to the Interconnection System Argentina (ISA)) was just 42 MW; that is to say, a very low volume considering that the total of the power installed of the Wholesale Electric Market for 2014 was 31.377 MW, as it can be seen in the chart 'Availability of Power' on page 33 of the referred

17. According to CAMMESA's annual report, large big users demand 16% of the generated energy whereas the minor large users demand 4%; the remaining 1% is demanded by the Self-generators.
18. Cf. Laithou and Eliaschev (2015) p. 373. These authors report on this matter based on the information given by CAMMESA as of 31 Oct. 2014. As we will *see* here, this situation has worsened.
19. In fact, from the 2.560 MW of power that, according to CAMMESA, will be incorporated to the WEM only about 740 MW are from the Atucha II Nuclear power station. The remaining 1.820 MW represents thermal power stations projects. Vuelta de Obligado Power Station of 560 MW, Rio Turbio Power Station of 240 MW, Brigadier López Power Station Power Station of 150 MW, Ensenada de Barragán Power Station of 300 MW and Central Guillermo Brown Power Station of 600 MW.

report. Nevertheless, the report seems to show that this issued had been sorted out saying that 'in the short-term' the incorporation of 2.560 MW of power was expected, coming from several projects, in which the National State had relevant participation (e.g., Atucha II) or in which the electric energy generators would be participating under the fund for necessary investment allowing the Increment of the offer in the Wholesale Electric Market ('FONINVEMEM').

(3) The average monomic price for 2014 was ARS 550/MWh, representing an annual increase of 41%, vis-à-vis ARS 389/MWh, the average monomic price for 2013.

56. Even though the average monomic price for 2014 was ARS 550/MWh, The monomic price 'collected' by the distributors was 95, ARS 2/MWh, representing about 17.3% of the monomic price recognized for the generators. That is to say, that the distributors and thus the end users do not pay the electric energy cost recognized by the National State:

(1) The aforementioned is not a minor issue, since the demand of the distributors represents 79% of the demand of energy. Hence, 79% of the demand of energy only pays 17.3% of the monomic price recognized by the Department of Energy for the generators.
(2) In addition to all this, only 12% of the demand has a fixed-term agreement with a generator.
(3) About 64.1% of the energy generated in 2014 was of a thermal origin, which implies a very strong relationship between the hydrocarbons and the electric energy generation sectors. Moreover, of 2560 MW of power estimated to be incorporated to the Wholesale Electric Market, 72% represents new generation plants of a thermal origin, what means a greater dependence on the hydrocarbons from the part of the generation sector. Thus, the electric energy generation and the electric sector together cannot disregard the hydrocarbons sector.

57. Thus what were the causes leading to that situation?

§3. How Were the Prices Fixed in the Wholesale Electric Market ('WEM') Before the Enactment of Law No 25561?

58. After the aforementioned, as follows there is a brief report on the way the WEM used to operate commercially and the different prices they used to operate with until the enactment of the Law No 25561, which declared the pubic emergency and the reform of the exchange regime.

59. Again, it is worth remembering section 35 of the Law No 24065 that after establishing that the technical dispatch of the system would be in charge of a partnership in which the National State would be a shareholder,[20] it stated the principles for the load dispatch setting forth that: 'The Department of Energy shall set the standards that DNDC[21] will have to comply with for its operation, which will guarantee transparency and equity in the decisions, having to take into consideration the following principles: a) To allows the execution of contracts freely agreed upon between the parties, deeming them as the generators (with the exception of those mentioned in section 1° of the Law No 23.696 and the Argentinean part of the binational entities), large users and distributors, (futures market); b) to dispatch the required demand, based on the recognition of prices of energy and power set forth under the following section, the ones the actor in the market shall commit to explicitly accept to be entitled to supply and receive electricity not freely agreed upon by the parties.'

60. Moreover, section 36 of the Law No 24065 expressly provides that: 'The Department of Energy shall pass a resolution with economic dispatch rules for the energy and power transactions contemplated in subsection b of the preceding section [with reference to the Spot Market] that will be applied by the DNDC. The referred rule will set forth that the generators receive due to the sold energy a uniform fee for all the points of delivery fixed by the DNDC, based on the economic cost of the system. For the calculation, the cost that represents the energy supplied for community should be taken into account. Moreover, it is set that the demanding parties (distributors) shall pay a uniform tariff, stabilized every ninety days, measured at the points of reception, which will include those received by the generators for the items aforementioned and the costs of transport in the points of supply and reception.'

61. From the section transcribed, it is inferred the following would gather in the WEM:

- a futures contract, with quantities, prices and conditions freely agreed upon between the seller and the buyer;
- a Spot Market, with prices fixed by schedule based upon the economic production costs, different from the Futures Market where the price is freely agreed upon between the seller and the buyer. To this market, not only does the demand have access, but also the generators to acquire the missing parts that can be necessary for the compliance of the future market contracts;

  The electric energy demand and the cost thereof varied according to the time of the year, the climate conditions, days of the week and time of the day.[22]

---

20. That role being in the end developed by CAMMESA, created by Decree 1192/92.
21. With reference to the National Load Dispatch exercised by CAMMESA.
22. 'All these variables are easy to explain: in winter, the days are shorter, and so there is more demand of artificial, electric heating, etc.; in contrast, in summer there is less demand of light requirements, but the consumption of air conditioners and refrigerators increases in general. On the other hand, the demand is not the same on working days and on weekends, and in the 24 hours of the day the requirements are different, that is why there exist peak hours, valley hours and remaining hours. In

In turn, they influence in the offer of the prices, and the availability of fuels used by the generators to produce energy and the availability of the machines generators to produce energy every hour.

'Regarding, price-fixing in the Spot Market, the marginal cost of the system correspond to the least efficient machines [or the most expensive] in operation, at a certain time',[23] making it clear that CAMMESA, knowing about the situation of the demand and the availability of offer, have to dispatch the machines, being able to meet that demand are the most economical ones, and being the price of the Spot Market of every time, that of the cost declared by the most expensive machine dispatched at that time.

– a market of prices stabilized every three-month periods of the prices established for the Spot Market. These stabilized prices have to be calculated by CAMMESA, based upon the arising projections, among others, the information supplied by the very same agents.[24] Those calculations drafted by CAMMESA have to be then approved by the Department of Energy and are destined to the purchase of electric energy from the part of the distributors in the Spot Market. This stabilization system is due to the fact that it is not easy for the distributors to transfer to the tariff the energy acquired by the distributor in the Spot Market with prices upon schedule which the end users pay on a monthly or two-month basis.

62. So, sections 35 and 36 of the Law No 24065 clear refer to three types of markets existing at the same time, with three different types of prices.

---

times of economic growth the demand of energy requirements increases, and in times of crisis, it decreases. That is why in the economic analyses of energy consumption is a diagnosis factor to be specially considered.' Barreiro (2002) p. 596.

23. Bastos and Abdala (1993) p. 193, also cited by Barreiro (2002) p. 597. As an example the authors '... give a simple model of price-fixing in the *spot* the following: there are three machines generators available, with different capacity generation (the first 300 MW, the second 300 MW and the third 100 MW) and with increasing operation costs (USD 20/MWh, USD 25/MWh and USD 30/MWh, respectively. At a certain moment – let us remember that in this market prices are fixed hour by hour –, the demand is up to 300 MWh. So, such demand is met by the first machine, and it is not necessary for the other two to work. The marginal cost will be USD 20/MWh, the one corresponding to the first machines. If the demand increases more than 300 MWh, up to 500 MWh, it is necessary to cover the difference by means of the use of another machine, the one producing at USD 25/MWh. How then is calculated the remuneration of the first machines? Is the remuneration still USD 20/MWh? If the marginal cost is the increase of the "total" cost when the cost of production is increased in a unit which is applied to the whole production, that is to say that the operation of the first machines will be remunerated at the operation cost of the second machines, which represents then, an earning for the first machines over its production costs. If the demand exceeds 500 MWh, the third machine has to be used, thus being the three machines remunerated at the cost of the last one, which is the least efficient in terms of costs'.

24. Bastos and Abdala *supra* p. 205 and following inform about the aspects take into account by CAMMESA for the program. Among others: (i) the demand of electric energy expected for the period; (ii) the load curves of demand of electric energy according to days and times; (iii) the introduction of the new generation equipment; (iv) the hydraulic offer based upon the rivers, reservoirs and the historical records of the rivers (v) availability of natural gas and carbon. Even though it is not cited by the authors mentioned, the bio fuels and the liquid fuels should also be considered; (vi) the prices of the fuels; (vii) the maintenance programmes on the generation plants determining their availability for the period analysed; (viii) the importation and exportation of electric energy; (ix) the cost of the energy not supplied; (x) the possible restrictions in the transmission system.

63. It is important to repeat that the Futures Market, there is a freely concerted agreement between the electric generator, on the one hand, and the distributor or large user on the other in which the parties negotiate and agree or should freely agree upon the price.

64. And a Spot Market and a market with stabilized prices, in which the price is fixed according to the cost of generation; that is to say, it has to reflect the economic cost of the system. Besides, the same regulation fixed an additional incentive for the efficiency so that the most efficient generators can receive the higher income than its cost of the generation if, at a fixed time, a more expensive or inefficient machine is dispatched at the same time, fixing that machine the market price of that time that all the generator in operation are receiving, at that very same time, even though a lower price was declared.

§4. Inconvenience Generated When Definite Solutions Are Not Taken on Time

65. In this section, we will briefly summarize those resolution which most influenced, from our point of view, in the condition of the context arising from CAMMESA's Annual Report from 2014.

66. Moreover, we will refer to the latest measures adopted by the National State to try and recompose the price the generators would receive even though, for our money, they are not meeting the objectives set under Law No 24065 and the results are not the ones expected by the authorities.

67. Due to the enactment of Law No 25561 under which the Public Emergency was declared in terms of social, economic, administrative and exchange matters, and the convertibility regimes of the peso under Law No 23298 was derogated. The National State, through the Department of Energy, started to take a series of measures with the aim of attenuating the effect of the devaluation in several prices established by the WEM, on which the US currency has a great influence to fix the costs.

68. Among the measures adopted we would like to elaborate on the following.

Resolution D.E. 240/03

69. Until August 2003, the Department of Energy had omitted to sanction a sufficient seasonal price which allowed the adequate remuneration of the generation prices, and that caused a deficit in the Stabilization Fund.

70. So as not to worsen the deficit of the Stabilization Fund and as they were not fixing the suitable seasonal price, the Department of Energy adopted Resolution No 240/03.

71. First, the resolution was temporarily adopted.[25]

72. Moreover, in it, there is a reference to an abnormal situation in the supply of gas to the power stations that caused an increased used of liquid fuels. The, resorting to the attributions conferred under section 36 of the Law No 24065,[26] it is resolved to modify the methodology for the fixing of prices being used by the WEM, discarding the Spot Price upon schedule of the fuels used for the electric generation, thus changing the fixing price system in relation to the economic operational costs of the electric system.

73. So, under section 1, of this resolution, the Department presupposes that the full availability of gas to generate from the part of the thermal generators, independent from the real availability to generate.

74. The consequence of this measure is that cost of the thermal machines using liquid fuel and the value of the water used for the economic dispatch of the hydroelectrical centres, were not considered for the fixing of the prices any more, causing a fall in the income of the generators.

Resolution D.E. 406/03

75. First, it is worth noticing that the resolution was passed on a temporary basis[27] and would be applied as from the WEM's economic transactions due in September 2003.

76. The reason for this resolution was the deficit of the Fund of Stabilization evidencing that '… differences between the collection of the prices and charges billed to the demanding agents and the amounts to be effectively paid to the Creditors Agents of the Wholesale Electric Market (WEM) would not be offset and covered'.[28]

77. It is worth mentioning that the deficit was caused by the very same Department of Energy that was not fixing the seasonal price that, in a suitable way, would pay the electric energy generation, by means of the recognition of the costs.

78. Instead of facing the underlying problem, consisting in fixing the adequate seasonal price, in the Resolution 406/03 of the Department of Energy it was set forth that every month the amounts owed were to be paid based upon the availability of funds collected with a due date in the same month and the pending payable to the

25. Cf. Whereas 5° of the resolution '… the provisions contained in the resolution herein constitute partial and temporary rules, of necessary and urgent passing in the frame of the emergency affecting the economy of the country as they have as well an impact on the Wholesale Electric Market. (WEM)'.
26. Cf. Whereas 4° of the resolution.
27. Cf. s. 8 of the resolution.
28. Cf. Whereas 2 of the resolution.

creditors of the WEM, should conform a debt of the Fund of Stabilization to be honoured when the fund had the necessary resources available to that end.

79. Moreover, it was set forth that the unpaid debts should be consolidated accruing an interest rate and with an order of priority for the payment of amounts owed to the WEM's agents.

§5. The FONINVEMEM

80. By means of Resolution 712/04 the Department of Energy creates the 'Fund for the Necessary Investments allowing to increase the Offer of Electric Energy in the Wholesale Electric Market (WEM)' ('FONINVEMEM') which allow the electric energy generators, as WEM's creditor agents to invest part of their sales Liquidations ('LVFVD') with a due date to be defined under the provisions of Resolution DE 406/03.

81. Among the whereases of the Resolution 712/04, the Department of Energy stated that:

– Due to the emergency, 'it was necessary to moderate the impact of the great seasonal increase necessary to implement distributing it in the future, which would impact in the Stabilization Fund of the Wholesale Electric Market (WEM) which had been in deficit since June 2003; and this is the reason why the 100% of the debt with the creditor agents of the Wholesale Electric Market (WEM) has not been covered with the resources collected with the billing to the demands'.[29]
– Due to the deficit registered in the Stabilization Fund and as the amounts owed could not be covered with the resources collected with the billing from the demand, Resolution 406/03 was adopted establishing a 'temporary mechanism' for the allocation of insufficient funds collected by CAMMESA[30] and due to that '… the electric power stations have accumulated documented credits with Liquidation Sales with a maturity date to be fixed for the great quantities of money'.[31]
– That based upon the report drafted by CAMMESA entitled 'Mid and long-term Risk Evaluation – Period 2004–2007' there is a risk of not meeting the increasing electric demand if the offer in electric energy remains stagnated.
– That it is not foreseeable in the short-term the realization of the necessary investments in generation by venture capitals, causing a risk in lack of supply.

82. Based upon the afore-elaborated, the Department of Energy proposed to the generators, as agent creditors with LVFVD to express their decision to convert the

29. *Ibid.*
30. Cf. Whereas 3 of the resolution.
31. Cf. Whereas 4 of the resolution.

65% of their accumulated amounts owed from January 2004 until December 2006, to participate in two projects of combined cycles called Thermo-electrical Manuel Belgrano and José de San Martín.

83. It is worth mentioning that the LVFVD contributed to the FONINVEMEM are converted into US dollars with an annual yield of Libor rate + 1% and in 120 consecutive equal instalments payable on a monthly basis, as from the commercial commissioning of the combined cycles they committed themselves to build.

84. Moreover, the Department of Energy committed the generators to express their irrevocable decision to commit the 50% of the LVFVD issued for the period of January and December 2007 to build the CTMB and CTJSM.

85. Between January and February 2010 the CTMB and CTJSM construction and commercial commissioning were performed, so as from March to April of 2010 they started to pay the respective instalments.

Resolution D.E. 220/07

86. Upon this Resolution, the Department of Energy recognized the objective of the Law No 24065 '… about fostering the necessary investments to guarantee the long-term supply'[32] and expressly points out 'that in the current circumstances, so as to boost and bring new energy offer, it is convenient to prepare the basis on applicable regulations, giving the necessary economic signals and disposing of the ways of action to follows by the Wholesale Electric Market Agents (WEM), or by the one pretending to be, for the installations of the new offer of generation'.[33]

87. It is worth mentioning that for last seven years,[34] the Department of Energy has been accepting the need to boost the installation of new generation by means of suitable economic signals.

88. This means that the Department of Energy again recognizes the need for making investments in the generation sector, and at the same time sees something that is even more important; the fact that there are no suitable economic signals for the remuneration of the generation, after the policies implemented as from the enactment of Law No 25561.

89. According to this resolution:

– new contracts are projected with the new offer of generation to be installed in the WEM;

32. Cf. Whereas 1 of the resolution.
33. Cf. Whereas 2 of the resolution. Even though this resolution was not originally for the generators without the State's participation, by means of Resolution 200/09, the Department of Energy included majority-stake State generators and State-controlled agencies.
34. In fact we could say eleven years if Resolution DE 712/04 is considered.

- the buyer is the WEM represented by CAMMESA and not the distributor or large user;
- the term fixed for the contract of supply is ten years; however, the Department of Energy is planning a shorter term;
- the remuneration to be paid to the new generation shall be determined 'upon the costs accepted by the Department of Energy';[35]
- the contract of supply must provide the sanction regime for non-compliance regarding the WEM's affectation;
- even though the generator must present an offer to the Department of Energy showing the units that will affect the supply, the term of the contract, and the breakdown of the fixed and variable costs, and the financing, the Department of Energy must analyse the information provided and will fix a remuneration to receive on a monthly basis taking into account the annuity of the installation cost and the fixed and variables costs for the operation and maintenance;
- the costs 'could be revised', when any of the component present significant variations, to guarantee that said cost is covered by the remuneration assigned under the contract of supply;
- it is established that as long as Resolution D.E. No 406/03 is applicable, the obligations of payment derived from the contracts of supply, will have priority of cancellation the same as those provided under section 4° subsection. E) of such resolution and it is made clear that, if the priority in the order of payment were to be modified, the new priority to be fixed should grant the contracts of supply a priority '*... that shall not be inferior to the one corresponding to the recognition of the operative costs of the thermal generators*'.[36]

90. We understand that the fact of fixing a different remuneration for the new generation to be incorporated and to only recognize to it its costs, also breaches the principle of uniform price-fixing pursuant to sections 35 and 36 of the Law No 24065.

91. The questioned resolution can also cause doubts for some sector interested in investing in new generation projects, as although it is indicated that the remuneration should guarantee the significant variations of costs coverage, in fact it is established that the Department of Energy 'can', that is to say has the power, but not 'must', carry put the necessary adjustments to the remunerations in case there are significant variations in the costs.

92. On the contrary, the fact of setting a Specific Regime of Sanctions in the contract in case of failure to meet the supply, it is also proof of the variation in the economic signals in the electric market and of the tight power reserve of the WEMs.

93. In fact, as from the enactment of Law No 25561, the generator that failed to respect the commitment assumed under the contract of the Futures Market due to failure of dispatch since their cost was superior than that of the Spot Market of each

35. Cf. s. 3 subs. d) of the resolution.
36. Cf. s. 8 of the resolution.

hour, they knew that such failure was covered by the Spot Market offsetting the difference, in a way, between the agreed price of contract and price of the Spot Market at the time of covering the contract.

94. Due to this, until Law No 25561, in the Futures Market contracts there was no regime of sanctions, as the Spot Market covered those failures of the Futures Market contract and the higher brunt, if any, was borne by the generator.

95. Moreover, the recognition of costs intended by the Department of Energy to foster investments of the new generation, is left out when in section 8 of the resolution, Resolution D.E. 406/03 is mentioned, which is one of the main reasons causing the WEM's problems, when keeping the deficit of the unified fund and hence the lack of income to cancel all WEM's costs.

96. Hence, it seems that this is yet another partial solution, seeking to solve of consequence of the problem generated, but not providing a final solution.

Resolution D.E. No 724/08

97. In this resolution, especially whereas No 3 thereof, the Department of Energy clearly recognizes that, due to the adoption of the Resolution 406/03, the generators '… are not guaranteed the disposal of the necessary economic resources to face the costs originating a greater repair, the replacement and/or modification for the repowering of the equipment's generators of great power and/or of their associated installations, that they may, in principle, be not be fully covered by the Variable Costs of the Production recognized by the WEM'.

98. It is also recognized that '… there have been long-term failure in generation equipment, which have increased the risk of supply of the demand in the required Security and Reliability conditions'[37] and to improve the offer of energy, '… it is convenient to modify the basic rules applicable, having the suitable standards to give predictability to the perception, to the generator, of the corresponding remuneration, when it has high costs repairs or repowering of the generation equipments as a priority'.

99. Again, it is clear that the measures taken by the Department Of Energy have affected the generators' remuneration, hampering them to have the necessary income to carry out the most important maintenance operations or replacement or repowering of the installations.

100. So in this context, the Department of Energy solved:

- To give the possibility to subscribe contracts of supply commitment to the generators who submit plans for repair and/or repowering, for which they have to

37. Cf. Whereas 4 of the resolution.

demonstrate that the cost thereof will not be higher than the 50% of the earnings forecasted in the Spot Market, during the term of the contracts.

- That the contracts of supply subscribed are for a term of thirty-six running months, with the option of unique renewal of six months.
- The seller is the generator and the buyer is CAMMESA.
- A sanctions regime for failure to supply the units of generations committed or failure to execute the jobs shall be included in the contracts.
- To set certain priority for the payments established in the contract of supply regarding the concepts established under Resolution 406/03, and it is expressly states that in the case of any change in the priorities of payment set forth in such resolution, the remuneration the generator receives shall not be inferior to the one corresponding to the recognition of the operative costs of the thermal generators.

101. It can be noted in this resolution that the Department of Energy recognize the income the generators receive are insufficient for the realization of major repairs or repowering in their installations.

102. Moreover, the resolution modifies the provisions under Law No 24065, since the contract is between the generator and CAMMESA and there is no recognition of uniform prices for the generators.

103. On the contrary, although the generators subscribing this type of contracts are guaranteed priority for the payment of their remunerations, the Department of Energy keeps in full force Resolution 406/03 and does not fix remunerations corresponding to the good operation of the WEM's, and thus this accentuates the debt with the generators.

104. Thus, this entails a partial solution which does not solve the real problem.

Resolution D.E. No 95/13

105. By means of this resolution, which was adopted and applied as from the transactions of February 2013, the DE tried to find the resources to guarantee the sustainability of the activity of generation and to ensure the long-term supply, recognizing that the generation that was incorporated by means of contracts of supply or energy plus had a differential remuneration, in comparison with the generation previously installed, and recognizes that it is necessary to adjust the remuneration received by the generators not covered by the new contracts that had regulated.

106. In the Resolution 95/13: (i) the concept of 'Availability Objective' was defined, which consisted in the average availability of the last three years, according to the technology; (ii) a new scheme of 'Remuneration of Fixed Costs' was established in pesos which considers the Power at Disposal at times of remuneration of power (hrp), according to the type of generation, the technology and the scale, establishing that a percentage of the remuneration set forth in Annex I will be charged depending on the fulfilment of the Availability Objective. Thus, as from the remuneration concept, the intention is to fix an incentive to improve the availability of the generation park; since the higher the availability, the higher the percentage to be perceived by the generator regarding the Remuneration of Fixed Costs. Moreover, it is set forth that the hours of non-availability in the generation equipment due to scheduled maintenance by CAMMESA, shall not be considered for the calculation of non-availability; (iii) 'Remuneration of Variable Costs' in pesos, the fuel excluded is approved that varies according to the type of generation and the scale; (iv) an 'Additional Remuneration' also fixed in pesos according to the type of generation and the scale is approved; however a percentage of that is destined to a Trusts to be reinvested in the financing of new generation projects; (v) although it is established that provisions under Resolution 406/03 shall not be applied, for the payment of the remunerations, the proportionality for the payment of the credits with CAMMESA's funds will be applied; Fixed Costs Remunerations, fuels costs and variable costs remuneration (not fuels) will be first paid; and then the generator's Additional Remuneration; (vi) it is established that, as the contracts with the generators and suppliers are terminated, costs associated to the operation shall stop being recognized; (vii) CAMMESA will be in charge of the fuel management and dispatch, so as to optimize and minimize costs in the fuel supply of the power stations; (viii) the possibility of subscribing new contacts in the Futures Market is temporarily postponed, and once the current contacts are terminated, the large users shall be forced to request their demand directly from CAMMESA.

107. As a condition to receive their remuneration under the resolution, the generator has to previously renounce to administrative or judicial claims against the national states, due to the measures taken by the latter which had affected the activity of generation.

108. It is clear that this resolution is aimed at improving the generators' remuneration, but with the singularity that the remuneration is fixed in a standardized ways, according to the technology and scale of the generator, leaving aside the price – hour criteria of the WEM's, fixed by the most expensive machine dispatched every hour.

Resolution D.E. No 529/14

109. The same as what happened with Resolution D.E. No 95/13; it seems that the Department of Energy has been noticing the need for disposing of new increase in the remunerations of the generators, in force as from the economic transaction corresponding to February 2014, to allow the sustainability of the sector.

110. This is construed from the whereas of the resolution when it clearly indicates '… by means of Resolution No 95 dated on 22 March 2013, the amendments to the regulations from the WEM were introduced in aspects related to the remuneration of the generator agents … so as to allocate the resources that shall guarantee the sustainability of the activity and thus to ensure the supplies for the end users in the whole country … that the adequacy of the remuneration covers mechanism that guarantee the electric energy supply at reasonable prices compatible with the maintenance of the competitiveness in the local economy, fostering the sustainable development of the sector. That is it necessary to ensure the generation of electric energy in reasonably foreseeable economic conditions in time, so as to guarantee the economic growth continuity and the social development that characterized Argentina in the last decade'.[38]

111. As it can observed, in this resolution it is recognized the need to ensure long-term policies, also to grant predictability and sustainability to the generation sector and effectively increase the remunerations. This can be considered as advancement in the right way by the authorities, seeking to restore the objectives set by Law No 24065, and abandoning former policies.

112. Now, the increases in the remunerations fixed under this resolution were also set due to the need for 'ensuring the continuity of economic growth and social development'.

113. So it seems that the Department of Energy, so as to give an increment in the generators' incomes, defines its reasoning according to a delicate balance between predictability and sustainability to be guaranteed to the generator, and the need to ensure economic growth and social development.

114. Thus, although a policy tending to recognize predictability and sustainability for the generator of electric energy has been commenced, if the total costs are not recognized we believe that there will be no predictability or sustainability, even worse when the income of the generators is conditioned to factors beyond the structure of their costs such as economic growth and the social development.

115. In fact, we have to take into account that the remunerations fixed in the resolution, are expressed in pesos and nowadays Argentina is immersed in a context of high inflation, without the prevision of validity term for the remunerations set or a term for the revision thereof.

116. The same as what happened to Resolution DE 95/13, the generator wanting to receive the remunerations fixed in the resolution under analysis must submit a waiver of rights in administrative and judicial claims, before the National State, the Department of Energy and/or CAMMESA associated with the 'Agreement for The Management and Operation of projects, Increase in Thermal Generation Availability and Adaptation to the Remuneration of Generation 2008–2011' and with Resolution DE 406/03.

117. In relation to the remunerations fixed in this resolution, it is worth mentioning that: (i) remunerations provided under Resolution 95/13 are kept and the values provided thereof are increased, and are still in pesos; (ii) in relation to the Fixed Costs Remuneration and the calculation of availability, the minimum and the maximum are increased and the availability according to the months of the year in

38. Cf. Whereas 3, 5 and 6 of the resolution.

which the demand of energy is higher is taken into account; (iii) the concept 'Remuneration of the Non-recurrent Maintenance' is incorporated; however LVFVD shall be issued by said remuneration and the funds will be destined to the finance higher maintenance; (iv) in the 'Variable Costs Remuneration' (not fuels) a remuneration for bio fuels is incorporated.

118. Lastly, this resolution, the same as Resolution 95/13, fixes remunerations according to the technology and the scale to be received for each generator and in this way the unique on-schedule price system determined by the price of the most expensive machines dispatched every hour is left aside.

§6. The Generators' Credit Risk with CAMMESA

119. As it was previously said under the deep elaboration of the resolutions adopted by the Department of Energy as from the enactment of Law No 25561, the most important issue has not been solved yet and this can be seen and perceived as a risk for the generators.

120. In this sense, from the Consolidated Financial Statements of the principal energy groups in the country it is clearly seen and worth pointing out that: ' … there is an increasing deficit between the payments received by CAMMESA and the debit balance of the generation companies regarding such entity. This occurs because the price perceived by CAMMESA in relation to electric energy commercialized in the Spot Market is regulated by the National Administration and it is lower than the generation marginal cost of electric energy that CAMMESA has to reimburse to the generators. The national government has been covering this deficit by means of contributions of the treasury. As those contributions are not enough to cover the total of the amounts owed in favour of the generators, CAMMESA's debt with them has increased throughout the time. It is not possible to know if CAMMESA will continue honouring the debts with the generators, due to both the energy and the power sold. … CAMMESA's inability to pay the amounts owed to the generators could have a substantially adverse effect on the cash payments and as a consequence on the results of the operations, its financial standing and with the risk of impacting on the ability of payment of the Partnership'.[39]

121. It is also notable the uncertainty caused in the generators due to the delays in payments from the part of CAMMESA and the risk of the Exchange rate.[40]

---

39. Cf. Note 6.1.2 de Pampa Energía (2015).
40. In the note 6.1.1 de Pampa Energía (2015) it is expressly indicated ' … the Partnership receives the majority stake if its earnings from CAMMESA that in recent years has registered important delays in the payment terms. Even though a very big portion of the transactions are expressed in US dollars, they are billed in Argentinean pesos converted at the Exchange rate of the month they are performed. In the case of the earnings derived from the contracts of supply in the frame of the Res. DE No 220/07, such amount in pesos is charged afterwards to CAMMESA on an average of 100 days after the date of the transaction but the Exchange rate difference is recognized by CAMMESA only on the maturity date, that is to say in approximately 45 days. In case of an important devaluation

122. We are pointing out the reference to Pampa Energía S.A.'s Consolidated Financial Statements since until 31 December 2014 it was one of the groups that mostly grew in the energy sector after the enactment of Law No 25561.

123. From the successive measures taken by the National State as from 2003, and previously referred to, it can be observed the following ones for the sector of electric energy generation:

- The fixing of prices to be paid by the demand which do not cover the generators' costs. Apart from the economic and financial inconveniences that this has caused in the generation, it has as well made a negative impact on the residential demand, which when acquiring a product, the electric energy, at a lower price, gets the wrong impression regarding the cost; as it is economical, compared to other goods of the economy, the residential user understands that it is abundant and increases its demand, initiating a vicious circle that cause harm to the system.
- The new way of fixing prices for the generation of energy, provoked that the spot prices and thus the stabilization funds stopped being an economic signal for the efficiency and the investment from the part of the generators, discouraging at the same time the Futures Market.
- The fixing of prices to the demand for the energy received, without recognizing its real cost, has been generating a market debt with the generators, whose recognition in the FONINVEMEM and instrumentation by means of the LVFVD has delayed to be instrumented and has meant higher costs and bureaucracy, beyond the renouncement from the part of the generators for at least receiving the formal recognition of their debit balance.
- This situation has caused that in some cases the generators do not have enough money to perform the maintenance of their equipment; so the Department of Energy has created a mechanism by means of which they could use the debit balance with the market or the possibility to solicit a loan to CAMMESA in exchange for committing the supply of the repaired machine.
- Even though the National State tried to take measures to promote the installation of new generation, such as the contractual regime of the future market provided in the Resolution 220/07, the reality, together with the inconsistencies of the policies adopted by the authorities who kept the temporary measures despite the passing of the time and the fact of not addressing the real issue, made that the effect of the plan got stuck half way.
- As from 2013, it seemed that the National State started to understand the reality of the sector and to see the generation costs. Although the recognition as from 2013, represented an improvement for the sector, they were just focused on the fixing of the prices, which was far away from the reality of each generator. In fact,

between the maturity date and the collection to CAMMESA of such amount in the dollars, as it happened in January 2014, the Equivalent US dollars the Partnership will receive will be significantly reduced, thus reducing its effectiveness of the coverage in relation to the Exchange rate'.

sustainability, predictability and long-term measures are mentioned, but the fixing of the remuneration is not considered for the costs structure of each generator. Moreover, it seems that the remunerations recognized were fixed taking into account factor disconnected from the generators, and so they may change.
- The measures adopted for the sector implied a new paradigm, except for the case of the contracts with Energía Plus and the contracts of supply subscribed for example under Resolution 220/07, as the generators are no longer freely connected with the demand to fix prices and quantities with autonomy, as Law No 24065 so set forth; and neither can contracts with the future market be subscribed, thus centralizing the supply by means of CAMMESA.
- This measure, the fixing of prices not related to the specific circumstances of each generator and the fact that the generator – without contract – receives remuneration according to the technology and scale and not based upon the cost – time of the WEM, has discouraged the generators from commercially competing with another to win new demand.
- Another new paradigm posed for the generators as from 2013 is that they stop being in charge of the fuels management, discouraging the thermal generators from competing with another to guarantee the most economical fuel supply that would allow them to achieve the better margin of the price.
- Due to the fact that up to date there is still the fundamental issue yet to be solved, that is that CAMMESA's billing to the demand is lower than what they have to pay to the generators and that the National Administration cannot cover the amounts owed to the generators, CAMMESA's debt has increased and the generators, at least some of them,[41] see they cannot assure that CAMMESA will continue paying the respective amounts owed regarding power and energy.

124. This adoption of measure caused an exodus from the part of many important international actors in the generation sector. Those actors who stayed made great efforts in the context of many uncertainties, a big sacrifice in terms of profitability and thanks to the commitment of their shareholders and the efficiency and wit of the *management* and the employees to adapt to the new circumstances as from 2003.

125. Thus, apart from the profitability being affected, just to give an example, some thermal generators had to cope with higher costs to face the maintenance by means of the use of liquid fuels such as fuel oil or gas oil which have been used as a replacement of gas throughout the years.

126. Moreover, in the face of insufficient income and many difficulties to obtain finance from the part of the local and/or foreign creditors to perform the tasks of maintenance, they were forced to solicit and negotiate financing payable with future sales to agree with CAMMESA by means of contracts of supply.

127. They also had to deal and cope with their income in pesos to face and honour the debts they had taken in dollars in the past to make some investment in

41. We refer to the case of Pampa Energía S.A.

their plants, to acquire spare parts, to contract maintenance services, and to deal with the pay rises set forth with the authorization of the National State which rejected to recognize the real cost of the energy generated, or if recognized, it did not pay and generating a debt.

§7. A Proposal for the Solution

128. Just In the same way as we try to challenge with the title of the study herein, the proposal we intend to expose is aimed to seek a definite solution to stop causing harm that then is pretended to patch with another measure not solve the problem once and for all.

129. Setting aside the differences, as at that moment the activities of generation, transport and distribution of electric energy were in the hands of the National State, the situation that the electric sector is going through in general, and that of generation in particular is similar to the one the sector went through in 1992.

130. In that sense, it is interesting to cite Bastos and Abdala who, when trying to make a diagnoses of the situation before the structural changes produced as from the enactment of Law No 24065 and the segmentation and further privatization of the State companies, stated that: '… Any experienced observer, kind of familiarized with the electrical sector in Argentina in the last decade, has surely noticed the progressive decadence of the system. They may as well have noticed that the theory to face and overcome the crisis was too far from the reality and the results of the measures taken. The objectives of the companies were not especially characterized by economic efficiency and development of the sector in the long run. For example, the creation of employment and the use of tariff as a tool of economic politics and or redistributive politics have been present in the past. The use of the price of the electricity to control the inflation or to implement subsidies in favour of certain users made it clear the conflict derived from the multiplicity of Administration objectives, which in general is in detriment of the companies' management.'[42]

131. Reading the aforementioned quote, we seem to be in front of a déjà *vu*, that even though it is not the same as what happened and incited the transformation in the electric sector, it has similar aspects, and although in the last years there has been signs of increase in the generators' remunerations, in fact a long-term comprehensive politics cannot be seen in the horizon.

132. On the contrary, nowadays and the same that had happened until the reform of the electric sector originated as from the enactment of the Law No 24065, the price of the energy was used as an instrument of economic and redistributive politics. Likewise, the price of electricity was fixed as an element to control the inflation or to implement subsidies in favour of certain users.

42. Bastos and Abdala (1993) pp. 1–3.

133. Also these policies highlight the conflict derived from the objectives of the public policies against the efficient company management, and it is clear that the one who bears the brunt, now and then, is the companies, in the case of the generation. The other affected party is the end user since even though he seems to receive a benefit in the short-term as he does not pay the real cost of the energy, sooner or later he will pay it with the risk of getting lower quality service and restrictions in the supply if this situation continues throughout the time.

134. We seem to be at a turning point, in which all the sectors involved but especially the political actors should define which way to take.

135. As it can be noticed, the political actors are also mentioned, since for a policy to be sustainable and long-standing, a wide consensus from all political sectors is required, not only from those who have been elected through a democratic process to 'temporarily' exercise the power but also from those who have a role in the opposition since the energy sector – and the generation as part of it, requires long-term public policies, and to that end it is necessary for them to be independent from those who preside over the fortunes of the country.

§8. Some Objectives Legally Fixed for the Generation Sector

136. We think it is convenient to put on the table these principles, as they are in full force, and not derogated as it seems if we consider the measures taken by the National State in the last years.

137. On the contrary, to make our proposal, we will consider these principles as the basis thereof.

138. To that respect, section. 2° of the Law No 24.065 establishes a set of objectives for the national politics regarding supply, transport and distribution of electric energy and among them it sets forth: (i) to foster competitiveness among the production;[43] (ii) to encourage investment to ensure the supply in the long run;[44] (iii) to incentivize the supply and the efficient use of electricity;[45] and (iv) 'to encourage the realization of private investment in production … guaranteeing competitiveness wherever possible'.[46]

139. These objectives, together with the provisions under 35 of the Law No 24065, are persuading us to go back to the reality of the text in Law No 24065; to stick to the law. This is our proposal.

---

43. Cf. Whereas b) s. 2 Law No 24.065.
44. *Ibid.*
45. *Ibid* .
46. Cf. Whereas f) s. 2 Law No 24.065.

140. Unfortunately, throughout this study, we have been forced to recite and reiterate once and again the laws 24065 and 15336, precisely because we understand that by observing these legal provisions, we can solve the problem of the generation sector; and of the remaining ones such as the transport, distribution and large users.

141. Moreover, we have also pointed out, on purpose, that many of the cites legal provisions are in force, as we want to emphasize the fact that they contradict and clash with the voluminous infra-legal set of rules passed by the National State, in this case the Department of Energy as from 2003.

§9. Contractualization: Costs Recognition

142. Considering the situation the generation sector is going through, we believe it is important to gradually adopt the following measures in the context of a comprehensive programme for the whole energy sector to rechannel the activity and to allow the development of investment, seeking to meet the objectives set under Law No 24065 for the activity of generation.

143. Hence, we propose:

(a) To look into the last decisions taken by the Department of Energy tending to sincere the real costs for the activity of generation which will allow the generators to cover the total costs and to obtain a suitable profitability inside a frame of competitiveness seeking to foster a more efficient electric energy generation, going back to a system of unique price on schedule, determined by the least efficiency machine of every hour.
(b) To transfer the whole demand, the cost representing the activity of generation. The assumption of the real costs from the part of the demand, with no distortion at all, is an economic signal to be considered by the latter, which will stop considering the energy as an abundant resource and will contribute to a more efficient use thereof. Besides, this way the generators should collect the total of the amounts owed and the WEM will stop the endless debt they have with each generator.
(c) So as to make the aforementioned sustainable and effective, profitability and the situation of each of the links conforming the energy chain should be analysed. Especially, the distributors of electric energy demanding approximately the 70% of the energy consumed, should be able to transfer the cost of the energy acquired to their clients, the end users.
(d) That the electric energy generators resume their commercial role for the energy they produce inside a framework of competence.
(e) To establish the obligatory nature and the respective incentives so that the demand, mainly the distribution sector, subscribe contract in the Futures Market with the generators, for the supply of electric energy required by their clients. However, for this to be effective and possibly inside a comprehensive and consistent politics as regards energy, the distributor has to be authorized to transfer the total costs to the users. In that sense, a transition period should be

allowed to attenuate the impact caused due to the whitening of the costs, by means of a rethinking of the subsidies policy, so that they can be rechannelled to some final users of the distributor, not affecting the sustainability of the links before the final end user, the distributor included.

§10. Challenges to Meet to Implement the Suggested Proposal

144. As follows we will describe those challenges that should be welcome so as to re-establish the principles and objectives provided in the regulatory frame of the Law No 24065.

§11. The Economic Emergency

145. As we have seen throughout this study, the measures taken by the Department of Energy which have affected the activity of generation, are rooted in the public emergency established as from the enactment of the Law No 25561 and was successively extended until 31 December 2015.

146. Unfortunately, Argentina has been in a state of emergency for more than thirteen years.

147. Such emergency was supposed to conclude on the 31 December 2015; a few days after there had been a change in the National Executive Power and the renovation of the Senate and the representatives.

148. In that sense, it has been said that the successive extension of the Law No 25561 implied the abandonment of the economic system protector of the private property, '… migrating to a kind of interventionist and statist state, with intentions of welfare condition'.[47]

149. The possibility of implementing the proposal, will depend if the public emergency will be extended again or not.

150. The presentation of a bill form the National Executive Power soliciting the Congress to extend again the emergency, or the decision from the part of the National Congress to extend the emergency, will be a bad start if the intention is to normalize the situation of the energy sector in Argentina.

§12. The Civil and Commercial Code

151. Between 1992 and 2001 there were great investments from the private sector in the activity of generation, which allowed an increment in the power installed.

47. Crivelli, July (2013).

152. These investments, even though they were made in a context of competence and risk, they were made due to the reasonable regulatory framework set forth by Law No 24065, but also because of the convertibility,[48] which allowed to express the prices in dollars in a context of very low inflation.

153. By means of the Law No 25561 the convertibility regime under Law No 23928 was set aside, and thus some contractual relations which were previously agreed in dollars were converted into pesos; however, nowadays, there exist a context of very high inflation affecting the peso as a currency to obtain long-term financing in the country.

154. This context motivates that the parties involved in long-term contracts of great magnitude, choose to agree to the prices in US dollars.

155. The enactment of the Civil and Commercial Code of the Nation,[49] whose section 765 establishes that if 'it was stipulated in a currency that is not a legal tender in the country, the obligation has to be deemed as many other things, the debtor can pay the amount in the equivalent legal tender', and this is an issue that the generators will have to face.

156. In that sense, if an interested party wants to resort to finance to build or repower a plant of generation, he will surely take the obligation of payment in dollars under a contract subject to the foreign law with a creditor or supplier from overseas.

157. To that respect, it has to be said that the remunerations fixed to the generators by the Department of Energy under resolutions 95/13 and 529/14 were established in pesos, and so the generator should plan how to face with those pesos the obligations owed in dollars that he may have taken with foreign supplier, assuming the exchange risk.

158. On the contrary, if the generator subscribed contracts in the Futures Market with a distributor or large user, he will surely offer them as a guarantee for the payment of the credit he receives. So, in those contracts, the way of payment has to be carefully studied and agreed, to allow the generator to show his creditor that he will receive enough dollars to pay him what he had committed to pay.

§13. Law No 26991

159. In the case there is no extension of the public emergency, to its maturity date which is 31 December 2015, we observe there is yet another evident challenge that could affect or put at risk the proposal herein.

---

48. Law No 23928.
49. Law No 26994.

160. This challenge is the Law No 26991, known as the Law of Supply.

161. Due to the application of this law and the general interest of the activity of generation for many sectors in the economy established in Law No 24065, utility margins, reference prices, maximum and minimum levels in the prices of the energy to offer to the generators could be established.

162. On the contrary, even when the contracts of supply can be subscribed in a direct way and freely with the distributors, those contracts could be revised and changed by the authority of application with the basis on Law No 26991.

163. The application of this law to a generator, does not mean that he can resort to the justice to claim for the pre-emptive right guaranteed in the National Constitution, as long as he can prove he has suffered from a real and concrete damage owing to the measure that could be taken by the National Executive Power under this law.

§14. Concentration and Horizontal and Vertical Relations in the Energy Sector

164. In this section, we will make reference to the phenomenon pointed out by Laithou and Eliaschev[50] about the importance of the hydrocarbons in the activity of generation and the vertical integration process between the '*upstream*' and the generation, with important actors such as YPF S.A.,[51] Central Puerto S.A.,[52] Grupo Enel[53] and Pampa Energía S.A.[54]

165. One of the aspects to consider for the recontracting of the demand, integrated mainly by the distribution, is the way in which it will be performed.

50. Cf. Larthou, Juan and Eliaschev, Nicolás (2015) pp. 373–375.
51. Laithou and Eliaschev mentions the creation of YPF Energía Eléctrica S.A., fully controlled by YPF S.A. that has taken over the power stations located in El Bracho, Tucumán, before operated by Pluspetrol S.A., which at the same time has a participation in Central Dock Sud with a power of 870 MW and in minor power stations such as Central Filo Morado. It also refers to the relationships between YPF with the power stations Ensenada and Luján de Cuyo, of SADESA Group and the relationships with Pampa Energía S.A.
52. In the case of Central Puerto S.A., it controls the power stations Nuevo Puerto and Puerto Nuevo (1,795 MW), Lujan de Cuyo (540 MW), Ensenada (127 MW), Piedra del Aguila (1,400 MW), has a participation in Central Vuelta de Obligado S.A. (800 MW), Distribuidora de Gas Cuyana S.A. and Distribuidora de Gas del Centro S.A.
53. Participating in the Hidroeléctrica El Chocón S.A., Central Dock Sud S.A. and Endesa Costanera S.A.
54. In relation to Pampa Energía S.A., from the Consolidated Financial Statements corresponding to the fiscal year ending on 31 Dec. 2014, arises their participation in Hidroeléctrica Los Nihuiles S.A. (265 MW), Hidroeléctrica Diamante S.A. (388 MW), Central Térmica Güemes S.A. (361 MW), Central Térmica Piedra Buena S.A. (620 MW), Central Térmica Loma de la Lata S.A. (553 MW), Central Térmica Piquirenda (30 MW), Transener S.A., Transba S.A., Edenor S.A. and Transportadora de Gas del Sur S.A. – TGS –, Petrolera Pampa S.A. with participation in six areas and forty-five productive wells.

166. In that sense, considering the end users' interest, a bid of prices could be realized by the distributors or through CAMMESA, acting on their own behalf, so that there is a comparison of prices which will end up benefiting all final users.

167. Then, when realizing the comparison or bidding of prices through CAMMESA, it is almost impossible that the Department of Energy would have any objection about the price obtained from the bid that will end up being paid by the users.

168. On the contrary, considering the influence of the thermal generation, the management of fuels becomes relevant as well. Specifically, the convenience of managing the acquisition thereof through CAMMESA or directly through the generators should be analysed again.

169. Moreover, if the generators could freely subscribe contracts with the distributors in the Futures Market, being able to get the adequate price in this way, it would seem reasonable that they dealt with the fuels management and the risk it entails. In that case, it should be verified that those groups simultaneously controlling a generator of energy and a producer of hydrocarbons are not breaching the general economic interest.

170. Furthermore, let us consider that when concentrating all the management of the fuels of the WEM on CAMMESA, its negotiating power against the producers should be stronger than that of a generator and thus, it could obtain more advantageous conditions.

171. Nevertheless, considering that CAMMESA registers delays in payments, and that for a significant part of the amounts owed they require the National State's contributions, these risks could be translated into in a higher price offered by the interested parties.

172. Moreover, how the WEM would go about when buying fuel should be taken into consideration. For example, if the acquisition will be concentrated on only one supplier or on more than one. In the case of wanting to acquire fuel by means of several contracts or suppliers the volumes for each of them and the schedule to call for price bids should as well be considered.

§15. Strategic State Energy Policy I: Hydropower Energy

I. At a National Level

173. It could be said that an electrical matrix that includes a proportion of energy sources fitting the country's natural resources allows a better production planning and improves the management of the electrical system. Specialists assert that having 40% of hydroelectric generation seems a reasonable working assumption in order to strengthen energy security due to the consequent reduction in dependence on liquid fuels at present.[55]

174. The Argentine hydroelectric sector, for various reasons, has suffered a setback in recent times, a situation that originates as a result of the decisions taken in the early 1990s of the twentieth century, when the operation of the power plants was concessioned hydroelectric plants executed by the National State, without taking the necessary provisions for the expansion of the hydroelectric generation system. At that time, the intention was to transfer to the private sector the decisions related to the incorporation of new hydroelectric projects, but in practice it was concluded that none of the concessionaires was interested in the execution of such uses. Currently, it would be a key moment to resume the development of the hydroelectric sector because there is consensus on the enormous potential that renewable energy presents for the country.

175. It can be confirmed that the growth in the demand for electrical energy in the past twenty years (1993–2012) registered an average accumulated annual rate of 4.33%, with intercalculated periods close to 6% of annual average growth. Considering a growth of the total population in the next two decades in the order of 13%, a hypothetical average rate of growth of demand of 5% accumulated annually and reaching a 40% share of water sources in the electricity matrix, the country would need to incorporate an additional water supply that provides 73,000 GWh/year of average annual energy and 16,000 MW of hydraulic power.

176. As set forth at the beginning of this section, the National Hydroelectric Regime (NHR) is part of the WEM, but due to the importance of water as a vital and strategic natural resource, it falls under special regulations defined by Law No 15336.[56]

A. *National Hydroelectric Regime*

177. Law No 15336 defines the normative difference between hydraulic energy and its related water. In effect, section 5 clearly states:

> The energy of waterfalls and other hydraulic sources, including seas and lakes, is legally considered different from the water and the lands that make up these sources. The right to use hydraulic energy does not imply modifying the use and purposes for which these waters and lands were intended, except in the strictly essential measure required by the installation and operation of the corresponding training works systems, driving and generation, in accordance with the particular provisions applicable in each case.

---

55. *See* MALINOV.
56. *See* Law 15336, OB 21/12/1967.

178. Consequently, section 6 declares national jurisdiction of power generation when:

(a) related to national defence;
(b) related to trade and commerce between the City of Buenos Aires (Capital Federal) and other provinces, or between a province and the Province of Tierra del Fuego, Antarctic and Southern Atlantic Islands;
(c) subject to National Congress's special normative;
(d) applying hydroelectric or maritime power generation;
(e) belonging to the WEM;
(f) applying to international power trade or interconnection;
(g) applying nuclear power generation; or
(h) I National Congress defines pursuant to general interest and convenience.

179. Law No 15336 also defines that the Executive Power is responsible for the promotion of hydroelectrical power. Nevertheless, any transboundary development (rivers, lakes, or maritime) requires a National Congress law. Also, expropriation shall apply in order to fulfil the aims of this law. The Executive Power is in charge of time limited/unlimited concessions as well as the exercise of police power and jurisdiction, including usage of federal land and tax exemptions. Thus, local systems and grids are subject to local normative, police power, and jurisdiction. Regulation provides for the national concession of hydroplants over 500 kV as well as public service of power transportation and distribution. In addition, It provides that concessions must explicitly regulate the following: water usage (whilst domestic consumption and land irrigation precede power generation); water navigation, land floodage, water domestic usage, land usage, straddling fish conditions, local tourism development, and environmental and ecosystem protection; the power standard and the maximum generation capacity; the concession works term; the exploitation term, when applicable; the transfer conditions, when reversion to the State is foreseen; the termination causes and conditions; the notification periods, either for time limited or unlimited concessions; and the corresponding concession fee. Hydroelectric concessions can be transferred upon approval of the Executive Branch.

180. In order to fulfil the NHR goals, the concessionaire is entitled to the following: to temporarily occupy the land required for the water reservoir as well as water flow, either subterranean or uncovered, pursuant to local regulation; to require from the Executive Power expropriation in case an agreement is impossible with the land owner. Private subjects can use hydroelectric generation for their industrial or personal usage as long as the generation capacity remains under 500 kV, it doesn't affect other generators, and it doesn't interfere with power policy plans.

181. Law No 15336 also provides water location provinces shall receive 12% of perceived income (equitable percentage when there is more than one province).

182. Pursuant to Law No 15336, Argentine hydroelectric generation boosted unbelievably, mainly since the 1970s (Figures 7 and 8).

Figure 7 Hydroelectric Power Generation Capacity (1936–2012)

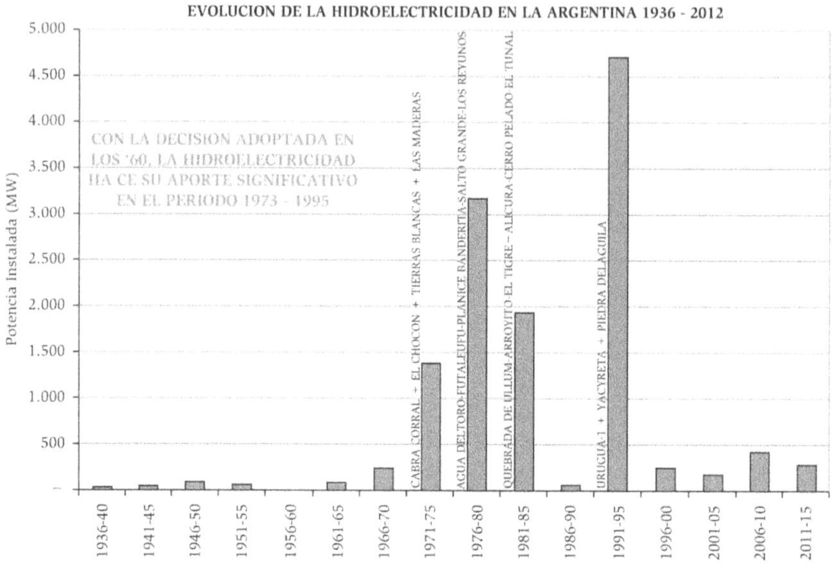

Figure 8 Hydroelectric Power Generation Facilities

Table 1 Operating Hydroelectric Power Generation Facilities

DAM	*CAPACITY(MW)*	*OPENING*	*LOCATION*	*RIVER*
Yacyretá	3,100	1998	Corrientes w/Republic of Paraguay	Río Paraná
Salto Grande	1,890	1979	Entre Ríos w/Uruguay	Río Uruguay
Piedra del Águila	1,400	1992	Neuquén – Río Negro	Río Limay
El Chocón	1,260	1973	Neuquén – Río Negro	Río Limay
Alicurá	1,050	1985	Neuquén – Río Negro	Río Limay
Río Grande	750	1986	Córdoba	Río Tercero
Futaleufú	472	1978	Chubut	Río Futaleufú
Planicie Banderita (Cerros Colorados)	472	1978	Neuquén	Río Neuquén
Pichi Picún Leufú	285	2000	Neuquén – Río Negro	Río Limay
Los Reyunos	224	1983	Mendoza	Río Diamante
Agua del Toro	150	1976	Mendoza	Río Diamante
Arroyito	128	1979	Neuquén – Río Negro	Río Limay
Los Caracoles	121.4	2009	San Juan	Río San Juan
Potrerillos (Cacheuta)	120	2003	Mendoza	Río Mendoza
Urugua-í	120	1991	Misiones	Arroyo Urugua-í
El Nihuil II (Aisol)	110	1968	Mendoza	Río Atuel
Manuel Belgrano (Cabra Corral)	100.5	1973	Salta	Río Salado
El Nihuil I	72	1947	Mendoza	Río Atuel

Punta Negra	64	2015	San Juan	Río San Juan
Potrerillos (Álvarez Condarco)	61	2003	Mendoza	Río Mendoza
Casa de Piedra	60	1996	Río Negro – La Pampa	Río Colorado
Florentino Ameghino	60	1963	Chubut	Río Chubut
Los Molinos I	52	1957	Córdoba	Río Segundo
Quebrada de Ullúm	45	1980	San Juan	Río San Juan
El Nihuil III (Tierras Blancas)	42	1971	Mendoza	Río Atuel
Ullum	42		San Juan	Río San Juan
Benjamín Reolín	33		Córdoba	Río Tercero
Las Maderas	30.6		Jujuy	Río Perico
Escaba	24	1948	Tucumán	Río Marapa
Central San Roque	24	1959	Córdoba	Río Primero
El Nihuil IV (Valle Grande)	18	1965	Mendoza	Río Atuel
El Carrizal	17	1971	Mendoza	Tunuyán
Ingeniero Cassafousth	16.2	1954	Córdoba	Río Tercero
La Viña	16	1959	Córdoba	Río de los Sauces
Pueblo Viejo	15	1968	Tucumán	Río Pueblo Viejo
Río Hondo	15	1967	Santiago del Estero	Río Dulce
El Tigre	14	1983	Mendoza	Río Diamante
Celestino Gelsi (El Cadillal)	12.6	1966	Tucumán	Río Salí
Cuesta del Viento	10.55	1997	San Juan	Río Jáchal
Fitz Simon (Embalse)	10.5	1955	Córdoba	Río Tercero

DAM	*CAPACITY(MW)*	*OPENING*	*LOCATION*	*RIVER*
Martín Miguel de Güemes (El Tunal)	10.52	1972	Salta	Río Salado
Los Divisaderos	10	1980	La Pampa	Río Colorado
Salto Andersen	8	2012	Río Negro – La Pampa	Río Colorado
Río Reyes	7		Jujuy	Río Reyes
Los Coroneles	6.64	1970	Mendoza	Río Diamante
General San Martín	6.48	1950	Mendoza	Río Mendoza
Piedras Moras	6.3	1979	Córdoba	Río Tercero
Julián Romero	6.2		Río Negro	Río Neuquén
Cipolletti	5.4	1956	Río Negro	Río Neuquén
Guillermo Céspedes	5.2	1963	Río Negro	Río Negro
Los Molinos II	4.5	1958	Córdoba	Río Segundo
Central Hidroeléctrica La Calera	4	1911	Córdoba	Río Primero
La Florida	2.4	1953	San Luis	Río Quinto
Loma Atravesada	2		Río Negro	Río Azul
Los Quiroga	2	1963	Santiago del Estero	Río Dulce
La Lujanita	1.7		Mendoza	Río Mendoza
Emilio Frey	1.2		Río Negro	Guillelmo
General Roca	1.2		Río Negro	Río Negro
Saladillo	1.2	2011	San Luis	Río Quinto
Salto de la Loma	1.2		San Juan	Río Jáchal
Cruz del Eje	1.1	1943	Córdoba	Río Cruz del Eje

La Carrera	1	Catamarca	Río del Valle
El Mollar	0.5	Tucumán	Río de los Sosa
Perito Moreno	0.428	Río Negro	Río Gutiérrez
Barrealito	0.424	San Juan	Río de los Patos
Las Chacras	0.4	San Luis	Río de las Chacras
Los Sauces	0.345	La Rioja	Río Grande de La Rioja
Cuesta del Ternero	0.14	Río Negro	Arroyo El Ternero
Mallín Ahogado	0.1	Río Negro	Río Quemquemtreu

Table 2 Projected or Developing Hydroelectric Power Generation Facilities

DAM	*PROVINCE*	*RIVER*	*CAPACITY kW*
Corpus	Misiones w/Paraguay	Paraná	3,800,000
Patí o Machuca Cué	Corrientes – Santa Fe	Paraná	2,912,000
Chapetón	Entre Ríos – Santa Fe	Paraná	2,300,000
Garabí	Corrientes w/Brasil	Uruguay	1,600,000
Cordón del Plata	Mendoza	Mendoza	1,528,000
Cóndor Cliff	Santa Cruz (en construcción)	Santa Cruz	1,140,000
Panambí	Misiones Brasil	Uruguay	1,048,000
Chihuido I	Neuquén	Neuquén	637,000
Michihuao	Neuquén – Río Negro	Limay	621,000
La Barrancosa	Santa Cruz (en construcción)	Santa Cruz	600,000
Los Blancos	Mendoza	Tunuyán	324,000

DAM	*PROVINCE*	*RIVER*	*CAPACITY kW*
Collón Curá	Neuquén	Collón Curá	376,000
Potrero del Clavillo	Catamarca – Tucumán	Gastona	240,000
Zanja del Tigre	Salta	Bermejo	234,000
Chihuido II	Neuquén	Neuquén	228,000
Portezuelo del Viento	Mendoza	Grande	210,000
La Elena	Chubut	Carrenleufú	102,000
El Tambolar	San Juan (en construcción)	San Juan	75,000
Nahueve	Neuquén	Nahueve	4,000
Aluminé	Neuquén	Aluminé	3,500
Arroyo Catarata	Neuquén	Catarata	2,700
Lago Aluminé	Neuquén	Aluminé	2,500
San Martín II	Neuquén	Calbuco	2,000
Cuyín Manzano	Neuquén	Cuyín Manzano	250
Moquehue	Neuquén	Moquehue	250
Roblecillos	Neuquén	Roblecillos	200
Malargüe[37]	Mendoza	Malargüe	108
Arroyo Pereira I	Neuquén	A. Pereira I	60
Pino Hachado	Neuquén	A. Mendoza	55

183. Law No 17574 provided the State corporation *Hidroeléctrica Norpatagónica S.A.* (HIDRONOR) with the concession to develop (i.e., *build*) and operate *Complejo El Chocón-Cerros Colorados* (Limay – Neuquén rivers, provinces of Neuquén and Río Negro).[57] Later on, HIDRONOR acquired the operation of *Alicurá* (Limay River), *Collón Curá* (Collón Cura River), and *Piedra del Águila* (Limay River).[58]

184. In addition to HIDRONOR's emblematic developments, there are over fifty relevant hydroelectric dam facilities (Table 1), among which: *El Nihuil* dam, inaugurated in 1947 (Atuel River, Mendoza Province); '*Rio Grande*' dam (Cordoba Province), inaugurated in 1986; Ameguino, Futaleufu, Agua del Toro, Río Hondo, San Juan, el Cardial Tucumán, Belgrano, Río Juramento.

185. As mentioned, Law No 23696 privatized HIDRONOR along with most State corporations (Table 1).[59] In order to proceed with the privatization, Decree 287/93 provided for the incorporation of *'Hidroeléctrica Alicurá S.A, Hidroeléctrica El Chocón S.A., Hidroeléctrica Piedra del Aguila S.A., Hidroeléctrica Pichi Picún Leufú S.A.,* and *Hidroeléctrica Cerros Colorados'.*

186. The Executive Power – former Ministry of Economics, Development and Public Services –, called for an open-based international bid in order to sell 59% of the shares (51% 'Class A' shares and 8% 'Class B' shares).[60] Thus, most State-owned hydropower corporations and shareholding were privatized between 1991 and 1995.[61] Typical concession contracts were eventually signed.

187. The hydroelectric operations of the National State operated by the former companies Agua y Energía Eléctrica and Hidronor, which have an installed capacity of 5,849 MW, were organized during the privatization process of the early 1990s in the twentieth-century Business units (Figure 7). The same has also indicated the expiration date of each concession, showing that these maturities will begin in 2023, that is, within a decade.

188. In most cases, the concession contracts explain how the end of the concession will be due to the expiration of the agreed term, mentioning that the ownership and possession of the concessionaire's equipment will be transferred by right to the Grantor (National State), without that the latter must pay the concessionaire a price or consideration of any kind. There are two exceptions, the Concession of Hidroeléctrica Los Nihuiles S.A. and that of Hidrotérmica San Juan S.A., in which two contracts were signed, one with the National State and the other with the respective provincial states.

---

57. OB 21/12/1967.
58. Law 2050, OB 28/12/1972.
59. Law 23696, OB 17/08/1989.
60. Resolution MEDPS 364/93.
61. *See* a detailed evolution at https://www.minem.gob.ar/www/830/25774/introduccion-al-quinquenio-1991-1995.

189. In the concession contract with the provincial State for the use of water for the exclusive production of hydroelectric energy, it is stated that the ownership and possession of the equipment of the concessionaire (own property) will be transferred by right to the provincial State, without that the latter must pay the concessionaire a price or consideration of any kind. In the case of the El Nihuil Hydroelectric Use (A.H.), the reason for this double contract is because the hydraulic work was built in the 1940s by the province of Mendoza to regulate the water of the Atuel river. Subsequently, this work was transferred to Agua y Energía Eléctrica S.E., the company that built the Nihuil 1 hydroelectric power station. Therefore, upon concessioning the project, it was agreed that the work would return to the provincial state at the end of the concession period.

190. The same position was adopted by the Province of San Juan with the A. H. Quebrada de Ullum on the grounds that it was built by the provincial State, for which it was agreed that the undertaking would return to the provincial State at the end of the concession period.

191. Since the reform of the National Constitution of 1994, the provinces, as expressed in Article 124, are the owners of the original domain of the natural resources existing in their territory, in particular water resources, and therefore are those that are capable of granting the concession to use water for electricity generation, a procedure that must be endorsed by laws sanctioned by the respective provincial legislatures.

192. It is also the responsibility of the National State to intervene in those cases in which the water resource covers two or more jurisdictions, and an agreement must be reached between the jurisdictions involved.

B. Regime of International Development: Salto Grande

193. The Salto Grande Hydroelectric Complex was built in an area of rapids and rocky slopes, in the middle course of the Uruguay River, taking advantage of a natural slope called Salto Grande for hydroelectric generation. It is located at kilometre 342.6 of the Uruguay River, upstream from the cities of Concordia (Argentina) and Salto (Uruguay).

194. The Uruguay River is one of the most important rivers in South America, whose course is shared by Brazil, Argentina and Uruguay. It is born in the Brazilian state of Santa Catarina, in the Serra Geral, at the confluence of the Canoas and Pelotas Rivers. It has an extension of 1,770 km and covers a total area of approximately 370,000 km^2.[62]

62. *See* https://www.saltogrande.org.

C. Regime of International Development: Yacyretá

195. In 1973 Argentina and Paraguay signed the Treaty of Yacyreta. Work started in 1983, finishing in 1994. In 1998, a 20th turbine was included, providing for the generation of 19,800 GWh in 2014.[63]

§16. Strategic State Energy Policy I: Nuclear Energy

I. At the National Level

196. Upholding a 'peaceful sense towards the benefit of mankind', Decree 10936/1950 was enacted by the Executive Power at a very early stage of the international atomic energy development, pursuant to the following reasons and whereas:[64]

(a) It represents a public order State matter.
(b) It represents a military strategic national defence matter.
(c) It represents a public health matter.
(d) Atomic energy can always replace traditional generation means, altering the national socioeconomic balance in relation to industry, transportation, mining, etc.
(e) It requires public and private cooperation for research and development.

197. Decree No 10936/1950 consequently created an autarchic Executive Power organ, the National Atomic Energy Commission (CNEA),[65] with the following original functions:

(a) Coordinate and stimulate atomic research.
(b) Control public and private atomic research within the Argentine territory.
(c) Propose measures against radioactive damage.
(d) Propose measures towards beneficial usage of atomic energy.

198. In addition, Decree Law No 22498 defined:[66]

(a) Autarchy of the CNEA.
(b) Location, at the capital City of Buenos Aires.
(c) National jurisdiction over the entire territory.
(d) Assets, composed by those belonging to CNEA, DNEA and National Atomic Energy Plants, and any asset acquired thereby.
(e) Resources, composed by the National Budget allocation, incomes from operations and activities, donations and legacies, loans and finance funding.

---

63. *See* https://www.eby.org.ar.
64. Decree No 10936, OB 31/05/1950.
65. *See* s. 1, Decree No 10936, OB 31/05/1950.
66. *See* Decree Law No 22498, OB 18/12/1956.

(f) CNEA board composition: one president and five members, lasting five years, with a possibility for re-election; anyone directly or indirectly related to a development activity is foreclosed from the CNEA board.
(g) The CNEA board duties are: to research the financial and political domains of atomic development industry; to assess the Executive Power in relation to atomic security; to assign assessing commissions; to establish direct relations with foreign atomic development institutions; to make presentations at meetings and conferences; to make agreements with public and private entities; to regulate the CNEA functioning, the exploitation and importation of atomic materials, the instalment of atomic energy facilities, the permanent control over radioactive substances and materials; to define fees and sanctions; to prepare and approve its budget; to appoint, ascend, translate, and remove personnel; to prepare scientific and technical personnel; and to propose new elements to be declared of nuclear strategic importance by the Congress.
(h) Special authorization from the Executive Power for the exportation of atomic materials, the enactment of societies,[67] the establishment of foreign offices, the request of foreign credit, and the agreement with the Provinces to develop nuclear mining within their jurisdiction.[68]
(i) The CNEA president is entitled as the organ of legal representative.

199. Lastly, original CNEA functions were expanded as follows:[69]

(a) Promote transference of nuclear technology.
(b) Regulate atomic waste.
(c) Regulate nuclear generation facilities retirement.
(d) Manage the property of nuclear fuel.
(e) Develop, build, and operate experimental reactors.
(f) Develop nuclear appliance to medicine, biology, and industry.
(g) Control nuclear mining.
(h) Promote general research agreements.

200. Regarding the early experience of atomic energy research and development, Decree No 2842/1955 approached the issue of atomic minerals' acquisition and management:[70]

(a) It determined that the CNEA was the only State organ with competence to acquire Uranium and related compounds.
(b) Mining producers must inform their technical development issues to the CNEA.

67. For example, Decree No 1719/1981, OB 26/10/1981 authorized the CNEA to enact a corporation (*Inc.*) to develop the Ezeiza Plant.
68. For example, Decree No 1669/1981, OB 21/10/1981 regulated an agreement between the Nation and the Province of Mendoza.
69. *See* Law No 24804, OB, 2/4/1997. *Also,* Decree No 1390/98, OB, 27/11/1998.
70. *See* Decree 2842, OB 28/02/1955.

201. Decree No 1540/1994 created a National Atomic Regulation Agency (ENRA), which was to be empowered with all CNEA competences except for the exploitation of nuclear energy generation, transferred to the new State-owned corporation *Nucleoeléctrica Argentina S.A.* in order to operate *Atucha I, Embalse de Rio Tercero,* and to finish and operate *Atucha II.*[71] Transmission of CNEA to ENRA never happened, remaining public atomic energy competences to CNEA as a General Secretariat of the presidency's organ.[72] In the meantime, the ENRA was succeeded by the Nuclear Regulation Authority (ARN): 'The Nuclear Regulatory Authority will be in charge of the function of regulating and supervising nuclear activity in all matters related to nuclear and radiation safety, physical protection and control of the use of nuclear materials, licensing and control of nuclear facilities, and international safeguard, as well as advising the National Executive Power on matters within its competence.'[73]

202. Broadly, it is possible to assert that Law No 24804 states that CNEA is mainly entitled to general atomic energy public policy matters, whilst ARN is entitled to atomic security, and atomic energy generation permits provisions and controls.[74]

203. The ARN is therefore an autarchic organ with full legal capacity,[75] and any atomic activity in the Argentine territory is consequently subject to the ARN regulation, including:[76]

(a) Safety and non-proliferation.
(b) Insurances in order to preclude or compensate nuclear damage according to the Vienna Convention on Civil Liability due to Nuclear Damage.
(c) National jurisdiction in relation to tribunals.
(d) Environmental impact assessment in relation to nuclear activities.
(e) Regulate the safety of nuclear development activities as well as materials and waste transportation.
(f) Evaluate, concede and retrieve atomic energy development licences.
(g) Evaluate, concede, and retrieve atomic minerals development licences.
(h) Inspect and control nuclear and nuclear–related facilities.
(i) Propose to the Executive Power the cession or replacement of a licensee.
(j) Prosecute civil or criminal actions in relation to nuclear activities.
(k) Apply sanctions.
(l) Decommission nuclear materials and close facilities.
(m) Protect sensitive technological, commercial or industrial information.
(n) Inform the Executive and Legislative Powers of the annual balance of activities.

---

71. Decree No 1540/1994, OB 30/08/1994.
72. *See* Decree No 1450/2002, OB 09/08/2002.
73. *See* s. 7, Law No 24804, OB, 2/4/1997.
74. *See* ss 7 and 8, Law No 24804, OB, 2/4/1997.
75. *See* s. 15, Law No 24804, OB, 2/4/1997.
76. *See* s. 9, Law No 24804, OB, 2/4/1997. *See* Resolution ARN No 14/1997, OB, 23/02/1998.

(o) Any other measure required to fulfil the aims and goals of the law.

204. Nuclear waste disposal locations and plants are suggested by the CNEA and approved by the ARN.[77]

205. The ARN is directed by a six–member board, representing during six years the Senate (2), the Chamber of Deputies (2) and the Executive (2). Anyone directly or indirectly related to a development activity is foreclosed from the ARN board.[78] The ARN board's duties are to: implement and control atomic normative; regulate the ARN functioning; regulate its personnel activities; prepare its annual budget.[79]

206. Regarding nuclear energy generation tariffs, section 26 asserts:

> The licensees holding an authorization or permit, or legal entities whose activities are subject to the control of the authority will pay annually and in advance, a regulatory fee to be approved through the general budget of the Nation. In the case of nuclear power plants, this annual regulatory rate may not be greater than the value equivalent to the annual average price of one hundred megawatt hours (100 MW/h) in the Wholesale Electricity Market determined based on the prices in force in that market in the year Immediately previous. Said sum shall be paid per rnegawatt of nominal nuclear power installed until the removal of irradiated fuel from the reactor at the withdrawal stage is completed by the operator of said facility. The new nuclear power plants must also pay, also annually and in advance, the regulatory fees corresponding to the construction and the licensing process, which will be approved by the national Executive Branch. For the rest of the licensees holding an authorization or permit subject to regulation, the Nuclear Regulatory Authority will dictate the corresponding licensing and inspection fee regime, which may not exceed zero with five percent (0.5%) of the income or equivalent indicator of the activity subject to regulation of the previous fiscal year. The delay in the payment of the fee or the fines provided for in Article 16, paragraph g) will be automatic and will accrue the punitive interests determined by the enforcement authority. The debt certificate for non-payment issued by the Nuclear Regulatory Authority will be sufficient title to enable the executive procedure before the federal civil and commercial courts.

207. It is essential to mention CNEA and ARN personnel – other than the board members – are subject to the General Labour Law Act No 26088.[80] In addition, they are subject to Administrative Proceedings Law No 19549.[81]

---

77. *See* s. 13, Law No 24804, OB, 2/4/1997.
78. *See* s. 18, Law No 24804, OB, 2/4/1997.
79. *See* ss 23–25, Law No 24804, OB, 2/4/1997.
80. *See* ss 3 and 27, Law No 24804, OB, 2/4/1997.
81. *See* s. 28, Law No 24804, OB, 2/4/1997.

208. Also, regulation states that 'the national State shall be the sole owner of the special fissionable materials contained in the irradiated fuel elements when executing an activity covered by this law, as well as of the special fusible materials that may be introduced or developed in the country'.[82]

209. Since Decree No 1390/1998, nuclear energy generation is performed by State–owned *Nucleoeléctrica Argentina Sociedad Anónima (NaSa)*, which operates all three facilities (*Atucha I, Atucha II,* and *Embalse*).[83] NaSa was to be privatized, but that never happened due to its strategic importance.

II. At the International Level

210. In the implementation of nuclear policy, the obligations assumed by the Argentine Republic are subject to the following international agreements: the Treaty for the Prohibition of Nuclear Weapons in Latin America and the Caribbean (Treaty of Tlatelolco); the Nuclear Non-proliferation Treaty; the Agreement between the Argentine Republic, the Federative Republic of Brazil, the Brazilian-Argentine Agency for Accounting and Control of Nuclear Materials, and the International Atomic Energy Agency for the Application of Safeguards, as well as the commitments assumed by virtue of membership to the Group of Nuclear Supplier Countries and the National Regime for Sensitive Export Control.

82. *See* s. 32, Law No 24804, OB, 2/4/1997.
83. Decree No 1390/1998, OB, 27/11/1998; *see* http://www.na-sa.com.ar.

Chapter 3. Transport

§1. Introduction

I. Unbundling & Public Service

211. As clearly stated, Argentina followed the 'unbundling' model originally applied in the United Kingdom to media and telecommunications, which was later generally used in similar industries in order to pursue privatizing schematics according to the '*Washington Consensus*'.[84]

212. According to '*unbundling*', neither can transportation companies buy or sell power nor can generators, distributors or great consumers be transportation companies' major shareholders.[85]

213. Notwithstanding the 'monopolistic character' of transportation and distribution of power, these stages remained under the 'public service' umbrella, affecting: their synergies with users; operational characteristics; tariffs characteristics; investment and maintenance; and their relationship with governmental organs.[86]

II. Privatizing: Concession Method

214. Law No 24065 promoted privatizing through international bid rounds and renewable fixed-term concession method.[87]

§2. The Interconnection System in Argentina

215. The ISA is composed by the transmission lines originally foreseen in Law No 15336, plus all subsequent enlargements and modifications.[88] The later – enlargement and modifications – must be approved by the regulator (National Power Regulatory Agency (ENRE)).

§3. The ISA Operation: CAMMESA & The Procedures

216. Law No 24065 sets the operative burden of the ISA on the above-mentioned CAMMESA company:

84. Cf. s. 1, Law No 24065.
85. Cf. ss 30 and 31, Law No 24065.
86. Cf. ss 2 and 3, Law No 24065.
87. Cf. ss 3 and 53, Law No 24065.
88. Cf. s. 11, Law No 24065.

The technical office of the Argentine Interconnection System (SADI) will be in charge of the National Cargo Office (DNDC), a body that will be established in the form of a corporation whose capital must be represented by non-endorsable registered shares and whose majority shareholding will be initially, at the head of the Ministry of Energy, and in which the different actors of the Wholesale Electricity Market (MEM) may have a shareholding. The state participation, initially majority, may be reduced by the Executive Power up to ten percent (10%) of the share capital, however this percentage must ensure the participation and veto power in the board.

The Ministry of Energy will determine the norms to which the DNDC will adjust for the fulfilment of its functions, which must guarantee the transparency and equity of decisions, according to the following principles:

a) Allow the execution of the contracts freely agreed between the parties, understanding as such the generators (with the exception of those included in article 1 of law 23,696 and the Argentine part of the binational entities), large users and distributors (market I finish it);
b) Dispatch the required demand, based on the recognition of energy and power prices established in the following article, which must be explicitly committed to accept the market players, to have the right to supply or receive electricity not freely agreed between the parties.[89]

217. Further on, Law No 24065 set the general basis for the ISA operative framework: 'The Procedures'.[90]

§4. Tariffs

218. Criteria for tariffs' regulation was also clearly stated by Law No 24065:

The services provided by the carriers and distributors will be offered at fair and reasonable rates, which will comply with the following principles:

a) They will provide carriers and distributors who operate in an economic and prudent manner, the opportunity to obtain sufficient income to satisfy the reasonable operating costs applicable to the service, taxes, amortizations and a rate of return determined in accordance with the provisions of article 41 of this law;
b) They must take into account the reasonable differences that exist in the cost between the different types of services considering the form of provision, geographical location and any other characteristic that the entity qualifies as relevant;

89. Cf. s. 35, Law No 24065.
90. Cf. s. 36, Law No 24065. Also, https://portalweb.cammesa.com/Pages/BackupBotoneraAneriorIzquierda/Normativa/procedimientos.aspx.

c) In the case of distributor tariffs, the sale price of electricity to users will include a term representative of their purchases in the WHOLESALE ELECTRIC MARKET. For this purpose, a reference price will be calculated that will be made up of the price of the contracts that the distributor enters into under the terms of article 21 of this law, the hourly spot price per node resulting from the provisions of article 36 of the this law and the associated transportation costs, both with the modifications introduced by articles 8 and 9 respectively of this decree;
d) Subject to the fulfilment of the requirements established in the preceding paragraphs, they will ensure the minimum reasonable cost for the users compatible with the security of supply.[91]

In addition, tariffs 'must enable a reasonable rate of return to those companies that operate efficiently. Likewise, the rate must: a) Be related to the degree of efficiency and operational effectiveness of the company; b) Be similar, as an industry average, to other activities of similar or comparable risk nationally and internationally'.[92] Tariffs review proceeding is also defined:

> The concession contracts to carriers and distributors will include an initial rate table that will be valid for a period of five (5) years and will comply with the following principles:
>
> a) It will establish the initial rates that correspond to each type of service offered, such bases will be determined in accordance with the provisions of articles 40 and 41 of this law;
> b) Subsequent rates will establish the maximum price to be set for each class of services;
> c) The maximum price will be determined by the entity in accordance with market indicators that reflect changes in the value of goods and / or services. These indicators will in turn be adjusted, more or less, by a factor designed to stimulate efficiency and, at the same time, investments in construction, operation and maintenance of facilities;
> d) The rates will be subject to adjustments that allow reflecting any change in the costs of the concessionaire, which the latter cannot control;
> e) In no case may the costs attributable to the service provided to a user or category of users be recovered through rates charged to other users.[93]

91. Cf. s. 40, Law No 24065.
92. Cf. s. 41, Law No 24065.
93. Cf. s. 42, Law No 24065.

Chapter 4. Distribution

§1. The Distribution Segment

219. Pursuant to the 'unbundling' model, the distribution is the last stage between power producers and users/consumers.

220. It is worth mentioning, 'Distributors will be responsible for serving any increase in demand in their concession area to end users, so they must ensure their supply, entering into block sale contracts, as they deem appropriate. They will not be able to invoke the insufficient supply of electrical energy as an exemption from responsibility for the breach of the quality of service standards established in their concession contract.'[94] Also, 'Carriers and distributors are obliged to allow indiscriminate access by third parties to the transport capacity of their systems that is not committed to supply the contracted demand, under the conditions agreed by the parties and in accordance with the terms of this law.'[95]

§2. Tariffs

221. Tariffs criteria mentioned for transportation applies to distribution.

§3. After Law No 25561

222. The normalization of prices and tariffs for electrical energy also contemplated, from its beginnings, gradual increases in prices paid by users supplied through distributors (typically residential users, commercial and industrial). The first of these increases occurred in late January 2016 with the publication of MINEM Resolution 6/2016, which set the price as a reference without subsidy for the whole country as established in Article 2 of Resolution 1,301 of 7 November 2011 of the then Secretary of Energy, which still represented a smaller percentage of the real cost of supplying national demand. It should be noted that demand segmentation was substantially eliminated from this rule, so that all users with demands less than 300 kW started paying the same seasonal price of energy, regardless of its use (lighting, residential, commercial). The Resolution also created the Social Rate programme, in which the price of energy at which the public service providers buy from electrical distribution to eligible users (MINEM Resolution 219/2016 and amendments), consisting of a consumption block of 150 kWh/month in which 100% of the price of energy was subsidized and another block equivalent in which 50% was subsidized. Subsequently, in June 2016, through the MINEM Resolution 1111/2016, the first block was doubled (300 kWh/month) for eligible users residing in NEA provinces. It should be clarified that, as of 1 January 2019, and by virtue of the Fiscal Consensus signed on 13 September 2018 approved by Law No 27,469,

94. Cf. s. 21, Law No 24065.
95. Cf. s. 22, Law No 24065.

the provinces agreed to define the differential electricity rate based on the socioeconomic conditions of residential users under its jurisdiction. Subsequently, new prices for energy, power and transport were fixed, with the aim of gradually and predictably approaching the price which pays the demand at the cost of generation. Listed below are the relevant administrative acts, from 2016 to the present:

(a) MINEM Resolution 6 dated 25 January 2016.
(b) SEE Resolution No 41 dated 25 April 2016.
(c) Resolution SEE 384/2016, dated 27 October 2016.
(d) Resolution SEE 20/2017 dated 27 January 2017.
(e) Resolution SEE 256/2017 dated 28 April 2017.
(f) Resolution SEE 979/2017, dated 1 November 2017, in force until the end of the Public Hearing called by Resolution 403 dated 25 October 2017 of the Ministry of Energy and mining.
(g) SEE Resolution 1,091 dated 30 November 2017.
(h) SSEE 44 provision dated 14 May 2018.
(i) SSEE 75 provision dated 31 July 2018.
(j) SSEE 97 provision dated 24 October 2018.
(k) Resolution SGE 366 dated 2 January 2019.
(l) SRRyME Resolution 14 dated 29 April 2019.
(m) SRRyME Resolution 38 dated 22 October 2019.

Part II. Regulatory Framework Concerning Oil and Gas *Upstream*

§1. Introduction

223. Argentina is a federal country. The same as Australia or Canada, gas and oil resources belong to the provinces where the hydrocarbon fields are (except for those deposits farther than 12 nautical miles, which belong to the National State). Different from Australia or Canada, the federal government has the exclusive authority to establish the basis of the regulation applicable to the gas and oil activity. However, the provinces act as the authority of application of those regulations.

224. Since its creation in 1907, the hydrocarbon industry in Argentina was highly regulated and was characterized by a great influence from the State through one of the first NOCs (National Oil Companies) in history, YPF created in 1922. However, during the 1990s, the activity was widely opened to independent and international oil companies by means of deep deregulation of the sector and the privatization of YPF.

225. On 29 June 2010, the first non-conventional well was drilled (of shale gas in the Loma La Lata field) in Argentina. In April 2011, the Energy Information Administration from the USA published the already famous 'World Shale Gas Resources: An Initial Assessment of 14 Regions outside the United States', a report that placed Argentina as a region with vast shale gas and shale oil resources (especially, in its formation Vaca Muerta). Six years later, 639 non-conventional wells had been drilled. After the USA and China, Argentina is the country with the highest development of non-conventional hydrocarbons.

226. However, on the arrival of the non-conventional there exist different opinions. Some people believe that they broke into the market as a 'game changer' both in the industry and the global energy geopolitics. For others, it is just a mere 'bubble' that will eventually explode, or even 'act of despair' of the producers to escape from near 'peak oil'. We favour the first option.

227. Some argue that the Shell gas or non-conventional gas is present as an environmentally friendly 'bridge' between the carbon dioxide energized world and global energetic matrix ruled by renewable energy sources. Others counter-argue that the Shell gas revolution (In the practice, low prices in gas and hence low prices in electricity) will postpone the moment in which the renewable energy will be finally competitive without subsidies. We also favour the first option.

228. The truth is that the energy sector is facing a new paradigm. Some analysts suggest that thanks to the non-conventional hydrocarbons, the USA will finally turn into a 'self-sufficient' country, after seventy years have passed since last time they were a 'net exporter'. Beijing, China, another potential key player in the shale gas wave, these countries – accounting for the 40% of the global consumption of energy, will emancipate from the imported natural gas and crude oil volumes, putting the leading role of Russia and Other Middle East countries at risk as the main suppliers of energy for the USA, Europe and Asia.

229. But beyond this so optimistic forecast, there emerges the debate on the question about sustainability of the shale among the most diverse groups of interests, both in developed and developing countries having considerable non-conventional resources. The saying that reads 'there is not such a thing a free lunch' extrapolated to the field of the non-conventional hydrocarbons indicates that the vast number of hydrocarbons that have been 'rediscovered' brought about together with them, from well below the earth, a great challenge.

230. The technology used for its commercial exploitation (the so-called hydraulic fracking or 'fracking') has a significant ecological footprint. Thus, the dilemma for the developed economies (such as The USA, Canada, the United Kingdom, Continental Europe) as well as the developing economies (China, Argentina, Poland, for example) consists in deciding if they will or will not exploit the resources available, and if they decide to do so, the challenge will be 'how to exploit it'. The way in which the dilemma is solved will have substantial effects in the twenty-first century global economy.

§2. Operative Modality

231. The hydrocarbons exploration and exploitation is an activity of an intensive capital and great technological development. This explains the dynamic character of the companies exploiting the conventional hydrocarbon fields as they have to be adapted not only to the regulatory changes being implemented but also to the technological changes in constant evolution.

232. The hydrocarbon gas starts as the exploratory well, which if it is successful is converted into appraisal well, until it gets to be a production well. The release of gas generated from the well will derive into a gas flow. In a non-conventional development, the shale gas/oil is found in the mother rock, the 'kitchen' where the hydrocarbon is created. The mother rock contains high levels of organic material ('rich gas or oil'), and little porosity and permeability. Hence there is no flow of hydrocarbon present in the rock. This is the reason why it is called 'non-conventional hydrocarbons'.

233. The operators historically considered the formations of shale gas/oil as indicators of the presence of hydrocarbons in nearby formations of greater permeability (the so-called reservoir rock). The reservoir rocks and the shale rocks can be found underneath the same extension of the earth. One may be at 1,500 m deep, while the other may be at 3,000 m under the earth. That is why the conventional and non-conventional exploitation can 'coexist and overlap'.

234. The combination of the advancements of two exiting techniques up to date unleashed the 'shale gas revolution'. In fact, the only way 'up to date' to economically exploit the shale rocks is through a dual technique: horizontal drilling and hydraulic fracking. This is the reason that the shale formations are a 'technology product'. We highlight 'up to date' as the industry is characterized by the innovation and the ongoing technological breakthroughs in such a way that what we say today (July 2017) can be inaccurate in some years' time.

235. The recovery factors of the shale gas are lower in comparison to the conventional reserves, and the decline rhythm of the shale is much faster than that of the gas of the conventional reserves. This requires a greater amount of wells (higher costs), and hence many argue that the shale gas is a 'price-driven revolution'.

236. The shale gas formations tend to extend throughout geographical areas significantly bigger than those of conventional gas. As a consequence, in certain places (for instance, Europe) the shale exploitation tends to affect 'highly dense areas'.

237. In the same line, areas with non-conventional potential are not always those with a strong tradition of gas and oil. That is why the shale exploitation, has aggravated the question of the 'political acceptance'.

238. The scale of necessary industrial operation to obtain a set volume of shale gas production is much higher than that required for the conventional production. In fact, the technique is called 'factory drilling'. This means that the activities of drilling and production can be considered more invasive, involving and generally greater 'environmental footprint'.

239. Finally, the 'hydraulic fracking' crates a complex challenge: (i) it uses great quantities of water, (ii) the chemicals injection creates the possibility of pollution in groundwater, (iii) the explosion partially underground carried out during the fracking or the reinjection of produced water can provoke quakes and (iv) the great quantity of water injected flowing back to the surface, creates the question of its sustainable disposition.

§3. Regulatory Frame for the Hydrocarbons Exploration and Production

240. Law No 17319, (The 'Hydrocarbon Law'), passed in 1967, conceives a system of exploration permits and exploitation concession given by the State (federal or provincial, depending on the place of the deposits), under which the companies have exclusive rights to explore, develop, exploit and acquire the production property in the mouth of the well in exchange for royalties and of the application of the general tax regime.

241. In 2014, Law No 27007 was sanctioned and its objective was to modify the Hydrocarbons Law to give regulatory tools to help boost the hydrocarbons projects economically speaking according to the geological reality of the country: matured fields, non-conventional formations, or offshore fields, which require a series of contract and economic conditions which a fifty-year-old law does not contemplate at least not appropriately.

242. In general, Law No 27007 tries to promote the development of the hydrocarbon projects by means of the following:

- Predictability for the investor regarding royalties and terms in the exploitation concessions terms.
- Longer exploitation terms to allow the return on investment of long-term intensive capital.
- The reduction of the setting of maximum limits to provincial 'government-take' to improve the return on investment for the respective projects.

243. Before the reforms under Law No 27007, most of the exploitation concessions were due around the years 2025/2027. That is to say, they had ten years of mining right left.

244. This combined with the fact that the current concession lacked appropriate schedules to develop non-conventional projects, gave place to the solution provided Law No 27007.

Chapter 1. Production

245. An exploration permit holder has the exclusive right to perform the necessary or appropriate operations for the hydrocarbons exploration inside the area specified in the permit. Each exploration permit can cover only *non*-tested areas not exceeding 10,000 km^2 (15,000 km^2 offshore).

246. Law No 27.007 establishes the basic terms of the conventional hydrocarbon-exploration permits. The first and second *basic* period of a conventional exploration permit is up to three years, and the extension term is up to five years. Regarding the non-conventional exploration, the law extends the term of the exploration permits up to a maximum of thirteen years; the terms of the first and second period are for up to four years, and they as well granted an extension term for up to five years.

247. This eliminates the restriction of the permit holding of more than five exploration permits at the same time, whether direct or indirect. It also establishes the flexibility of the obligations to reinvest a portion of the area for the term of the exploration permit. At the end of each of the first two basic terms, the areas covered are reduced at least 50% of the remaining area covered by the permit, and the permit holder can decide which part he keeps. At the end of the basic periods, the permit holder shall give back the remaining area to the Argentinean government unless he asks for an extension term and so he will keep 50% of the area.

Modification of the terms

248. Section 1 of the Law No 27007 replaces section 23 of the Hydrocarbons Law by the one indicated as follows. *The* removals of the Hydrocarbons Law are crossed out. Modifications and incorporations to the project are in **bold type**.[96]

Hydrocarbons Law	*Law No 27007*
Section 23. – The terms of the exploration permits shall be fixed in each tender with maximums as follows: Basic Term: 1st period for up to four years. 2nd period for up to three years. 3rd period up to two years.	**Section 23.** – The terms of the exploration permits shall be fixed in each **tender by the** Competent Authority, **in accordance with the objective of the exploration**, based on the description as follows: Basic term: Exploration with a conventional objective.

96. The format of removals cross-out and modifications incorporations **bold type** is repeated every time sections are compared.

Hydrocarbons Law	*Law No 27007*
Extension Period: for up to five years.For the excavation of the continental shelf (CS) each one of the basic term periods can be intended for one year. The extension under this section is optional of the permit holder. The partial transformation of the area with an exploration permit in concession of exploitation carried out before the permit basic term expiration, pursuant to section 22, authorizes to add a term of concession to the time not passed for the exploration permit, the extension term excluded. At any time the permit holder shall be entitled to renounce to all or part of the area covered with the exploration permit, notwithstanding the obligations set forth under section 20.	1st period for up to **three years**. 2nd period for up to **three years**. Extension Period for up to five years. **Exploration with an unconventional objective**: **1st period for up to four years,** **2nd period for up to four years,** Extension Period for up to five years For the exploration of the CS and **the territorial sea**, each of the basic terms of exploration with **a conventional objective** can be extended for one year. The extension set forth in this section is an optional for permit holder who **has made the investment and has fulfilled the other remaining duties at his expense.** The partial transformation of the area of the exploration permit in concession of exploitation carried out before the end of the basic term pursuant of section 22, gives the right to add to the term of the concession the time not passed of the exploration permit, the extension term excluded. At any time, the permit holder shall be entitled to renounce to any and all part covered by the exploration permit, notwithstanding obligations set forth under section 20.

249. As *follows* analysis of the amendments in further detail:

Law No 27007 establishes a difference between the applicable terms according to the exploration objective (i.e., conventional or non-conventional). This distinction was not present in the Hydrocarbons Law.
Law No 27007 reduces the maximum exploration terms since: (i) It eliminates the possibility of a third period inside the basic term, and (ii) for the exploration with a conventional objective, it reduces the maximum term for the first period from four to three years' time.
Law No 27007 clearly adds as a condition for the extension of the exploration term that the permit holder '*has made the corresponding investment and fulfilled the other remaining duties at its expense*'. This would have been an implicit condition in the original text of the Hydrocarbons Law; however its inclusion, in clear terms, strengthens the concept.

Removal of the limit in the number of simultaneous permits

250. Section 2 of the Law No 27007 replaces section 25 of the Hydrocarbons Law for the content as follows:

Hydrocarbons Law	*Law No 27007*
Section 25. – The exploration permit will cover areas with no more than one hundred de (100) units. And those granted over the platform shelf will not exceed one hundred and fifty (150) units. No physical or legal person can simultaneously have five exploration permits whether directly or indirectly.	**Section 25.** – The exploration permits will cover an area with no more than one hundred de (100) units. And those granted over the platform shelf will not exceed one hundred and fifty (150) units.

Law No 27007 formally eliminates a restriction that in the practice is not applied.

Modification of the reduction regime of the exploration area after the maturity of each period

251. Section 3 of Law No 27007 substitutes section 26 of the Hydrocarbons Law for the content as follows:

Hydrocarbons Law	*Law No 27007*
Section 26. – When each first and second basic terms of an exploration permit are due, the permit holder will reduce his area, at least, a 50% of the remaining area covered by the permit when the respective period is finished. The remaining area shall be equal to the original one minus the areas previously restored or converted into lots of an exploitation concession. At the end of the basic term, the permit holder will give back the total of the remaining area, unless he wants to exercise the right of extension; in such circumstance the area will be reduced to 50% of the remaining area g before the last period of such basic term is due.	**Section 26.** – When the basic term is finished, the permit holder **will decide if he continues exploring the area, or if he gives it back in total to the State. The permit holder shall be entitled to keep all the area originally granted, as long as he has duly fulfilled the obligation emerging from the permit.** At the end of the basic term the permit holder shall restore the total area, unless he exercises the right to use the extension period, and so the restoration shall be limited to the 50% of the remaining area (50%) before the maturity of the second period of the basic term.

Chapter 2. Exploitation

§1. Areas Award

252. The mechanism of award of a new area (which is not a concession deriving from an exploration permit or an existing subdivision) shall be by means of a public tender, and the criteria of selection shall be the investment amount compromised.

253. The Ministry of Energy and Mining and the provinces will draft a model Terms and Conditions[97] to be used by the different awarding authorities and they may add further special conditions for the area to be solicited.

254. The provinces will not be able to reserve areas in favour of public entities or companies or with a State participation, whatever its legal status.[98] But the areas reserved before the enforcement of the law shall continue to be awarded and exploited under the mechanisms of association pursuant to section 95 of the Hydrocarbons Law.

§2. Handling System

255. Section 18 of the Law No 27007 bans the handling system during the development stage. Regarding the areas that had been reserved in favour of provincial entities or companies, with a State participation (e.g., G&P), associative schemes can be realized (e.g., joint venture contracts), in which the participation of such State entity during the development stage will be proportional to the investment compromised and in relation to the ones effectively carried out by them. However, the handling system is not prohibited in the exploration stage. Hence, the provinces could impose it under a system in which the producers would not have the right to recover the costs during the production stage: 'free carry'.

§3. The Concession

256. If a permit exploration holder discovers quantities commercially exploitable of gas or oil, he has the right to obtain the exclusive concession to produce and exploit those hydrocarbons. Both the permit exploration holder and the concessioner are guaranteed confidentiality regarding the data acquired, unless the information has been disclosed, is about to be disclosed or due to legal issues were to be disclosed.[99]

---

97. *See* s. 47 of the Hydrocarbons Law.
98. *See* s. 91 *bis* of the Hydrocarbons Law.
99. Daniel Casal, 'Panorama de los Contratos de Operación para la Actividad Hidrocarburífera' Revista Argentina de Derecho de la Energía, Hidrocarburos y Minería, No 1, May–July 2014.

257. An exploitation concession also gives the holder the right to carry out the necessary or appropriate activities for the production of hydrocarbons, as long as those activities are not interfering with the activities of other permit exploration holder and exploitation concessions. An exploitation concession gives the holder the right to obtain a transport concession so as to evaluate the hydrocarbons produced in the area.

258. Law No 27007 establishes that the hydrocarbons exploitation concessions will be in force for thirty years as from the date of giving the exploitation concession, plus the time not passed of the exploration permit, minus the term of the extension, and it can be postponed for ten more years, subject to the approval of the terms and conditions by the giving authority at the moment of the extension.

259. Regarding the Non-conventional Hydrocarbons Exploitation Concessions, Law No 27007 incorporated to the Hydrocarbons Law a new type of commissioning for the exploitation of hydrocarbons: the Non-conventional Hydrocarbons Exploitation Concessions (hereinafter the '*CENCH*') consisting in a thirty-five-year term, an up to five-year 'Pilot Plan' included to be defined by the concessioner to determine the commercialization of the fields.

§4. Concession Extension

260. The concessioners will have to right to ask for an extension, each of them for a ten-year period, regardless of the extensions obtained prior to the passing of the new law.

261. The royalties aliquot is limited to an 18% in the cases of extension; that is to say, the giving authority could increase by 3% the aliquot of the first extension awarded (reaching a fee of 15%), and another 3% in the second extension (reaching a fee of 18%), but in any and all extension the giving authority awards, it cannot make further increase in the aliquot.[100]

262. The giving authority could establish for the extensions the payment of an 'extension bonus' whose maximum amount will be equal to the result of multiplying the remaining proved reserves associated to the conventional hydrocarbons exploitation at the end of the current period the concession by the 2% of the average basin price applicable to the respective hydrocarbons for the two previous years to the moment of giving the extension.

§5. Permits Expiration

263. The exploration permits and the exploitation or transport concessions can expire in any of the following scenarios:

100. *See* s. 27 of the Law No 27007.

- lack of payment of an annulment of the respective fee within three months of the maturity date;
- lack of payment of a royalty within three months of the maturity date;
- substantial or unjustified failure to comply with conditions set forth about productivity, conservation, investments, works or special advantages;
- repeated failure to submit the required, to allow the inspection to the corresponding authority of the application or to observe the appropriate techniques in the realization of the work;
- in the case of exploration permits, the failure to ask for the exploitation concession within thirty days of having determined the existence of commercially exploitable quantities of hydrocarbons and the failure to submit the application corresponding to the development programmes and investment commitments thereof;
- the concession or permit holder's bankruptcy;
- the passing away or finalization of the legal existence of the concession or permit's holder; or
- if the hydrocarbons were not transported for third parties on a non-discriminatory basis or the repeated breach of the tariffs authorized for such transport.

264. The Hydrocarbons Law establishes that before the declaration of expiration, the authority of application will have to give to the permit holder and/or concessioner who had failed to comply, a reasonable period to pay for the penalty.

265. When the concession is due or ended, all the hydrocarbons wells, the operation and maintenance equipment and the facilities will be automatically transferred to the province where the reservoir is placed or to the national government in the case of a reservoir of federal jurisdiction (i.e., to say place in the CS or offshore farther than 12 nautical miles), with no compensation for the concession's holder.

Chapter 3. Transport

Transport Concessions

266. Law No 26197[101] ('Ley Corta') establishes that the national government retains the power to give transport concessions to: (i) transport concessions placed in the territory of two or more provinces and (ii) transport concessions directly connected with exportation gas pipelines and destined to exportation. Consequently, transport concessions placed inside the territory of only one province and that are not connected to exportation installations, are transferred to the provinces.[102]

267. The term of any transport concession used to evacuate the hydrocarbons production and its derivatives of an exploitation concession (whether conventional or non-conventional) will be thirty-five tears as from the moment of the adjudication. The term of a transport concession can be extended for an additional period of ten years after the extension has been solicited to the corresponding authority. When that term is due, the installations will be under the State's domain without charge or tax whatsoever and operative of law.

101. 'La Ley Corta' was in full force as from 3 Jan. 2007.
102. *See* s. 3 of the Law No 26197.

Chapter 4. Tax

268. In Argentina, resources belong to the provinces in general, and to the federal government (which only has resources placed as from 12 nautical miles from the base lines –territorial sea – and up to the exterior limit in the CS – 200 nautical miles). Even though, the royalty corresponds to the provinces, the aliquot is established by a law of the National Congress, 'any and all possibility of competence between the provinces by the settlement of the companies' excluded. In the USA, on the other hand, the resource belongs to the owner of the installations and the royalty rate is applied in each concession contract, causing competition among the states. The system of royalties inside these two federal countries can also be differentiated regarding the royalties distribution. Different from Argentina where there is no distribution of royalties collected by the provinces (or the State), 'in the USA, there are funds with specific aims, that, somehow entails a distribution beyond the states where the exploitation is located'. The purpose of the royalties is 'to provide the owner of the reserve with a stable flow for the irreplaceable loss derived from the non-renewable resources extraction done by the producer'.

269. The Hydrocarbons Law establishes that a royalty of 12% will be paid for the value of well head (minus transport, treatment costs and other deductions), and 15% to the exploration permit holder. The difference between aliquots is established by the State to 'act as an incentive to speed the decision of soliciting a concession and to massively develop the area'. The value is calculated on the basis on volume and sales price of the produced gas and oil, minus the costs of transport and storage. Law No 25.561 that established the export retentions set forth that they were not to be deducted from the export price so as to calculate the 12% royalty. The awarding authorities shall be entitled to reduce the royalty up to 5% taking into consideration the productivity, condition and place of the wells pursuant to Law No 27007. The very same law says the royalties shall be the one and only mechanism of income for those authorities.

270. The production tertiary and extra heavy oil and offshore projects could obtain a reduction of royalties of up to a 50%, with the prior approval of the awarding authority and the Planning Commission.

271. The concessioners will be able to obtain a reduction of 25% of the royalties applicable to non-conventional hydrocarbons for the following ten years at the end of the 'Pilot Plan', if they require Non-Conventional Hydrocarbons Exploitation Concession for the following three years after Law No 27007 comes into force.

272. Apart from the payment of the royalties, under sections 57 and 58 of the Hydrocarbons Law, the holders of exploration permits and exploitation concession should pay an annual fee for each square kilometre or fraction of area of the permit of concession which varies depending on the phase of operation, that is to say, exploration or exploitation; and the case of the former, depending on the period of the exploration permit. The concessioner bears the expense indirectly, as in case of lack of payment the exploration or exploitation of the field may be suspended.

Chapter 5. Easements

273. Section 66 of the Hydrocarbons Law provides that the permit holders of Exploration, Exploitation and Transport concessioners of the hydrocarbon fields have the rights guaranteed by the Mining Code regarding the real estate of fiscal or private property placed inside the area affected by their work. The opposition of the owner of the affected facility, whether that be about the occupation or the compensation regime, shall not suspend or hinder the realization of the works authorized by the authority of application, as long as the concessioner take the necessary precautions for eventual risks they could generate. This right is – as well – applicable to, in the case of areas granted which are covered by sea, rivers and lake waters, the coastal terrain boarding thereof or the nearest coast.[103]

103. *See* s. 67 of the Hydrocarbons Law.

Chapter 6. Non-conventional Formations Exploration and Production

274. Once a country has been granted a permit to develop *shale* gas, parallel to an environment legal regime, a strategy should be designed about how to explore and exploit the non-conventional resources.

275. Give the unique characteristics of the *shale* gas industry, the regulatory authorities should consider if the existing regulations applicable to the *upstream* activity are appropriate, or else, if it is necessary to adopt a new regulatory framework specially designed for the non-conventional industry.

276. Whatever the decision, so as to have a successful result, the regime should give the potential investors clear guarantees and security in relation to the activity, and should as well consider the issues as follows.

§1. Terms of Access to the Non-conventional Resources

277. The property rights over the *shale* gas/oil in the USA correspond to the owner of the land. This has been one of the reasons for the rapid growth of the industry in the USA, as they have lower entrance barrier than in countries where the ownership of the minerals is in the government, and so that ownerships is subject to the times of the administration's agendas.[104]

278. In such countries, the regulatory authorities should consider what type of contract they will concede (e.g.: licences, *production sharing contracts*, service contracts, etc.), if the State were to participate in the operations (directly or through a State-owned company),[105] and if the concession of contracts shall be performed by means of a tender or by an open negotiation.

§2. Separation of the Rights on Mineral Substances

279. The conventional and non-conventional hydrocarbon reserves can be found underlying the very same extension of the earth. In these cases, the first could be under exploitation and second could not. The coexistence of conventional and non-conventional resources under the same extension of land opens a new paradigm in hydrocarbons exploitation.

---

104. *See* 'Second Report Stevens', *supra*, p. 9.
105. For instance, in Argentina, Neuquén (where '*Vaca Muerta*' is placed) an oil 100% State-owned company was created ('*Gas y Petróleo del Neuquén S.A.*') with the almost exclusive right to participate in the '*production sharing contracts*' given by the province for the *shale* gas exploration and exploitation in Neuquén.

280. The owners of the resources can consider the possibility of separating the rights on the minerals in different strata (such a '*deep rights*' and '*shallow rights*'). The separation of these rights was originally thought to incentive the exploration and production of non-productive areas, and to increase the quantity of available rights for sale. With the revolution of *shale* gas/oil, such separation can be used to efficiently exploit the two types of resources: the conventional and non-conventional ones.[106]

§3. Taxation

281. The success of the *shale* gas industry in the USA is footed in the small independent energy companies the independent energy (the so-called *momma and poppa companies*), which took the risk of being the pioneers in entering into the technically challenging *shale* industry – One of the reasons for that is the '*Energy law in the USA from 1980*' which gave the producers (i) fiscal credits of up to 50 cents per BTUs' million,[107] and (ii) introduced the rule of '*drilling intangible cost*'[108] typically covering more than 70% of the wells' development costs[109]

282. Similarly, Alberta province (Canada) offers reduced royalty tariffs for '*deep drillings*' (deeper than 2.500 m) and for less productive wells.[110]

283. The fact that the non-conventional is more expensive to exploit than the conventional[111] demands a decision if a special fiscal regime should be established aimed at releasing the investments (especially in the countries where the *shale* formations are not developed).

---

106. Alberta and British Columbia in Canadá have established different legal regimes which set two types of right over the minerals ('deep rights' and 'shallow rights') to foster the public reversion of any portion of the strata not being explored or exploited by producers (*See* Allan Ingelson & Will Randall, '*Shallow Rights Reversion: Uncertainty and Disputes*'. *HeinOnline* 48 Alta.L. Rev. 397 2010–2011). In the United States, the private rents ('*leases*') sometimes contain clauses about depth vertical separation called '*Pugh clause*' that, up to a certain extent, can be used to separate the right originally contained in the lease in case no investment has been performed in a determined area.
107. To reduce the incentive of passing products derived from gas to products derived from oil whenever the oil prices fall, such drop was accompanied by an increase in the fiscal credit.
108. The intangible costs of drilling include the necessary for the drilling and the beginning of the production, including but not limiting the salaries, supplies, contractors' services and similar overheads for which there is no residual value.
109. *See* STEVENS second report, *supra*, p. 2. *See also* Daniel Yergin, *The Quest*, *supra*, 326.
110. *See 'The New Royalty Framework'* (25 Oct. 2007), at www.energy.gov.ab.ca.
111. At least during the development stage '*when the offer increases and the production capabilities are honed, the costs drop, and shale gas can be even cheaper to produce than the conventional natural gas*' (*see* Daniel Yergin, *The Quest*, *supra*, 329).

§4. Prices Regime

284. The *shale* gas/oil industry in the USA took off in the decade when the prices of oil and gas were significantly high.[112] The price of oil and natural gas in the USA are based especially on the offer and demand laws, as well as on the influence of *hedgers* and speculators.[113]

285. However, many of the countries with great expectation for the development of *shale* gas have opted to control the prices (e.g., China and Argentina) a decision that can really hinder any real possible development for the non-conventional gas. These countries have taken different courses of action to deal with the issue.

286. Some prefer to take out the prices controls and to adopt a regime of price based on the laws of the markets, for instance, what China decided in their twelfth 'five-year plan'.[114]

287. Others can proceed with the prices-control scheme, but allowing higher prices for the *shale* gas in comparison to the conventional gas; or even control the conventional gas prices and let the market control the price of the *shale*. This approach of '*double regime*', which was first elaborated by the USA in the '*Natural Gas Law of 1978*' regarding intra and interstate production, was also introduced in Argentina under the programme known as 'Gas Plus' or several programmes of 'Incremental Production'.[115]

§5. Commercialization of the Production

288. Together with the prices regime, the operators will be as well worried about the regulation of the commercialization of the *shale* production.

---

112. Between 2000 and 2008, the price of the natural gas *Henry Hub* was stable at an average of USD 6.73 per MMBtu, at a stable dollar in 2010. But as the production of *shale* started to increase in significant volumes in 2009 and 2010, the price was reduced at an average of USD 4.17 per MMBtu (at stable dollars 2010). In October 2011, it was further reduced at USD 3.50 per MMBtu (at stable dollars 2010). In 2016, the price was about USD 2.25 p/MMBtu (*see 'The Economic and Employment Contributions of Shale Gas in the United States*' (December 2011, report written by *IHS Global Insight*, at www.ihs.com *(see also* 'Second Report Stevens', *supra*, p. 4).
113. At the end of 1980 and the beginning of 1990, NYMEX included natural gas to their indexes. *Henry Hub*, Louisiana, is an important transmission and transaction point of natural gas and it is the reference for NYMEX for the sale of contracts of futures of gas in their Exchange market.
114. *See* IEA, *supra*, p. 118.
115. Generally, the '*market dual systems*' operates on the premise of '*new*' gas (Extracted from the wells drilled as from a certain date) with a deregulated price and the '*old*' gas (of the wells drilled up to a certain date) are still subject to price controls. This approach could be useful to attract investments of new drillings and a new production, but it can also be counterproductive when increasing the amount of disputes over the contracts of '*old*' gas (i.e., to say the '*take or pay*' battles arising from Natural Gas Law of 1978 in the United States) and when incrementing the transaction and monitoring of the costs of '*old*' and '*new*' investments (*See* Jeffrey C. King, *supra*, p. 5).

289. Different from the crude oil, the characteristics and the use of the natural gas in most countries (e.g.,: electricity generation, domestic and commercial heating, the raw material in the industry), make for the regulators a totally different '*ball game*' when considering the '*priorities in the use of gas*', as such:[116]

- The use of gas for reinjection to keep or improve the production of oil.
- The use of gas for generation of de electricity in the field by the producers.
- Obligation of domestic supply for the internal market in general or a specific segment (for instance, demand for residential and commercial heating, generation of electricity).
- Sales for exportation through oil pipelines or GNL.

290. The regulators will have to clearly define the scope and privileges of those supplies destined to the rendering of the public service or the order of priority and to confirm the producers' capacity to make spot and long-term sales of non-conventional gas, without the rerouting of the hired volumes to other consumers.

§6. Extension and Stages in the Contracts

291. The hazy line delimiting the stages of exploration and exploitation of a *shale* gas development project is another key item the regulators have to consider when marking the regulatory frame.[117] In the *shale* gas industry, the exploration is not an unusual obstacle as the existence of bedrock is already well known.[118]

292. The real obstacle is the '*assessment period*' (or '*appraisal*'). An intensive drilling is usually necessary to verify the size, the shape and the nature of the resources of the s*hale* and to carry out a financial analysis of the area. While each well appraisal of a conventional deposit tends to increase the knowledge on the deposit structure and its limits in general, in the case of the *shale* formation is much more difficult to extrapolate the results of the individual appraisal wells to the area as a whole[119]

293. Many legal regimes did not have any provision to face the situation in which the period exploration is too short to allow the assessment of a discovery that could take several years.[120] The non-conventional gas demands from the regulators to consider introduction of longer periods of exploration or an '*intermediate*' stage

116. *See* Claude Duval et al., *supra*, p. 184.
117. *See* IEA, *supra*, p. 53.
118. *Ibid.*, p. 22. '*In fact there is no true exploration of non-conventional gas. However, the amount of gas present and specially the amount of gas that can be technically and economically recovered is uncertain until a number of Wells have been drilled and tested*'.
119. *See* IEA, *supra*, p. 53. *See also* 'First Report Stevens', *supra*, p. 14, where the economist highlights that 'due to the big geological differences, *not only in between the oilfields, but also between the Wells of the same formation, the extrapolation of one formation or well to another has to be treated with great care*'.
120. *See* Claude Duval et al., *supra*, p. 135.

between the exploration and the exploitation in which the producers can appraise and value the commercial viability of the *shale* gas exploitation.

294. There are some experiences of regulations in this sense. In the 1980s, Australia implemented in its formations of gas *offshore* '*retention contracts*' allowing the producer to keep the area of the contract (instead of resigning to it) for a certain period of time (between five and ten years), while he was analysing the discovery and defining its commercialization.[121] In the 1990s, Argentina created a similar regime called '*Suspension of the Declaration of de Marketability*', that mainly released the producers from the obligation of investing in and developing the market of the gas, in the case of the existence of the following conditions: (i) non-availability of the transport to commercialize the natural gas, (ii) lack of demand of natural gas in the market, (iii) impossibility to industrialize natural gas, or (iv) lack of commercial capacity for any GNL project.

§7. Access to the Transport Capacity

295. The promise of the great quantities of natural gas as from the non-conventional formations can only be realized if there exists an adequate capacity of gas pipelines for the transport of such production to the consumers.[122]

Experts affirm that the access of third parties to the gas pipelines in the USA has been one of the main factors to succeed for the *shale* gas, as it guaranteed the small gas producers that their new gas production would be capable of entering the market and this is way they encouraged the investment[123]

296. In the USA, the ownership of the rights of the transport capacity is separated from the property of the gas pipeline. This separation ('*unbundling*') of the rights of capacity of the property of the installations makes is possible for the producer to access to the market through tenders of the gas pipelines capacity.[124]

297. The regulators have to consider that the *shale* gas development will be delayed if there are no transparent rules about the way to assign the available capacity, the types of services (for instance, firm and non-interruptible and firm with '*interruptible windows*'), the applicable tariffs and the extension of the gas pipeline capacity.[125]

121. *See* David AW Maloney, '*Stranded Gas: Australia's Offshore Retention Leases*', 22. J. Energy & Nat. Resources L. 357 2004.
122. *See* Michael J. Byrd et al., '*Exploring Common Legal Issues in U.S. Shale Plays*', at www.bakermckenzie.com, January February 2010.
123. *See* IEA, *supra*, p. 53; *See also*, Kenneth B. Medlock III et al., '*Shale Gas and US National Security*' (July 2011), p. 14, *James A. Baker III Institute for Public Policy, Rice University*, available at www.bakerinstitute.org.
124. *See* Robert Means and Deborah Cohn, '*Common Carriage of Natural Gas*', pp. 553, 59 Tul. L. Rev. 529 1984–1985.
125. *86 See* Fred Bosselman et al., *Energy, Economics and the Environment* (Foundation Press, 2006), p. 598).

§8. Flexibility in the Operations

298. The industry of the *shale* gas services is an '*oligopoly controlled by the USA*'.[126] The revolution of the *shale* gas/oil was possible in the USA thanks to a great fleet of earth drilling equipment operating in the country. Nowadays, there is no other '*onshore*' services industry equal to that globally speaking. This situation will delay the rhythm of development in the country willing to follow the revolution of *shale* gas of the USA, such as Poland, China and Argentina.[127]

299. For those reasons, there are a series of standard obligations in international oil agreements that the regulators will have to modify to make the non-conventional oil operation financially feasible: (i) the obligatory execution of the compromised works (e.g., the drilling of the wells) within specific and rigid terms[128] (ii) ' *local hiring*' and availability of '*citizenship*' under which the producers have to hire local labour and service companies for the development of their areas and (iii) restrictions to the importation of goods in the way of importation duties or long administrative proceedings.[129]

300. In brief, the regulators eventually will have to consider if the producers have the right to (I) to suspend the period of validity of exploration and/or exploitation if it is impossible to render the service due to lack of equipment, (ii) to release the producer from the obligation of '*local hiring*' and of '*citizenship*' if the hiring of local labour or local services companies are not possible due to the lack of local personnel or companies with the necessary qualifications to carry out the operations and (iii) to freely and automatically import the necessary capital goods for the *shale* gas operations, at least until the local industry is developed.

§9. Concession of Non-conventional Exploitation

I. Introduction

301. As it was mentioned before, Law No 27007 incorporated into the Hydrocarbons Law a new type of commissioning for the exploration of hydrocarbons: the CENCH exploitation.

---

126. *See* IEA, *supra*, p. 91.f. Nowadays, the global drilling activity is centralized in the United States where more than half of the world's drilling fleet of equipment is located (about 2,000 active gas and oil drilling equipment, including those used for *shale* gas) to supply only 9% of the production of oil and 19% of gas in the world. In July 2010, there were only thirty-four drilling equipment on earth in all Western Europe. Only in the non-conventional way *Barnett*, in 2008, 199 drilling equipment were operating (*see* 'Second Report Stevens', *supra*, p. 9).
127. For instance, regarding costs, the drilling of a well of *shale* gas in Poland is three times as expensive as in the United States (USD 12 million versus USD 4 million) (*see* 'Second Report Stevens', *supra*, p. 9).
128. *See* Claude Duval et al., *supra*, p. 128.
129. *Ibid.*, p. 167.

302. Even though Decree No 929/2013 (the 'Decree 929'), which created the so-called Regime of Investment Promotion for Hydrocarbons Exploitation, already contemplated the figure of the CENCH, Law No 27007 gave it a legal frame and introduced significant modifications to its regulation.

303. This chapter describes the CENCH, and elaborates on the special characteristics that distinguish it from the concession of the hydrocarbons exploitation (hereinafter 'Conventional Concession'),[130] explains the changes introduced by Law No 27007 to the figure of the CENCH regarding the Decree 929, and analyses some of the specific aspects in detail.

II. Description of the CENCH

304. The place of the CENCH in the text of the Hydrocarbons Law (regulated in section 30 of Title II, called 'Concessions of exploitation') indicates that this is a kind inside the genre 'Concessions of Hydrocarbons Exploitation'.

305. Hence, all the provisions of the Hydrocarbons Law related to hydrocarbons in general apply to the CENCH,[131] which includes, *Inter alia*, section 27, first paragraph, which sets forth that 'the concession of exploitation confers the exclusive right *of exploiting the field of hydrocarbons existing in the areas comprised in the respective title of concession during the term fixed under section 35*'.

306. According to the last paragraph of the new section 27 *bis* of the Hydrocarbon Law, the CENCH shall have as its main objective 'The Non-Conventional exploitation of Hydrocarbons', defined in the first paragraph of the same section as 'the extraction of liquid and/or gaseous hydrocarbons *through non-conventional stimulation techniques applied in fields in geological formations of shale gas or shale oil, arsenic and compact (tight sands, tight gas, tight oil), coal coats (coal bed methane) and/or characterized in general by the presence of low permeability rocks*'.

307. However, the rule clearly sets that the owner of a CENCH 'will be able to develop complementary activities of conventional hydrocarbon exploitation.'[132]

130. The term Conventional Concession will be used as it facilitates the distinction with Non-conventional Exploitation Concession. However, let us make it clear that Conventional Concession entitles the owner of the right to exploit hydrocarbons conventionally and non-conventionally, having as a main objective one or the other type of exploitation.
131. Only provision such as s. 33 from the Hydrocarbons Law which establishes in its first paragraph '[c] *each of the lots in a concession shall coincide, the most possible, with all or part of the productive trap of hydrocarbons commercially exploitable*' no not apply to the CENCH as they are not compatible with non-conventional hydrocarbons exploitation. According to the geologists' elaboration, in the non-conventional hydrocarbon formations, there are no 'productive traps', when the hydrocarbons are placed inside the bedrock, acting a reservoir. *See* Instituto Argentino del Petróleo y Gas (2013).
132. Section 27 *bis in fine* of the Hydrocarbons Law, incorporated by s. 5 of the Law No 27007.

308. The CENCH has a term of thirty-five years, a 'Pilot Plan Period of up to five (5) years included, to be defined by the concessioner and approved by the Authority of Application at the moment of initiating the concession'.[133] The regime of extensions also applies to the CENCH under section 35 of the Hydrocarbons Law that – after the changes introduced by Law No 27007 – establishes indefinite extensions of ten years to each of them.[134]

309. Apart from the special cases of tender of vacant areas in tested zones[135] and assignment of participations in areas already given as a concession,[136] a CENCH can be accessed as from: (a) the ownership of (a) an exploration permit or (b) a Conventional Concession, without the need for the tender in none of the cases.[137]

310. Regarding access to the CENCH through a Conventional Concession, the new section 27 *bis* of the Hydrocarbons Law provides that 'The exploitation concessioner, *in the area of the concession, shall be entitled to request a subdivision of the existing area in new non-conventional exploitation areas of hydrocarbons and the award of new concession of a Non-Conventional Hydrocarbons Exploitation. Such request shall be funded in the development of a new pilot Plan that, in accordance with acceptable technical-economic criteria, has the exploitation commercial objective of the field uncovered. The National or provincial Authority of Application, according to the case, shall decide within the term of sixty (60) days and its validity will be computed in the way set forth under section 35.*'

311. In that case, the Conventional Concession corresponding to the area not affected to the CENCH will be ruled by the pre-existing terms and conditions, being the awarding authority forced to collect the respective title to the resulting extension of the subdivision.[138]

---

133. Section 35 subs. b) of the Hydrocarbons Law – Section 35 of the Hydrocarbons Law was amended by s. 9 of the Law No 27007.
134. To request an extension, the owner of the concession (CENCH or Conventional Concession) should: (i) have complied with all the requirements as the exploitation concessioner, (ii) be producing hydrocarbons in its corresponding area, (iii) submit an Investment Plan consistent with the development of the concession and (iv) make the formal request within at least one year in advance before the expiration of the concession.
135. Section 29, second paragraph, of the Hydrocarbons Law sets forth that 'The National, or Provincial Executive Branch, *as applicable, shall* [...] *have the power to give exploitation concessions on tested areas to those who meet the requirements and respect the specific procedures under s. 5* [Adjudications] *herein.*
136. Section 72, first paragraph, of the Hydrocarbons Law sets forth that: '*The permits and concessions granted pursuant to this Law can be transferred – with the previous authorization of the Executive Branch – to the ones meeting and complying with the terms and conditions to be the permit holder or concessioner, as applicable*'.
137. *See* s. 27, second paragraph, of the Hydrocarbons Law, incorporates by s. 4 of the Law No 27007.
138. *See* s. 27 *bis*, third paragraph, of the Hydrocarbons Law.

312. Moreover, the owners of the CENCH that are simultaneously owners of an adjoining pre-existing Conventional Concession, shall be entitled to request a unification of both areas as only one CENCH, '*as long as it is irrefutable proved the geological proximity of both areas*'. Such request should be based on the development of a Pilot Plan.[139]

313. Last but not least, it is worth mentioning that section 28 of the Law No 27.007 created an incentive for the hydrocarbons producers who ask for CENCHs within the first three years of the validity of the Law No 27007,[140] when providing that 'the national or provincial Executive Power, according to the case, as the Awarding Authority, *shall be entitled to reduce up to twenty five per cent (25%) the amount corresponding to royalties applicable to the hydrocarbons production and for the term of the following ten (10) years to the end of the pilot project,*[141] *in favour of companies requesting a Non-Conventional Hydrocarbons exploitation Concession, in the terms under section 27 bis of the 17.319 and its amendments, within thirty six (36) months as from the date of validity of the present law*'.

III. Changes Introduced by the Law No 27007 to the Figure of the CENCH Regarding Decree 929

314. The figure of the CENCH had been incorporated to the Argentinean Hydrocarbon regulation in 2013, through a Decree 929 which created the Promotion Regime of Investment for the hydrocarbon exploitation. Law o 27007 gave legal status to the CENCH, and introduced significant amendments in its regulation.[142]

315. The differences presented in the new text of the Hydrocarbons Law for the CENCH, under Decree 929, are as follows:

- Under the regime of the Decree 929, to access a CENCH it is necessary (i) to be the owner of the Conventional Concession, and (ii) to have been included in the Promotion Regime of Investment for the Hydrocarbons Exploitation created by Decree 929 (the '*Promotion Regime*').

---

139. *See* s. 27 *bis*, second paragraph, of the Hydrocarbons Law.
140. Law No 27007 was in force as from 8 Nov. 2014.
141. Section 28 of the Law No 27007 uses the expression 'pilot project' instead of 'Pilot Plan', but it refers to the same concept.
142. Law No 27007 also modified the conditions of Access to the Promotion Regime when expanding the benefits under Decree 929 to the hydrocarbon projects which involved the direct investment in foreign currency of a value no less than USD 250,000,000 to be invested over the first three years of the Project. Under the original Promotion Regime the minimum investment was USD 1,000,000,000 to be invested during the first five years of the Project. Furthermore, Law No 27007 establishes that for the cases of 'offshore exploitation', the percentage of hydrocarbons which the benefits were to be applied was – under Decree 929 – 60%, instead of 20% applicable to the conventional and non-conventional exploitation projects. This additional benefit for the offshore projects was not contemplated in the original Promotion Regime. *See* s. 19 of the Law No 27007.

- However, the Hydrocarbons Law regulates the CENCH as a new kind of concession to which, anyone who is an owner of (a) an exploration permit or (b) a Conventional Concession, whether or not it is included in the Promotion Regime can have access to.
- Under the Regime of the Decree 929, the term of the CENCH was twenty-five years, 'to which a 10-year extension could be added in advance or simultaneously (…) (…), *under the condition of effective compliance of all the obligations established in the hydrocarbons legislation for the exploitation concession*'.[143]

316. In the new wording of the Hydrocarbon Law, the term of duration of the CENCH is thirty-five years, without being necessary to use the anticipated extension.

317. The aspects of the CENCH which are common to Decree 929 and the Hydrocarbons Law are as follows:

- The possibility of unification, as a unique CENCH, the CENCH and a pre-existing Adjoining Conventional Concession, as long as it is irrefutably proved '*the geological proximity of both areas*'.[144] Law No 27007 added a requirement for the unification that was not contemplated in the Decree 929, *that is to say*: '*such request should be funded in the development [of a] pilot plan*'.[145]
- A CENCH's owner's power is to develop complementary exploitation conventional hydrocarbon activities in the perimeter of the CENCH. Both the Decree 929 and the Hydrocarbons Law provides: '*it is established that the new Exploitation Concession of Non-Conventional Hydrocarbons shall have as its main objective the Exploitation of Non-Conventional Hydrocarbons. However, the owner shall be entitled to develop complementary exploitation activities of conventional hydrocarbons, in the frame of Section 30 and concordants of the* [Hydrocarbons Law]'.[146]

IV. Access to a CENCH Through an Exploration Permit

318. It is possible to access a CENCH through: (a) an exploration permit, or (b) a Conventional Concession.

319. The access to a CENCH by means of a Conventional Concession is clearly regulated in the new wording of Hydrocarbons Law. The owner of the concession

143. Section 14, second paragraph, Decree 929.
144. Section 15, Decree 929, and s. 27 *bis*, second paragraph of the Hydrocarbons Law.
145. Second paragraph *in fine* of s. 27 *bis* of the Hydrocarbons Law, incorporated by s. 5 of the Law No 27007– The requirement of the Pilot Plan for the unification of one CENCH with one adjoining and existing Conventional Concession was incorporated by the Senate. The original project did not have that into account.
146. Section 16 of Decree 929, and s. 27 *bis*, third paragraph, of Law No 27007.

who has the intention to access a CENCH should '*solicit a subdivision of the existing area into new non-conventional hydrocarbons exploitation areas and the award of a new non-conventional Hydrocarbons Exploitation Concession should be based on the development of a pilot plan that, in accordance with acceptable technical-economic criteria, has the objective of the commercial exploitation of an uncovered field. The national or provincial Authority of Application, as applicable, will decide within sixty (60) days and its validity will be calculated in the way set forth under section 35*'.[147]

320. However, the Hydrocarbons Law seems to be inconsistent when regulating the access to a CENCH by means of an exploration permit.

321. The new last paragraph of section 27 establishes that 'the *owners of an exploration permit and/or a hydrocarbons exploitation concession* shall be entitled to solicit to the Authority of Application an Exploitation Concession of Non-Conventional Hydrocarbons, *in the terms provided in Section 22 or Section 27 bis, as applicable*'.[148]

322. This provision seems to indicate that in the cases of access to a CENCH by means of an exploration permit requirements, under section 22 of the Hydrocarbons Law should be met, and such section establishes that: 'Within thirty *(30) days of the date on which the permit holder, in accordance with the acceptable technical-economic criteria, determines the field is commercially exploitable, he shall express – before the application authority – his will to obtain the corresponding exploitation concession, and he complies with the requirements under section 33, paragraph 2.*[149] *The concession should be given within the following sixty (60) days and the validity term will be calculated according to what is set forth under section 35.*'[150]

323. The doubt posed here is if the holder of an exploration permit wishing to acquire CENCH should meet the requirements of section 22 in the same way as if he intended to get a Conventional Concession, or if, on the contrary, has the power to base his request in the development of the Pilot Plan, the same as the individuals trying to get access to a CENCH by means of a pre-existing Conventional Concession.

324. It is to be considered that section 35, subsection (b) of the Hydrocarbons Law, when establishing the duration of the CENCH, provides that the thirty-five years term '*will include a Pilot Plan for up to five (5) years to be defined by the*

147. Section 27 *bis*, first paragraph, of the Hydrocarbons Law.
148. The emphasis is ours.
149. Section 33, second paragraph, establishes: '*The concessioner shall be bound to perform the measurement of all the lots [i.e.: the exploitation lots], and he shall adjust the limits according to his best knowledge about the productive traps*'.
150. Section 22, first paragraph, Hydrocarbons Law.

Concessioner and approved by the Application Authority when initiating the concession'. This provision seems to indicate that the CENCH, whatever its origin (i.e., *to say*: exploration permit or Conventional Concession), should include a Pilot Plan.

325. Moreover, if characteristics of the non-conventional hydrocarbons exploitation are considered, it seems that the clear and simple application of section 22 (i.e., without its combination with the figure of the Pilot Plan) – for the cases of access to a CENCH by means of a permit – would be inappropriate.

326. The experience of several producers in *shale* projects has proved that in the case of non-conventional hydrocarbons formations it is necessary to carry out a Pilot Plan with a considerable term (i.e., between one and five years) to be able to confirm that the massive development of the area will be viable from the commercial point of view.

327. The Association of International Petroleum Negotiators (*AIPN*) has recognized this practice of introducing the figure of the Pilot Plan in its new model of Joint Operating Agreement (JOA) for non-conventional projects.[151]

328. Hence, it is reasonable to conclude that the owners of the exploration permits intending to be awarded a CENCH have the power to combine the commerciality statement with the presentation of the Pilot Plan.

329. When this happens, logically the commerciality statement will not imply the economic viability of the massive development of the area (for that, it is necessary to execute a Pilot Plan), but it will imply that the producer sufficiently trusts in the commercial potential of the project so as to execute the Pilot Plan.

330. So it is important to consider if the permit holder should develop a Pilot Plan in the frame of an exploration permit, and once the commerciality of the massive project is confirmed, to request the CENCH under the terms of section 22 of the Hydrocarbons Law. However, the new section 35 subsection (b) of the Hydrocarbons Law discards this hypothesis as it clearly establishes that the Pilot Plan is part of the exploitation stage, and not of the exploration one.

331. The fact that the law provides that the Pilot Plan conforms the exploitation stage presents the following advantages for a CENCH's owner: (i) the Pilot Plan is initiated having the producer the right to exploit el the area for a period of thirty-five years, and (ii) the production obtained in the frame of the Pilot Plan pays a 12%

151. The new model of the JOA of AIPN for non-conventional products defines the pilot project as follows: '*Pilot Project means the set of operations, activities, wells and facilities needed to evaluate the non-conventional exploitation methodologies to be used to exploit specified Sub-Area(s) in an Unconventional Resource in order to determine the commercial viability of a large scale exploitation of such Unconventional Resource*'.

– royalty instead of the 15% – royalty, which is the applicable aliquot to the hydrocarbons production obtained in the frame of the exploration permit.[152]

V. The Pilot Plan

332. As seen before, the Hydrocarbons Law contains a new concept associated with the figure of the CENCH: the Pilot Plan, cited in section 27 *bis* and 35 subsection (b).

333. Section 27 *bis* establishes that the owner of the Conventional Concession, who pretends to subdivide the area to obtain a CENCH, should submit a request '*based on the development of a pilot plan that, in accordance with the acceptable technical-economic criteria, has the objective of commercially exploiting the uncovered field*'.

334. Section 35 subsection (b) provides: 'In accordance with the following classification, the exploitation concessions shall have the validities established as follows, which will be counted as from the date of the resolution awarding them, plus the additional resulting from the application of section 23: […] (b) Non-Conventional Hydrocarbons Exploitation Concession: thirty five (35) years. This term will include the Period of the Pilot Plan of up to (5) years, to be defined by the concessioner and approved by the Authority of Application at the moment of the initiation of the concession.'

335. Furthermore, section 28 of the Law No 27007 mentions 'pilot project', a term used as a synonym of Pilot Plan.[153]

336. The introduction of the concept Pilot Plan of the Hydrocarbons Law brings about the following queries:

- Does the Pilot Plan imply to assume a commitment of investment with the authority the same as happens with the exploitation permits? Or it is just a mere tentative schedule of activities.
- This text of the Hydrocarbons Law does not respond this issue. It is possible to think that the Pilot Plan implies a commitment of investment; however, it may happen that the awarding authorities, when approving and controlling the pilot plans, construes it as a tentative schedule of activities.

152. Thus, s. 21, second paragraph, of the Hydrocarbons Law sets forth: '*The hydrocarbons extracted during the exploitation shall be subject to the payment of a 15%-royalty (15%)*'.

153. Section 28 of the Law No 27007, already referred to (*see 4. I) ii) and 4. I) vi)*), provides that: 'The Executive Branch – national or provincial – *as applicable, as the Awarding authority, shall be able to reduce up to a twenty five per cent (25%) the amount corresponding to royalties applicable to the production of hydrocarbons and for the term of ten (10) years after the finalization of the pilot project*, in favour of the company requesting the Non-conventional Concession Exploitation of Hydrocarbons, in the terms of section 27 bis of the law 17319and its amendments, within thirty six (36) months as from the valid date of the law herein'.

- Due to the characteristics of the non-conventional projects, it would be reasonable that even of the Pilot Plan effectively implied a commitment of investment; there exists some flexibility so that the producers can change the terms as they advance in the execution.
- What would happen if *before* the end of the Pilot Plan the owner of the CENCH determines that the exploitation of that formation is not viable from the commercial point of view? Should he make the investments programmed in the Pilot Plan anyway?
- It would seem anti-financial to ask the owner of a CENCH to continue with the investments in the Pilot Plan when the exploitation of that formation will not be viable from the commercial point of view.
- Thus, if, before the Pilot Plan is ended, it is determined that the project is not commercially viable, it is possible to think that the owner of the CENCH could give the area back[154] to the awarding authority without having to complete the Pilot Plan.
- What happens if when the Pilot Plan ends the owner of CENCH considers that the massive development will not be viable from the commercial point of view?
- Again, the text of the Hydrocarbons Law does not expressly regulate anything for this alleged situation. We believe that, if when the Pilot Plan concludes the owner of the CENCH considers that the area's massive development is not viable from the commercial point of view, it will be reasonable to give the area back to the awarding authority.[155]
- It is neither clear, in case the CENCH had been awarded due to the Pre-existing Conventional Concession ownership. When the area covered by the CENCH is reversed, the rights of a Conventional Concession are valid again up to the end of the original term of the Conventional Concession. The affirmation seems to be the logical option, as the right of the concessioners to solicit a CENCH is intended to stimulate the non-conventional hydrocarbons formations development, and as such, it should not place the concessioner in the less favourable context than the one he had before to exercise such power.
- Why does the Law No 27007 fix a maximum term of five years for the Pilot Plan? What would be different without that maximum term?
- The maximum term for the Pilot Plan would suggest that during such term attenuated conditions apply regarding the investment commitments.
- Section 28 of the Law No 27007 establishes the possibility of obtaining the reduction in the amount of royalties applicable 'for the term of the following ten (10) years after the pilot project ends in favour of the companies soliciting the Non-Conventional Hydrocarbons Exploitation Concession under the terms in section 27 bis within 36 months counting as from the validity date of this law'.
- It is not clear yet (i) the reason for this benefit to be applicable after the conclusion of the Pilot Plan, and (ii) the conditions for the authorities to grant that benefit.
- Assuming that the objective of the Pilot Plan is to confirm the commercial viability of the non-conventional project, the sequence, according to section 28 of the

154. Cf. s. 37 and concordant of the Hydrocarbons Law.
155. *Ibid.*

Law No 27007, would be the following: (i) the owner of the el CENCH should confirm the commerciality with the 12% – royalty, and (ii) once this milestone is achieved, the owner requests a reduction in the amount of royalties.

- The question triggered is why the authority would reduce the amount of the royalties for a commercially viable project with a royalty of 12%.
- Presumably, this provision had been thought for the cases in which the massive development proved to be commercially viable only with a reduction of the royalty. We believe that Law No 27007 should have clearly established that.

VI. Comparison Between the Conventional and Non-conventional Concessions

337. The differences between the CENCH and the Conventional Concession are just a few but significant ones. They are elaborated as follows:

- The CENCH has a term of thirty-five years, while the term for the Conventional Concession is twenty-five years.[156]
- The CENCH must have as its main objective the Non-Conventional Hydrocarbons Exploitation (apart from the option of developing complementary exploitation activities).[157] This restriction does not exist in the case of a Conventional Concession as its main objective can be the conventional and non-conventional exploitation of hydrocarbons.[158]
- Apart from the special cases of tenders of vacant areas in tested zones[159] and assignment of participation in areas already awarded in concession,[160] the only way to access the Conventional Concession is through an exploration permit. Whereas, the access to the CENCH can be by means of (a) an exploration permit or (b) a Conventional Concession.
- The CENCH includes a first of up to five-year term called 'Pilot Plan', whose objective is to test the commerciality of the Project; on the contrary, the Hydrocarbons Law does not provide anything like that for the Conventional Concession.
- Last but not least, it is worth mentioning that the possibility to access to a reduced royalty under section 28 of the Law No 27007 only applies to the CENCH.

---

156. As afore-elaborated (*See* 4 I) ii) the extension regime in the same.
157. *See* 4. I) ii) and 4. I. ii).
158. *See* 4. I) i).
159. Section 29, second paragraph, of the Hydrocarbons Law establishes that '[The]*e National Executive Branch national or provincial, as applicable, shall* […] *grant exploitation concessions over tested areas to those who meet the requirements and comply with the specific procedures under Section 5* [Adjudicating] *of the Title herein*'.
160. Section 72, first paragraph, of the Hydrocarbons Law provides that: '*The permits and concessions awarded under this law can be transferred, with previous authorization of the Executive Branch, in favour of those meeting the requirements and conditions set forth to be a permit holder or concessioner, as applicable*'.

338. Is it possible to have a Conventional Concession and a CENCH in the same area?

Previous to the reform of the Hydrocarbons Law, it was posed – in doctrine – if it was possible the coexistence of different exploitation concessions horizontally delimited according to the depth in the same area (for instance, a concession giving the right to exploit hydrocarbons from the surface up to 2,000 m deep and another giving the right to exploit hydrocarbons deeper than 2,001 m).[161]

The incorporation of the figure of the CENCH to the Hydrocarbons Law, and the possibility of access to it by means of a Conventional Concession poses a further issue: if it is possible – with the new wording of the text in the law – to subdivide horizontally an exploitation concession to give place to a CENCH delimited by levels of depth, so that Conventional Concession (for instance, from the surface up to 2,000 m deep) and a CENCH (for instance, as from 2,000 m deeper down) can coexist in the same area.

Not only does the Hydrocarbons Law clearly prohibit this option, but also some provisions seem to discard it. For example, section 27 *bis*, second paragraph, setting forth the power to unify a CENCH with a pre-existing Adjoining Conventional Concession, established that such unification will result in a unique CENCH. Does not this solution suggest that the Hydrocarbons Law discards the possibility of horizontally delimiting the Conventional Concessions and the CENCHs? We think it does.

Furthermore, the third paragraph of section 27 *bis*, referring to the alleged case of the subdivision of the Conventional Concession into a CENCH, establishes that '*the concession corresponding to the area duly given in concession and not affected by the new Non-Conventional Hydrocarbons Exploitation Concession, will be valid under the pre-existing terms and conditions, having the Awarding Authority to collect the respective title of the resulting extension of the subdivision*'.[162] Upon this prevision, it can be inferred that the title of the subdivided concession should be accurately readjusted as the law does not allow the coexistence of the Conventional Concession and a CENCH on the same area.

Additionally, the fact that the law expressly allows the development of complementary activities of conventional exploitation inside a CENCH[163] seems to be a solution for the cases in which in the area (vertically divided) there are different types of formations, at different levels of depth.

However, this does not prevent two co-owners of a concession from signing an agreement so that one can exclusively exploit the shallow and the other the deep.[164] Such agreement will be valid and binding for the parties, but not enforceable for the awarding authority. For the awarding authority, there will still be only one concession, vertically delimited and with two co-owners.

---

161. *See* Borderes (2014).
162. The emphasis is ours.
163. *See* s. 27 *bis*, third paragraph, Hydrocarbons Law.
164. '*Shallow*' and '*deep*' are terms used in the oil Anglo-Saxon jargon to refer to the rights of exploitation according to the depth of the area.

VII. Colophon

339. In spite of certain unavoidable ambiguities in any and all regulation, the figure of the CENCH incorporated to the Hydrocarbons Law as from the Reform of 2014, appropriately responds to the needs of the development of the novel activity of non-conventional hydrocarbons exploitation, which nourishes itself from other more developed countries regarding the activity and its regulation. This virtue is a privilege in Argentina where it is usual that the laws are sanctioned full of gaps, inconsistencies and silly mistakes as a consequence of our flippancy and lack of competency in the exercise of the legislative technique.

340. One of the harshest criticisms to the regulation of the CENCH has been the possibility of access as from the pre-existing Conventional Concession. This preference, unadvisable in abstract, will be justified in the need for boosting a rapid development of the non-conventional activity, which would be delayed if the current concessioners did not have incentives to transform their current rights into the CENCHs.

341. A sound implementation of the CENCH would be pending from the part of the awarding authorities, especially regarding the Pilot Plan, more exposed to future regulation and practice.

342. Besides, despite the advantages of the CENCH and in general of all the Reform of 2014 to the Hydrocarbons Law, as an efficient regulation of the non-conventional hydrocarbons activity, the success of the activity does not only depends on this new regulation, but also on other still pending factors; among them, the necessary changes of the exchange regime and, regarding natural gas, the normalization of the tariffs and the modification of the regulations that are now limiting the firm sale of natural gas in long-term contracts.

Chapter 7. Environmental

343. The environmental dangers of the hydrocarbons were first noticed in 1970 approximately, in Argentina as well as at a global level. Even though the Hydrocarbons Law had already mentioned the environmental requirements, under section 67 establishing the adoption of the necessary measures to prevent from damages to the fields, farming activities, as well as the water, it was in 1992 that the first environmental rules were passed. In 1992, Resolution 105 was adopted intended to regulate the environmental aspects of the different stages in the oil activity; such resolution provides the submission of environmental tests among other provisions elaborated herein.

344. The very same year, Law No 24051 was passed.[165] The substantive law is applicable to whole national territory. Among others, there are the criminal rules. Sections 55–58 of the Law No 24051 of Hazardous Waste represses, with the same punishment established in section 200 of the Criminal Code,[166] to those people who, using the waste referred to in the law, shall poison, tamper, or pollute in a dangerous way the health, soil, water and atmosphere or the environment in general. Law No 24.051 also punishes with imprisonment those who willingly or unwillingly pollute the health, the water, the soil, the atmosphere or the environment with dangerous substances. As it was mentioned before it is the National State the one who has to define the substantive legal frame regarding hydrocarbons. However, the provinces have the original domain of the hydrocarbons and take responsibility for the administration and they are the authority of application of the national rules regarding hydrocarbons in their respective jurisdictions. The provinces should, then, control and apply the Hydrocarbons Law in relation to the environment pursuant to section 2 in fine, of the Law No 26197.

345. Even though it is the provinces' responsibility to promote and guarantee the least harmful hydrocarbons exploitation, the permit holders themselves have to assume the responsibility regarding environmental damage. Not only shall they compensate for damages, but also they shall have the prioritized obligation of taking the necessary actions, measures and policies to eradicate the damage caused to the environment.

346. Section 28 of the Law No 25675[167] establishes that 'the one causing environmental damage shall be objectively responsible for restoring that to the way in which it was prior to its production. In case it was not technically feasible, a substitute compensation determined by the intervening ordinary justice, shall be deposited in the Environmental Compensation Fund created thereby, which will be administer by the Authority of Application, notwithstanding other possible corresponding judicial actions'.

---

165. Law No 24051 (Law of Hazardous Waste) was in full force as from 8 Jan. 1992.
166. Confinement or imprisonment of three to ten years – if the act was followed by the death of a person, confinement of imprisonment of one to twenty-five years.
167. Law No 25675 (General Law of Environment) was in force as from 27 Nov. 2002.

§1. Treatment of Flow Back Water

347. The oil exploitation process demands a great volume of water for what is called secondary recovery. This consists in putting water in the production structures, keeping the pressure of the well and generating sufficient force to sweep along the greatest possible quantity of oil to those wells by means of the force exercised by the vertical water.

348. Section 4.4.1 of the Annex I of Resolution No 105/92 of the Department of Energy provides that 'the operator shall preferably use the same water of production and once it is treated, re-inject it to the stratum of origin, as long as the field does not have a natural water thrust of formation. However, and according to the commerciality of the oil exploitation, the operator will be able to use underground fresh water provided that it exceeds the average value of salt dissolved of the underground drainage basin where the wells are drilled'. Thus, they shall be entitled to choose the underground water dispatch zone to obtain the worst quality water that will be used by the drainage basin without compromising the secondary recovery plans.

349. As they are considered vitally important resources, the water from the rivers, lakes and ponds shall not be injected in the oil productive formations in the secondary recovery process. Those fields that are now using fresh water from these sources should be slowly changing the drainage source for the secondary recovery tasks as an immediate and sudden change could damage the productive structure. The date of commencement for the replacement of the drainage sources shall be as from the first year of enactment of such regulations.

350. As it was aforementioned, part of the water and the chemicals injected in the field go back as *flow back water*[168] which is not suitable for the superficial dispatch or to be sent to municipal facilities of water treatment.[169] Regarding the non-conventional hydrocarbons exploitation, some states in the USA such as Virginia, have observed that the provision of waste water is '*maybe the greatest challenge*' in the hydraulic fracking operations.[170]

351. The alternatives for the secure management of *flow back water* could be: (i) to build special *flow back water* – treatment facilities for its dispatch (Even though its cost is higher than the other options), (ii) to treat and reuse the *flow back water* in future *frackings,* as long as the industry allows higher salinity in the water injected, as the technique of reutilization would have a very high costs otherwise, or (iii) to have the *flow back water* through a deep injection well (this alternative of

168. Less than 10% of the chemical injected products go back to the surface. Between 16% and 35% of the water flows back to the surface. The '*flowback water*' gets a part of mineral content of the field (sodium, magnesium, calcium), increasing the salinity of the water being injected. (*See* Vikram Rao, *supra*, p. 41).
169. *See* Vikram Rao, *supra*, p. 41.
170. *See* Susan L. Sakmar, *supra*, p. 402.

provision is, in fact, the cheapest; however, there is evidence of earthquakes in Oklahoma and Ohio presumably related to deep wells).[171]

352. One was to implement these alternatives is to obligatory demand the adoption of any of them, giving the operators the chance to choose the most economically and environmentally efficient. Or a specific technique could be directly demanded, with variations authorized in certain cases.

§2. Reduction of Drinkable Water

353. One of the most important critiques to the technique of *fracking* is that it uses very high quantities of fresh water. Of course, the issue is even worse in areas where there is shortage of water.

354. Among solutions available for this issue we found: (i) the reuse or recycle of *flow back water* (although this would not cover the 100% of the water used for each operation of *fracking*), and (ii) the use of the water from salty aquifers not used for the human consumption or in farming.[172] The regulating authorities should consider these methods in the shale gas/oil operations.

355. There is something else to consider regarding water consumption. The oil and gas contracts, in general, do not take into account the right to use of water; so the producers should buy the access to water to the government of the land's owners of the (depending on the legal regime). When regulating the activity, the authorities should also remember how to rule the use of water concession, the coverage of such concessions and the tariffs to be charged.[173]

§3. Prevention from Well Water Pollution

356. There are two possible ways in the operations of *shale* gas/oil that can pollute the aquifers. The first is in the leak of chemical products used in *fracking.* The second one is through the infiltration of the methane produced in aquifers. Both risks are generally attributed to the deficient construction of the wells.[174]

357. Thus, the main solutions to solve this issue suggest that the regulators take into account:(i) specific requirements that should be met by the wells' operators (e.g., to carry out tests in the water wells before the drilling, well cementation from

171. *See* Vikram Rao, *supra*, pp. 41/42.
172. *Ibid.*, p. 45, 'The use of fresh water as a fluid base for the operations of *fracking is not necessary anymore. The seawater with little or no value at all for human consumption or the agriculture can be used'*.
173. For examples, the Argentinean provinces through the non-conventional field '*Vaca Muerta*' collect approximately USD 5,500 for every 20,000 cubic metres of water consumes during the drilling of a well.
174. *See* Vikram Rao, *supra*, p. 29.

top to bottom, double *casing*, *logging*, etc.,[175] (ii) drilling permits only awarded to companies with good background in the oil industry so as to maximize the possibilities of due diligence in the well construction and (iii) the operations near the water wells subject to special limitations (e.g., space between the wells).[176]

358. The Resolution No 105/92 gives solutions that can be applied to the conventional and non-conventional hydrocarbons exploration. Section 3.2.7 of the Annex I coincides with the solution mentioned about the requirements that should be met by the operators as it sets forth that 'before opening waste and mud pool of drilling and termination, the operator has to demonstrate that there is not fresh water underground'. In case there is fresh water, the water and mud pool must be coated with removable plastic lamina, so as to prevent from water pollution. Moreover, the resolution establishes that the permit holders and the concessioners must: (i) control the accumulation of waste, (ii) make a septic tank for sewage liquids (iii) a waterproof seal to collect leaks of oil, grease and gas oil.[177] Finally, section 3.2.4 from Annex I establishes that '*the planning of the well will have to consider the protection pipeline cementation up to the surface to guarantee there is no pollution risk with surface brackish water*'.

359. Decree No 33589 of 1933 exemplifies the evolution of the environmental paradigm regarding the care of the waters. Section 15 of the decree establishes that, '*the concessioners must appropriately isolate the waters – through the methods approved by the Mining Authority – during the course of any drilling containing oil or gas may as the water may pollute them*'. At that time, the oil was more important than the water. Nowadays, there is more awareness regarding the pollution of the water.

§4. Handling of Drilling Residue

360. Furthermore, Resolution No 105/92 includes operative modalities to control the waste produced by the drilling. Among the most important provisions, it is worth mentioning item 4.3.1.2 which establishes that when there is a small oil spill, it has to be mixed with resin for the asphalt of internal field ways. The resolution also establishes that the heavy hydrocarbons 'that cannot be recycled in situ, may be eliminated using them to consolidate ways spreading them in the field under certain conditions or, commercializing them as heavy oil'.[178] Finally, for the handling of non-burnable metal waste, section 3.2.8 sets forth that 'for the steel wires and the pipes of up to 1' (25 mm of diameter), it is convenient to cut them with a blowtorch

175. In this sense, one of the standards to meet for the AIE is '*to isolate well and prevent leaks*', apart from the requirement as follows: '*Set strict rules about wells, construction, case hardening and tests of integrity, as part of a general regulation for performance due to which the gas formations must be totally isolated from the strata penetrated by the well, especially those of fresh water.*' *See* IEA, *supra*, p. 13.
176. *See* Vikram Rao, *supra*, p. 29.
177. *See* s. 2.1.1 of the Resolution 105/92.
178. *See* s. 4.3.1.2 from Annex I of the Law No 105/92.

long enough to facilitate the accumulation in the recipients available to that end. Those recipients with non-burnable metal waste should be buried in a suitable place to that end, or in the mud pools of abandoned wells, to promote the biodegradation and/or natural chemical degradation.

§5. CONTROL OF AIR EMISSIONS

361. During the termination of the well, the capture of gases requires investments in the separation of gas and installations of processing not occurring in all the cases. The venting and/or flaring[179] (mainly methane[180]) in this stage the process has become one of the greatest worries related to the greenhouse gas emissions.

362. The regulators aim at achieve zero venting and a minimum flaring of gases through: (i) setting of restrictions to those practices and demands of equipment installations contributing to minimize the emissions, and/or (ii) a tax to the greenhouse gases released during the operations of conventional and non-conventional gas, the same as with 'tax on carbon' created by Alberta province (Canada) regarding the exploitation of 'tar sands'.[181] The resolution of the former Secretary of Energy No 236/1993 establishes the rules about venting of gas in the oil fields. Section 3.1 allows the venting of well gas as long as the RGP of the Venting Point is not higher than 1 m3/m3. Nevertheless, the following subsection '*prohibits the venting of gas produced in any and all wells whose RGP were higher than 1500m3/m3, whatever the composition of the gas produced. These wells shall remain closed while they do not meet the conditions for gas capture and use*'. The resolution also contains regulations about the gas that allows the venting providing that the permit holders and concessioners perform the flaring through appropriate procedures reducing to a minimum the noxious gases emissions.

---

179. In the course of refinery operations of gas and oil production, *flaring* is the controlled firing of natural gas, whereas the vetting is the controlled release of gases to the atmosphere (*See 'Flaring & venting in the oil & gas exploration & production industry'* (2000) of the *International Association of Gas and Oil Producers* available at www.ogp.org.uk/pubs/288.pdf).
180. *See* Vikram Rao, *supra*, p. 29.
181. A barrel of tar sand adds a 5 to 10% more of carbon dioxide (CO_2) to the atmosphere that an average barrel of conventional oil. (*See* Daniel Yergin, *The Quest*, *supra*, 257). Alberta province requires that those emissions producing more than 100,000 tons greenhouse gases a year have to obligatory meet some reduction objectives. In a typical system of '*cap and trade*', those not being able to do so, shall buy compensation or pay a fine of 15 pesos per ton, which they must deposit in a Clean Energy Fund which nowadays has a value of USD 257 million. According to Alberta's government, this program has contributed to prevent from almost 24 million tons in the province since July 2007. *See 'Carbon Tax Here to Stay: Alberta Energy Minister'* (7 Sep. 2011), available at www.risk.net/energy-risk/news/2107127/carbon-taxstay-alberta-energy-minister.

§6. Regulatory Strategies

363. In all issues regulations, the regulators must decide if they adopt an approach of '*command and control*' defined by an administrative control with clear criteria, obligations and specific requirements (e.g., complete disclosure of hydraulic fracking fluids), an incentive regime based on the imposition of punishments and rewards to the companies (for instance, the tax on greenhouse gases released during operations of exploitation), or a combination of both depending on the topic to regulate[182]

364. In relation to this, the International Energy Agency (IEA) suggests to the regulators 'striking a balance in the formation of policies between the regulation of command and control and the one based on incentives with the aim to guarantee high operational standards and to promote technological innovation and improvement'.[183]

365. Regarding shale gas operations, a good initiative to facilitate the award of a social licence would be that the industry regulated itself by means of security standards for the operations issued by prestigious organizations such as the *Society of Petroleum Engineers.*

§7. Abandonment of Wells

366. The abandonment of the hydrocarbon wells ('wells') is ruled by Resolution No 5/96 of the former Department of Energy (the 'Resolution') adopted in January 1996 that can be summarized as:

> The abandonment of a hydrocarbons well implies, from the technical point of view, the execution of a set of tasks expressly regulated by several authorities of application of the Hydrocarbons Law. From the financial point of view, a well abandoned through the technique of the resolution establishes two types of abandonment in the well: temporary and permanent, being the concessioner the sole responsible to determine, due to technical marketing or operational reasons, the type of abandonment. A well can be temporarily abandoned when, according to the concessioner's view there are valid reasons to foresee its reutilization in the future. However, the resolution only accepts the definite abandonment of a well situated in urban areas or 100 m away from such urban areas.

182. *See* Robert Baldwin and Martin Cave, *Understanding Regulation* (Great Britain, Oxford University Press, 1999), p. 37.
183. *See* IEA, *supra*, p. 9.

§8. CATEGORIES OF WELLS

367. The resolution distinguishes three types of wells:[184]

(1) Based on its location ('Category A'):
  - A.1. Wells located in urban areas. To that end, an urban zone is an area with permanent houses or buildings, to be used daily or occasionally, different from the buildings constructed specifically for the hydrocarbons activities.
  - A.2. Wells located 200 m away from a farming area, forest or currents or sources of water, the sea excluded.
  - A.3. Wells located in areas not previously described.

(2) Based on its condition ('Category B'):
  - B.1. Active wells: To that end, active wells include wells which are temporarily disused due to maintenance or other activities related to the continuation of its use.
  - B.2. Inactive wells: They include the wells in which the exploration and/or exploitation have ceased or have not commenced and in relation to which the concessioner has to decide if it is convenient or not to abandon them.
  - B.3. Abandoned wells: These are the wells abandoned by the concessioners on the date of the resolution, due to technical and/or economic or commercialization reasons, or that will be abandoned in the future due to the requirements of the resolution.

(3) Based on the level of priority ('Category C'):
  - C.1. The resolution establishes four levels of priority (1 to 4) that are established according to criteria such as the risk of localization, production background, age of the well, maintenance conditions, presence of corrosive fluids, accidents previously occurred in the area, USD 1.

§9. TERMS TO ABANDON A WELL

368. The resolution imposes the obligation to abandon the wells according to its category, based on the following schedule.[185] These terms of abandonment are applied to all the wells that the moment the resolution was adopted, (i) were categorized as 'subject to abandonment', or (ii) were 'inactive' and in a condition to be abandoned:

(a) (PGH) Category A.1 wells and well that qualify as Priority 1 wells:

   These wells will have to be abandoned within five years as from 9 January 1996, the date when the resolution was adopted, with the possibility of extended that period for one more year if a duly justified request is submitted and supported by the concessioner and approved by the Department of Energy.

184. *See* Chapter 2 from Annex I of Resolution No 5/96.
185. *Ibid.*

(b) Category A.2 wells and well that qualify as Priority 2 and 3 wells:

> These wells will have to be abandoned within ten years as from 9 January 1996, with the possibility of extending the term by one additional year, if a duly justified request is submitted and supported by the concessioner and approved by the Department of Energy.

(c) Category A.3 wells and wells that qualify as Priority 4 wells:

> These wells are to be abandoned within fifteen years as from 9 January 1996.

369. It is worth mentioning, however, that the concessioner is entitled to, before the exportation of the terms aforementioned and with base in the activities duly supported from the technical point of view, recategorize the wells, subject to the approval from the Department of Energy. Notwithstanding the aforesaid, the resulting terms of such recategorization for the abandonment of the inactive wells, shall not extend further than four years before the termination of the concession or beyond the time of the total or partial delivery of the exploration area in which the well is located.

§10. Requirements to Abandon a Well

370. The resolution recommends detailed specific techniques for the abandonment of the wells. It is worth saying, though, that the concessioners can use other techniques or methodologies for the abandonment of the wells, as long as they meet the security and environmental requirements and are not objected by the Department of Energy.

§11. Environmental Issues for the Design of Non-Conventional Hydrocarbons Policies

I. 'To Ban or Not to Ban': An Energy Policy

371. Any and all adoption of policies implies a decision-making process. Energetically speaking, there are quite a few decisions to make when designing policies: should the administration in our country implement an energy industry '*low in carbon dioxide*'?[186] Should we, due to security, close down the nuclear plants and concentrate on the production of natural gas and renewable energy sources for the

186. For instance, the United Kingdom is currently designing a '*Transition Plan*' to become a low carbon dioxide country ('*low carbon*') *See 'The UK Low Carbon Transition Plan'* at www.decc.gov.uk.

generation of electricity?[187] And topics such as diversity in the offer, security in the supply thereof, the liberalization of the energy markets, among others will bring about other questionings.

372. Among the countries full of non-conventional resources, the decision in the hands of the authorities is basically *to allow or not its development.*

373. Some authorized the exploitation of *shale* gas ('*hydraulic fracking*' technique included) from the very beginning,[188] others imposed a temporary suspension which was then lifted once studies and tests performed confirmed the possibility of sustainable development and after the necessary changes in the legislation had been made,[189] still others imposed a more '*permanent*' *suspension.*[190]

374. The regulating authorities should take into account if there are contracts or drilling permits *prior to* any suspending decision, and at the same time, if such investors have already commenced the activity of *fracking* in their respective awarded areas. In that case, the regulators should decide between respecting the acquired rights pursuant to such contracts, or else, exposing themselves to claims and judicial actions filed by those investors.[191]

---

187. After the '*Fukushima*' disaster in Japan, Germany seriously started considering this option. *See 'Germany's Energy Supply Transformation Has Already Failed'* at www.eike-klima-energie.eu.
188. For example, Texas and Louisiana states where the formations '*Barnett*' and '*Haynesville*' have been under exploitation for the last decade.
189. For example, *fracking* was banned in the United Kingdom in May 2011, after two light earthquakes were detected near the only hydraulic fracking operation in the country in the Bowland basin, to the East of Blackpool in Lancashire, north of England. Almost two years later, the United Kingdom administration lifted the measure. *See 'Fracking for shale gas gets green light in UK'*, The Guardian, Thursday 13 Dec. 2012.
190. For example, in the states of New York, Nueva Jersey and Maryland, *fracking ban* was imposed while they were completing the environment-impact tests and due to the need of a change in regulations. In Europe, this policy has been introduced in France, Switzerland and Bulgaria. Some authors comment that these administrations are adopting the principle of '*make a virtue of getting late*' or '*fast follower*', as they could profit from the experience of the areas where *shale* gas has been exploited under the '*trial and error*' approach (e.g., in Barnett's formation). (*See* Vikram Rao, *supra*, p. 118).
191. Of course, this will depend on the drilling permit conditions and in the introduction of a clause of stabilization comprising environment standards (*See* Peter D. Cameron, '*Stabilisation in Investment Contracts and Changes of Rules in Host Countries: Tools for Oil & Gas Investors*', p. 93, Association of International Petroleum Negotiators (AIPN) July 2006, *available at* www.aipn.org). For example, Oil and Gas drilling Company *Lone Pine* initiated an arbitration against the Canadian government under Chapter el 11 of TLCAN claiming that they had invested millions of dollars in the development of non-conventional resources in Quebec before the government presented a bill in the National Assembly in May 2011 to give force of law to the temporary suspension of *shale* exploitation in the whole province and to the reversal of specific permits regarding *shale* deposits (*see 'Canada's Energy Policies Spark NAFTA Claims*', Magazine GAR, 27 Nov. 2012).

375. Furthermore, the fact that the *shale* formations are located throughout large geographical areas going through different states/provinces or oven countries[192] creates the possibility of '*inter-jurisdictional conflicts*' between the states that share the non-conventional resources and keep opposed positions regarding hydraulic *fracking*, (e.g., in the formation '*Marcellus*' of the USA, Pennsylvania allows the technique; however New York does not). This, at the same time, can call the federal intervention in federal countries such as the USA, Australia or Argentina.[193] Such contingency can even extrapolate to the European in which countries such as Poland allow the exploitation of *shale* gas, while in others such as France such exploitation is forbidden.[194]

376. If the energy policy is to go ahead with the non-conventional hydrocarbons development, the interested parties will demand to know the measures taken to mitigate the environmental risks inherent to the activity

II. 'Licence to Operate': A Socio-environmental Policy

377. The campaign against *fracking* initiated by NGOs such as *The Sierra Club*[195] or the public in general reflected in the documentary '*Gasland*' that came out in 2010 in the USA[196] has been gradually increasing. An aggravation on the social resistance is the fact that the production of *shale* gas/oil is being performed not only in areas where gas and oil are traditionally produced, but also where there is no historical background of production.

378. In this section, we will analyse the socio-environmental key issues to be addressed when drafting policies on the subject. A suitable socio-environmental regulation for the development of *shale* gas/oil and its full application by the authorities and its due fulfilment by the industrial actors are essential whether or not this *shale* gas/oil prevails.

---

192. Such as the formation of '*Marcellus*', comprising the states of New York, Pennsylvania, Maryland, West Virginia, Virginia and Ohio, or the '*Panonia-Transilvania Basin*', comprising Austria, Hungary, Romania, Bulgaria and Croatia.
193. Regarding the environment, there exist two main situations justifying the creation and application of the federal regulation of the theory: '*the race for the deep*' and the principle '*transborder pollution*'. The first situation arises when the jurisdictions compete to attract or retain industries when minimizing the environment demands. The second situation occurs when a State sending pollution to another State gets the working and fiscal benefits of the economic activity generating pollution, but they do not bear the total costs of the activity.
194. Ver J. Gorski, *Could the EU Impose a Ban on Shale-Gas Extraction and Would This Prevent Exploitation of the Fossil Fuel in Poland?* OGEL, 10(5). The author reaches the conclusion that '*the EU legislator has competence to adopt a legal measure applicable at a community level banning the hydraulic fracking; however each member state would keep the right to vote*'.
195. *See* '*Beyond Natural Gas (Protecting our Air, Water and Communities)*', Natural Gas campaign of *The Sierra Club* (*at* www.sierraclub.org/fracking).
196. Documentary 'Gasland' (2010) at www.youtube.com/watch?v=dZe1AeH0Qz8.

III. Complete Disclosure of the Chemical Products

379. An issue posed the interest groups refers to the underground water pollution as a result of the use of chemicals in *fracking*. Due to '*commercial confidentiality*' invoked by producers and service companies, *shale* gas producers in the USA have not disclosed the products used in the fracking fluid so far.[197]

380. The regulatory authorities should decide if they will keep the professional secret of the products used in *fracking* pursuant to the protection rights of data claimed by producers and service companies, or if full disclosure shall be demanded so that the exception of exclusivity of the products of the producers is not used as a shield.[198] The second option is, as it seems, a question of law solved.

381. On the contrary, the increasing pressure exercised nowadays to disclose the chemicals have resulted in several companies openly declaring the name of the products.[199] Moreover, in the USA, a country where the services companies used to invoke 'confidentiality' of the chemical used, it is now obligatory to disclose them by law.[200] Furthermore, the IEA suggests imposing '*obligatory full disclose of the additives for fracking fluids and volumes*'.[201]

IV. Prevention of Earthquakes

382. The UK authorities imposed a suspension of almost two years for the hydraulic *fracking* operations after an earthquake of 2.5 in the Richter scale registered on 1 April 2011 which was related to *flow back water injection*.[202] Thus, the correlation between the increase in the *shale* gas production and the increasing risk of earthquakes is another worrying factor.

383. Experts allege that moderate seismic movements can be produced when the well in the fractures intercept and reactivate an existing '*fault*, hence it is recommended that the operators carefully study the geology of the area to determine if the

---

197. The US Energy Policy of 2005 clearly excluded the *fracking* from the scope of control of *Environmental Protection Agency's (EPA)*, a clause known as a legal loophole of '*Cheney and Halliburton*', in honour of Vice President Dick Cheney, former CEO with Halliburton.
198. *See* Vikram Rao, *supra*, p. 161.
199. *See* Vikram Rao, *supra*, p. 38; explaining that water together with sand or ceramic pearls (el '*proppant*'), represent more than 99% of the fluid of the typical fracturing; although the mix of additive chemicals is also used to give the fluid all the necessary properties for the fracture. A friction reducer (in general polyacrylamide) commonly used in diapers for babies, a scale inhibitor (generally phosphonate) commonly used in detergents, in biocide (generally a chlorine dioxide) frequently used as chlorine in the municipal water supplies, and a surfactant (surfactant agent) generally used in soap.
200. *See 'Obama Tightens Fracking Regs, Requires Chemical Disclosure'* at http://www.usnews.com/news/articles/2015/03/20/obama-tightens-fracking-regs-requires-chemical-disclosure.
201. *See* IEA, *supra*, p. 13.
202. *See 'Written Ministerial Statement by UK's Secretary of State for Energy and Climate Change on Exploration for Shale Gas'*, 13 Dec. 2012, available at www.decc.gov.uk/en/content/cms/news/wms_shale/wms_shale.aspx.

faults represent an increased risk of earthquake, and so avoid drilling or fracking in such zones.'[203] 'The conventional techniques permit to identify such faults and so the interaction with them can be prevented.'[204] Besides, during the drilling or the fracking, the operators have to monitor any seismic activity and to stop their operations in case they find signs of an increase in seismic activity.[205]

384. The UK authorities lifted the prohibition of hydraulic fracking due to these requirements[206] and other regulators from other countries could follow suit.

V. Well Pad

385. *Shale* gas/oil exploitation has changed the paradigm of exploitation of gas and oil in faraway isolated areas. The '*Marcellus*' non-conventional formation is the perfect example of how *shale* gas exploitation has affected geographically high-density areas.

386. The well pads consist in one way of production in which multiple wells (any number between five and forty) are drilled from one location or '*pad*'. This technique reduces the traffic associated with pumping trucks, decomposition of the water and it mitigates the damage in the ways and soil of the communities in question. Moreover, it facilitates the water treatment operations thank to the economies of scales.[207]

387. The regulatory authorities should consider if this technique has to be binding or not, and in case it is, in which circumstances (e.g., in densely populated areas).

VI. Social Licence

388. Practically only the USA in the whole world adheres to a system of property conferring the owner of a land the ownership of the minerals underlying the surface on that extension.[208] Thus, those owners located near the operations that

203. *See* IEA, *supra*, p. 26.
204. *See* Vikram Rao, *supra*, p. 57.
205. *Ibid.*, p. 57.
206. *See 'Written Ministerial Statement by UK's Secretary of State for Energy and Climate Change on Exploration for Shale Gas'*, 13 December 2012, available at www.decc.gov.uk/en/content/cms/news/wms_shale/wms_shale.aspx.
207. *See* Vikram Rao, *supra*, Glossary. In the year 2011, approximately 30% of the new *shale tight gas wells* in the USA and Canada were '*well pads*' (*See* IEA, *supra*, p. 23).
208. *See* Claude Duval et al., *International Petroleum Exploration and Exploitation Agreements: Legal, Economic & Policy Aspects*, Second Edition (2009), Barrows Company, p. 14.

potentially suffer from such obstructions are also directly benefited. This income perspective would be enough to obtain an implicit '*social licence*' for *shale* operations[209]

389. However, the owners' acceptance may vary depending if he is or not economically benefited with the drilling activity,[210] and even among those who could be benefited there could also be a question of '*principles*' not to accept due to environmental impact.

390. In the international context, the problem of the '*social acceptance*' is greater as the owners of the land are not the owners of the resources of the soil, and hence they do not receive a part of the earning coming from the *shale.*

391. The operators on the area know that the energy resources development without the public's acceptance is a short-term approach, since the operations can be stopped by oppositions *de iure* (e.g., by means of injunctions or other judicial orders) or de facto (e.g., with demonstrations) once the stranded costs have been invested. On the contrary, the public officers do know this approach may not be useless for the future elections.

392. One tool the regulators have to consider for the activity to gain social acceptance is the public hearings or consulting administrative proceedings where the affected citizens have the opportunity to express their opinion and suggest way to mitigate damages in their daily lives. In the second stage, the regulators should consider if such opinions shall or shall not be binding for the operators. However, the key issue is that the '*social licence*' is essential for the long-term *shale* gas exploitation.

§12. Environmental Issues Regarding Non-conventional Hydrocarbons in Argentina

I. The Unconstitutionality of the Ban of Fracking from the Part of the Municipalities

393. On the 22 August 2013 Allen municipality passed the Ordinance No 046/2013 (the '*Ordinance*') prohibiting the use of hydraulic fracking methods for the extraction of hydrocarbons inside the limits of the City of Allen (*fracking).*

394. In this context, Rio Negro province filed a complaint ab initio or unconstitutionality of the Ordinance before the Provincial High Court (the '*Court*') that

209. *See* 'First Stevens Report', *supra*, p. 13.

210. In the United States, the owner may receive a bonus or royalties when letting their land to an oil company so as to develop the resources.

sustained the petition declaring the Ordinance unconstitutional due to lack of municipal competence to pass an anti-fracking Ordinance.[211]

395. The sentence determined that sections 121 and 124 of the National Constitution, as well as section 79 of the Provincial Constitution and sections 2 and 6 of the Law No 26197 give the provinces the regulatory powers over the exploitation of hydrocarbons performed in their territory. The exclusive competence was given to guarantee the uniform order of the hydrocarbons activity in the territory of Río Negro. When the municipality prohibits the practice of hydrocarbons exploitation, they are considered to be invading the provincial competence in terms of natural resources policy. In this sense, the Court considered appropriate to declare the exclusive competence of the provincial State regarding hydrocarbons legislation.

396. Moreover, the decision also establishes the limits on the environmental attributions conferred to the municipal autonomies, saying that '*such powers cannot trespass the municipal interest itself (sections 225 and 229 subsections 15 and 16 of the provincial Constitution, section 38 subsection p of the Municipal Charter of Alem)*'. So, the municipal autonomy will not be an 'Interference source' of the municipalities regarding the competencies of the province and the nation, harmony is established among the three entities. In line with the municipal limitations, the decision establishes that 'even though the municipalities exercise their powers of environmental policy in their territory *(Articles 225, 229 inc. 15 y 16 of the Provincial Constitution), they should do so without invading the limits of the provincial competences*'.

397. Similarly, on 7 April 2017, the District Attorney of Neuquén requested the High Court of Justice to declare the Ordinance No 783/16 passed by the Vista Alegre municipality (the 'Ordinance') unconstitutional; such rule was passed the Vista Alegre municipality. The Ordinance was passed to ban the fracking in the whole municipal territory of Vista Alegre due to the environmental and social impact causing it.

398. The same as the previous case, (*see* item 6.3. A. i.), the District Attorney stated that the Ordinance interfered with the exclusive competence of the province and clarified that the Constitution never gave the municipality the authority to legislate regarding hydrocarbons. It was also considered that when applying the Ordinance, a precedent would be established that could have a harmful impact on the provincial management.

II. Decree No 1483/12 of Neuquén: Non-conventional Resources

399. On 13 August 2012 Decree No 1483/12 of the province of Neuquén was passed which approved Annex XVI 'Rules and Procedures for the exploration and

211. *Provincia de Río Negro v. Municipalidad de Allen about conflict of powers (City Ordinance No 046/ 2013,* Supreme Court of Río Negro, File 26731/13-STJ.

exploitation of non-conventional reservoirs' as an integrating part of the Decree No 2656/99 of the Law No 1875 about preservation, conservation, defence and improvement of the environment

400. The Decree No 1483/12 (the 'Decree') is aimed at establishing the environmental guidelines about the shale gas, tight gas, shale oil and tight oil well drilling in non-conventional reservoirs that the hydrocarbons operators have to follow in the province, to prevent, mitigate and minimize the environmental impacts that can be caused by such drillings.

401. In that sense, section 3 of the decree establishes that non-conventional exploitation and exploration projects should have an Environmental Licence before its execution.

402. Pursuant to section 4 the environment report should contain the following requirements:

- Description and process of the flow back treatment system of the water used in the hydraulic stimulation of the well.
- Sworn statement of the fluids composition used in the termination of the wells through hydraulic stimulation utilized in the process with security sheet of each chemical product or substance.
- The endorsement of the project by Mining and Hydrocarbons Under Secretariat.
- Authorization of water use and discharge of effluents issued by the authority of application.
- Moreover it is established that any modification the permit holder, concessioner and/or the operator should make after the issuance of the Environmental Licence, pursuant to section 5, should be submitted to the applicable environmental authority.

403. On the contrary, section 7 of the decree also determines that the permit holder, concessioner and/or operator shall submit the sworn statement with the information of the estimated volume and the source of provision of water to be used, during the stages of drilling and termination of the well and to pay the tariff due to the industrial use of public waters whatsoever the application authority imposes.

404. Section 9 prohibits the use of underground water, during the non-conventional well drilling and termination, capable of meeting the supply the population or for irrigation.

405. Another aspect to point out of the decree is that section 10 determines the flow back water should be totally submitted to a treatment system that guarantees what is set forth under Law No 899 (Code of Waters of the province) for the following reuse and decomposition alternatives:

- Reuse in the hydrocarbons industry.

– Reuse in risk associated to an environmental productive or decomposition process of the intervened area, with the approval of the authority of application.
– Final decomposition of the drain well pursuant to what the regulations establish.

406. In that sense, section 11 establishes that the water coming from flow backs, whatever its condition, shall neither be poured over bodies of superficial waters, and nor can it be stored before or during its treatment in containers open pit.

407. Section 12 of the Decree provides that the non-conventional development wells of the field should be designed in such a way so as to optimize the use of the location fit for multiple wells, minimizing the impacts produced by the movement of its ground and accesses.

408. Regarding the storage pools of water for the termination of the wells, section 13 determines that they have to be waterproofed. Furthermore, the environmental report should contain location, size, shape, way, depth, characteristics of the waterproof used, time of operation, sanitation of the abandonment and further requirements the authority of application would solicit.

409. Section 14 establishes that the permit holder, concessioner and/or operator shall submit all the physical chemical tests of the flow back water to the environmental authority, so that they are informed of the quality and quantity thereof. Such presentation shall be done periodically as long as there is the flow back.

410. Finally, section 15 determines that the permit holder, concessioner and/or operator shall submit the plan of the non-conventional drillings of each area to the authority of application every six months.

III. Bill about the Fundamental Principles of Environmental Protection in the Exploration and Exploitation of Hydrocarbons in the Province of Neuquén

411. The bill sent to the legislature of the province of Neuquén aims at establishing the fundamental principles of environmental protection in the hydrocarbons exploitation and exploration in non-conventional field or reservoirs in the provincial territory.

412. Section 6 of the bill contemplates areas of exclusion inside of which it is prohibited to perform non-conventional wells exploitation operations, or exploration projects or potential economic evaluations of the specific activity. These areas are determined in the following way:

– distances shorter than 1,000 m away from native forests;
– distances shorter than 1,000 m of the bank of natural or artificial rivers, streams, lakes or lagoons;

- minimum distance of 600 m away from a house or construction taken as a domestic house for people to temporarily or permanently live and that are isolated from urbanized centres;
- minimum distance of 8,000 m away from any urbanized centre considering the limit of the municipal place if any or the limit of the maximum constructions whether it is a village, town or city or cohabitation conglomerate of any type;
- minimum distance of 1,000 m of any drilling, pool or drainage of thermal water;
- distance shorter than 600 m of any concrete work or structure which is an elevated road functioning as a means of communication means or bridges;
- minimum distance of 600 m from distribution or high-tension electrical energy transformation centres (more than 13.4 Volts);
- minimum distance of 600 m from high-tension regulation plants of gas or compressor station of gas or high-tension pipeline (heavier than 39 kg/cm^2);
- distance shorter than 6,000 m from dams, contention dams, works of river channelling, or stored water level compensation structures.

413. Chapter IV of the bill is about environmental responsibility. In that sense, section 8 establishes that the exploration permit holder or CENCH owner is objectively responsible for the environment where he develops the activity. Hence, he should re-establish or restore the place affected by the conditions prior to base line, being exclusively responsible for the implied environmental costs.

414. Moreover, section 9 determines that the economic costs resulting from mitigation and recovery actions made by the provincial State due to the permit or concession holder's omission will be paid by the provincial State; thus it will be allowed to take all the necessary measures tending to recover the refund of the sums derogated. Due to the impossibility to recover the original condition of the place, section 10 sets forth that the permit or concession holder must compensate the provincial State.

415. The bill, in section 11, determines that the permit or concession holder shall guarantee its activity by means of an environmental insurance in favour of the provincial State and section 12 establishes that in the event of an environmental incident, the owner shall report it to the authority of application with the details of the situation within twenty-four hours the event has occurred.

416. Section 14 determines that the transformation of a conventional productive well into a non-conventional is forbidden, unless the first is depleted or abandoned and it is not in an area of exclusion duly proved and certified by the authority of application.

417. On the contrary, Chapter VI is about the use of the water. Section 17 prohibits the use of underground water to meet the demand of the population, irrigation and thermal and therapeutic uses.

418. It is further established under section 18 that the water of flow back should be totally submitted to a treatment that guarantees the frame inside the physical and chemical parameters of discharge established by Law No 899 (Code of Waters of the province of Neuquén), furthermore, the discharge of water or any other fluid such as drilling water, connate water, purge water, fluids used in the termination of the well, cement grouts, emulsion of oil with water or any other waters coming from the hydrocarbon exploitation or exploration is prohibited.

419. Chapter VIII, dealing with owners and pre-emptive measure, determines under section 21 that the owner of an exploration permit or a CENCH should have an emergency plan identifying the resources available to that effect in the area where the activities are performed by the participating public agencies or bodies with environmental issue responsibilities.

420. In that sense, section 22 determines that a protecting and pre-emptive infrastructure shall be built near fragile areas. On the contrary, section 23 establishes that in case of a hydraulic fracture a control of measures of seismic parameters should be performed away from the fractured well, or in the concentrated configuration of the well.

421. In the case of the final deposition of waste coming from non-conventional hydrocarbons' activities in deep receptive formations, section 24 establishes that those formations have to be waterproofed sealed and have redundant vertical insulating barriers to the surface.

422. Moreover, Chapter X that deals with the administrative matters determines that the authority of application has the power to realize any and all tests, essays and the necessary further physic-chemical formalities to check the development of the project. Besides, the owner should submit:

- Certification of a good sealing of the pipes up to at least 400 m under the last useful groundwater aquifer determined by the use of well logs data.
- Certification of the flow back destination at the end and follow-up protocol of the flow back water.
- Protocols of action prior to the intervention and protocols of immediate action in emergency for damages caused to the environment.
- Finally, the responsible of the operation in a field shall submit the 'debt-free report' to the authority of application.

IV. Empirical Experience

423. As from the end of 2014 up to date twenty CENCHs have been awarded, all but one in the province of Neuquen in the Vaca Muerta Formation. Only one was awarded in the area CN-8 Puesto Guardian in the province of Salta.

V. *Loma Campana*

424. Even though the CENCH was not given according to provisions under the Hydrocarbons Law, *Loma Campana* case is the first evidence of a CENCH in Argentina.

425. By means of Law No 2867 of Neuquén, which ratified the provincial decree provincial No 1208/13, the exploitation concession awarded to YPF was extended on the area of Loma Campana. That is to say, the anticipated extension of the concession was awarded. The development, exploration and exploitation of the non-conventional hydrocarbons were based then upon provisions of Decree 929/2013 afore-elaborated.

426. The integral development plan of the area programmed a one-year non-conventional development Pilot Plan with the drilling of 115 vertical wells in the areas of Loma Lata Norte and Loma Campana with an investment of USD 1,146 million. Based on the successful result of the pilot, the massive development of the block, which will be done as from year 2 to year 35, will involve the drilling of 1,073 vertical wells and 489 horizontal wells with an investment of USD 15,360 million.

VI. Bajada de Añelo and La Amarga Chica

427. By means of Decree No 2693/14 of Neuquén on 18 December 2014, the joint venture (herein under UTE) conformed by YPF and YSUR was awarded the first CENCH's in the country for the area of La Amarga Chica and Bajada de Añelo for the term of thirty-five years.

428. In the decree which depicts the Memorandum Agreement of Investment – entered into between the Undersecretary of Mining and Hydrocarbons, Gas and oil and the companies – by means of which it is established, as a condition of the UTE contracts reconversion for the exploitation of the CENCHs areas in favour of the companies, the total of USD 41,000,000 for the province which will contribute six areas to GyP for an amount of USD 41,000,000.

429. For the area La Amarga Chica, whose extension is 188.6 km^2, the Pilot Plan programmes an investment of USD 422,000,000 for the first three years of the investment project, for the drilling of approximately twenty-four wells. Subject to the results of the Pilot Plan, it is estimated that the total investment will be up to USD 8,600,000 for the drilling of approximately 847 wells.

430. For the area of Bajada de Añelo, whose extension is 204.47 km^2, the Pilot Plan is making an investment of USD 447,000,000 for the first three years and six months of the project, for the drilling of approximately thirty-one wells. Subject to the results of the Pilot Plan, the development for the total investment will represent up to USD 10,158,000,000 for the drilling of up to 1,100 wells. YPF has participation on that CENCH of 85% and YSUR of the remaining 15%:

	La Amarga Chica (188.56 km^2)	*Bajada de Añelo (204.47 km^2)*
Reconversion payment	Reconversion bond of USD 41 million and assignment for six areas (value USD 41 million)	
Pilot plan term	three years	three years and six months.
Minimum investment engaged	USD 422 million (24 wells).	USD 447 million (31 wells).
Contingent investment (subject to the result of the Pilot Plan)	USD 10,158 million (1,100 wells).	USD 8,600 million (847 wells).
Royalty rate	12%	12%
Social Corporate Responsibility bond	USD 10.5 million (2,5% of USD 422 million)	USD 11.1 million (2.5% of USD 477 million)
Total tax stability	Yes, for 35 years.	Yes, for 35 years.

VII. Lindero Atravesado

431. By means of Decree No 1540/15 of Neuquén, on 16 July 2015 the joint venture (herein under UTE) Pan American Energy (PAE) having a 62.5% and YPF having a 37.5% was given a CENCH on the area of Lindero Atravesado, whose surface was 509.39 km^2. The CENCH will last for thirty-five years, a four-year Pilot Plan included.

432. The Pilot Plan intends to drill forty wells in the period as from 1 January 2015 to 31 December 2018, with an investment of USD 590,000,000 and a registration of 650 km^2 of seismic for USD 23,000,000. Between 2015 and 2025 the non-conventional development integral plan submitted by the companies' plans the previous evaluation and shale pilot in which fifteen wells will be drilled so as to evaluate the shale potential of the area and to implement a production pilot for the sum of USD 300,000,000. If the pilot is a success, the non-conventional development integral plan will be implemented with the drilling of 721 wells, the infrastructure development and the productions payment terms and a water-injection plant for the disposal of the drains; all of this implies an approximate investment of USD 11,200,000,000.

433. The decree also establishes that if the minimum investments provided in the Memorandum Agreement of investment, subscribed between the companies and the provinces and approved by the same decree, are made, the concession will be automatically extended for the term of ten years. Such investments are as follows: An additional programme of twenty wells with objective tight gas in the western part of the area for a minimum amount of USD 260,000,000, a pilot with a shale objective for a minimum amount of USD 200,000,000, that plans the drilling of approximately fifteen wells, the building of an installation of oil or gas treatment for the processing of the production resulting from both projects for an amount of USD 100,000,000.

434. On the contrary, for the concept of Corporate Social Responsibility and Exploitation bonus the companies will pay to the provinces the amounts of USD 14,800,000 and USD 7,400,000 respectively, whereas for the stamp tax, they will pay the amount of USD 4,100,000.

	Lindero Atravesado (509.39 km^2)
Pilot Plan term	4 years.
Minimum investment involved	USD 590 million (40 wells).
Contingent investment (subject to the result of the Pilot Plan)	USD 11,200 million (721 wells).
Royalty rate	12%
Stamp tax	USD 4,100,000
Social Corporate responsibility bond	USD 14,800,000
Local tax stability	Yes, for 35 years.

VIII. Bandurrias

435. By means of the Decree No 1541/15 of Neuquén it was resolved to subdivide the block Bandurria that had been given to the UTE made up by YPF, PAE and Wintershall Energía. In that sense, the areas called Bandurria Centro, Bandurria Norte and Bandurria Sur were created.

IX. Bandurria Sur

436. The Decree No 1541/15 gave one CENCH in the area of Bandurria Sur, whose extension is of 228.5 km^2, to YPF. The CENCH will last for thirty-five years and it will include a three-year Pilot Plan during which twenty wells are to be drilled and investments are to be made of USD 360,000.000. As from 2019 a massive development is planned according to the results obtained and around 1,140 horizontal wells are expected to be drilled with a total investment of USD 14,900,000,000.

X. Bandurria Centro

437. By means of Decree No 1543/15 PAE was given a CENCH over the area of Bandurria Centro, whose extension is 130 km^2. The CENCH will be valid for thirty-five years and the Pilot Plan for the term between 1 August 2015 and 31 July 2019.

438. The Pilot Plan programmes the drilling of sixteen wells with an investment of USD 304,000,000. Should the plan be successful, a non-conventional integral development plan will be implemented whose scope is expected to be: The drilling of a total of 404 wells for the development of non-conventional hydrocarbons and infrastructures for an amount estimated at USD 6,800,000,000.

439. Regarding Corporate Social Responsibility there will be a contribution to the province of USD 7,600,000.

XI. Bandurria Norte

440. The Decree No 1542/15 gave to Wintershall Energía a CENCH over the area of Bandurría Norte, whose extension is 107 km^2. The CENCH will be valid for thirty-five years and the Pilot Plan for the term of three years will be included.

441. The Pilot Plan consists in building a vertical well and four horizontal ones with an investment of USD 82,000,000. Based on the results of the Pilot Plan, a notional development plan will commence in 2019 with additional investments projecting the drilling of 136 horizontal wells. The investment will amount to USD 2,483,000,000:

	Bandurria Sur (228.15 km^2)	*Bandurria Norte (107 km^2)*	*Bandurria Centro (130 km^2)*
Pilot Plan Term	three years.	four years.	four years.
Minimum investment involved	USD 360 million (20 wells).	USD 82 million (4 wells).	USD 304 million (16 wells).
Contingent investment (subject to the result of the Pilot Plan)	USD 14,900 million (1.160 wells).	USD 2,400 million (140 wells).	6.800 million (404 wells).
Royalty rate	12%	12%	12%
Local tax stability	Yes, for 35 years.	Yes, for 35 years.	Yes, for 35 years.

XII. Sierras Blancas

442. The Decree No 1717/15 of Neuquén granted to the UTE formed by GyP, O&G Developments and Medanito a CENCH on the area of Sierras Blancas, whose extension is 166.3 km^2. Participation in the UTE by the companies is the following: GyP 10%, O&G (Shell Group subsidiary and operating company) 85% and Medanito 5%. The CENCH will be valid for thirty-five years and the five-year Pilot Plan will be included.

443. The works in the Pilot Plan amount to USD 130,000,000 and consists in drilling and termination of three horizontal wells, the construction of an oil and gas treatment plant with capacity for ten thousand daily barrels whose costs will be attributed jointly by the UTE Cruz de Lorena and the UTE Sierras Blancas to deal with the production of the areas and the corresponding evacuation ducts:

	Sierras Blancas 166.3 km^2)
Pilot Plan Term	five years
Minimum investment involved	USD 130 million (3 wells)
Contingent investment (subject to the result of the Pilot Plan)	–
Royalty rate	12%
Social Corporate responsibility bond	–
Local tax stability	Yes, for thirty-five years

XIII. Cruz de Lorena

444. By means of the Decree No 1718/15 of Neuquén the UTE formed by Gym, O&G Developments and Shell Compañía Argentina de Petróleo was granted a CENCH on the area of Cruz de Lorena, whose extension is 158,74 km^2. Participation of the companies in the UTE is the following: GyP 20%, O&G (operator) 40% and Shell Compañía Argentina de Petróleo 40%. The CENCH will be valid for thirty-five years and it will include a five-year Pilot Plan.

445. The Pilot Plan, with an investment of USD 122,000,000, projects the drilling and termination of three horizontal wells, one vertical well and the construction of an oil and gas treatment plant with capacity for ten thousand barrels whose cost will be paid together by the UTE Cruz de Lorena and the UTE Sierras Blancas to meet the production of both areas. Furthermore, the connection of the production wells to the treatment plant and the construction of the evacuation ducts are planned.

	Cruz de Lorena (166.3 km²)
Pilot Plan Term	five years
Minimum investment involved	USD 122,000,000 (3 horizontal wells and 1 vertical well)
Contingent investment (subject to the result of the Pilot Plan)	–
Royalty rate	12%
Social Corporate responsibility bond	–
Local tax stability	Yes, for thirty-five years

XIV. Bajo del Choique: La Invernada

446. The Decree 2444/15 of Neuquén awarded GyP, which integrates a UTE with ExxonMobil Exploration Argentina, a CENCH for the exploration, development and exploitation of the area Bajo del Choique – La Invernada, whose extension is 400,27 km^2. The CENCH will last for thirty-five years and will include a three-year Pilot Plan.

447. The Pilot Plan will consist in the drilling of 5 new horizontal wells of up to 2,500 m of side branch and twenty-five stages of fracturing, the building of an installation for production with capacity for separation and storage, the construction of a gas pipeline up to a point where the gas produced can be injected to evacuate the crude, and the connection to one existing production well, with an investment of USD 251,000,000. Subject to the results of the pilot, the project plans the drilling of 556 horizontal wells of 2,500 m with twenty-five stages of fracturing, with an estimated investment of USD 13,900,000,000.

448. The Decree No 2444/15 also establishes that ExxonMobil Exploration will have to pay to the province the amount of USD 8,000,000 as contract collection bonus:

	La Invernada and Bajo del Choique (166 km²)
Pilot Plan Term	five years
Minimum investment involved	USD 251 million (5 wells)
Contingent investment (subject to the result of the Pilot Plan)	USD 13,900,000,000 (556 wells)
Royalty rate	12%
Contract collection bond	USD 8,000,000

	La Invernada and Bajo del Choique (166 km^2)
Local tax stability	Yes, for thirty-five years

XV. Aguada Federal

449. The Decree No 0128/15 of Neuquén gave GyP, which forms a UTE with Wintershall Energía, a CENCH for the area for the exploration, development, and exploitation in the area of Aguada Federal, with a valid term of thirty-five years with a two-year Pilot Plan for the drilling of six wells and an investment of USD 162,000,000:

	Aguada Federal (166.3 km^2)
Pilot Plan Term	two years
Minimum investment involved	USD 162,000,000 (6 wells)
Contingent investment (subject to the result of the Pilot Plan)	–
Royalty rate	9%
Social Corporate responsibility bond	–
Local tax stability	Yes, for thirty-five years

XVI. Rincón La Ceniza and La Escalonada

450. The Decree No 0191/15 of Neuquén awarded to the UTE formed by GyP, Total Austral Argentinean branch, O&G Developments, Shell Compañía Argentina, a CENCHs for the areas of Rincón La Ceniza and La Escalonada, whose extensions are 220,77 km^2 and 239 km^2 respectively, which will be developed and exploited together due to their proximity. The CENCHs will be valid for thirty-five years and will include a two-year Pilot Plan.

451. The Pilot Plan includes five 1,000-m horizontal wells and ten fracturings and one well with connection to the Gas pipeline of the Pacific for the area Rincón La Ceniza. For the area La Escalonada, the acquisition and processing of 3D seismic, one vertical delineation well, one 1,500-metre horizontal well and fifteen fracturings are planned. The construction of an early production plant and lines of connection for the joint use for the areas La Escalonada and Rincón La Ceniza are as well projected. The investment for such plan amounts to USD 344,000,000.

452. If the Pilot Plan succeeds, an integral development plan will be performed that will include the total drilling of 590 wells, the building of installations for the hydrocarbons production, whose investment will amount to USD 12,892,000,000.

453. Moreover, the companies will have to pay a total USD 8,600,000 for social responsibility:

	Rincón La Ceniza (220.77 km²)	*La Escalonada (239 km²)*
Pilot Plan Term	two years	
Minimum investment involved	USD 344 million (6 wells for Rincón La Ceniza and 1 well for La Escalonada)	
Contingent investment (subject to the result of the Pilot Plan)	USD 12,892 million (590 wells)	
Royalty rate	–	
Social Corporate responsibility bond	USD 8,000,000	
Local tax stability	Yes, for thirty-five years	

XVII. Rio Neuquén

454. By means of Decree No 0776/16 of Neuquén Petrobras Argentina was granted a CENCH on the area of Rio Neuquén, whose extension is 232,85 km^2. The CENCH will be valid for thirty-five years, a five-year Pilot Plan included.

455. The Pilot Plan is projected to drill twenty-four wells and to adequate installations in the period from 2016 to 2020 whose investment will amount to USD 346,000,000. According to the results obtained, a massive development of the field is planned which implies 160 wells drilled together with the necessary installations for the production whose investment will represent a total of USD 2,218,000,000.

456. Moreover, as regards social corporate responsibility Petrobras will make a contribution to the province equivalent to USD 8,650,000. On the other hand, regarding the exploitation bonus the company will pay USD 5,700,000 and related to the stamp tax a total of USD 2,422,000. In total, they will contribute USD 16,772,000 to the province:

	River Neuquén (232.85 km²)
Pilot Plan Term	five years
Minimum investment involved	USD 346,000,000 (24 wells)

	River Neuquén (232.85 km²)
Contingent investment (subject to the result of the Pilot Plan)	USD 2,218 million (160 wells)
Exploitation bond	USD 5,700,000
Social Corporate responsibility bond	USD 8,650,00
Seal tax	USD 2,422,000
Local Tax Stability	Yes, for thirty-five years

XVIII. Punta Senillosa

457. By means of Decree No 1054/16 of Neuquén Tecpetrol was awarded a CENCH on the area of Punta Senillosa, whose extension is 24.39 km^2. The CENCH will be valid for thirty-five years and the Pilot Plan will last for thirty months as from 1 July 2016.

458. In the Pilot Plan, the drilling of four wells and the adequation of installations are projected and this will entail an investment of USD 20,600,000. Based on the results obtained, a massive development of the field is programmed which will imply seventeen drilled wells plus the necessary installations for the production; all this will represent an investment of USD 61,000,000.

459. Moreover, in relation to social corporate responsibility the company Tecpetrol will make a contribution to the province equivalent to USD 515,000. On the contrary, the company will pay USD 144,200 for the stamp tax, making a total contribution of USD 659,200,000 to the province:

	Punta Senillosa (24.39 km²)
Pilot Plan Term	thirty months
Minimum investment involved	USD 20,600,000 (4 wells)
Contingent investment (subject to the result of the Pilot Plan)	USD 61 million (17 wells)
Royalty rate	12% until 2026. 18% as from 2026
Social Corporate responsibility bond	USD 515,000
Seal tax	USD 144,200
Local tax stability	Yes, for thirty-five years

XIX. Fortín de Piedra

460. By means of Decree No 1055/16 of Neuquén Tecpetrol was awarded a CENCH on the area Punta Senillosa, whose extension is 249.45 km^2. The CENCH will be valid for thirty-five years together with a Pilot Plan of thirty months as from 1 July 2016.

461. In the Pilot Plan, the drilling of 1 vertical well, 4 horizontal wells are programmed, 3D seismic and the installation which will imply an investment of USD 200,000,000. Based on the results obtained, a massive development of the field will be commenced which will entail a total 500 wells drilled that together with the necessary installations for the production will represent an investment of USD 6,000,000,000.

462. Furthermore, regarding social corporate responsibility Tecpetrol will make a contribution of USD 5,000,000 to the province. On the contrary, the company will pay USD 1,400,000 for the stamp tax making a total contribution for the province of USD 6,400,000:

	Fortín de Piedra (249.45 km^2)
Pilot Plan Term	five years
Minimum investment involved	USD 200,000,000 (5 wells)
Contingent investment (subject to the result of the Pilot Plan)	USD 6,000 million (500 wells)
Royalty rate	12% until 2026/ 18% as from 2026
Social Corporate responsibility bond	USD 5,000,000
Seal tax	USD 1,400,000
Local tax stability	Yes, for thirty-five years

XX. CN-8 Puesto Guardián

463. By means of Decree No 3015/15 of Salta, Presidente Petroleum S.A. was awarded a CENCH on the area of CN-8 Puesto Guardián. The CENCH will be valid for thirty-five years and a two-year Pilot Plan will be included with a possible extension of a period up to twelve months:

	CN-8 Puesto Guardían
Pilot Plan Term	two years (with a possible extension of twelve months)
Minimum investment involved	–

Contingent investment (subject to the result of the Pilot Plan)	–
Seal tax	–
Local tax stability	Yes, for thirty-five year
	CN-8 Puesto Guardían
Pilot Plan Term	two years (with a possible extension of twelve months)
Minimum investment involved	–
Contingent investment (subject to the result of the Pilot Plan)	–
Seal tax	–
Local tax stability	Yes, for thirty-five years

XXI. Empirical Experience 2016–2019

464. As of November 2019, in the space of unconventional exploitation of gas, Argentina already had completed 2,541 wells, doubling the December 2015 number of 1,254 wells. In the case of the shale gas, it already had reached 1,196 wells, 97% above the 606 completed until 2015, while in the case of the tight-sands gas, it had reached 1,345 wells, 108% above the finished ones until December 2015. In terms of activity, the number of stages of monthly fracture performed by company, as can be seen, whereas in 2015 they averaged about 98 monthly fracture stages, almost exclusively per YPF account, the average between January and November 2019 amounted to 542, more than quintupling the activity in relation to 2015, involving more companies.

Figure 9 Shale Fracking 2016–2018

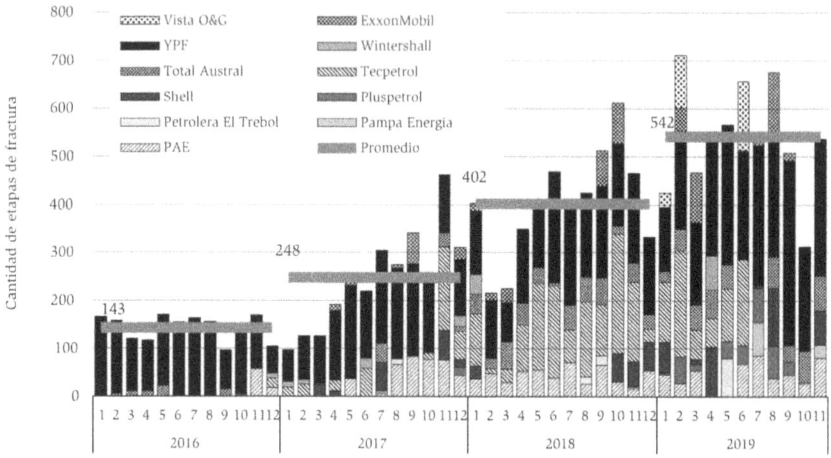

Fuente : Luciano Fucello-Country Manager NCS Multistage.

Chapter 8. Offshore Oil and Gas

465. Hydrocarbons (O&G) offshore can give rise to an endless succession of questions.[212] Conventional approaches – even worse when compounded by undue haste – could simply lead to considering a model's *convenience*. However, haste is not the best counsellor in social studies (even less so when the debate is on the substrate, basis and founding of a modern economy, i.e., primary energy sources). Consequently, the right analysis begins by considering the *benefits* (short, medium or long term) of a model, pass through to the review of the *efficiency* of a model, and conclude with its *viability* or *feasibility*.

466. This monograph aims to examine what are the most suitable answers for Argentina. In order to achieve this objective, this work shall: (i) start by conducting a review of the foundations of offshore oil and gas development; (ii) review and compare seven models which are particularly representative and illustrative of the industry (the UK, Norway, Malaysia, Nigeria, Brazil, Angola and Mexico); (iii) review the existing model in Argentina; and (iv) present findings and conclusions. The choice of the study cases was made upon their governmental system, geographic distribution, industrial strength and model diversity.

§1. Offshore Development Milestones

Oceans and offshore oil and gas development

467. The sea is an immense source – proven and potential – of hydrocarbons exploitation.[213] By 2001 there were over 8,000 offshore platforms and 700 exploration wells located along 5,000 offshore basins scattered among over 100 states.[214]

468. According to Figure 1, exploration and exploitation have extended from State territorial seas to exclusive economic zones (EEZ) and CS of coastal states. Article 55 of the 1982 UN Convention on the Law of the Sea (UNCLOS) affirms:

> [t]he exclusive economic zone is an area beyond and adjacent to the territorial sea, subject to the specific legal regime established in this Part, under which the rights and jurisdiction of the coastal State and the rights and freedoms of other States are governed by the relevant provisions of this Convention.[215]

212. This monograph defines the moSEl as a set of political, regulatory and trade measures implemented as part of the offshore energy activities.
213. G. Blake, M. Pratt, C. Schobasin & A.A. Brown (eds), *Boundaries and Energy: Problems and Prospects* (London: Kluwer Law International, 1998), p. 9.
214. H. Esmaeili, *The Legal Regime of Offshore Oil Rigs in International Law* (London: Ashgate, 2001), p.1.
215. Article 55.

469. On the other hand, Article 76 of UNCLOS determines that:

> [t]he continental shelf of a coastal State comprises the seabed and subsoil of the submarine areas that extend beyond its territorial sea throughout the natural prolongation of its land territory to the outer edge of the continental margin, or to a distance of 200 nautical miles from the baselines from which the breadth of the territorial sea is measured where the outer edge of the continental margin does not extend up to that distance.

470. Article 76 also provides for the possibility and procedure of the coastal State to establish a CS between 200 nm and 350 nm.

471. The jurisdiction of coastal states is determined by the provisions of UNCLOS, which preserves for the benefit of all states the freedom of navigation, overflight, and of the laying of submarine cables and pipelines, as well as other internationally lawful uses of the sea related to these freedoms. In the EEZ, the coastal State has sovereign rights for the purpose of exploring and exploiting, conserving, and managing the natural resources of the seabed and subsoil. Similarly, in connection with the establishment and use of artificial islands, installations, and structures, and as provided in Article 60 and related articles of UNCLOS, provides as follows:

> in the exclusive economic zone, the coastal State shall have the exclusive right to construct and to authorize and regulate the construction, operation and use of:
>
> a. artificial islands;
> b. installations and structures for the purposes provided for in Article 56 and other economic purposes;
> c. installations and structures which may interfere with the exercise of the rights of the coastal State in the zone; and
>
> the coastal State shall have exclusive jurisdiction over such artificial islands, installations and structures, including jurisdiction with regard to customs, fiscal, health, safety and immigration laws and regulations.

472. Article 60 deals with the exclusive right of coastal states to build, authorize and regulate the construction, operation, and use of the three objects in the EEZ (artificial islands, installations and structures for the purposes of exploration and exploitation of natural resources sea, and other facilities and structures for economic purposes). It may seem that Article 60 excludes the construction and use of other types of facilities such as military installations. However, paragraph(c) of Article 60 refers to the right of the coastal State over 'installations and structures which may interfere with the exercise of the rights of the coastal State in the zone' – a general provision which can extend a State's authority to almost all facilities and structures in the EEZ. This means that the rights of other states to establish any kind of artificial island, oil platform or other facility is strictly limited to individuals authorized by the coastal State. However, under Article 60(1)(c), facilities for purposes other than exploration and exploitation of natural resources of the sea and other economic effects, such as military installations, can be established by states other than the coastal State (only if the construction of such structures does not interfere with the exercise of the rights of the coastal State in the area). The article states the power to issue regulations to regulate the exploration and exploitation of natural resources of the sea in the EEZ (particularly the construction and operation of oil platforms). Although the position of the CS in international law has not been weakened by UNCLOS, the novel concept of the EEZ has created a degree of duplication and confusion. Speaking in broad terms, there are currently two legal regimes for the rights of coastal states in relation to natural resources in the area of the seabed in the EEZ and the CS; however, the CS is really only relevant when it extends beyond the EEZ of a given State. The coastal State has sovereign rights over its CS only for the purposes of exploration and exploitation of non-living natural resources; on the other hand, coastal states have sovereign rights in their EEZs for the purpose of exploring and exploiting natural resources, whether living or non-living, and sovereign rights over other economic activities such as the production of hydropower.[216]

473. There is some confusion regarding the creation and operation of oil platforms and artificial islands in the geomorphological continental margin beyond 200 nm. According to Article 80 of UNCLOS, the provisions of Article 60 of the Convention apply to installations on the CS. As already indicated, Article 60 gives the coastal State the exclusive right to construct, authorize and regulate the construction, operation and use of artificial islands and installations for the purpose of exploring and exploiting the natural resources of the sea and other economic purposes; the coastal State also has the exclusive right to construct, authorize and regulate the construction, operation and use of facilities which may interfere with the exercise of their rights. All this means that, under Article 80 it is the coastal State which has the exclusive right to establish (or determine) installations and artificial islands for all economic purposes if the geomorphological continental margin extends beyond 200 nm. However, to resolve potential conflicts – applying Articles 58, 60 and 87 of UNCLOS – non-coastal states may also establish artificial islands and offshore installations in the area of the geomorphological continental margin beyond 200 nm economic purposes if they do not interfere with the exercise of the rights of the coastal State.

---

216. To the extent that the exclusive economic zone and continental shelf coexist (within the 200 nm), an assailable legal regime applied mutatis mutandis. However, in cases where the continental margin extends beyond 200 nm geomorphological, or when a coastal State has not established an exclusive economic zone, only the legal regime governing the continental shelf applies. This means that these coastal states have the right to exercise jurisdiction over the adjacent continental margin beyond 200 nm, but its sovereign rights in that area are limited to the exploitation of non-living natural resources of the subsoil (more adjacent continental margin beyond 200 nm of the waters remains legally considered high seas).

Public policies and regulations

474. Development of offshore oil and gas led to the implementation by states of *public policy* and *regulatory frameworks* in relation both to energy and environmental issues at national and international levels. Regarding *public policy*, it is possible to assert that most governments currently promote *security of supply*, *efficient use* of energy resources, and the *substitution* of hydrocarbons by renewables or alternative sources of energy. Also, according to the importance of hydrocarbons exploitation in relation to a State's economy, *public policies* determine participation in oil and gas operations, the fiscal burden (taxes, royalties, etc.), benefit or production sharing, the treatment of foreign investments (including special schemes for procurement and *local content policies*),[217] any restrictions on the amount of production (due to market or environmental reasons).[218]

475. Regarding the *regulatory framework*, according to the *principle of sovereignty*, any State can wilfully adopt and implement international law normative. In addition, states can tailor normative pursuant to jurisdictional, legislative and constitutional criteria. Consequently, laws, decrees and regulations constitute the regulatory framework for the hydrocarbon industry (both nationally and sub-nationally), mainly including:

- the ownership of hydrocarbons (before and after extraction);
- the system of land and easements (right to explore and build);
- the system of licences and authorizations;
- the system of contracts and operations (including risk sharing clauses, operation, financing, confidentiality, corruption, termination, settlement of disputes, applicable law, etc.);
- the fiscal and management of income (including taxes, fees, royalties, payment in kind option, currency and banking system, etc.) regime;
- the environmental regime (including risk analysis, insurance, etc.);
- the labour system (rights and obligations of workers, safety standards at work); and
- the guarantee scheme (insurance, etc.) and responsibilities (contractual and tort).[219]

Offshore drilling

476. The normative framework or criteria for offshore platform location is not internationally harmonized. Neither international customary law nor codification

217. For a detailed policies to promote local contracts, *see* MZ Ngoasong, 'How International Oil and Gas Companies to Respond Local Content Policies in Petroleum-Producing Developing Countries: A Narrative Enquiry' (2014) 73 *Energy Policy* 471.
218. B. Taverne, *Petroleum, Industries and Governments* (London: Kluwer Law International, 1999), p. 87.
219. *Ibid.*, p. 139.

has been able to provide a satisfactory answer to the issues surrounding this topic. Even the UNCLOS Treaty – the broadest and most extensive applicable Treaty – fails when referring to wells and platforms, namely:

- definition and legal status of the wells and offshore platforms;[220]
- jurisdiction applicable to the wells and platforms in the sea according to maritime space;[221]
- protection of wells and platforms;[222]
- overlapping usage of maritime space;[223]
- environmental risk;[224] and
- the abandonment and disposal regulation of wells and platforms.[225]

In general

477. In 2012 the Republic of Argentina was the largest producer of natural gas and the fourth largest oil producer in South America. The freezing of tariffs and protectionist policies have limited its attractiveness to investors, while domestic energy demand and rapidly growing oil and gas production decreased, leading Argentina to rely on imports.

---

220. Public International Law and Maritime Law raises the dilemma over the possibility that certain types of exploitation platform can be considered a 'boat', with all the accompanying legal consequences: flag and jurisdiction, collision, collision, salvage, pollution etc. Alternatively, operating platforms, may fall within the category under UNCLOS for 'artificial islands, oil wells and other offshore facilities' (s. 60).
221. Practically, the right of the coastal State and other states to explore and build wells in the sea has been the subject of conflict for over half a century. Criteria and overlapping jurisdictions extending from the Truman Proclamation and the concept of the exclusive economic zone and the continental shelf have provoked conflicts over the massive development of offshore projects. Although the encoding, there are still many issues to resolve with regard to the rights of the coastal State in areas under their jurisdiction and offshore development (right to explore, build, Criminal and Civil Law and applicable jurisdiction, customs arrangements, taxation, immigration regime, status, health system, etc.).
222. The protection of wells and offshore facilities is a complementary issue to the Court. In this regard, UNCLOS applies, as well as the relevant resolutions of the International Maritime Organization (IMO or IMO, for its acronym in English), and particularly the 1988 Rome Protocol for the Suppression of Acts against the Safety of Fixed constructions located on the continental shelf.
223. The main problem that arises is how to resolve conflicts that may arise between the operations of the oil platforms and other legitimate activities at sea, such as fishing, navigation, the laying of pipes and cables and the recreational use of the sea.
224. The exploration and exploitation of offshore activity represents a high environmental risk. The use of drilling muds, drill cuttings, treated water and waste dumping pollute the marine environment. Although only a small source of marine pollution, the problem is becoming important in light of increased production of offshore oil and occurrence of international incidents.
225. The decommissioning of offshore oil rigs has become a contentious issue at international level (especially since 1995). The dispute over this began in early 1970s, when the rate of oil production in the sea rose and many facilities began arriving at the end of its economic life. The matter was complicated in 1982 when Unclos, unlike the 1958 Geneva Convention on the continental shelf, ordered a partial regime for the elimination of platforms. The inconsistency between two of the most important international treaties on the law of the sea, the lack of a general treaty, increased public attention and the high cost of the total removal have led to inconsistent practices by states.

478. Total primary energy consumption in Argentina in 2012 was 3.26 quadrillion Btu, out of which natural gas consumption represented approximately 52%, and consumption of petroleum products 34% (Source: BP Statistical Review of World Energy).

479. Natural gas is widely used in residential areas as the primary fuel for electricity generation and as an industrial raw material, while oil is the main fuel used in the transport sector (a smaller part of the total energy consumption country can be attributed to nuclear energy, coal and hydropower, which are used for generating electricity, while other renewable resources are used for the production of biofuels for transport).

Offshore Development Geography

480. The offshore basins of Argentina are located on the CS, mainly in two sub-basins: San Jorge Basin and Austral Basin.

'San Jorge' Gulf Basin

481. San Jorge Gulf Basin is a large irregular region located in the central Patagonia. In geological terms, the basin comprises the southern part of the province of Chubut, the northern part of the province of Santa Cruz and much of the CS in the Gulf San Jorge, covering inland and marine areas (65%) (35%).

482. The total area the basin covers approximately 200,000 km^2, out of which 70,000 km^2 (35%) contains recoverable oil (potential possible hydrocarbons) according to current knowledge and data.

483. Twenty thousand wells have been drilled in the basin area (only twenty-six on the CS); 10,000 wells were productive, with 5,000 oil and/or gas wells remaining.

484. While the higher levels have already been exploited in most sites with some intensity, there remains potential for exploration in nearly all deep levels. In addition, the mainland remains virtually unexplored (5,500 km^2), as well as the entire CS (20,000 km^2), beneath Paso Río Mayo and the vast region north of the Chico and Senguerr rivers.

'Cuenca Austral' Basin

485. Totalling an area of 170,000 km^2 (23,000 km^2 offshore), the basin extends into the south of the American continent, covering an important part of the Santa Cruz province of Argentina, Chile Magellan, the eastern part of the strait of the same name, Isla Grande de Tierra del Fuego and a portion of the CS bordering Argentina to the east.

According to the Hydrocarbons Law No 17,319:

- The Nation is the owner of hydrocarbon deposits that may be found from the 12 nautical miles measured from the baselines established by Law No 23,968, to the outer limit of the CS.
- Provinces own hydrocarbon deposits in their territory, including those in the sea adjacent to their coast to a distance of 12 nautical miles measured from the baselines established by Law No 23,968.
- The City of Buenos Aires owns hydrocarbon deposits within its territory.
- The Province of Buenos Aires or the City of Buenos Aires, according to their respective jurisdictions, own the hydrocarbon deposits that are in the seabed and subsoil of the Rio de la Plata, from the coast to a distance of 12 nautical miles that does not exceed the line established in Article 41 of the Treaty of Rio de la Plata and its Maritime Front and in accordance with the rules set out in Chapter VII of that instrument.
- The Province of Tierra del Fuego, Antarctica and South Atlantic islands, own those hydrocarbon deposits in their territory, including those in the sea adjacent to its coast to a distance of 12 nautical miles measured from the baselines established by Law No 23,968, respecting the provisions of the act signed agreement dated 8 November 1994, between the said province and the province of Santa Cruz.

Offshore Development Structure

486. In line with the National Constitution, Hydrocarbons Law No 17,319 of 1967 (as amended) provides that 'the deposits of oil and gas on the territory of Argentina and on its continental shelf are the inalienable and national heritage of the State or provincial States, according to the territory in which they are'.[226]

487. The Ministry of Energy (Ministry of Energy) regulates the overall energy sector; the National Gas Regulatory Body (ENARGAS) monitors and regulates this activity.

488. Thus, pursuant to the Hydrocarbons Law, 'the Executive Branch may grant exploration permits and temporary concessions and transportation of hydrocarbons […]'. Furthermore, 'licensees and dealers will have dominion over the hydrocarbons extracted and consequently can transport, market, process them and sell their products, in compliance with the regulations issued by the executive branch on reasonable technical and economic foundations which provide for the proper functioning of the domestic market and seek to encourage the exploration and exploitation of hydrocarbons'.[227]

226. *See* Title I of Law No 24145 'Federalizaci6n de Hidrocarburos', sanctioned on 24 September 1992.
227. Section 6.

489. However, in order to ensure that domestic demand is met, for years crude oil has been subject to export taxes and restrictions on export volumes, which limits the benefits that companies can generate from the Argentina selling production abroad.

490. With regard to the environmental framework, the following regulations apply:

- UNCLOS.
- IMO Resolutions.
- Convention Against Pollution 1973/1978 (MARPOL).
- Paris Convention for the Prevention of Pollution from Land of 1974.

491. Regarding market players, the NOC Yacimientos Petrolíferos Fiscales (YPF) is the largest oil producer in the country. In May 2012 the Argentine government approved a law confirming the expropriation of the YPF oil and gas company. Expropriation affected the 51% majority ownership of Repsol YPF. The second largest shareholder is oil producer PAE, owned by BP and Bridas Corporation (a 50/50 joint venture between China National Offshore Oil Corporation and Bridas Energy Holdings). PAE currently operates one of the largest oil basins in Argentina, Cerro Dragon basin. On the contrary, Chevron (USA), Petrobras (Brazil) and Sinopec Group (China) have slowly increased their presence in upstream oil production.

Energy Argentina SA (ENARSA)

492. ENARSA, a State-owned company, deserves special mention because until 2016:

- It owned, exclusively, the exploration permits and exploitation concessions on all national maritime areas not subject to such permits or concessions from the entry into force of its founding law.
- It aims at carrying out on its own, through third parties or associated with third parties, the study, exploration and exploitation of hydrocarbon deposits of solid, liquid and/or gas, transportation, storage, distribution, marketing and industrialization of these products and their direct and indirect costs as well as the provision of public service transport and distribution of natural gas, for which it may produce, process, refine, buy, sell, exchange, import or export and perform any other operation of its industrial or commercial activities necessary to achieve its goals.
- It can – individually, through third parties or associated with third parties – generate, transport, distribute and sell electricity.
- It can individually perform business activities related to energy goods and develop any of the activities included in its object, both at home and abroad.
- It may exercise all rights under the Law No 17,319 gives the holder of exploration permits and exploitation concessions on all national maritime areas which

are not subject to such permits or concessions from the entry into force of Law No 25,943 (with permits or concessions to areas included in the areas granted to the company reverting to the Nation).

- It can operate in any segment of the value chain in an integrated energy goods or independently through specific business units. It will promote technological innovation in its activities.
- It can intervene in the market in order to avoid abuses of dominant position arising from the formation of monopolies or oligopolies.
- It can perform by itself or in association with others for others, any financial operation, excluding those reserved by Law No 21,526 to specially authorized for that purpose entities.

493. In short, ENARSA was a monopolistic entity in a geographical sense (the entire Argentine maritime space) with full oligopolistic powers – as it is able to have input in every sector of the production chain.

494. Since 2016, pursuant to Law No 25,943, ENARSA has played a different role in the Argentine energy market. Offshore permit concessions were reversed to the State through the Ministry of Energy. Offshore exploration is planned to start in 2017 upon an agreement between YPF and the Norwegian NOC Statoil.

495. At the end of 2017, Decree 882 instructed the then Ministry of Energy and Mining to carry out the merger of ENARSA and EBISA in order to rationalize and make public management more efficient.

Exploration and Development

496. According to OGJ, in 2013, the proven oil reserves in Argentina were estimated at 2.8 billion barrels of oil equivalent. In the meantime, total oil production was 723,203 bbl/d, 103,000 bbl/d of which were liquid natural gas plant (Figures 10 and 11).

Figure 10 Argentina Crude Oil Production (1980–2013)

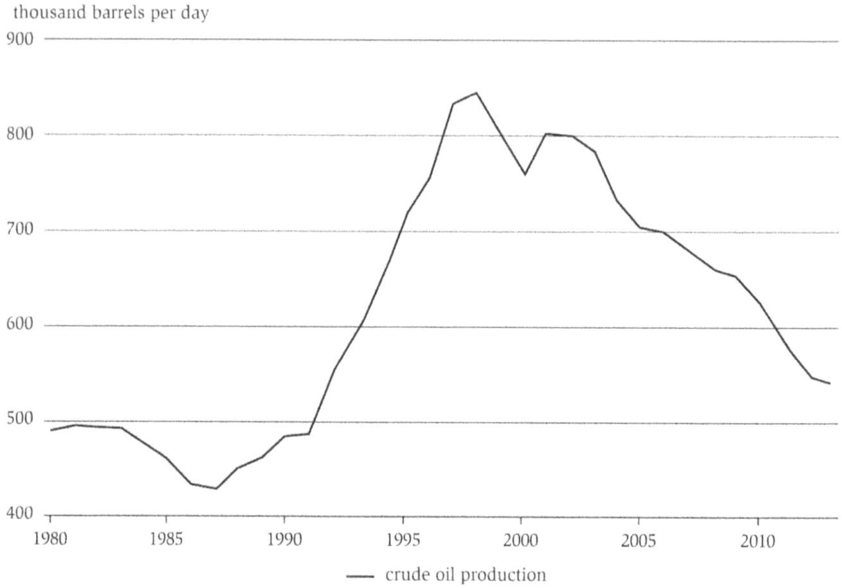

Figure 11 Argentina Oil Consumption (1980–2013)

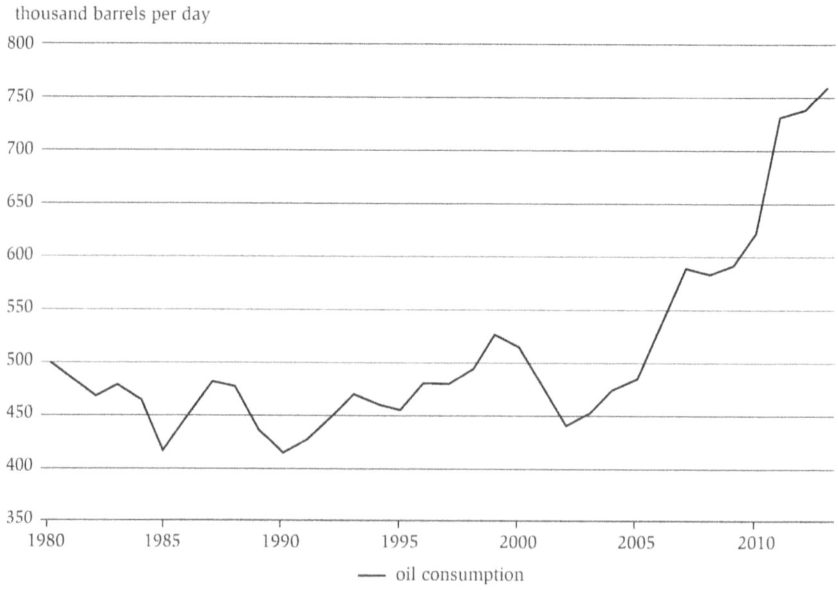

497. According to OGJ, in 2013, Argentina possessed 13.4 Tcf proven gas reserves – a significant decrease from a high of 27.5 Tcf in 2002.

Argentina produces more natural gas than petroleum liquids. However, natural gas production in the country fell for the sixth consecutive year to 1.3 Tcf in 2012 (Figures 12 and 13).

Figure 12 Argentina Natural Gas Production (1980–2013)

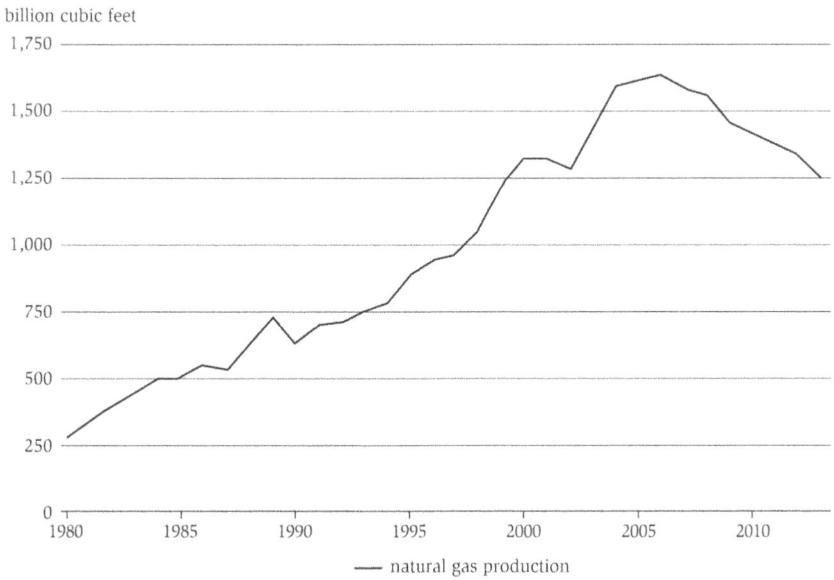

Figure 13 Argentina Natural Gas Consumption (1980–2013)

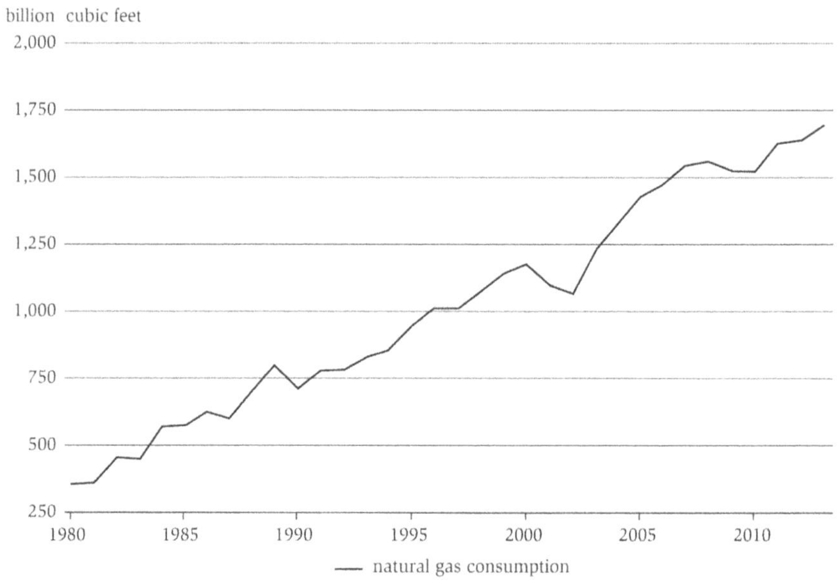

498. In 2018 – the last year reported in the National Energy Balance to date – more than 87% of the total internal energy supply came from hydrocarbons, which explains the importance of adequate policies due to their impact on the energy sector and in the rest of the economy. Total production of oil and gas in Argentina reached a maximum in 2003, measured in thousands of barrels of oil equivalent per day (kbbl/d). Since then, it began a decreasing trajectory until reaching its minimum value in 2014. In 2019, the activity has already resumed the path of growth, again reaching the 2011 levels.

499. In terms of hydrocarbon exploration, the Macri administration carried out after more than 30 years the first international public contest to grant coast exploration permits offshore. The bid was tendered for 38 areas, out of which 23 received bids and were awarded 18 areas on a surface of 94,804.51 km^2, for a total of 9 consortiums and with investment commitments higher than 724 MMUSD. The regulations that will allow Round 2 to be launched during the first half of 2020, where 25 new areas will be offered in the Colorado Basins, West Falklands, Northern Argentina and Southern Argentina.

Figure 14 Argentine Offshore Exploration Plan

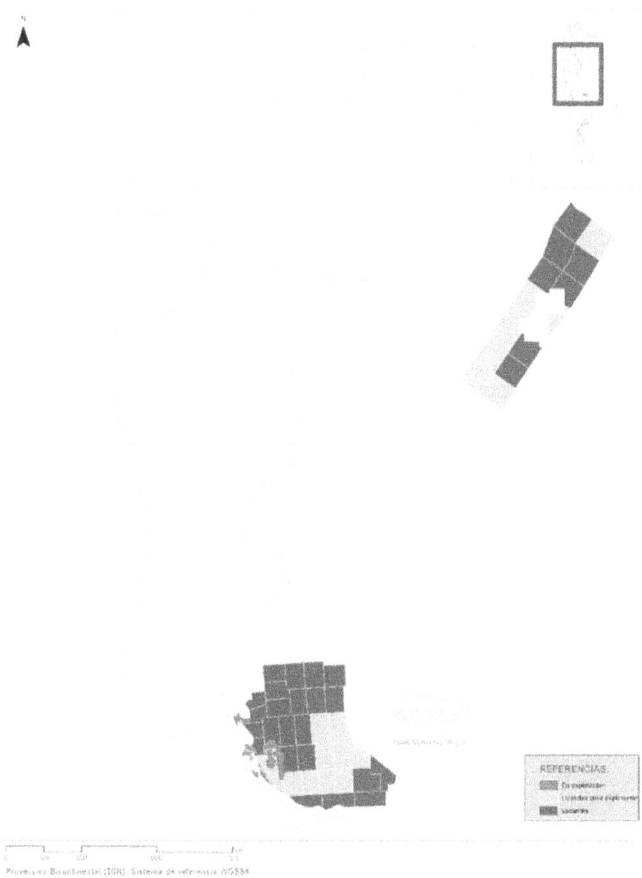

Fuente: Dirección Nacional de Información Energética-SSPE- Secretaría de Gobierno de Energía sobre la base de información de la Dirección Nacional de Exploración y Producción de Hidrocarburos.

§2. Conclusions

500. According to the data analysed and the behaviours/governmental trends described in this work, the following conclusions regarding the performance of offshore hydrocarbon exploitation can be identified:

Argentina	Low	Lack of juridical stability High levels of governmental intervention Lack of technical capacity

501. There is some debate on the merits of a gradual rearrangement improving many institutional factors. The latter approach, for example, might allow better coordination of reforms with political considerations, and may also yield benefits more quickly to provide credibility and maintain the momentum for reform. However, such larges deals are complicated by the lack of lasting institutions which can credibly negotiate and compromise with political concession holders.

502. The above discussion omits the vagaries of trying to explain the separation of the functions of model regardless of the institutional and political context. Although it may be felt that this model is best practice, it may still not be appropriate for every State oil sector in crisis or in the world. Thus, countries which lack the support conditions for best practice might be better off implementing second best choices.

503. Is a full reform required to improve offshore development in Argentina? No, it is not. Broadly, the Argentine O&G normative is acceptable – and the Energy 1990s reform led the country to advanced normative positioning. Argentina needs is a specific Promotion Regime for offshore development that compensates high costs and risks as well as market disadvantages. Should Argentina support a *specific* model, it would probably need to be a *hybrid* of the *Norwegian* rule-of-law and transparency model – which is the source and not the result of the system's achievements – and the *Indonesyan* model of strong mixed share-stakeholders' NOC, well positioned worldwide and privately administered.

Part III. Regulatory Framework Concerning Oil and Gas *Downstream*

§1. General Concepts

504. The oil activity is divided into (1) *upstream* – exploration and production –; (2) *midstream* – gas and crude oil transport –; (3) *downstream* – Refining of crude oil, gas treatment, transport, distribution and commercialization of derived products.

505. The three stages are of great importance, the coordinated and chained work of each of them will bring about efficiency and maximization of the use of crude oil that, as we all know well, is a non-renewable natural resource. Hence, optimization of its use is essential to obtain a sustainable operation.

506. Have you ever wondered what we would do with crude oil if the *downstream* did not exist? We could not do much. The crude oil has limited applications by itself. It is the refining process the one that makes the difference or the 'value added' to that raw material and makes it useful for a lot of activities.

507. The *downstream* represents an indispensable technological link between the *upstream* and the commercialization of the elaborated products or consumption. The configuration with which the refinery is to work is the initial strategic point to guarantee the sustainability and to meet the market needs.

508. The crude oil is the essential raw material for the development of the *downstream*; however this is the activity that adds the real value of use when the product is transformed to be consumed or to serve as the raw material for other industries such as the petrochemical, plastic, pesticides, fertilizers, etc. Up to date, there is no other raw material from which it is possible to extract a great quantity of derived products destined to different applications/uses.

509. Frequently we have heard that the *downstream* is the 'façade' of the oil industry. Importance lays upon arrival to the massive client by means of its refined derivatives (i.e., fuel) through the commercialization and branding process. In the oil industry this is known as *retailing*.

510. We could affirm that the *downstream* initiates with the arrival of crude oil to the processing plants called refineries. The refinery is known as the transformation centre where the physical separation of the crude oil in its different components takes place, apart from the chemical conversion of these components into different ones. Through these processes, products which are, in turn, the base for other industries or used for the clients' consumption, are obtained.

511. These products have to respect maximum quality specifications to be commercialized in the domestic market. The authority of application regulates the required quality in relation to the uses and the needs of the market.[228]

512. The more complex the refinery the higher the optimization to the crude oil. The technologies nowadays grant the maximum use of the crude oil reducing the generation of waste and/or residue.

513. As it was mentioned before, the crude oil is a non-renewable natural resource; hence, it is essential to optimize its use to achieve the sustainability of the activity. The optimization of such refining capacity will be in direct proportion to the availability of crude oil, apart from the technological and infrastructure factors. This is of the utmost importance, in general, as the refineries use mixes of different oils (heavy and light); the diversity of products destined to the market derives from them. This is known as 'crude diet'. Hence, the refineries require a configuration which has to do with the products demanded by the market and the availability of crude oil for the process.

514. The increasing severity of the environmental regulations, as well as the legal and administrative formalities – associated to the community requirements – adds the need for having operative and technological systems for the typical configuration of refinery which guarantees its sustainable operation from the social point of view. The social licence is very important as the refineries are usually placed near populated centres.

515. The refining activity is characterized by the presence of stranded costs and important economies of scale. This reduces the number of operators in the market. The stranded costs are those investment costs that produce a current of benefits in the long run, as they are not rapidly recovered. The economies of scale determine that the unitary costs decrease as the production increases.

516. These characteristics of the activity foster the vertical integration, especially with the commercialization link since, in general, the oil stations are identified with the brand of the refining company. They also constitute an important barrier to enter the market, limiting the potential competition of the importations (Figure 15).

---

228. Resolution of the Department of Energy (DE) No 1283/2006.

Figure 15 Scheme of the Hydrocarbons Value Chain

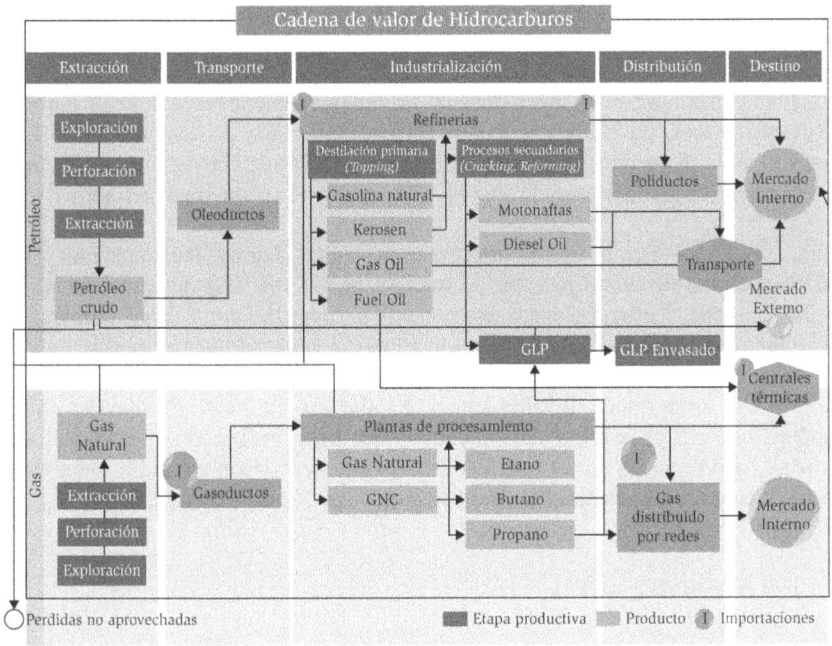

Source: Ministry of Public Finances, Nation's Presidency and Under Secretariat of Economic Planning, National Bureau of Sector Planning (July 2016) Hydrocarbons: *Report on the chain value*, *1* (6), 7–8. Recovered from: www.meco http://www.mecon.gov.ar/peconomica/docs/Complejo_Petroleo_y_Gas.pdfn.gov.ar/peconomica/docs/Complejo.

§2. Conversion of the Crude Oil into Consumable Products

517. The conversion is performed in the refineries through an engineering chemical process called 'refining', initiated with the separation of the crude oil in different distillation fractions. The fractions are further treated –, with methods such as cracking, reforming, alkylation, polymerization and isomerization –, to turn them into mixtures of products with more useful and net commercially oil *derivatives.*

518. These mixtures of the new components are separated by means of extractions of solvents or cracking for example. Impurities are eliminated with techniques such as dehydration and the removal of desalination or by means of elements such as sulphur and hydrogen.

519. The refining processes have been developed due to the changing demand for certain products; consequently, it is a dynamic activity that has to be in line with, environmental, technological advancements and the market needs.

520. As a result of the chemical engineering process, the crude oil is transformed into useful products such as liquefied petroleum gases, oil, kerosene, jet fuel, gas oil, fuel oil, etc. The elaborated products of higher value are fuel for transport. The fuel oils and the asphalt have a lower value.

521. The refineries are big industrial complexes that involve several units and auxiliary services. Each refinery has its own configuration and combination of processes, mainly determined by the location of the facilities, the desired products and the economic considerations. Probably, there are no two identical refineries.

522. With the arrival of the internal combustion engine, the main task of the refineries ended up being just the production of gas oil. The quantities of *gas oil* available of the distillation were not enough to meet the consumers' demand. So, the refineries started to look for ways to produce more and better quality gas oil.

523. The importance in this chain of the Argentinean Productive system responds to the high level of dependence of the local hydrocarbons energy matrix, to the so hard replacement of this resource by renewable energy and to the existing electric generation infrastructure, highly dependent from thermal energy.

§3. The Refining Process

524. In the refinery there are several processes whose result will be useful products for the clients or other industries. Each process is performed in different plants, which operate in a coordinated way. The main plants in a refinery are as follows:

> *The Crude oil Distillation Unit* (CDU)]: It is the first processing unit in, virtually, all the refineries. It distils the incoming crude oil in fractions that are then processed in other process units. Very often, the CDU is referred to as the atmospheric distillation unit as it lightly operates on the atmospheric pressure.
>
> *The vacuum distillation unit*: it distils the waste at the bottom of the CDU. The operation is carried out at lower pressure than the atmospheric to be able to fraction the heavier hydrocarbons without forming coal.
>
> *The visbreaker*: it improves the product at the bottom of the vacuum distillation by means of thermal cracking to obtain lighter fractions and a heavier lower – viscosity fraction destined to fuel oil.
>
> *The delayed coker and the fluid coker*: It converts very heavy waste fractions or bottom of the vacuum tower into gases, oil and diesel *oil* and petroleum coal.
>
> *The Fluid Catalytic Cracking* (FCC): it breaks the big molecules of the heavy high-boiling-point fractions of the crude distillation and transforms them into light-lower-boiling point fractions of a higher value. It uses high temperatures and a catalyst to get the cracking. As a result of the big molecules rapture, greater volumes of more profitable lighter fractions are

obtained. The catalyst is responsible for the selection of the rapture in getting desired products. Apart from the reactions of raptures, there are isomerization, cyclization reactions and hydrogen transfer that improve the quality of the products.

The hydro cracking unit: it uses hydrogen, adding it to the rapture process of big heavy-fraction molecules of crude (of the atmospheric distillation and vacuumed) by effect of the temperature and pressure on the solid base catalyst. More valuable products are obtained, similar to light atmospheric distillation products.

The oil reforming unit: it converts the disulfonated-oil molecules into higher-octane molecules to produce reformed oil, which is used as components of the commercial oil.

The isomerization unit: it converts linear molecules (straight-chain hydrocarbons, as the average pentane) into hydrocarbons branched-chain molecules with a higher numbers of octanes. The objective is to mix them in the commercial oil combination. It also converts the average butane into the isobutene necessary the same as the alkylation load unit.

The alkylation unit: it converts the isobutene and butylenes into alkylate, a high-octane component used for the formation of commercial oil

The hydro treatment oil unit: it uses hydrogen to disulphate the fraction of oil from the crude distillation unit and other units of the refinery.

The hydro-treating middle distillates unit: it uses hydrogen to disulphate *the* fractions of kerosene and gas oil from the crude distillation unit and similar fractioning cuts of thermal and/or catalytic cracking.

525. One indispensable element in all refineries is the torch, also called 'match'. It is a very important security device. It prevents certain gases from being released into the atmosphere and, in the event of an eventual overpressure of the refinery, it avoids leaks. The extra tip is that, in general, there are two torched: one is on and the other is off ready to be turned on whenever necessary.

526. Apart from the basically productive activity, there are other areas contributing to the efficiency and the sustainability of the refining; for example, the quality of the air, water and soil measurement; the contingency plans and the drills; the training; the renovation of the equipment and updating of the technology. The secured operation is the fundamental axis of this industrial activity.

527. The refining is a dynamic and ongoing process operating 24 hours a day; consequently, the workers are under the rotating shifts regime.

§4. Plants Maintenance

528. The refineries in Argentina are very old and no big investment has been made or no new refineries have been built in the last two decades. Hence, they have to be maintained which entails, in many occasions, what is called a 'shutdown of the plant'.

529. The 'shutdowns of a plant' are not something improvised in a so complex industrial establishment full of security measures. They take several days and are planned, unless an unexpected incident forces the shutdown of the plant.[229] Also, it has to be taken into consideration the progressive 'start-up' of the plants that were taken out of operation for their maintenance. These processes are done under strict security measures with the corresponding notification to the administrative and environmental authorities.[230]

530. The shutdowns and start-ups imply a very careful logistics, as they have to guarantee the *stock* of products to comply with the obligations, whether they are contractual and/or legal.

531. Even though, it is believed that the crude constitutes a strategic resource for the countries having it; however, the truth is the production of the derivatives is the crucial part of the process as they are the ones boosting the countries' economic activities.

532. Although a county may have and produce hydrocarbons, unless they have the necessary infrastructure to process them, they will be forced to import fuel oil and its derivatives for the development of this activity.

533. The refineries constitute strategic places requiring a lot of care and precision; since, different form the fields, most of them are located in populated places and near communities. Hence, the technological advances – seeking efficiency and optimization of the refineries operation and the use of the crude oil – are linked to the associated-risks reduction and to the environmental and social impact minimization.

§5. Impacts of the Refineries to the Environment

534. The environmental impacts of a refinery are the result of, above all, the emission of gases, la discharge of liquid effluents, solid waste, the noise and smell, apart for the visual an aesthetics effects plus the social and community impact.

229. Stop mechanisms having to do with contingency plans.
230. Many jurisdictions require the companies to inform the stops and starting of the plants.

535. The gas emissions generate the most difficult environmental impact to control. They are composed by particles, gaseous hydrocarbons, carbon monoxide, sulphur compounds (SO_x) and nitrogen compounds (NO_x). These harmful emissions may affect the surrounding areas of the refinery.

536. The liquid effluent of the refineries – oil, grease, ammoniac, phenol composts, sulphur, organic acids, chrome and other metals – are transferred to *waste waters treatment* plants. These contaminants are expressed in terms of their *Biological Oxygen Demand* (DBO_5), their *Chemical Oxygen Demand* (DQO) and the Total Organic Carbon (COT). No liquid effluent is discharged without the previous treatment.

537. The refineries generate great quantities of solid waste; the main ones are wasted catalysts, coke fines, iron sulphurs, the filter media and the different types of mud (from tanks cleaning, oil and water separators and wasted waters treatment systems). These residue, dangerous or not must be treated according to the applicable regulations.

538. The noise of the high-speed mechanical equipment; control valves; piping systems, turbines and engines; lighters; heat exchanger with air cooling; fans and cooling towers also generate impacts that have to be controlled so as not to cause harmful effects.

539. The refineries must have environmental management plans according to their site's characteristics and their activities. They must also have contingency plans.

Chapter 1. Production

540. Most of the crude oil processed in the refineries comes from different hydrocarbon basin in the country. The geographical place of the actors in the chain depends fundamentally on the location of the natural resources.

541. Argentina has five productive basins, in the provinces of Formosa, Salta, Jujuy, Mendoza, La Pampa, Neuquén, Río Negro, Chubut, Santa Cruz and Tierra del Fuego.

542. However the four most important refineries are in Buenos Aires province. They belong to a (1) YPF SA; (2) Shell C.A.P.S.A.; (3) Axion Energy SA; (4) Pampa Energía SA.

543. Even though Buenos Aires is not an oil province from the *upstream* point of view, it is from the *downstream* point of view.

544. For the refineries to work in a secure and efficient way, it is necessary to have *quantity, quality and continuity in the supply of crude oil.* As it was aforementioned, the refining is an ongoing process that implies the coordinated and concatenated work of various plants; any change in the supply could negatively impact in the production, and hence, in the products commercialization. If any of those oils were scarce or missing, the refinery would not work according to the initial configuration, and the derivatives productions would also be affected.

545. Unfortunately, the current circumstances do not allow long-term agreements for the crude oil supply. Due to this, refineries are constantly negotiating to obtain the supply.[231]

546. It is not only about having the necessary volumes of crude oil, since that raw material has to be treated so as to be transported to other processing places. In Argentina, the transport to the refineries is by means of a duct or in tank ships. This requires another logistics and costs. Without crude oil there is no *downstream*, and without *downstream* there are no derived products, which are the ones consumed in the market. To ensure the raw material supply is essential for the refinery.

547. During the first ten years of the twenty-first century, the light crudes production fell and this affected the light and medium products elaboration (oil and gas oil). Such decrease was combined with an increase in the demand of fuels in the domestic market. Hence, it was necessary to take measures by means of the passing of several rules to mitigate the lack of products due to an increasing demand from the domestic market. The measures included the importation of gas oil.

---

231. This depends on the oil company be integrated or not; but the price is essential due to the impact of the royalties, taxes, etc.

548. As the international conditions were not ideal to import, the free-tax coupons programme was created.[232] Between 35 and 40% of the price of the oil and gas oil pump are taxes, and so the importation free from taxes would mitigate the negative economic impact the importer would suffer.[233] The requests were done in the former National Secretariat of Energy, today the Ministry of Energy and Mining. The situation was such as the international price was higher than the local one.

549. When the price of the crude oil fell sharply years later, another alternative was analysed: the importation of raw material to process it in the local refineries and optimize its capacity of idle refining. Consequently, in January 2014, the former Planning and Strategic Coordination Commission of the Hydrocarbons Investment National Plan adopted the Resolution No 1/2014 which established a procedure for the light crude oil importation. The aim was to mitigate the local production fall of such raw material and not to negatively alter the crude diet in the refineries.

550. ENARSA had a leading role in these operations; it was the importer of crude oil and the seller in the local market each refinery according to the volumes requested. ENARSA acted as a trader, retaining the difference between the import price and the local sale price. The system benefited the State as well as since they collected the Value Added Tax (VAT) for the value of the local sale.

551. The Hydrocarbons Law (Law No 17319), under sections 6 and 7, strengthens the obligation of prioritizing the local supply and the disregard of the international prices when they significantly increased. However, the gap between the local and international prices – the former being for a very long time well below the external values –, has notably influenced on the relative prices of the chain and has discouraged investment.

552. The exportations have always been strongly regulated and controlled by the authority (Secretariat of Energy, today the Mining and Energy Ministry), as an exportation authorization certificate is required issued by such authority. The certificate must be submitted in the customs so that the exportation can be approved.

553. In 2017, The National Executive Power passed the Decree No 192/2017, which regulates the importation of crude oil, diesel and gas oil.

554. The local prices are strongly controlled by different instruments of the economic politics that systematize their incidence over the crude internal value vis-à-vis the *commodity* international price. However, instead of doing it by means of a regulation, which would guarantee legal security, it is performed through agreements between producers and refiners at the request of the authorities.

232. Law No 26022 about National plan of Gasoil Supply, Resolution 611/2005 of the Department of Energy and its supplementary.
233. During the period 2005–2013, the international price of the crude oil was much higher than that of the domestic market; and the same happened to its derivatives.

555. By means of these agreements, the refiners must buy volumes of local light crude oil at a price higher than the international one – something which is known in the market as 'criollo crude'. Consequently, the prices of the products in the local market are also higher. This measure produces loss of competitiveness in the international market, exportation and ranchos, as the parameters are the international prices. That is to say, the raw material is bought at a higher price, but the product must be sold as if the *commodity* has been bought at an international price. Nowadays, the market is highly intervened, with the aspiration of achieving a free market.

556. It is worth mentioning that the crude oil sold by the local producers is commercialized in US dollar, however, the derived products dispatched by the refiners are traded in pesos in the domestic market; thus the difference in the exchange causes an impact on the refiner.

Chapter 2. Normative

557. The *downstream* does not have a 'title' as the concession of the *upstream* and *midstream* would have.

558. Law No 17319 and its further amendments are focused more on the *upstream* and the *midstream*. It only mentions some activities of the *downstream* in sections 2, 3, 6 and 7.

559. The majority of decrees, resolutions, provisions, etc. of different jurisdictions (national, provincial and municipal) makes is difficult to construe and apply coherently and evenly with the subsequent impact in the dynamics of the activity.

560. So as to give a general view, some of the national most representative rules will be enumerated.

561. The installation of the refineries in our country is regulated by Law No 13660, that sets forth: 'the facilities of elaboration, transformation and storage of solid, liquid and gaseous mineral fuels have to adjust, in all the National territory to the rules and requirements of the Executive Power to guarantee the communities' security and health, of the mentioned facilities, the normal supply of public and private services and to meet the needs of the national defence'. This law is from 1949. After that, in 1960, the Decree No 10877/60 was passed.

562. In accordance with this rules, the refineries will have the areas as follows:

- *Area of distilleries operation – Zone I*: area occupied by the equipment and installations destined to the distillation process.
- *Area of storage tanks – Zone II*: this is the place where the storage tanks of raw materials, intermediate or finished products and set of installations destined to the movement of fluids are located.
- *Area of auxiliary facilities in distilleries – Zone III*: installations, equipment and buildings not included in the previous zones.

563. Among the several rules,[234] we also find the resolution of the Department of Energy No 419/98 which creates the Registry of Elaboration and Commercialization Companies before the Ministry of Energy and Mining.

564. The oil refineries, pursuant to Decree No 10877, must have an annual external audit security service for its facilities that guarantees the compliance of the rules. Such service is rendered by some National Universities commissioned by the Ministry of Energy and Mining and is regulated by Resolution DE 404/1994.

---

234. Due to the number of plants, places and products, there are also applicable rules in each place and for each product.

565. There is also the application of a Leaks Control National Programme of Air Tanks of hydrocarbons and derivatives storage, regulated by Resolution DE No 785/2005, whose main objectives are:

- To carry out a national census of the quantity and conditions of the air tank park of hydrocarbons and derivatives storage of in the whole country.
- To update, organize and systematize the information regarding the infrastructure and logistics of the air hydrocarbons and derivatives storage.
- To check the physical conditions of the air tanks of hydrocarbons and derivatives storage on a regular basis.
- To check and verify leaks of the air tanks of hydrocarbons and derivatives storage, as well as its possible polluting effects on the associated environment.
- To foster and verify the adoption of measures intended to correct, mitigate and control the pollution originated as from the air tanks of hydrocarbons and derivatives storage.

566. For a better understanding of the situation of the *downstream,* we have to consider the reforms done in the 1990s, the restructuring of the energy sector at the beginning of the decade was due to an extensive programme of reforms that reached different sectors of the economy.

567. The measures entailed the deregulation of the tradable energy markets, the opening to the participation of private actors, a greater level of freedom in the mobility of financial capitals and radical change of the State's role, which left its company role and focused on the role of control and regulation.

568. In the course of that decade, the deregulation in the oil industry was protected by mainly three decrees: (1) No 1055/89; (2) No 1589/89; (3) No 1212/89. The last one was more focused on the topic of the *downstream*. In general terms, it provided:

- The free exportation and importation of derived products.
- Freedom of prices.
- Free installation of refineries, with no requirement other than the compliance of the security and technical rules established by the general regulations in force.
- Free installation of manholes, submitted to the technical and security rules set forth by the Department of Energy.
- Free ownership of the manholes: the owners must meet the requirements of technical, commercial and economic capacity established by the competent authority, assuming all responsibility derived from the service.
- Free availability of a percentage of the money coming from exportations.

569. During the 1990s, all indicated that the trend would be a deregulated market; however, this assumption faded away, and the change in the governments was reflected upon the energy policy. The market was gradually being regulated.

570. Law No 25561, passed in 2002, declared the public emergency regarding social, economic, administrative and financial and exchange issues. It was extended many times. The National Administration, based on especially this law and Law No 20680 (Law of Supply),[235] which provided several rules regarding investment.

571. Due to the excessive delegation those rules gave, and still do, to the National Executive Power, most of the regulations were passed by the former National Department of Energy and the Domestic Trade Secretariat.

572. Many times, this intervention was done without considering that the oil activity acts in coordination with the *midstream* and the *upstream*. To regulate the last link without considering the other stages created a distortion that harmed the elaboration, transport, distribution and commercialization of derived products.

573. Without going into a deep analysis about the legality and legitimacy of the measures taken by the institutions, we will just describe some rules to analyse the risks and impacts they entail:

(1) *Decree No 645/2002*. Registry of Contracts of exportation operations, in which all gas oil export operations are to be registered, pursuant to the rules passed by the mentioned authority.
(2) *Resolution of the Energy Department No 1679/2004.* The refineries interested in exporting gas oil shall demonstrate that the demand is duly met or that the domestic demand has the possibility of acquiring gas oil.
(3) So as to credit the above-mentioned, they shall submit the sworn statement that will at least contain:
   - Faithful evidence that the commercialization chain dependent of the refinery is properly supplied.
   - In case the estimations done by the refinery were incorrect, the refinery will have to, at least, import a volume similar to the one it exports, at its own expense, and without the commercial chain being affected due to its errors of prevision and calculation.
   - Reliable evidence of the publication in a minimum of three pieces of massive written national media and the Official Bulletin (of Argentina) of an offer of gas oil sale to be exported directed to all the commercial chain of gas oil authorized to operate, the distributors and manholes included.
   - The commercial conditions offered must be basically the same as those offered by their commercial net, being the parties entitled to mutually change those conditions. Under no circumstances, shall potential buyers be solicited a price higher than the one in the domestic market for the commercial net in similar conditions, commercial discriminatory conditions or that directly or indirectly make the offer virtually inaccessible for the domestic

235. During this period there was a great debate between validity and applicability of the Law of Supply.

demand. The offer must have a term of validity. Such term shall not be shorter than ten working days and the buyers will be able to choose to buy all or part of the volume offered.

(4) *Resolution DE no. º 1834/2005.* It establishes a regime oriented to guarantee the domestic supply of liquid hydrocarbons, especially gas oil.

(5) *Resolution DE No 1879/2005.* The gas oil refineries registered in the Department of Energy that have contracts establishing a certain level of exclusiveness between the refining company and the fuel supplier, shall guarantee the supply for the domestic market in an ongoing, reliable, regular and non-discriminatory way, under penalty of application of The Procedures or sanctions set forth in the current regulations.

(6) *Resolution DE No 1338/2006.* It incorporates to the regime established by the Decree No 645/2002 oil, fuel oil and its blending, diesel *oil*; air kerosene or *jet fuel*; lubricants, asphalts, coke and derivatives for its petrochemicals.[236]

(7) *Resolution DE No 1334/2006.* The commercialization of all new types of fuels shall be previously authorized by the Under Secretariat of Fuels.[237]

(8) *Resolution of the Secretariat of Domestic Trade (SCI) no. º 25/2006.* The refining companies and/or wholesale distributors and/or retailers shall reasonably cover the total demands of gas oil, in accordance with the volumes required, as from the market's usual practices.

(9) *Resolution DE No 715/2007.* Obligation to import a similar volume of gas oil as the one to be exported.

(10) *Resolution of the Production and Economy Ministry (MEyP) no. º 394/2007.* It established the mobile retentions modality. I t supposed a total and radical change, as the retention for the products was up to that moment 5% and with the new regulation percentages were around 60%. Even though this rule was derogated by Resolution No 1077/2014 due to a drop in the international prices, and now retentions are lower, at that moment it caused a significantly negative economic impact on the *downstream.*

(11) *Resolution SCI no. º 14/2008.* The oil and its derivatives refineries must optimize the production so as to obtain maximum volumes for the capacity.

(12) *Resolution SCI no. º 295/2010.* It fixed the price of the liquid fuels commercialization. It was derogated by Resolution SCI no. º 543/2010.

(13) *Resolution SCI no. º 13/2011.* It fixed the new prices of the liquid fuels commercialization. It was derogated by Resolution SCI No 46/2011.

574. This cumbersome set of rules – whose timeliness, legality and legitimacy is not the subject matter of this work did not consider the real situation of the industry: (1) lack of light crude oil; (2) insufficiency in the refining capacity; (3) restrictions limiting the logistics; (4) increase in the demand; (5) disadvantages in the importations; (6) isolation from the international reality; (7) impact from the devaluation; among other circumstances. In a nutshell, the intention was to change a factual reality with legislation.

---

236. The procedure was made more flexible for some products, prior authorization of the Department of Energy.

237. The rule did not establish a procedure so the requirements are left at the authority's discretion.

575. Several policies have been applied to boost the production and incorporation of oil reserves: The Programme 'Petróleo Plus' and 'Refinación Plus', created by Decree No 2014/2008; however, they were not as successful as expected.

576. In 2012, Law No 26741, known as 'Law of Hydrocarbons Sovereignty' was created and it established that: (1) the oil activity is declared of public interest; (2) the National Executive Power will fix the policies in this matter so as to achieve the objectives of the rule; (3) the Hydrocarbons Federal Council is created; and (4) it expropriates the YPF SA and YPF GAS SA.'s shares. By means of this law, they intend this activity to be part of Hydrocarbons Investment National Plan. The aim is to recover the fuel self-supply. The plan was never informed and was just a wishful thinking.

577. The Decree No 1277/2012 – that pretended to issue the legislation of the Law No 26741 – has been *partially derogated by Decree No 272/2015* (1) establishes the objectives of Hydrocarbons Investment National Plan; (2) creates the Planning and Strategic Coordination Commission of the Hydrocarbons Investment National Plan;[238] (3) creates the National Registry of Hydrocarbons Investments; (4) sets the obligation of the submittal of an Annual Investment Plan by the producers, refiners, carriers and marketers.

578. The passage of these rules has neither boosted the increase in refining capacity either; however it has caused an increase in the administrative obligations that do not clarify the context at all.

579. The Decree No 1277/2012 was modified by Decree No 272/2015 that dissolved the Commission and gave those powers to the Energy and Mining Ministry.

580. Nowadays considering the international scenario (a fall of the crude oil price and its derivatives, obviously), the State is adopting measure aimed at mitigating the negative impact on the domestic market. The measures are made concrete basically by means of the agreements entered into between different players of the industry at the request of the National Administration.[239]

581. The prices of the derivatives, together with the price of the oil, are the result, first of all, of the price of the crude oil plus a margin of refining that includes the costs of the activity and taxes. Then, the transport, wholesaler and retailer commercialization margins and taxes are incorporated. This way, the policy of prices splitting of the barrel of crude oil made an impact on the prices of sub-products of the oil, modifying the internal price of reference.

---

238. The Department of Energy was part of the commission and there was an overlapping of competencies between them.
239. Some measures could be listed here: (1) the price of the local crude oil higher than the international one; (2) price of the derivatives higher than the international one; (3) CAMMESA's participation in the purchase of fuel oil for the power stations; (4) importation of products without taxes.

582. The price of the hydrocarbons had a high increase from the beginning 2011 to mid-2014. The barrel of oil historically peaked reaching a value of 125 dollars. The liquefied natural gas also increased significantly, and it reached a value of 18 dollars per BTU million between March and September of 2012.

583. As from mid-2014, the upward trend changes, and there was downward trend, instead, that reduced 47% of the average values of 2015 vis-à-vis 2014 (48.7 USD/bbl).

584. On the contrary, there exists a formal agreement about prices, volume supply by the producers and of obligation of purchase by the refiners at the request of the National State. There is no specific set of rules to regulate the prices, the margins, and the way to fix them in practice. The context does not give legal security and stability so necessary to attract investments.

Chapter 3. Tax

585. Without the intention of going too deep into fiscal topics, there follows a list of the taxes that impact the activity which has a strong fiscal component.

586. One of the biggest problems is the diversity and coexistence of jurisdictions on the same subject. The collecting agencies are different (Nation, province, municipality), it is very difficult to have some coordination; each of them collects with different objectives and applications.

587. The taxes collected by the Nation are:

- Income Tax and Minimum Presumed Income Tax
- Tax in Credit and Debit in Bank Accounts
- Value Added Tax
- Tax on Oil Transfers
- Hydro Infrastructure Rate
- Tax on Gas oil
- Customs Duties.

588. The taxes collected by the provinces are:

- Stamp Tax
- Gross Income Tax.

589. Taxes collected by the municipal authorities:

- Security and Hygiene Tax
- Marketing and Publicity Tax
- Light, Sweeping and Cleaning and Conservation of the Street Tax.

590. As it can be observed, the *downstream* market is remarkably distorted due to the tax burden.

Chapter 4. Distribution and Consumption

591. Once the crude oil arrived in the refinery, it was processed and converted into a product for commercialization and the most complex stage of the process begins from the business' point of view.

592. One thing is the negotiation of the refineries with the crude producers – who need each other and so they create a synergy, even though it is supposed that both oil companies know the rules of the market – a totally different thing is the sale the refinery will perform with the resulting product of the refining process. Due to the diversity of derivatives, the latter has to explore several markets ruled by different standards, parameters and paradigms.

593. The commercialization requires a very complex and precise strategy and logistics. Production and commercialization are closely related; there is no point in having products if there is no market to commercialize them afterwards. The reduction of the refineries is organized in accordance with the estimated demand of products and the availability of the raw materials to process.

594. In general, the products are channelled by different business units, each one having its own characteristics and features; a few just to mention: (1) *aviation*: it is in the sale of air fuel for domestic and international flights; (2) *navy*: it is in the sale of fuel for domestic and international ships; (3) *trading*: it is in the exportation of products that are not consumed in the domestic market; importation of products for the domestic consumption and the purchase of crude oil; (4) *lubricants*: commercialization of lubricants –local/importation/exportation –; (5) *bitumen*: sale of asphalts; (6) *retail*: retail or consignment to the oil stations – oil and gas oil –; (7) *commerce to industries*: sale of products to big industries, whether as final consumers or as raw material for other processes; (8) *chemicals*: solvents, turpentine and other basic products included; (9) oil liquefied gas;, etc.

595. These products are carried in truck for their final destination (most of them *Free on Board* sale (FOB) or *Cost Insurance and Freight* sale (CIF)) The products are transported first by ship to the deposits of the refinery companies in other provinces, and then distributed by truck. There is no suitable transport by duct for the derived products; thus, to guarantee the free circulation in sea as well as earth ways is essential to maintain the adequate supply for the market.

596. All operations are duly informed to the Energy and Mining Ministry which publish them in its webpage.

§1. International Market

I. Exportation

597. The companies wishing to export any product must follow the procedure established in Resolution DE No 1338/2006, already mentioned. In fact, only the cuts not consumed in the domestic market are exported. The exportation is not a profitable business anymore; first, due to the adoption of the resolution by Ministry of Economy and Production No 394/2007 and, nowadays due to the international prices.[240]

598. However, regardless of being profitable or not, there are technical, operative and logistics issues, demanding the need to evacuate those products (let us remember that refining is a dynamic process and the storage capacity of the derived products in the refineries is limited). The products have to be evacuated as they are produced.

599. The experience has proved that any type of delay in the issuance of authorizations, whether from the part of the authorities – today the Ministry of Energy and Mining – or the exporter itself has caused negative effects: (1) impact on the processes; (2) penalties in the delays of the ships; (3) contractual penalties; etc. that influence the margin of refining.

600. Even though it is prudent to keep the control over certain products, those controls should be dynamic effective and efficient for the activity they pretend to control. The application of the procedure described has only hindered the dynamism required by any commercial activity, has increased the costs, causing unnecessary delays in the means of transportation and, above all, it has built distrust in the buyers who are not certain if the governmental authorities will or will not authorize the sale of those products overseas.

II. Importation

601. Under Decree No 192/2017, the Registry of Crude Oil and derivatives (some) Importation Operation was created. Although it is called 'registry', it is – in fact – an authorization request for importers, similar to exports, but with another procedure.

602. The authority of application will be the Ministry of Energy and Mining; the procedure was regulated by the Hydrocarbons Resources Secretariat by means of Resolution No 47 E/2017.

603. In this way, the ministry has a wide control over the importations and exportations of crude oil and its derivatives authorizing or not the permits requested.

240. The crude oil in the local market is more expensive than in the international.

§2. The Domestic Market

604. Here we will briefly develop the commercialization of the products by the oil stations '*retail*', we will not address all the rules the oil stations have to comply with to operate since, again, we will fall into multiples jurisdictions; however, it is important to highlight that the Ministry of Energy and Mining is the authority with the highest competence in the subject due to the specificity the activity requires.

605. The competence of the ministry arises under section 2 from the Hydrocarbons Law (No 17319), which sets forth the exploration, exploitation, industrialization, transport and *commercialization of hydrocarbons* must adjust to the provisions of that law, to the regulations set forth by the National Executive Power.

606. We will just mention the security measures that the facilities must follow in the oil station:

- *Decree No 2407/1983.* It regulates the security standards applicable to the supply or sale in oil pump specially in: (1) elements against fires; (2) role of the fire and fight against it; (3) leaks control; (4) fuel reception and storage; (5) supply of fuel to customer/user; (6) specifications for the underground installations of fuel deposit and dispatch; (7) specifications for the oil stations and the fuel pumps construction; (8) specifications of the tank truck for the fuel transportation; (9) electric installations and equipment; (10) fuel pumps for the sale of fuels; (11) control, suspension, cancellation and interpretation of the standards.
- *Resolution DE No 1102/2004.* It creates the Registry of Liquid Fuel Pumps, Own Consumption, Stores, Distributors and Commercialization of Hydrocarbons and Natural Compressed Gas in bulk. Values of reference – Although the title of the rule says it creates the registry, there were registries already in force (e.g., of pumps) and a resolution (DE No 79/1999) that was derogated by Resolution No 1102/2004. This one completed and/or modified several further rules, not only regarding registries but also about penalties on security, underground tanks, conditions on temporary or definite close down of the activity, leaks controls, etc.
- *Resolution DE No 404/1994.* It created the Registry of National Universities for the Realization of Technical, Environmental and Security Audits. At first, those audits were to be performed by companies duly authorized by the Former Department of Energy; but then the Resolution DE No 266/2008 was adopted, and it excluded the companies to replace them by the universities. Many of the companies were subcontracted by the universities, as they lacked the necessary experience; at the same time, other companies set actions for protection of constitutional rights. In fact, universities and companies carry out the audits.
- *Resolution DE No 217/2001.* National Program of Oil Quality Control – Inspection Service.
- *Decree No 1028/2001.* It creates the Federal Information System of Fuels. Pursuant to this rule, all the economy agents, whether public or private, performing hydrocarbons and fuels exploration, exploitation, treatment, storage, transport, industrialization, fractioning and commercialization (wholesale and retail) activities are obliged to submit the technical, quantitative, qualitative and financial

information in accordance with the rules set forth by the authority of application, which are deemed necessary to evaluate the performance of the sector and to formulate policies regarding security care, preservation of the environment, development of investments allowing the sustainable growth of the activities and the competition conditions that guarantee the suitable consumer's protections.
- *Resolution No 314 E/2016.* It creates the System of Fuel Price Information on Line regarding the pump.

607. The oil company cannot dispatch fuel in the oil station, unless it has the registration and valid security audit certification (Resolution DE No 404/1994).

608. Resuming the topic of the commercialization through the oil station, they could be divided into:

- *COCO* (*company owned-dealer operated*): when the oil company is the owner of the facility and it operates the oil station, whether by itself or by a subsidiary.
- *CODO* (*company owned-dealer operated*): when the oil company is the owner of the facilities, but the oil station is operated by a third party called '*dealer*'.
- *DODO* (*dealer owned-dealer operated*): when the facility and the operation of the oil station are carried out by the third party (*dealer*).
- *Blanche*: when it is not associated to any company and they purchase fuel from anyone and sell it. There is no exclusiveness.

609. The most usual ways are COCO and DODO. The most complex is DODO relationship, as it adds a third party (*dealer*) with whom the oil company enters into a 'contract of fuel supply', which can be by consignment or resale. In the very same contract, the use of the brand is authorized in the facility. In the case the station wanted to have a '*shop*', another type of contract is additionally subscribed similar to a franchising.

610. In the sale by consignment, the oil company fixes the sale price for the consumer and the dealer, and in turn receives a commission (a percentage on the retail sale price). The company is the owner of the product and the dealer is the custodian.

611. On the contrary, the dealer fixes the retail price for the end user. The oil company sells the fuel to the dealer and the latter resells it getting a margin of income over the price. In this last case, the operation can be FOB (the *dealer* hires the transport) or CIF (the oil company hires the transport and delivers the product in the oil station).

612. The contract with the oil station manager or *dealers* has its own regulations and special features such as:

- Modality of commercialization
- Exclusiveness
- Conditions to deliver the fuel (FOB/CIF)

- Duration term
- Compliance of the applicable legislation
- *Stock* of products
- Conditions of the service and customer service
- Licence to use the trademark
- Publicity and promotions
- Insurances
- Quality and quantity control
- Audits and inspections
- Sanctions
- Transfer of the goodwill
- Sale/rent of the property – pre-emptive rights
- Environmental security
- Taxes
- Jurisdiction and applicable law.

613. In relation to the regulations, Decree No 1060/2000, and an extensive quantity of regulations adopted by the former Department of Energy, as well as the rules passed by the jurisdictions in which the stations are located are worth mentioning. As regards regulation, Decree No 1060/2000 is worth mentioning that it provides:

(1) Maximum validity terms for the contracts:
   - Eight years, in the case of the setting up of a new oil station.
   - Five years, in the case subscription, renewal and/or extensions of existing contracts with oil stations.
   - In the case of clauses or agreements, instrumented in whatever way, in breach of the maximum terms established shall be deemed not drafted null and void.
   - It sets a limit in the verticality of the contracts, setting forth that the oil companies and/or fuel supplies cannot have and/or operate directly a percentage higher than 40% of the total of the network of oil stations that commercialize their brands.

(2) Depending on the special features of the contract, there can also be associated contracts:
   - Gratuitous loan agreements for pumps, tanks and bill boarding.
   - Franchising for the convenience stores.
   - Loan agreements for working capital and/or works and improvements in the facilities.
   - Apart from the reasons for termination of the contracts agreed upon by the parties, the authority has also regulated over the termination thereof. The Under Secretariat of Fuels passed the provision No 157/2006, under which the oil stations, with contracts in force, which have agreed a certain level of exclusiveness with the refining and/or distribution oil company in any way whatsoever and, intend to finalize, for any reason, the contractual relationships, shall inform that to the Secretariat beforehand and the Department of Commerce shall intervene.

614. Process and Policies of Ethics and Compliance, Security and Hygiene are to be taken into account, as well, among the regulations each oil company applies and requires when entering into this type of contracts.

Part IV. Interaction Between Energy Law and Tax Law

Chapter 1. Introduction

615. The aim of this section is to describe the taxes and duties imposed on the energy in the national territory. To that end, in the first section we will find the distribution of competences in fiscal terms among the different levels of governments that the Nation's Constitution has established. Having been the competences determined, some general aspects that should be taken into account will be elaborated about taxes in force to, – afterwards – to look into the description of taxes currently in force, first national taxes, second the local taxes making a distinction between provincial and municipal taxes. Once the taxes levied on the companies in general are described, we will look into the concrete taxation aspects of each of the energy sources. Some special aspects of the different sources of energy regarding the general regime previously depicted will be analysed and then, specific regimes and taxes established for the corresponding source of energy.

Chapter 2. Distribution of the Taxation Competences

616. Argentina, pursuant to section 1° of the National Constitution, has adopted the federal form of government. Consequently there are two levels of government: federal and provincial. Moreover, the provincial governments, in turn, and through their constitutions, must guarantee the municipal autonomy (sections 5 and 123), which generates a third level of government. Thus, inside the territory, three levels of government coexist (federal, provincial and municipal), with powers to establish taxes on the individuals' activities and property, through the several expressions of taxation capacity: income, net worth and consumption.

617. The National Constitution, furthermore, establishes, in general terms, the way to finance the public sector expenditure. The federal government has the power to establish 'exportation and importation duties' and the 'contributions that the Congress will impose on the population in an equal and proportional way' (section 4). Among the powers of the Congress: (a) 'to legislate about Customs matters. To establish the importation and exportation duties, which, together with appraisals, will be uniform for the whole country' (section 75, subsection 1); (b) 'to impose indirect contributions as a concurrent power with the provinces' and 'to impose direct contributions, for a fixed period of time, proportionally equal in the whole territory of the Nation, as long as the defense, common security and well fare of the State requires it' (section 75, subsection 2); (c) 'to rule the commerce of other nations and of the provinces among them' (section 75, subsection 13).

618. Section 9 explains that 'in the whole national territory there will only be national customs offices which will be ruled by the tariffs approved by the Congress'. Similarly, section 10 reads that 'in the provinces inside the Republic, the national manufactured products as well as all types of goods dispatched in overseas Customs are guaranteed the right of the free circulation'. In the same way, section 11 establishes that 'the goods (…) passing from the territory of one province to another will be free from transit duties (…) and no other duty shall be imposed, whatever its denomination, as long as they transit inside the national territory'. As it can be noticed the National Constitution is clear about the prohibition of provincial customs.

619. Notwithstanding the aforesaid, the general rule is that 'the provinces keep all the power not delegated by this Constitution to the federal government, and the one expressly reserved by special powers at the time of their incorporation' (section 121) and. consequently 'the provinces do not exercise the power delegated to the Nation' neither can they 'pass laws about trade, domestic or international navigation, or set up provincial customs' (section 126).

620. As from the set of regulations elaborated, it can be inferred that: (a) regarding direct contributions the provincial governments have original jurisdiction whereas the power of the federal government is exceptional and only for a fixed period of time; (b) regarding indirect contributions the federal as well as the provincial governments can impose them concurrently; (c) as regards customs, the federal government, is the only one that can set up customs overseas, and the provincial governments are allowed neither to regulate the commerce, the navigation nor to create customs inside the territory.

621. It should be as well, considered the competences the federal and provincial governments have over the territorial sea, the adjacent zone, the EEZ, the CS.

622. It is necessary to point out that, notwithstanding the distribution of competences, the very same National Constitution provides that both direct and indirect contributions are co-participating, setting forth the institution of a law agreement (section 75, subsection 2), which has not been enacted up to date.

623. So far, only federal and provincial governmental competences have been depicted; however, as it was already said, there is a third level of government: the municipal one. So, it is necessary to highlight that the tax competences of the municipalities are limited by each provincial Constitution; hence, to know the extension and scope of the municipalities' fiscal powers we have to resort to the fundamental regulations of each jurisdiction. Finally, with the constitutional reform of 1994 and in the Second Title 'Government of Province', section 129 gives to the City of Buenos Aires 'an autonomous government regime with its own powers in jurisdiction and legislation'. Even though the judicial nature of the Autonomous City of Buenos Aires is controversial, for the purpose of this present and to simplify the analysis, the taxes will be looked into together with those of the other provinces as the fiscal regimes are similar.

Chapter 3. Generalities

624. In simple terms, a tax is an obligatory payment that is demanded from the taxpayer by the State in the exercise of its power and by virtue of law.

625. Taxes are divided into duties, rates and special contributions. In taxes, the payment is imposed of the taxpayer without direct counterbalance from the part of the State. In rates, the payment imposed upon the taxpayer constitutes the remuneration of an individualized or particularized activity or service of the State. Finally, in special contributions, the payment is imposed upon the taxpayer by virtue of the special benefits rooted in the work or other expenses from the State.

626. It is important to point out that the taxation is ruled by its own principles, so they should be analysed in the territory and upon the taxpayer. Among the principles, it is worth mentioning, for the purpose of this study, the principle of legality notwithstanding the relevance of the remaining ones –, by virtue of which 'no tax burden can be imposed without the pre-existence of a legal provision framed in the constitutional precepts and guarantees, that is to say validly created by the unique power of the State invested with such powers', with reference to the legislative power. Consequently, in the analysis herein proposed the texts of the laws passes by the National Congress and other legislative provincial as well as municipal powers – principal source of the taxes – will have supremacy. On the contrary, it is considered that the fiscal regime in Argentina, far from being a coordinated system of taxes, consists in an overlapping of several taxes with no planning and with a high level or normative dispersion horizontally – inside the same level of government – and vertically – among the different levels of government (federal, provincial and municipal). This entails that a very cumbersome almost impossible analysis of the fiscal regime as a homogeneous whole. With the aforementioned clarification, as follows the most important features of the national, first and then local taxes, with a distinction between provincial and municipal ones.

§1. National Taxes

627. At a national level, there are up to date more than twenty taxes in force. It is clear, though, that not all the taxes levied upon companies, the activities or the energy sources; however, many of them can indirectly have an impact thereon.

628. As follows, the most relevant features of the national taxes that can globally influence the companies and the activities related to energy.

I. Income Tax

629. The income tax is ruled under Law No 20.628 (t.o.by Decree No 649/1997), and is a direct contribution which was established by the national Congress due to emergency reasons, whose last extension was set forth for 31 December 2019.

630. In generic terms, it is established that all earnings of the persons are levied upon by the tax (section 1, first paragraph), making a distinction between person of visible existence (physical persons or individuals) and persons of ideal existence (judicial persons), and between residents and non-residents in the country.

631. The rule, then, makes a distinction when defining the earnings in relation to the subject. For the physical persons, the earning has to meet three requirements: periodicity, permanence and authorization from the source producing them (section 2, subsection 1). Whereas, for legal persons the theory of balance is applied, calculating their earning even if they do not meet those requirements (section 2, subsection 2). Moreover and for both cases, earnings shall be deemed as 'the results coming from alienations of personal property subject to amortization, shares, instalments and social participations, securities, bonds and other values whoever the owner is' (section 2, subsection 3).

632. In the category of legal entities, by virtue of section 69, the following are included as long as they were incorporated in the country: corporations, joint-stock companies, limited liability companies, limited partnerships, civil associations, foundations, mixed economy partnerships, State-owned agencies, corporation with majority stake, State-owned companies, trust and mutual funds (subsection a). Moreover, 'Commercial, industrial, farming, mining establishments and any other type, organized as stable company, belonging to associations, partnerships or companies, whatsoever their nature, incorporated overseas or belonging to physical persons residents in other countries' are also contemplated (subsection b).

633. For the purpose of law, all the legal entities aforementioned are considered residents in the country (section 119); hence it has implications over the fixing of the levied earnings.

634. In this sense, the residents 'pay for the total of their earnings obtained in the country or overseas, being able to compute as prepayment of tax, under this law, the sums effectively paid for analogous taxes over their activities overseas, up to the limit of the increase of fiscal obligation originated for the incorporations of the earnings obtained overseas' (section 1, second paragraph). All the persons listed under section 69 are applied the general aliquot 35% over the tax base.

635. Whereas the non-residents 'pay only for their earning from an Argentinean source' (section 1, third paragraph), being applicable Title V over the beneficiaries from overseas (sections 91 a 93).

636. Both for residents and non-residents, the most important thing is of the source of earnings. Notwithstanding the complexities of the topic, in general, 'earning from an Argentinean source are those that come from property located, placed or used economically in the Republic, from the realization in the national territory of any activity susceptible of producing a benefit, or that has happened inside the limits thereof, regardless of the nationality, domicile or residence of the owner or the parties participating in the operations, or the place of the subscription of the contracts' (section 5).

637. Earnings are divided into categories (Title II): (a) first category – land rent – (Chapter I); (b) second category – capital income – (Chapter II); (c) third category – benefits of the companies – (Chapter III); and (d) fourth category – earned income related to the job – (Chapter IV). The earning of the second and the fourth categories are assigned in the corresponding fiscal period based on the amount earned, whereas the first and the third are assigned for the criteria of the accrued (section 18).

638. In general terms, the tax base in calculated in the following way 'the net income is the gross income minus the necessary expenses to obtain it, in its case, to keep or maintain the source (…). To establish the net income subject to taxes the calculation is: the total of net income of the first, second, third and fourth categories minus deductions authorized by section 23. Under no circumstances, shall expenses related to exempted income or not covered by this tax shall be levied' (section 17) – moreover, 'to calculated the total of net income, the net results obtained in the fiscal year will be offset, inside each and between the different categories. When there is a loss in a year, this can be deducted from taxable income obtain in the years immediately after. If five years passed as from the time when the loss occurred, the taxpayer shall be entitled to no deduction of the remaining loss in successive years' (section 19).

639. In another level, the text includes a long list of exemptions subjective as well objective (section 20), with the limitations under section 21.

640. In the economic contest in our country, Title VI (sections 94 a 98), establishing a system of adjustment for inflation is worth mentioning. Notwithstanding the operation thereof, it should be noted that its application is postponed due to the set of sections 7 and 10 of the Law No 23.928, section 39 of the Law No 24.073, section 4 of the Law No 25.561 and section 5 of Decree No 214/2002. The National Supreme Court has without exception rejected the unconstitutionality of the legislations herein summarized; however it has authorized the use of inflation adjustment when the prohibition of applying it made the tax confiscatory.

Tax on undocumented departures

641. Under sections 37 and 38, the tax on undocumented departures is set forth. The first of the sections sets forth that 'when an expense fails to have the documentation and it is impossible to prove by other means the earning, keeping and conservation of such taxable income, no deduction shall be admitted in the balance sheet and it will subject to the payment of the 35% duty which is deemed definite', whereas the second section establishes the exemption from the payment when the tax collector 'presumes that the payment has been done to buy property ' or when 'it presumes that the payments (…) are not taxable income in the hands of the beneficiary'.

II. Tax on the Presumed Minimum Income

642. The tax on the presumed minimum income is included in the Title V of the Law No 25.063, an emergency tax which was initially for the term of ten years (section 1), further extended on several occasions. Section 76 of the Law No 27.260 has recently set forth the abrogation of the tax herein 'for the fiscal year initiating on 1 January 2019'.

643. Such tax was a supplement of the Income tax, and basically presumes, and no proof to the contrary shall be admitted, that an asset should produce a rent.

644. Specifically it imposes taxes upon the resulting assets at the end of the fiscal year, (section 1), among others, for the following entities (section 2): (a) the partnerships domiciled in the country (subsection a); (b) the companies or unipersonal exploitations located in the country, belonging to the persons domiciled therein (subsection c); (c) entities and agencies listed in section 1 of the Law No 22.016 (subsection d); (d) the trusts incorporated in the country, except for the financial trusts (subsection f); and (e) the stable facilities domiciled or located in the country (subsection h).

645. As follows the law lists the exemptions, (section 3), deemed of relevance to the purpose herein: (a) property located in the Province of Tierra del Fuego, Antártida and Islands of the South Atlantic Ocean (subsection a); (b) the property belonging to persons under the Regime of Investment for the Mining Activity (subsection b); (c) the property granted tax exemption, subjective or objective, pursuant to the national laws or approved international treaties (subsection d); (d) the shares and other participations of capital of other entities subject to the tax (subsection e); (e) the property awarded from trustors to trustees, in the case of financial trusts, certificates of participation and debt securities (subsection f); and (f) the property of assets levied in the country whose value altogether, determined under the rules of this law, be equal or lower to USD 200,000 (subsection j). On the contrary, the text reads that 'the total or partial exemptions referred to as bills, bonds and other securities, established or to be established in the future by special laws, shall be granted tax exemption under section herein'.

646. Then, the law extensively elaborates on the way to determine the tax base, upon which the 1% aliquot will be imposed (section 13), setting forth that 'the income tax determined for the fiscal years upon which the tax herein is calculated, shall be withheld as payment on account of the tax under this law'.

III. Value Added Tax

647. The VAT, created by Law No 23.349 (t.o. Decree no. 280/97), levies, according to the respective subsection of section 1: (a) the sale of personal property located or placed in the national territory; (b) the works, rents and services rendering performance in the national territory with the exclusion of those renderings carried out in the country but whose use or exploitation will be overseas.; (c) definite importations of personal property; and (d) transaction made overseas but whose use or exploitation will be effective in the national territory. Section 2 defines the notion of sale, whereas section 3 lists – including without limitation – the works, rents, renderings covered by the tax.

648. Then, section 4, in its respective subsections, establishes that the taxable persons are those: (a) whose usual work is the sale of personal property; (b) realize on their own name, on behalf of third parties sales and purchases; (c) import personal property in their name or on behalf of third parties; (d) are building companies performing certain works; (e) render levied services; (f) are lessors in the case of levied rents; (g) are renderers of the renderings realized overseas but whose use or exploitation will be effective in the national territory. Moreover, it adds that, 'are as well included (…) the joint ventures, company contribution groupings, consortiums, association with no legal entity as legal persons, non-partnership groupings or any other entity, individual or collective, in the context described herein'.

649. Then, the law provides the ways to establish the taxable event (sections 5 and 6). The law included an extensive Title II referring to exemptions, among the most important one the exemption to exportations (section 8, subsection d). The general aliquot of the tax is 21%; with a further increase of 27% and a reduced one of 10.5%, pursuant to 28. Notwithstanding the special feature of the regime, for the domestic operations – that is to say – the ones done in the national territory –, the tax to be paid is determined by the difference between fiscal credit and debit. As a tax base the law establishes 'the net sale price, of the rendering of the service', which 'will be the resulting one from the invoice or equivalent document issued by the taxpayer of such duty, net on discounts and similar ones done under the customs of the market' (section 10, first paragraph). So as to set the fiscal debit, 'the total amount of the net sales, rents, Works, or rendering or service prices levied (…), taxable on the current fiscal period, will be applied the aliquot fixed for all operations' (section 11, first paragraph). Then, the fiscal credit is subtracted from the fiscal debit, which consists in 'the tax that, in the fiscal period being settled, would have been billed due to a definitive purchase or importation of goods, rents, or rendering of service' (section 12, subsection a, first paragraph). Another case that can be relevant is the definitive imports. To that respect, the following should be taken into account, 'the aliquot shall be applied upon the definite normal price for the application of the importation duties to which all imports duties and levies shall be added' (section 25).

IV. Tax on Personal Property

650. Law No 23.966 (t.o. Decree No 281/97) incorporated the emergency tax on personal property, whose original validity was extended many time, the last one until 31 December 2019 pursuant to Law No 26.545 (section 1).

651. Taxable subjects are physical persons and undivided estates (section 17). Regarding those domiciled in the national territory, both the property located in the country and overseas is levied; whereas those with domicile overseas are only levied on the property they have in the national territory; in all the cases regarding the existing property on 31 December of each year (sections 16 and 17).

652. For the purposes herein, the most relevant of the tax consists in the partnerships have been incorporated as substitute responsible for the tax. Thus, the unnumbered section incorporated after section 25 sets forth that 'the tax corresponding to shares or other capital participations of the partnerships ruled under Law No 19.550 of Commercial Partnerships (…), whose owners were physical persons and/or undivided estate domiciled in the country or overseas, and/or partnerships, and/or any other type of legal person, domiciled overseas, shall be settled by the partnerships ruled under this law, and the aliquot to apply shall be cero point twenty five cents per cent (0.25%) over the set value (…). The tax so integrated shall be deemed as a unique and definite payment'. Moreover, the same section sets forth that 'it is presumed and no proof to the contrary shall be admitted, that the shares or capital participations of partnerships ruled under Law No 19.550 of Commercial Partnerships (…), whose owners were partnerships, any other type of legal person, company, permanent establishments, trust fund or exploitation, domiciled, settled or located overseas belong indirectly to the physical persons domiciled overseas or to undivided estate settled there'. Furthermore, for the Trusts, the section establishes that 'the tax shall be calculated and settled by those acting as trustees', applying the aliquot of 0.25% over the value of the goods integrating the Trusts on the 31 December every year and adding that 'the tax settled in that way shall be deemed unique and definite' and that 'it is presumed and no proof to the contrary, that the goods of the Trust belong to persons directly or indirectly subject to the tax imposition'. Last but not least, section 26 sets forth, for the purposes herein, that ' the taxpayers of the minimum presumed income tax (…) and any other existing legal person (…) domiciled in the country having a co-ownerships, possession, use, usufruct, disposition, deposit, withholding, custody, administration or physical custody of goods subject to the tax belonging to [‘physical persons domiciled overseas and the undivided estate overseas] (…), shall pay a unique and definite payment calculated on the basis of the value such goods (…) on 31 December of each year: For the year 2106, the cero point seventy five cents per cent (0.75%). For 2017, the cero point fifty cents per cent (0.50%). –As from 2018 and the following, cero point twenty five cents per cent (0.25%)’.

V. Taxes on Credits and Debits in Bank Accounts and Other Operations

653. Law No 25.413 created an emergency tax on credits and debits of bank accounts and other operations.

654. The tax would be imposed originally ‘as from the following day of its publication and shall be valid for credits and debits done until 31 December 2002’ (section 7). However, it has been subject of successive extensions, being the last one established under section 1 of the Law No 27.199 up to 31 de December 2017.

655. The law established the application of the aliquot of 0.6% on ‘credits and debits performed in account – whatsoever its nature – open in the entities ruled under the Financial Entities Law’ (section 1, first paragraph e subsection a).

656. Furthermore, it sets forth an aliquot of 1.2% for ‘the operations performed by [financial] entities in which the beneficiaries do not use accounts indicated therein’ (section 1, subsection b) and for ‘all of their own flow of funds or those of third parties, even in cash, that any person, included in Financial Entities Law, does on their own behalf or on behalf of third parties’ (section 1, subsection c).

657. As regards the fixing of the duty, ‘the tax shall be fixed over the gross amount of the credits and debits and levied operations, without making any deductions or increases whatsoever due to commissions, expenses, or similar items, indicated separately in a clear way in the corresponding receipts’ (subsection 1, last paragraph).

658. As regards exemption from taxes, notwithstanding the list made by the rule, it is established that ‘Objective and/or subjective exemptions pursuant to other national, shall not be applied – even in the case general, special or statutory laws-, decrees or any other rule of inferior normative hierarchy’ (section 2, fifth paragraph), empowering ‘The National Executive Branch to establish total or partial exemptions of the tax herein in those case it considers relevant’ (section 2, sixth paragraph).

VI. Social Insurance Contributions

659. The social insurance contributions regime consists in a complex scheme of rules.

660. Namely, there are two modalities of work based on the way it is developed: (a) under a contract of employment; or (b) self-employed.

661. Owing to the profusion of rules, only the general aspects and global percentage will be depicted as a painstakingly analysis would exceed the limits and purposes of this study.

A. Regime for Workers under a Contract of Employment

662. A regards the regime for workers under a contract of employment, there are two types: (a) the contributions made by the employer as the responsible for his own debt; and (b) the payments corresponding to the employee made by the employer at the moment of the paying salaries and wages.

Contributions

663. The global general percentage of the contributions of the employer for each worker amounts to 23% over the salary, which can be divided into the following way: (a) 10.17% corresponds to the Social Security System in Argentina; (b) 1.5% corresponds to National Retired and Pensioners Social Service institute; (c) 4.44% corresponds to the National Regime of Family Allowances; (d) 0.89% to the National Employment Fund; (e) 6% corresponds to social insurance. Furthermore, there is the obligation of hiring insurance with a Labour Risk Insurance Company whose amounts varies according the corresponding quotation.

Payments

664. The employer must retain for the worker's salary a global 17%, which can be divided into: (a) 11% corresponds to the Social Security System in Argentina; (b) 3% corresponds to National Retired and Pensioners Social Service institute; and (c) 3% corresponds to social insurance

B. Regime for the Self-Employed Worker

665. Regarding the self-employed workers, it can be briefly elaborate that there are several categories according to the activity, each of them with reference taxes and duties and whose percentage of contributions amounts to 32% of the taxable income, 27% of that corresponds to Social Security System in Argentina and 5% corresponds to National Retired and Pensioners Social Service institute.

VII. Customs Duties

666. The customs duties are regulated in the Customs Codes (Law No 22.415); furthermore, it should be considered that under Law No 26.795 the MERCOSUR Customs Code was incorporated to the regulation thereof.

667. Notwithstanding the special features of customs regulations, the following general aspects are to be considered.

668. The Customs Code has a Preliminary Title which defines, among other issues, the customs territory (Chapter I) where it is established at the same time that 'importation is the introduction of any good into the customs *territory*' (Chapter II, section 9, subsection 1) and that 'exportation is the extraction of any good out of the customs territory' (Chapter II, section 9, subsection 1).

669. In section IX – Taxes Set Forth by the Customs Legislation: all taxes demanded by the customs are established there.

However, the most important ones are as follows.

A. *Importation Duties*

670. The Customs Code establishes that 'the importation duty levies a tax for consumption' (section 635) and that 'importation is for *consumption* when the goods are introduced in the customs territory for an indefinite period of time' (section 636).

671. The text establishes the dates on which the import duty is to be applied (sections 637 and 638). On those same dates, for liquidation purposes, the validity of 'the customs regime, the aliquot, the tax base and the exchange rate for the *conversion* of the foreign currency into national legal currency' are defined as well (section 639).

672. After that, it is provided that '*the* import duty can be ad valorem or specific' (section 640).

673. The 'ad valorem is that whose amount is obtained by means of the application of a percentage over the customs value of the goods *or* over the official CIF prices if they were higher' (section 641); it should be considered that 'the customs value of the imported goods for consumption is the normal price' (section 642). The aliquots can be established by the National Executive Branch (sections 664 and 667) and they range from 0% and 35%, whereas 'the specific one is the one whose value is obtained by means of application of a fixed sum of money for each unit of measurement' (section 660). Moreover, 'the specific import duty can operate as a unique import duty or as a maximum, minimum or additional of the ad valorem import duty' (section 662). Even though the 'specific import duty is established by law', immediately after that National Executive Branch is given the power to fix it in certain cases (section 663).

B. Exportation Duties

674. The law establishes that 'the *export* duty levies the exportation for consumption' (section 724) and that 'the exportation is for consumption when the goods are taken out of the customs territory for an indefinite period of time' (section 725).

675. Notwithstanding other provisions of law, '[the export duty] is applicable (…) established by the law in force on the date of the registration of the corresponding exportation consumption request' (section 726). Moreover, 'for the purposes of *calculation* of the export duties and further taxes that levy exportation for consumption, the tax regime, the aliquot, the tax base and the Exchange rate shall be applicable for the conversion of the foreign currency into legal national currency' in force on the date of the request (section 728).

676. The same as the importation, the export duty 'can be ad valorem or specific' (section 733).

677. The ad valorem export duty 'is the one whose amount is obtained by means of the application of a percentage over the value levied on the goods or, over official FOB prices' (section 734). In this sense, 'the value levied on the goods to be *exported* for consumption is the FOB value in operations done by sea or air and the FOT value or the FOR value according to the means of transportation used, in operations done by land, between the buyer and the seller independent from each other (…) as a consequence of a sale in cash' (section 735). The aliquots can be established by the National Executive Branch (sections 755 and 757) and are fixed for each specific good.

678. On the contrary, the specific export duty 'is the one obtained by means of application of a fixed amount of Money for each unit of measurement' (section 752) and 'it should be established by law' (section 754).

679. Furthermore, the export incentives regime under section X should be considered: Drawback (Chapter I, Refunds and Reimbursements (Chapter II).

C. Statistics Rate

680. The Customs Code establishes that 'the importation or exportation, whether definite or temporary, about which a general statistical service shall be rendered, can be levied with an ad valorem rate for such concept' (section 762), whose tax base 'is the corresponding customs value of the good. Such value is defined so as to calculate the corresponding import or export duty, if applicable' (section 763). The applicable aliquot is 0.5%, projecting maximum amounts for the importation operations according to the import tax base.

§2. LOCAL TAXES

I. Provincial Taxes

681. After the elaboration on National taxes, let us now analyse provincial taxes that could globally affect the energy, even in the Autonomous City of Buenos Aires, as the same taxes are applicable.

682. In the analysis of the Provincial Tax Competences, the Law No 23.548 of Federal Co-Participation of Fiscal Resources should be taken into consideration.

683. Notwithstanding specific aspects, section 9 of such law provides that:

> The observance of each province will be done by means of a law that provides that: a)They accept the regime in it without reservation or limitation whatsoever. b) They commit themselves and their administrative and municipal agencies, whether they are or not autonomous, not to apply local taxes similar to the national ones set forth under this law. In compliance with this obligation, no taxes, rates, contributions or other tributes shall be levied, whatever their characteristics or denomination, on the items subject to national taxes distributed or raw material used in the elaboration of products subject to taxes under this law; this obligation does not cover rates for services effectively rendered (…). From this obligation, (…) provincial taxes on the real estate, on the gross income, on the property, establishment, circulation or transfer of vehicles, of seals and free assignment of goods are expressly excluded.

684. In other words, the ample provincial fiscal powers set forth in the National Constitution, are, in fact limited to the establishment of just a few taxes. As far as this study is concerned, the taxes to be analysed are on the list as follows: (a) real estate tax; (b) gross income tax; and (c) stamp tax. As already mentioned, they also govern the Autonomous City of Buenos Aires.

685. In the frame of this so limited provincial competence frame, the municipal governments will only be able to exercise the competences their constitutions and their corresponding organic laws empower them to do so. So, the municipal taxes substantially defer in each jurisdiction; thus, no thorough analysis will be done, just the general criteria to be considered.

686. Last but not least, it is necessary to mention that there are several instruments that regulate the fiscal relationship between the federal government and the provinces. To that respect, it is only worth mentioning that the Federal Pact for the Employment, Production and Growth from the 12 August 1993 constituted a commitment of the provincial governments and the National State regarding the then municipality of the City of Buenos Aires – in relation to taxes, especially those concerning amendment to the gross income tax, the stamp tax and taxes on the real estate. For a number of reasons, the provincial governments never upheld the commitment or only did it in part.

687. As a clear consequence of the aforementioned, it can be understood that in the country there is a different fiscal regime for each province, in the Autonomous City of Buenos Aires and in each municipality, so dynamics of the most relevant taxes will be elaborated in general terms.

A. *Gross Income Taxes*

688. Each provincial jurisdiction has the power to establish the gross income tax in its territory. Nowadays, every province and the City of Buenos Aires have a Fiscal Code and such tax is provided therein. In this situation, as it was established, there are as many tax regimes as jurisdictions (twenty-five in total).

689. Generically, it can be said that a tax levies the habitual fiscal exercises of an activity for a payment inside a jurisdiction, independent of the result or profit and the individual developing it. The fiscal codes include lists of activities levied by the tax and activities not levied. The tax base is determined based on a total amount of the gross income accrued in the fiscal period for the activity taxed, with lists of enumerations of incomes exempted. The fiscal period is on an annual basis, with the prevision of monthly payments in advance. The tariffs laws, updated in general on an annual basis determine, by means of a list, the aliquots applicable to each activity – in some cases, with a general aliquot. As a general guideline, all activities are applied aliquots of 3%, 3.5%, 4% and 5% on the tax base. Moreover, there are usually minimum amounts that are to be included by activity. The jurisdictions usually set differentiated aliquots according to the activity realized inside or outside the jurisdiction, or whether the company has or not facilities inside the jurisdiction. Furthermore, nowadays, all jurisdictions have established different retention and perception tax regimes, applicable even when the individual is not settled in the jurisdiction.

Multilateral Agreement

690. Due to the characteristics of the tax, several jurisdictions could consider that the taxable activity has been developed inside those territories; this situation is called double or multiple taxations.

691. So in this case, the Multilateral Agreement subscribed by the provinces and the former municipality of Buenos Aires dated on 18 August 1977 established a system of distribution of the tax base among the jurisdiction. Such agreement is applied to the activities that 'are exercised by the same tax payer in one, several or all stages in two or more jurisdictions, but whose gross income, as they come from a unique process, economically inseparable, must be considered al together' (section 1).

692. For the distribution of the income, the agreement set several special regimes (sections 6 to 14) and a general regime (sections 2 to 5) of secondary application for the situations not expressly provided for, determining two bodies of application: the Plenary Commission (sections 16 to 18) and the Arbitration Commission (sections 19 to 26).

B. Stamp Tax

693. This tax levies the traffic, through the setting of an imposition over the instruments (public or private) of certain acts, contracts and operations (judicial acts) of a pecuniary nature. So as to be levied the instrument must be given in the jurisdiction or has an effect in it or have a relationship with it.

694. Law No 23.548 of Federal Co-participation of Federal Resources establishes that the tax 'levies on acts, contracts and operations of a pecuniary nature instrumented, on contracts of a pecuniary nature formalized by correspondence, and on operation in money representing delivery and reception of money accruing interests, done by Financial Entities' (section 9, subsection b, sub-paragraph 2, first paragraph).

695. The jurisdictions include in the tax – in accordance with the text transcribed – both acts performed between persons present or those carried out between absent persons (by correspondence).

696. In all the cases, according to Law No 23.548, 'all deeds, papers or documents arising from the performance of the acts, contracts and operations (…) shall be deemed as an instrument, in such a way that the paper has the characteristics of a judicial title by which the compliance of the obligations can be demanded without the need for another instrument or further acts performed by the taxpayers' (section 9, subsection b, sub-paragraph 2, second paragraph).

697. According to this precept, the tax is ruled by the principle of instrumentality, by which the law prohibits that the jurisdictions levy acts encountered in more than one instrument (what is called 'instrumental complex') or that, despite being instrumented, require other acts to be levied. Notwithstanding the ban, there are in the fiscal codes rules contravening them, and the national Supreme Court has declared the unconstitutionality of those rules on several occasions.

698. So as to determine the tax base, the fiscal codes establish the amounts to be considered to fix for certain judicial acts. Generally, the tax base in the value attributed to a legal act, that can be determined, undetermined but determinable – being the tasks of the taxpayers' to do so –, or if indeterminable – in many cases fixing the tax as a set amount.

699. The corresponding aliquot is applied on the tax base. The aliquots of this tax have significant oscillations for each judicial act; thus in some cases there are differential aliquots according to the place of imposition or progressive aliquots.

700. Nowadays, all jurisdictions have established in their fiscal codes the stamp tax, so, the same as with the gross income tax, it may happen – and it does happen – a double or multiple impositions over the same instrument. However, there is no agreement to solve such issue, there are only some provincial rules tending to moderate the load.

C. Real Estate Taxes

701. The Real Estate Taxes levies in the ownership of some real estate located inside the jurisdiction, covering both rural real estate – in general, at a provincial level – and urban real estate – in general, at municipal level. The fiscal valuation is determined by each jurisdiction and it constitutes the tax base. The aliquot is applied over the tax base and, in general, it is progressive set in the tariffs law. Depending on the jurisdiction, the aliquot ranges from 1% to 2%, 3% or 4%. In many cases, there is a basic tax and an additional or complementary one – covering the set of properties of one taxpayer –, as well as the increase on vacant lands. As this is about an impersonal property tax, there is no overlapping among taxes of different jurisdictions.

II. Municipal Taxes

702. In Argentina, there are more than 2,000 municipalities and their tax competences are established under the provincial constitutions, the organic law and Law No 23.548 of Federal Co-participation of Federal Resources. The municipal tax power is considerably restricted due to the fact that the provincial administrations have delegated in the Federal Administration most of the powers, and the rest of the remaining tax competences have been exercised by the provinces themselves. A detailed elaboration would exceed – due to its extension and complexity – the scope herein; thus, the most common regulated taxes will be named as examples, with variations in the legislations of the vast number of municipalities. The main taxes levied by the municipalities are the service retribution tax. However, many municipalities have introduced other types of taxes of a judicial nature difficult to determine; some of them have been established as duties and others directly as taxes. In some duties, the same as in the provincial context, there are differential aliquots depending if the taxpayer has or not a shop in the municipality; or else he is imputed as tax base the gross income of the taxpayer. Regarding the last provision, section 35 of the Multilateral Agreement is relevant, in relation to the inter-municipal distribution of the tax base, and in that sense it is provided that:

> in the case of the activities subject matter of the agreement herein, the municipalities, boroughs and other similar local entities of the adhered jurisdictions,

shall be entitled to levy taxes, inspection duties or any other tax whose application be allowed by the local laws over shops, industries or activities performed in their respective jurisdictional area, only the part of gross income attributable to those adhered fiscal authorities, as a result of the application of the rules in the agreement herein. The distribution of such taxable amount among the cited jurisdictions will be agreed upon the provisions herein, unless there was an inter-jurisdiction agreement replacing the cited distributions in each adhered provincial jurisdictions. When the legal rules in force in the municipalities, boroughs and other local similar entities of the adhered jurisdictions only allowed the collection of taxes in those cases in which there was a shop, facility or office where the levied activities is performed, the cited jurisdictions in which the taxpayer has the corresponding commissioning, shall be entitled to levy the 100% of the taxable amount corresponding to the provincial fiscal authority. The provisions herein do not compromise the jurisdictions if they dispute expressed constitutional provisions.

A. Security and Hygiene Inspection Tax

703. There is a wide variety of taxable amounts as well as names, tax base, aliquots used regarding this tax, and so only general characteristics will be elaborated; however to determine the scope of the tax it is important to resort to the corresponding ordinances of a given municipality.

704. In general terms, it can be defined as a retribution – from the part of the taxpayer – for the rendering of a service – by the municipality –, in general, of inspections in the office, shop, or industrial facility, so as to control the security, health and hygiene – among many other items – thereof. According to municipality, the description can be more or less detailed, including, in some cases, the comment of attributing any service not levied by other tax.

705. Regarding the tax base, many municipalities take the gross income of the taxpayer's; whereas some other calculate it based on the quantity of employees, extension, location, or a combination of all the indexes together. The aliquots applicable over the tax base vary from jurisdiction to jurisdictions.

B. Publicity and Advertising Duties

706. In this case, the tax is more homogeneous than the security and hygiene inspection tax, but the main problem here is to determine its exact judicial nature.

707. Notwithstanding that, it can be established, in general terms, that the existence of publicity in the street, or the one visible from the street, or the one placed in venues of public access is levied. As regards the tax base and the aliquot, they are determined upon the size of the advert.

C. Fees on Private use of Public Thoroughfare

708. The fee or duty on private use of public thoroughfare among the names that the municipalities can give to it due to the discussion over its judicial nature – levies on the areal, surface or underground use and pays back for the authorization of occupation or usufruct of a public municipal domain space.

709. The tax base, in general, can be established upon the linear m, square m, or other units of measurement that can be considered to assess the level of use or occupation – days, quantity of determined good, among others – upon the tax base, the aliquot or corresponding fixed amount is applied.

Chapter 4. Special Aspects

710. In the previous paragraphs, the most important taxes have been elaborated which are globally applied according to the different levels of government. To that respect, it should be considered that, by principle, general aspects shall be applied and only as an exception specific rules and regulations shall be enforced.

711. In this section, special aspects presented for each source of energy will be analysed. Preliminary, remember that at a national level there are quite a few rules establishing exemptions, deductions, differential aliquots over the general regime; likewise, at a provincial level there are quite a few provisions in the fiscal codes and the tariff laws, so just some exemptions to the general regime will be mentioned.

§1. Oil, Gas and Derivatives

I. At a National Level

A. Value Added Tax

712. Section 3 of the Law No 23.349 expressly establishes those providing service of gas are affected (subsection e, sub-paragraph 5).

713. In general, the taxable amount, in this case of sales, is calculated at the moment of the delivery of the good, issuance of the respective invoice, or equivalent act, the previous one (section 5, subsection a). However, there are specific provisions: (a) in the case of the gas regulated by a meter, the taxable amount is assessed at the moment of the maturity of the term fixed for the payment of its price or that of total or partial perception, the previous one (sub-paragraph 1); and (b) in the case of primary products commercialization coming from extractive activities of crude oil and gas, in those whose fixing of the price is after the delivery of the product, the taxable amount is assessed at the moment of the fixing of such price (fourth paragraph).

714. As it was exposed, the general aliquot of the tax is 21% (section 28, first paragraph). However, it is established: (a) the aliquot of 27% for the sales of gas regulated by meter (second paragraph); and (b) a reduced aliquot of 10.5% for the sales and importation of propane, butane, liquefied petroleum gas (subsection k).

715. Section 7, subsection h, sub-paragraph 13, grants tax exemption to 'international transport of passengers, and loads, those done on the borderline crossing by water included'. To that respect, section 34 of Decree No 692/1998 establishes that such exemption covers the transport of liquefied gas and hydrocarbons, in the national territory by means of pipelines, when destined for exportation.

716. Section 23 establishes a special regime, according to which 'when the rendering for [jobs done in other people's premises] was the exploitation concession, the tax base to fix the fiscal debit will be the total of income received by the concessioner, in a direct way or due to exploitation'.

B. Customs Duties

717. So as to fix the taxable value to calculate the ad valorem export duties, in that value the total of the expenses incurred in should be included up to 'the place where the last ship measurement was practiced for the goods to be exported by oil pipelines, gas pipelines, multi-products pipelines' (section 736, subsection d), of the Customs Code).

C. Hydrocarbons Regime

718. Law No 17.319 establishes the regime applicable to hydrocarbons, setting forth some special features about taxation.

Tax stability

719. Section 56 prescribes the principle of tax stability. Thus, subsection a) provides that the exploration and exploitation concession permit holders 'shall be liable to pay all the existing provincial and municipal taxes up to the date of the adjudication. During the term of the permits and concession the provinces and municipalities will not be entitled to either levy new taxes or increase the existing one on the holders, except for the service retribution taxes and contribution due to improvements or general increases of taxes'.

720. The subsection d) points out that 'Shareholders or other direct beneficiaries of the earning are granted tax exemption regarding other present or future national taxes of any nature or kind even those that could be imposed to – related to the activity (…). However, they are not granted such exemption due to service retribution taxes, improvements contributions, and for taxes levied to third parties that the permit holders or the concessioners have taken responsibility for.'

Special Income tax

721. The law has established a special income tax that levies the exercise of the activity as permit holder or concessioner (section 56, subsection c).

Hydrocarbon Fee

722. Section 57 establishes that 'the exploration permit holder will annually pay and in advance a fee for each square kilometre or fraction', according to a scale.

723. Whereas section 58 establishes that 'the exploitation concessioner will annually pay and in advance a fee per square kilometre or fraction covered by the area of four thousand five hundred pesos ($ 4.500)'.

Extension bonus

724. Section 58 *bis*, first paragraph, provides that 'the authority of application shall be entitled to establish that for the exploitation concession extension, the payment of a bonus extension whose amount will be equal to the result of multiplying the remaining proved reserves at the end of the term in force for the concession by the two per cent (2%) of the basin average price applicable to the respective hydrocarbons for the term of two (2) years prior to the award of the extension'.

Exploitation Bonus

725. Section 58 *bis*, second paragraph, establishes that 'for the case of complementary activities of conventional hydrocarbons exploitation, as from the maturity of the awarded concession term and in the Non-conventional hydrocarbons exploitation concession, the Authority of Application shall be entitled to set the payment of an exploitation bonus whose amount will be equal to the result of multiplying the remaining proved reserves associated to the conventional hydrocarbons exploitation at the end of the term of the awarded concession and by the 2% of the basin average price applicable to the respective hydrocarbons for the two years prior to the award of the Non-conventional hydrocarbons exploitation concession'.

Hydrocarbons Royalties

726. The law establishes that in terms of royalties a percentage of 12% over the production of the liquefied hydrocarbons extracted in well heads, as well as on the volumes extracted and effectively used of the natural gas productions (section 59, first paragraph). Those will be collected in cash, unless the State wanted to collect them in kind. In the first case, the amount will be calculated over the value of the crude oil in the well head.

D. Tax on Liquefied Oils and on Compressed Natural Gas

727. In Chapter I from Title III of the Law No 23.966 (t.o. Decree No 518/1998) tax on liquefied fuels is created. It levies taxes on 'the transfer for payment or free of charge of the national or imported products', in such way that it only affect in one of the circulation stages (section 1).

728. The text includes in section 4, a list of products, the corresponding aliquots and a minimum amount to charge.

729. Notwithstanding the particular cases, the tax base represents 'the net sale price arising from the invoice or equivalent document to operators in resale regimes in dispatch plant, extended by the imposed party as a condition for earnings' (section without number added after section 4).

730. The taxable amount is determined, pursuant to section 2: (a) as a general criteria, with the delivery of the good, issuance of the invoice or equivalent document, the previous one; (b) in the case of products consumed by the very same taxpayers, with the withdrawal of the fuel for consumption; (c) regarding well heads of liquefied gas – automobile use, at the moment of the control of the holding of goods.

731. The taxable payers pursuant to section 3, are: (a) in the case of importations, the importers themselves; (b) the companies that refine or commercialize liquefied oil and/or other derivatives of hydrocarbons in all its ways; (c) the companies producing, elaborating, manufacturing or getting levied products directly or through third parties; (d) in the case of liquefied gas for automobile use, the fuel well heads and fuel storage for private consumption owners shall be levied.

732. Finally, notwithstanding some special features, under section 7, transfer of products are granted tax exemption when: (a) they are destined to exportation; (b) they are destined to ranch of overseas boats, international flights aircrafts, or fishing boats; (c) they are destined to be used as raw materials in set chemical and petrochemical processes; (d) they are destined to be used in an industrial process for vegetal oil extraction; (e) they are destined for the consumption in the provinces of Neuquén, La Pampa, Río Negro, Chubut, Santa Cruz, Tierra del Fuego, Antártida and islands of the Atlantic ocean, de Patagones District in Buenos Aires province and Malargüe in Mendoza.

733. In Chapter II in the same Law No 23.966, the tax on compressed natural gas is created which levies upon 'the natural gas distributed by networks destined to compressed natural gas (G.N.C.) to be used as automobile fuel' (section 10, first paragraph).

734. The 16% aliquot applicable on the retail sales price applicable (section 10, first paragraph, in fine), this price deemed as the net price billed to the oil stations, to which an amount or representative percentage will be added to the margin of the well head to the public (section 10, second paragraph).

735. The taxable amount will be assessed the day of the maturity of the corresponding invoices (section 11), being the distributors of the product the taxpayers thereof (section 12).

E. Tax on Gas Oil and Liquefied Gas for Vehicle Use

736. Pursuant to Law No 26.028, a tax with specific affectation was created (section 1, first paragraph, first part).

737. Such tax levies 'the transfer for a valuable consideration or free of charge, or importation, of gas oil or any other liquefied fuel replacing it in the future', so that it only affects once in the stages of circulations and in full force until 31 December 2024 (section 1, first paragraph, second part).

738. Especially, regarding biodiesel as liquefied fuel in the generation of electrical energy, it is determined that is exempted until 31 December 2016.

739. The rule further clarifies that the tax 'contained in the transfers or importations of fuels levied shall not be computed as compensation and/or payment on account of any national current or future tax' (section 11).

740. The 22% aliquot under section 5 is applied upon the same tax base provided in section unnumbered incorporated after section 4 of the Title III of the Law No 23.966 – net sales prices.

F. Tax on Oil and Natural Gas Destined to CNG

741. Law No 26.181 creates the tax on transfer – for a valuable consideration or free of charge, or importation – on certain oil and natural gas distributed by network and destined to natural compressed gas for the use of automobile fuel, or over any other liquefied fuel replacing it in the future, in full force until 31 December 2035 (section 1, first paragraph, second part), applying it in such a way that it only affects once in the stages of circulations.

742. The rule further provides that the tax 'contained in the transfers or importations of fuel levied shall not imputed as a compensation and/ payment on account for any national current or future tax' (section 11).

743. Regarding the oil, the applicable aliquot is 4% on the net sales price, defined in the already mentioned unnumbered section contained immediately after section 4 of the Title III of the Law No 23.966 (section 2).

744. Regarding natural compressed gas, the aliquot of 5% will be applied upon the net sales price, set forth under section 10 of Title III of the Law No 23.966 (section 2).

745. In both cases, the minimum amount of USD 0.05 per litre of oil or per cubic metre of compressed natural gas is established for its use as fuel for automobiles.

G. Surcharge to Natural Gas

746. Section 75 of the Law No 25565, establishes that 'a surcharge of up to 7.5% over the natural gas price at the point of entering the transport system, for each cubic metre of 9,300 kilocalories, that will be applied on the total of the cubic m consumed and/or commercialized by networks or pipelines in the national territory whatever the final utilization thereof' (second paragraph).

747. Such surcharge was established so as to finance the Fiduciary Fund for Residential Consumption Subsidies of gas.

H. Specific Charges

748. Law No 26.095 creates, with specific purposes, 'specific charges for the development of Works (…) as a contribution to a Trust Funds constituted or to be constituted for the development of infrastructure work of the gas and electricity services' (section 2), which 'shall neither be considered nor computed as a tax base of any tax of national origin, with the exception of the value added tax' (section 3, first paragraph); empowering 'the National Executive Branch to fix the value of the specific charges and to adjust them as well' (section 4).

749. Moreover, it is established that such specific charges 'shall be in full force until the full payment of the titles issued by the Trusts constituted or to be constituted are verified to deal with the investments related to the infrastructure Works of the energy sector' (section 5).

750. Notwithstanding the doubtful legal nature of the specific charges, the National Supreme Court disregarded the tax nature thereof.

I. Tariffs Charges

751. Decree No 2067/2008 created a fiduciary fund, which was integrated, among others, by 'by the tariff charges payable by the users of the regulated services of transport and/or distribution, by the consumers of gas receiving the gas directly from the producers without making use of natural gas transport and distribution systems, and the companies processing natural gas', saying that such charges 'shall not be deemed as tax base of any tax from national origin, with the exception of the value added tax' (section 2).

752. The rule give the administration the power 'to fix the value of the charges and to adjust them, whenever they deem it necessary, so as to deal with the payment and/or repayment of natural gas importations' (section 6) and to 'exempt categories of users for the payment and/or repayment of gas natural importations' (section 7).

753. It is important to say that the National Supreme Court established the tariff charged do not have a tax nature

J. Hydrocarbons Export Duties

754. Section 6 of the Law No 25.561 created 'a Hydrocarbons Export Duties for the term of five years giving the National Executive Branch the power to establish the corresponding aliquot (…). Under no circumstances, shall the Hydrocarbons Export Duties reduce the value of well head, for the calculation and payment of royalties to the provinces producers'. That duty was successively intended and it was in full force in January 2017.

755. Resolution No 1077/2014, currently in force, of the former Ministry of Public Finances and Economy defines as crude oil international price (PI): PI: Brent Value of reference from month N minus USD 8 per barrel (8,0 USD/bbl); being: 'Brent Value of reference: is the average price for the ICE Brent first line or month immediately published by "Platts Crude Marketwire" under the heading "Futures Settlements" as from the day 21 of the next preceding second month (month N-2), and the day 20 of the next preceding month (month N-1) included. "N": means the month of exportation' (section 2).

756. According to the aforementioned resolution, such international price in applicable to a long list of hydrocarbons under Annexes I, II and III of the norm, upon which aliquots under sections 4, 5 and 6 will be established, respectively for all those annexes.

II. At a Provincial Level

A. Gross Income Tax

757. Law No 23.548 Federal Co-participation of the Fiscal Resources – section 9, subsection b, sub-paragraph 1 – set forth two special issues: (1)that the gross income 'shall be determined upon the basis of the income of the period, the tax base of amounts corresponding to domestic taxes for the fuels fund … excluded'; and (2) that 'in relation to fuels derived from oil, with official sale price, the imposition shall not levy the production stage' and that 'in the following stages the difference between acquisition and sale price can be levied'.

758. In another level, on the research of the fiscal codes, in some provincial jurisdictions the following special features are observed:

(a) In the case of the provision of gas, the gross income is calculated at the moment the term is due for its payment or as from the total or partial or total perception, the first to occur.
(b) The tax on liquid fuels and compressed natural gas are excluded from the tax base.
(c) Cooperatives dedicated to the production, distribution and/or rendering of natural gas are exempted.

(d) Establishments providing a supply of gas and located in a provincial jurisdiction are exempted.
(e) Those whose earnings come from the rendering of gas service in a provincial tax-free zone are exempted.
(f) Certain activities are levied reduced aliquots between 0.48% and 1.5%: generation, extraction, production, industrialization, refining and/or distribution of oil and gas.
(g) The wholesale or retail commercialization of liquid fuels derived from oil and natural gas are exempted or levied with a reduced aliquot of up to a 2%.
(h) The commercialization of liquid fuels derived from natural gas and oil with some requirements is exempted.
(i) In some situation, it is established that the tax base will be calculated upon the difference between the purchase price of and the sale price.

B. Stamp Tax

759. Based upon a research on fiscal codes, the following special features are observed in some provincial jurisdictions:

(a) Cooperatives rending a gas service by networks are exempted.
(b) Accession agreements about gas are exempted.
(c) Contracts destined to the hydrocarbons exploration and exploitation are imposed to pay an aliquot of 1%.
(d) Gas and fuel supply contracts for the generation of electric energy are exempted.

C. Taxes and Duties

760. Several provincial jurisdictions establish specific duties and tariffs for related activities.

D. Tax on Fuels Derived from Oil: Province of Salta

761. The Fiscal Code, under its Title X, regulates the tax on fuels derived from oil.

762. Thus, section 341 provides that 'for each litre or kilogram of oil derived fuel, destined to mechanical traction, sold or introduced in the province, a tax shall be paid', thus, section 342 establishes that the taxpayers are those selling to the public, and section 343 further establishes that 'the tax is to be paid as from the date of commercialization or introduction of the products in the Province and the payment shall be honoured (…) by the companies distributors acting as retention agents'.

§2. ELECTRIC ENERGY

I. At a National Level

A. Value Added Tax

763. Section 3 of the Law No 23.349 clearly establishes that suppliers of electricity are subject to the tax, except for the public lightning service (subsection e, sub-paragraph 5). In the case of the supply of electricity regulated by meter, the taxable amount shall be assessed at the moment of maturity of the fixed term for the payment of the price or that of the total or partial perception, the first to occur (sub-paragraph 1).

764. As it was afore-elaborated, the general aliquot of the tax amount to 21% (section 28, first paragraph). However, for the sale of electric energy regulated by meter, the aliquot will ascend to 27% (second paragraph).

765. Section 7, subsection h, sub-paragraph 13, sets forth the tax on 'the international passengers and load transport, the ones of frontier crossing by water included'. To that respect, section 34 of the Decree No 692/1998 establishes that the transport of electrical energy shall be granted tax exemption, when it is performed in the national territory by means of the use of a transmission line destined to exportation.

766. Section 23 establishes a special regime, under which 'when the rendering [of jobs done in a third party's property] is carried out in an exploitation concession, the tax base for fixing the fiscal debit shall be the total of income the concessioner receives, whether directly or due to exploitation'.

B. Customs Duties

767. So as to fix the tax base to calculate the ad valorem export duty, the total expenses incurred in until 'the place where the last ship measurement was performed for the goods to be exported (…) by electricity network' shall be included (section 736, subsection d), of the Customs Code.

C. Surcharge on Tariffs

768. Section 30 of the Law No 15.336, with the amendments under section 70 of the Law No 24.065, creates the national fund for electric energy, which 'shall be fixed by a surcharge of [$ 0, 0054686] by kilowatt hour over the tariffs paid by the wholesale market buyers, that is to say companies distributors and large users, as well as by the reimbursements plus the interests of the loans granted with the Fund's resources'.

D. Surcharge on the Sale Price

769. Law No 23.681 establishes 'a surcharge over the electricity sales price of six by one thousand (6‰) of the tariffs in force in each period and in each zone of the country applied to the end users, with the exception of those granted tax exemption over energy created under Law No 15.336' (section 1); the surcharge will include 'in the invoice of the end users', on the total amount billed, minus any other tax charge levied by electricity consumption (section 2).

E. Hydroelectric Royalties

770. Law No 15.336, under section 15, provides that 'in the concessions for the use of hydro electrical energy source of national jurisdiction (…), the following clauses and conditions are to be established: (…) 9. The fee the concessioner shall pay regarding royalties for the use of the source which will be included in the National Fund of Electric Energy'.

771. Whereas section 43 sets forth that 'the provinces where the source of hydro electrical energy are located will monthly receive a twelve per cent (12%) of the amount resulting from applying the energy sold to the consumption centres (…). In the case of the hydro electrical source located in bordering rivers between provinces or where the river flows among more than two provinces, the twelve per cent (12%) will be equally and rationally divided among them'.

II. At a Provincial Level

A. Gross Income Tax

772. Based on the research of the fiscal codes from some provincial jurisdictions, the following peculiarities are observed:

(a) In the case of the electric energy supply, the gross income is accrued at the moment of the maturity date for the term fixed for its payment or as from the total or partial perception, the former one.
(b) Electrical services companies or cooperatives due to specific activities are granted tax exemption.
(c) Sale operations in the Wholesale Electric Market are exempt.
(d) In some contexts, the electricity supply is allowed tax exemption.
(e) Contracts or acts related to certain works or installations are granted tax exemption.
(f) Electricity service supply in provincial duty-free zones is not subject to local gross income tax.
(g) The activity of generation is exempt or levied a reduced aliquot between 1% and 1.75%
(h) Certain related taxes are excluded from the tax base.

B. Stamp Tax

773. Based on the research of the fiscal codes from some provincial jurisdictions, the following peculiarities are observed:

(a) Electric services companies and cooperatives are allowed tax exemption.
(b) Operations made in the Wholesale Electric Market are granted tax exemption.
(c) Sales purchase contracts of electric energy entered into between distributors and generators in the Wholesale Electric Market are provided tax exemption.
(d) Certain acts and contracts related to works and installations are granted tax exemption as long as they meet specific requirements.
(e) Regarding contracts of supply aliquots between 1% and 1.5%, or reduced aliquots of 0.5%, or else they allowed tax exemption.
(f) Accession distribution contracts are provided tax exemption.

C. Real Estate Tax

774. Based on the research of the fiscal codes from some provincial jurisdictions, it is observed that properties destined to public services of electric energy or those affected for easement of conduits are allowed tax exemption.

D. Taxes and Duties

775. Several provincial jurisdictions establish taxes and duties for specific activities.

E. Electric Regulatory Frame: Province of Buenos Aires

776. The provincial Law No 11.769 establishes the Electric Regulatory Frame in the Province of Buenos Aires, in which under Chapter XVIII regulates the Provincial and Municipal tax regime. Thus, it is established that 'the agents of the electrical activity (…), for the sales operations performed with the end users, shall pay on a monthly basis to the Province of Buenos Aires, a contribution equivalent to [0.6%] of the gross incomes, net of taxes, collected for the sale of electric energy in this jurisdiction with the exception to public lighting supply – which will be discriminated and transferred to the end user's invoice' (section 74, first paragraph). In the same sense and with identical guidelines, they will monthly pay to the municipalities of the respective districts, a contribution equivalent to 6% (section 75, first paragraph).

F. Contribution on the Electricity Companies: Buenos Aires – Autonomous City

777. The fiscal code, under Title X, establishes a contribution that affects the Electricity Companies.

778. Thus, section 395 sets forth that 'the Electricity Companies are obliged to pay a unique tax (…) on the gross income coming from the electric energy in Buenos Aires-Autonomous City, once the supply destined to public lighting has been deduced. The payment of this unique tax does not exempt the companies from paying the retributive duties for services ad improvements'. Nowadays, the aliquot is 6%.

§3. Mining

I. At a National Level

A. Income Tax

779. The income tax of the Law No 20.628 provides that 'the taxable value of the mines (…) will be calculated based on the cost attributable to them, plus, if applicable, the expenses incurred in to obtain the concession. When the exploitation of such goods implies the consumption of the producing substance of the rent, the proportional deduction of the use of such substance shall be assessed, calculated in relation to the extracted units' (section 75).

B. Value Added Tax

780. Law No 23.349 sets forth that, for the case of extraction of minerals in which the price-fixing is calculated after the delivery of the product, the tax is calculated when fixing such price. (fourth paragraph).

C. Customs Duties

781. Pursuant Decree No 349/2016, an aliquot of 0% was fixed for the exportation duty of the goods in the taxable categories of the Chapters 25 and 26, as well as other categories in Chapter 27, all corresponding to the Common MERCOSUR Registry.

D. Investments Regime for the Mining Activity

782. Law No 24.196 creates the Investments Regime for the Mining Activity (section 1), established for physical persons domiciled in the country or legal entities incorporated in the country that 'develop by themselves the mining activity in the country or are settled in the country to that end' (section 2).

783. The rule sets forth the activities imposed by the regime (section 5) and those excluded from the regime (section 6).

784. In Chapter IV – Fiscal Treatment of the Investments: it is established that the persons developing covered activities shall be imposed the general tax regime with the amendments introduced by the commented law (section 7).

Fiscal Stability

785. The covered mining projects 'shall have fiscal stability for the term of thirty years counting as from the date of submittal of their Feasibility Study' (section 8).

786. The fiscal stability 'covers all taxes, such as direct taxes, duties and tax contributions … as well as the export and import duties, levies and other taxes' (sub-paragraph 1.1) and 'this means the companies … shall not suffer an increment in their tax burden, considered separately in each determined jurisdiction when submitting … the Feasibility Study, in the national, provincial or municipal level, those adhering' (sub-paragraph 1.2).

787. The text specifies that 'in the payment of interests to financial entities and agencies overseas, covered in Title V of the Incomes Tax Law … the fiscal stability also applies to: i) the increment of the aliquots, duties and amounts in force and, ii) the alteration on the percentages and/or mechanism of fixing the presumed net income of Argentinean sources, when the companies under the regime of such law, have assumed under contract such tax at their expense' (sub-paragraph 3).

788. There are further topics included which are neither breaching not covered by fiscal stability (sub-paragraph 4).

789. It is further established under this law that 'fiscal stability is as well applied to Exchange and Tariffs regimes; the Exchange parity, reimbursement and refunds and/or devolution of tax due to exportations are excluded' (sub-paragraph 6).

790. Section 9 excludes the VAT from the fiscal stability.
Last but not least section 10 provides that 'any and all change to the principle of fiscal stability … by the provinces or municipalities adhering … shall entitle the damaged party to claim before the national or provincial authority, as applicable, to retain the co-participant funds corresponding to the non-compliant fiscal authority, the amounts paid in excess, so as to compensate the taxpayer'.

Income tax

791. First, it is set forth that 'the persons under the present investment regime shall be entitled to reduce the tax balance of the income tax, the one hundred per cent (100%) of the amount invested in prospection, exploration, special studies, mineral and metallurgical essays, those of a Pilot Plan, those of applied research, and further jobs destined to determine the technical-economic feasibility thereof' (section 12).

792. Second, an amortization optional regime is set forth (section 13).

793. Third, it is set forth that 'the earning coming from contributions on mines, and mining duties, as capital stock, in companies developing activities covered … shall be provided tax exemption of income tax'; moreover, 'the capital extension and shares issuance that would give place to the capitalization of the contribution mentioned herein-before shall be exempted from the stamp tax' (section 14).

Benefits on exportations

794. The fiscal credits originated in imports and acquisition of goods and services, affecting exploration companies registered in the regime and destined to mining activities such as prospection, exploration, mineral essays and applied research, 'shall be reattributed according to the procedure, way and conditions established by the National Executive Power'. It is important to highlight that 'the retribution … shall not be performed when the referred fiscal credits have been financed under the regime established by Law No 24.402' (section 14 *bis*).

Minimum presumed income tax

795. Section 17 establishes that 'the persons registered in the present investment regime for the mining activity are exempted from the tax on assets, as from the fiscal exercise at the moment of the registration'.

796. In concordance, section 3 of the Law No 25.063 establishes that '(…) b) the goods belonging to the persons covered by the investment regime for the mining activity (…) that are affected by the development of the activities mentioned in such regime are exempted from the tax'.

Financing Regime

797. In general terms, under Law No 24.402 'A financing regime, destined to the payment of the value added tax was established and levies: a) Purchases of Definite Importation of new capital goods. b) The investments made in physical infrastructure Works for the mining activity' (section 1), that 'will be implemented through credit lines, which financial entities … could give to the individuals … , destined to pay said tax' (section 4).

Mining Royalties

798. It is provided that 'the provinces adhering to the regime (…) that perceive royalties or decide to perceive them, shall not be entitled to collect a percentage higher than three per cent (3%) over the pithead' value of the extracted mineral (section 22).

799. To that effect, it is understood as 'pithead' mineral as the 'mineral extracted, transported and/or previously accumulated to any transformation process'. Furthermore, the 'pithead' value of the minerals and/or metals declared by the producer is defined as 'the value obtained in the first stage of commercialization, minus the necessary operative and/or direct costs to take the pithead mineral to such stage, with exception of the direct or indirect expenses and/or costs inherent to the extraction process' (section 22 *bis*).

E. Mining Taxes

800. The Mining Code (Law No 1.919) says that 'mines are given to individuals by means of an annual tax for possessions that will be fixed periodically by the national law and that the concessioner will pay the National or Provincial government, according to the jurisdiction the mines are located in' (section 213).

801. Regarding the tax regime, it is established that 'for the first five years of the concession … no other contribution will be imposed on the ownership of the mines' and that 'the fiscal exemption … is granted overall tax or duty, whatever its denomination whether national, provincial, or municipal present or future, applicable to the exploitation and commercialization of the mining production', being excluded 'rates on reciprocation of services and the actuation sealing, which will be, in any case, the one ruled by the judicial and administrative order' (section 214).

802. Finally, it is established that 'the fee will paid in advance and in equal parts in two six-month periods, that will be due on June 30 and December 31 of each year, considering fraction of a semester as a complete semester' and that 'the mine concession is due ipso facto due to lack of payment of an annual fee after two months of the maturity date' (section 216).

F. Federal Mining Agreement

803. Pursuant to Law No 24.228, the Congress of the Nation ratified the 'Federal Mining Agreement', subscribed by the provinces on 6 May 1993.

804. For the purpose of this work, it was agreed that 'the provinces will foster the abolition of those municipal taxes and duties directly affecting the mining activity' (clause 9) and 'in concordance with the measures taken by the Nation, the provinces will eliminate stamp taxes on all those judicial acts related to prospection, exploration, exploitation and benefits of mineral substances, with the exception of solid. Liquid and gaseous hydrocarbons' (clause 10).

II. At a Provincial Level

A. *Gross Income Tax*

805. Based on the research of the fiscal codes from some provincial jurisdictions, the following peculiarities are observed:

(a) The mere purchase of mineral products to be industrialized and sold in another jurisdiction as well as the mining exploitations are levied regardless of the frequency of the operation, that is to say they are levied even if they are occasional.
(b) Reduced aliquots are established between 0.5% and 1.75% over mining exploration and exploitation activities.
(c) The primary mining activity is tax exempted in general terms.
(d) When the activity is under the mining investments regime is allowed tax exemption.
(e) For some cases, the tax base will be calculated over the difference between the price of purchase and the price of sale.
(f) Some related taxes are granted tax base exemption.

B. *Stamp Duties*

806. Based on the research of the fiscal codes from some provincial jurisdictions, the following peculiarities are observed:

(a) Leasing contracts are granted tax exemption, when the lessee develops the mining activity.
(b) Contracts related to the mining activity or the prospection and exploration of mineral substances are allowed tax exemption.
(c) Mines assignment contracts are exempt.
(d) A reduced aliquot of 0.5% is established on the mining establishments' assignments.

C. Taxes and Duties

807. Several provincial jurisdictions establish specific taxes and duties for each related activity.

D. Mineral Extraction Duties: Province of Entre Ríos

808. The Fiscal Code, in Title VII, sets forth minerals extraction duty. Thus, section 295 sets forth that the extraction of the mineral substance shall pay such duty; being 'taxpayers (…) physical or legal persons performing the extraction' and responding 'in solidarity for their payment, the holders of the fields, quarries and banks whatever the title and those commercializing or transporting the material in their own name' (section 297). Regarding the tax base, section 296 sets forth that 'it will consist in the quantity extracted measured in cubic m'.

E. Mineral Extraction Duties: Province of Jujuy

809. The Fiscal Code, in Title VII, sets forth minerals exploitation duty To that respect, section 334 prescribes that 'the duties on exploitation of mineral fields located in the Province and destined to commercialization and/or industrialization shall be paid (…) in relation to the production of minerals'. Section 335 makes it clear that it covers 'all types of minerals that the Mining Code classifies as first or second category'.

810. Section 339 provides that 'the taxpayers are (…) physical or legal persons dedicated, to the exploitation of minerals coming from the field located in the Province, as their main activity or as accessory to others'.

811. As regards the tax base, it is set forth that 'they will be determined and applied on the basis of the quantity of minerals extracted in "pithead", with clarification – in each case – of its original origin and the condition in which the commercialization is done', whereas sections 342 provides that 'the value of the minerals will be the one arising from the sales or judicial businesses performed by the taxpayer, of the national or international market price – the higher one, being them based upon pit head mineral, or in the case of elaborated products over the price of the first stage of commercialization, subtracting the costs added as from the extraction to the agreement on the sale conditions in the stage considered'. Upon this basis, the aliquot of 3% will be applied (section 344).

812. On the contrary, Chapter V establishes reductions, the non-taxable minimum incentives and an exploration fund.

813. Finally, section 350 provides that 'the mining exploitation activities at the moment of this law being in force, and those imposed under its regime, shall have fiscal stability and invariability pursuant to the laws 24.196 and 25.161'.

§4. Renewable Energies

I. At a National Level

A. National Wind and Solar Energy Regime

814. Law No 25.019 provides, for the purpose of this study, that 'the capital investments destined to wind or solar equipment installations and/or central installations shall be entitled to defer their payments of the value added tax for the term of fifteen years as from the enactment of this law. The deferment owed will be paid afterwards in fifteen annuities as from the maturity of the last deferment' (section 3).

815. Moreover, It was determined that 'all activity of wind or solar generation that give energy to the wholesale market and /or is involved in the rendering of the public service under this law, shall have fiscal stability for the term of fifteen years, counting as from the enactment of this law; fiscal stability being deemed as the impossibility of affecting the business with a total higher tax burden, as a consequence of the increases of the tax contributions and duties outside its denomination in the national context, or the creation of some new ones that may affect them as holder of legal right there of' (section 7).

B. National Regime of National Development

816. Law No 26.190 created an 'investment regime for the construction of new works destined to the production of electric energy generated as from renewable source of energy' (section 7), establishing that the beneficiaries will 'holder of investments and concessioners of new electrical energy Works generated as from renewable energy source … settled in the national territory, whose production is destined to the Wholesale Electric Market (WEM) or the rendering of a public services' (section 8) and 'and they shall have the promotional benefits … as long as the project has an effective commencement of execution before 31 December 2017, included' (section 9, first paragraph).

817. Section 9 provides the promotional benefits:

> As regards the value added tax and the income tax, they shall be applied with certain modifications, the Investment Promotion Regime in capital goods and infrastructure works set forth under Law No 26.360 (subsection 1), which basically consists of the anticipated devolution of the value added tax corresponding to goods or infrastructure works included in the project proposed and/or to apply in the income tax the accelerated amortization thereof. None of these benefits are mutually exclusive, allowing the beneficiaries to access simultaneously both fiscal options. (subsection 1.2)
>
> The compensation on losses with earning with the income tax shall be valid for the term of ten years. (subsection 2)

818. The goods affected by the activities promoted do not integrate the tax base of the presumed minimum income tax. (subsection 3)

819. It is allowed to deduct interests from the losses of the partnerships and the differences originated for the project finance. (subsection 4)

820. When a 60% of integration of national components can be unequivocally proved in the electromechanical installations, the civil works excluded, those individual or entities shall be entitled to receive as an additional benefit a fiscal certificate to be applied to the payment of national taxes, for the value equivalent to 20% of the national component of the electromechanically installations (subsection 6).

821. Section 11 sets forth that certain cases shall not be entitled to adhere to the regime.

C. Amendments to the National Investment Regime

822. Law No 27.191 initiates the 'Second Stage of the National Development Regime for the use of renewable sources of Energy Destined to the Production of Electric Energy – Period 2018–2025' (Chapter II), apart from making amendments to the Law No 26.190 (Chapter I)

823. Basically, Law No 27.191 extends the terms of access to the benefits of the Law No 26.190 and introduces some specification for this new period.

824. The changes incorporated to the aforementioned regime are as follows: (a) for the investments realized between 1 January 2018 and 31 December 2021, included, the benefit of the anticipated devolution of the VAT shall be effective after a minimum of two fiscal periods counting as from the one in which the investments have been made; (b) for the investments realized between 1 January 2022 and 31 December 2025, included, that benefit shall be effective after a minimum of three fiscal periods calculated in the same way; (c) regarding the benefit of accelerated amortization in the income tax for investments, the beneficiaries performing them shall be entitled to opt for the realization of the respective amortizations as from the fiscal periods of concession of the good pursuant to the regime established in the law.

825. Besides, it is worth mentioning that 'the beneficiaries of the regime (…), whatever the date their project are initiated or developed, shall be entitled to transfer the Price agreed upon in the contracts of renewable energy supply entered into, the highest costs derived from taxes and levies, contributions or national. Provincial, municipal increases, and those of Buenos Aires-Autonomous City produced after the subscription of such contracts' (section 13, first paragraph).

826. Besides, A Regime of importations is incorporated (Chapter VI), and will be in force until 31 December 2017 (section 16), under which 'they shall be exempted from the payment of import duties and from any other duty, special tax, or levy correlative or statistics rate, with the exclusion of the other retributive rates of services, due to the introduction of capital goods, special equipment or part or spare part of the goods, new in all the cases, and of items (…) necessary for the execution of the investment project'.

II. At a Provincial Level

A. Duties and Levies

827. Several provincial jurisdictions establish duties and levies for related activities.

B. Promotion and Development Regime for Solar Energy: Jujuy Province

828. The provincial Law No 5.904 sets forth a Promotion and Development Regime for Solar Energy establishing under Chapter II a Promotion and Development Regime for Solar Energy, being the beneficiaries of such regime 'physical and/or legal persons holders of the investments and/or concessioners of the projects of installations of centrals generating electric energy as from the use of Solar Energy (…) settled in the provincial territory, whose productions will be destined to micro generation, to the Wholesale Electric Market and/or the rendering of public services' (section 14).

829. In tax matters, the following benefits are granted: (a) exemption from the stamp tax (section 15, subsection I); (b) exemption from gross income tax (section 15, subsection II); and (c) fiscal stability for the term of fifteen years for 'all activities of electric generation as from the use of Solar Energy destined to in the Wholesale market and /or the rendering of public services' (section 16).

Part V. The National Agencies: Regulators of Gas and Electricity in the Argentinean Law

Chapter 1. The Development and Legal Regime if the Regulatory Agencies in Argentina

830. The same as in other Latin American countries, the creation of the regulation agencies in Argentina occurred in the frame of a deep reform process of the State and the privatization of the public services[241] carried out in the 1990s as from the enactment of Law No 23.696[242] in 1989.[243]

831. In this scenario, in which the State stopped, basically, participating in the production of goods, and the rendering of services, and started to have a control and regulation role, a countless number of new administrative structures appeared which were called regulatory agencies, which were given the main role of ensuring the good operation from the privatized sectors and to that end were granted administrative, normative and in some cases jurisdictional powers by the judicial order.

---

241. Nallar Dera and Daniel Mauro, *Regulación y control de los servicios públicos,* Marcial Pons, Bs. As., Madrid, Barcelona, 2010, p. 355 and the following. 'The privatization process in Argentina was deep and accelerated. The transfer of the assets from the public to the private sector was initiated in 1990. As evidence of that accelerated process, it is worth remembering that after three years of the beginning of such process, the most expensive agencies had already been sold, and a total of 9 billion dollars in cash had been collected and the external debt had been reduced for a value market of approximately 4,600 million dollars. The amounts for the sales of assets during the decade were 24,000 million dollars, if considered both the cash obtained and liabilities transferred. The privatization included oil companies, banks, railways, natural gas and electricity production, transportation and distribution companies, telecommunication companies, ports, water and sanitary services, iron and steel industry companies, chemical companies and those on the area of defence among others. The volume in sales for privatizations represented the 9% of the annual average GDP corresponding to the period 1990–1994' (Gerchunoff, Pablo; Greco, Esteban and Bondorevsky, Diego, 'Comienzos diversos, distintas trayectorias y final abierto: más de una década de privatizaciones en Argentina, 1990–2002', Serie Gestión Pública No 34, Instituto Latinoamericano y del Caribe de Planificación Económica y Social (ILPES), CEPAL, Santiago de Chile, April de 2003, p. 11, http://cdi.mecon.gov.ar/biblio/doc/cepal/gespub/34.pdf).
242. O. B. 23/8/89.
243. It is worth mentioning MATA, after the State Reform, the role of planning and setting of policies, service rendering, regulation, award of commissioning of rendering and control of services to the actors of the system were basically separated (MATA, Ismael, *Ensayos de derecho administrativo*, RAP, Bs. As., 2009, p. 104 and 'Panorama del control de los entes reguladores', EDA, 2001–610).

832. Thus, most of the regulatory frameworks gave the regulatory agencies the tasks as follows: (a) to make comply with the provisions of the regulatory framework and the concession contract, (b) to control the security and the service rendered by the regulated entity, (c) to prevent from anticompetitive and monopoly behaviours, (d) to apply sanctions to the companies due to the non-compliance of the obligations assumed, (e) to approve – if applicable – the expansion and improvement plan of the service and to control its compliance, (f) to deal with the users' claims, (g) to approve tariff schemes, (h) to create the favourable atmosphere before the National Executive Power for the assignment, extension and termination of contracts, etc.

833. The importance given to these entities determined that in the reform produced in the National Constitution of 1994 constitutional recognition was conferred to them in the new section. 42, paragraph 3.[244]

834. Even though the model adopted in Argentina was that of independent agency in the section, taken from '*Independent Regulatory Commission*' of the USA., the Argentinean regulatory agencies have substantial differences if compared with the model of references aforementioned.

835. In fact, in our country the regulating authorities are constituted as from the traditional figure of the continental European regime of the autonomous administrative entity,[245] in the context of the Public Administration. This was also the format used by other administrative agencies of regulation and control of economic sectors, already in existence at the moment of the creation of the regulatory agencies of public services, for instance, the Central Bank of the Republic[246] and the Office of the Superintendent of Insurance.[247]

---

244. *See* what we further elaborated in Chapter II. Régimen jurídico de los entes reguladores argentinos. Variedad institucional.

245. Cassagne, *Curso de derecho administrativo*, 11th ed., Thomson Reuters La Ley, Bs. As., 2016, t.I, pp. 318/319. As Marienhoff puts it an autonomous entity is a '*public state person that, with legal aptitude to administer itself, performs specific public roles*' (Marienhoff, Miguel S., *Tratado de Derecho administrativo*, 2nd ed., Abeledo-Perrot, Bs. As., 1977, t. I, p. 384).

246. The Central Bank is a national autonomous agency (s. 1, Law No 24.144 and its amendments). Section 4 from the Organic Chart, according to the amendment introduced under s. 3 of the Law No 26.739, sets forth: '*The powers and roles of the bank are: a) to regulate the operation of the financial systems and to apply the Law of Financial Entities and the rules therein set forth; b)The control the quantity of Money, the interest rate and to guide the credit; c) To act as the financial agent of the State and as the country's depositary and agent before the international monetary, banking and financial institutions to which the nation has adhered, as well as to have an active the role in the international integration and cooperation; d) To concentrate and administer the reserves in gold, Money and other external assets; e)To contribute to the good operation of the capital markets; f) To execute the exchange policy in complete agreement with the legislation enacted by the Honourable Congress of the Nation; g) To regulate, as far as its powers' concern, the systems of payment, the liquidation and compensation chambers, the fund remittances, the money carriers, as well as any other activity in relation to the exchange and financial activity; h)To grant the protection the rights of the users of financial services, the defence of competences coordinating its role with the competent public authorities on those matters. In the exercise of its powers and functions, the bank shall not be not subject to orders or instructions from the National Executive Branch,*

836. Thus, the Argentinean regulatory agencies are public State persons forming part of the Decentralized Public Administration, they do not depend on the legislative power, and, with some exceptions, they are under tutelary powers of the Executive Branch and they are submitted to its authority regarding appointment and removal of authorities, revision of decisions, the regulatory policy development and their budgetary support.[248]

837. This form of organization and framework of the regulatory entities is based upon the text of section 99, subsection 1° of the National Constitution that confers to the Executive Power the ownership of the leadership of the Public Administration and the role of the maximum political responsibility in the country's administrative organization.[249] However, such argument has been refuted by those who consider the constitutional category of the regulatory entities in the third paragraph of section 43 of the National Constitution under the denomination 'agency of control',[250] which allows to say that they are constitutional organs of necessary existence having wide operational autonomy, and so they have to operate independently from the powers of direction of the Executive Branch.[251]

---

neither shall it be entitled to undertake obligations of any kind and nature conditioning, restricting or delegating those powers without the expressed authorization of the Honourable Congress of the Nation'.

247. The Office of the Superintendent of Insurance is an autonomous entity in charge of exercise the supervision of the insurance and reinsurance in Argentina with the purpose of having an efficient, stable, solvent market (ss 64 and 65, Law No 20.091).

248. *See*: Cassagne, *Curso de Derecho Administrativo*, cit., t. I, p. 319.

249. *See*: Comadira, Julio R., 'Los sujetos reguladores en la postprivatización', RAP n° 183, p. 28.

250. The rule establishes: '*the legislation shall set forth efficient procedures for the prevention and solution of disputes, and the regulatory frameworks of the public services of national competences, providing the necessary participation of the consumers' and users' associations, and of the interested provinces, in the agencies of control*' as it can be read, the constitutional clause is very basic and it does not give many elements to understand what an '*agency of control*' means. In fact, in it there is no reference regarding the concrete role of such authorities, neither does contain any reference to the institutional design of the agencies of control, as it happens with other provisions incorporated by the same Constitution of 1994. For example s. 85 that when referring to the General Auditory of the Nation's, in which it clear establishes its roles and that it has '*operational autonomy*', or s. 86 regarding the Ombudsman, in which it is provided that '*it is an independent agency instituted by the Congress of the nation that will act with full functional autonomy, without receiving any instructions from any authority*'. Despite the laconic way of the text of s. 42 of the Constitution, it is implicit therein that for development of the role of control it is established the need that the agencies have the suitable and sufficient functional independence (autonomy) to that end award of differentiated judicial personality is instrumentally convenient.

251. Reiriz, María Graciela, 'Autoridades administrativas independientes para la regulación y control de los servicios públicos', collective work *Topic of Administrative Law in honour to Prof. Doctor Agustín A. Gordillo,* Editora Platense, la Plata, 2003, p. 277. In this sense Mario Rejtman Farah affirms that: 'These agencies are not, for our Money, similar to the autonomous institutional ones traditionally known, they do not have the modalities or characteristic thereof, pursuant to the traditional administrative organizational principles. Their aims, competences and functions and the special regulation set forth for them under 42 of the National Constitution give them differentiating notes and special features in comparison to the other ones.' (Rejtman Farah, Mario, '¿Independencia de los entes reguladores?'AA.VV *Cuestiones de intervención estatal Servicios públicos,* RAP, Bs. As., 2011, pp. 509 and the following).

838. Beyond the referred discrepancies, nationally speaking. the reality shows that most of the regulatory agencies of public services, have been constituted as autonomous entities,[252] and thus, as it was expressed by the Attorney's Office of the National Treasury, they conform to the Public Administration, and although they do not depend on the National Executive Branch in terms of hierarchy, such organ exercise the administrative or tutelary control over them, which does not cover the technical functions exclusively given to the regulatory agencies in their technical capacity, unless there is a case of an arbitrary act.[253]

839. All regulatory entities in Argentina are directed by a collegiate body called Board of Directors, which seeks to give to the regulatory decision more debate, derived from plurality of opinions, as well as more transparency. Moreover, so as to guarantee the technical aptitude and independence of the agencies, in general, in the sector regulatory frameworks, the members of the boards appointed must have a technical and professional background in the subject,[254] a system of incompatibilities and exclusive diligence in the execution of their role is established.[255]

840. The regulatory agencies of public services, whose regulation belongs to the Federal Administration, are subject to the control of Sindicatura General de la Nación[256] and the Auditoría General de la Naciòn[257] with exception of some specific formalities that have been specially regulated (e.g., administrative challenges and procedures for citizens' participation in the decision-making processes[258]) they are applied the rules of administrative procedures contained in the Decree Law No 19.549 and its regulatory Decree, 1759/72 (t.o. 1991).[259]

---

252. *See*, e.g., ENARGASENARGAS (s. 51, Law No 24.076); ENRE (s. 55, Law No 24.065); ORSNA (s. 16, Decree 375/97); ERAS (s. 2 of the Tripartite Treaty subscribed among the National State, the Province of Buenos Aires and the Administration of Buenos Aires Autonomous City, approved under Law No 26.221).
253. Judgments, Book 239, p. 115.
254. *See*, e.g., s. 58, Law No 24.065; 54, Law No 24.076 and 14, Decree 1.185/90.
255. Sections 59, Law No 24.065 and 55, Law No 24.076.
256. The Sindicatura General de la Nación (SIGEN) is the agency in charge of the internal control of the national public administration (ss 7 and 96 of the Law of Financial Administration and of the Control Systems in the National Public Sector, 24.156).
257. The Auditoría General de la Nación is a constitutional agency, with functional autonomy, technically assisting the Congress of the Nation in the exercise of the external control of the National Public Sector (s. 85 of the National Constitution and ss 7 and 118 of the Law No 24.156, in Financial Administration and the Control Systems in the National Public Sector).
258. In some regulatory frameworks, the public hearing was adopted for certain specific decisions. For example that is the case of the regulatory framework of the gas (ss 6, 16, 18, 29, 46, 47 and 68, Law No 24.156) and the electric regulatory framework (ss 11, 32, 49, 73 and 74, Law No 24.065).
259. Thus it is provided under ss 65, Law No 24.076 and 71, Law No 24.065; *see*: Tawil,, Guido S., 'El procedimiento administrativo ante los entes reguladores', in AAVV. *Procedimiento Administrativo*, Ciencias de la Administración, Bs. As., 1998, p. 253; and in *Estudios de Derecho Administrativo*, Abeledo-Perrot, Bs. As., 2012, p. 21; Fonrouge, Máximo 'Cuestiones del procedimiento Administrativo ante los entes reguladores', AA.VV., *Cuestiones de procedimiento administrativo*, Ediciones RAP, BS. As., 2006, p. 955 and Cicero, Nidia Karina, 'El procedimiento administrativo en los entes reguladores de los servicios públicos', AA VV., *Procedimiento Administrativo*, Tawil, Guido Santiago Director, Abeledo-Perrot, Bs. As., 2010, p. 543.

841. Apart from the common features afore-elaborated and present in most of the regulatory agencies in Argentina, they have substantial differences in their judicial regime that makes it difficult to systematize them.[260]

842. The reason for the heterogeneous panorama in the country is, contrary to other countries, where there was no master plan to define certain basic guidelines and premises to be considered in privatization projects, which was manifested in the respective regulatory frames and the creation of the regulatory bodies.[261]

843. Moreover, in the privatization operations not always were there homogenous objectives, clearly reflected in their economic and judicial regime. Thus, for instance, in the first privatizations, carried out in the early 1990s in a compelling macroeconomic framework, the priority was in fiscal matters due to the losses being generating by the public companies and the need for having fresh funds to finance the enormous budgetary deficit of the National State.[262] Consequently, the focus was on making those operations being attractive and successful more than making them efficient and competent.

844. The experience has demonstrated that those privatizations that were performed motivated by fiscal reasons had a more precarious design, which derived in a limited regulatory efficiency[263] and an evident lack of capacity in the use and development of instruments of control, all of which was clearly reflected in the regulatory administrative structure.[264]

---

260. Cassagne, *Curso de derecho administrativo,* cit., Book I, p. 318.
261. Martínez de Vedia, Rodolfo, *Los servicios públicos nacionales (situación actual)*, RAP, Bs. As., 2010, p. 16.
262. Gerchunoff, Pablo, Greco, Esteban and Bondorevsk, Diego, 'Comienzos diversos, distintas trayectorias y final abierto: más de una década de privatizaciones en Argentina, 1990–2002', Serie Gestión Pública No 34, Instituto Latinoamericano y del Caribe de Planificación Económica y Social (ILPES), CEPAL, Santiago de Chile, April 2003, http://cdi.mecon.gov.ar/biblio/doc/cepal/gespub/34.pdf.
263. In many cases, certainly, there had been initial mistakes that were further corrected and as consequences there were better and more satisfactory results.
264. Gerchunoff, Pablo, Greco, Esteban and Bondorevsk, Diego, 'Comienzos diversos, distintas trayectorias y final abierto: más de una década de privatizaciones en Argentina, 1990–2002', Serie Gestión Pública No 34, Instituto Latinoamericano y del Caribe de Planificación Económica y Social (ILPES), CEPAL, Santiago de Chile, April 2003, http://cdi.mecon.gov.ar/biblio/doc/cepal/gespub/34.pdf. In that sense, OSLAK points out: 'in several cases, the 'urgency' to privatize demoted the efficient design of the regulatory frame. The Argentinean case is paradigmatic in that sense. In the first stage of the reform of the State, the priority was to restrict the State intervention, what was verified, among other things, in the transfer of public companies to the private sector. This political orientation had great influence upon the sequence followed for the privatization of the services, the enactment of the regulatory frames and the creation of the corresponding regulatory agencies. The main problem, which would help explain the delayed creation of some regulatory agencies, was the lack of preset criteria about the expected way of operation of the services and the very same agencies of control.' (OSLAK, Oscar, 'Privatización y capacidad de regulación estatal: una aproximación teórico metodológica', published in the collective work *Política y gestión pública*, Bs. As., 2004, CLAD-Fondo de Cultura Económica, p. 24).

845. In contrast, in the cases where efficiency and progress were prioritized in the competitiveness of the economy, and in which the experience gained could be profited from, in general, had a more organized institutional design and a consistent regulatory design. Faithful is the example of the privatizations of gas and electric energy performed under the frame of the dispositions of Law No 24.076 and 24.065 that, as seen further on, are in general terms laws model in relation to powers conferred to the respective regulatory agencies created therein, that is ENARGAS and ENRE.[265]

846. Due to the serious crisis of the end of 2001, which originated the enactment of the Law of Emergency No 25.561, the Argentinean reality from that moment until 10 December 2015 – with the general claim of an ideological change regarding the role of the State in the economy – revealed a very deficient operation in the national regulatory agencies of public services, which became bureaucratic structures subordinated to the administration's political management. As a consequence, their technical independence was resented, and their regulatory and control capacity diminished as well; this due to the fact that there was a discordance between the situation of contracts affected by the economic emergency declared by Law No 25.561, the regulatory frameworks, and countless provisional measures taken in the context of the emergency in stark contrast with the pre-existing regulatory design.

847. Even though the institutional design of many entities contributed to the afore-elaborated situation – truth is told – not even those agencies with suitable regulatory designs could prevent the political authorities' interference and co-option. This was instrumented by means of irregular practices such as: the appointment of public officers without respecting the selection procedure provided to that effect, the transformation of collegiate agencies into unipersonal ones,[266] and even the administrative intervention in the regulatory agency.[267]

265. Bogo, Jorge, 'La organización institucional de los servicios públicos: una posible agenda de reformas', document drafted for the project 'Balance del proceso de transformación de los servicios de infraestructura en la República Argentina', Bs. As., 2004, p. 5 (http://www.fundacionfines.org.ar/12-2004/documents/Bogo/Jorge%20BOGO%20-%20Paper.doc).

266. Cf. s. 2 of Decree 1414/05, which modified s. 6 of Decree 87/01 when setting forth the Controller Agency of Traffic Concession would be in charge of and administered by an executive director instead of a Board of Directors as it had been formerly established in the decree which created such agency.

267. For example, this is what happened to the National Commission of Transport Regulation (CNRT), successively intervened as from the passing of Decree 454/01, with the National Commission of Telecommunications (CNC), whose intervention was established by the Decree 521/02 and which was intervened until its dissolution as a consequence of the creation of Federal Agency of Communication and Information Technology (AFTIC). The same was the National Regulatory Agency of Gas (ENARGASENARGAS) was intervened as from 2007 (Decree 571/07), for the term of ten years until the passing of Decree 594/2017 (O. B. 31/7/2017) which disposed the cessation of the intervention and the appointment of, previous corresponding method of selection, its vice president and three directors. Pursuant to s. 4 of such decree it was established that the President of ENARGASENARGAS' Board of Directors was going to be chosen by the National Executive Branch, and the role was going to be temporarily in charge of the Vice President of the collegiate body. Since the person elected to be the President of ENARGASENARGAS' Board of Directors – by bid

848. As from the change of governments occurred on the 10 December 2015, a process of normalization of the regulatory agencies operation was initiated by means of the application of regulatory frameworks and the integration of the authorities thereof pursuant to the regulations of the respective frameworks.[268]

– resigned, by means of Resolution 205-E/2017 from the Energy and Mining Ministry, there was a new bid to cover the vacant position. In relation to Interventions of the Regulatory Agencies *see*: Oteiza, Mariano, La Intervención Administrativa en Entes Reguladores. ¿Control efectivo u oportunismo gubernamental? in Revista de Administración Pública, nº 337, pp. 141 and the following.

268. So regarding the ENRE, by means of Decree 258/16 the appointment of the person as President of the Board of Directors was ratified, pursuant to its appointment under Decree 54/14; furthermore the vice president and first and second members of the board were appointed until the appointment of the professionals elected as a result of the application of the open bid procedure to be carried out pursuant to the terms of s. 58 of the Law No 24.065. In turn, under Decree 433/16 the first member of the Board was appointed. Pursuant to Decree 258/16, by means of Resolution 204 – E/2016 the Mining and Energy Ministry summoned the open bid for the appointment President, Vice President and first member of the Board of the ENRE and instructed the Electric Energy Department in the case they require from the Federal Council of Electric Energy, the presentation of the three 'eligible candidates' by this Council, so as to proceed to cover the post of Second and Third Member of the Board of the ENRE, pursuant to s. 58 of the Decree 1.398/92 and the procedure approved by said Council. With regard to the position of President of ENRE's Board, by means of Resolution 205-E/2017 a second call of election was summoned. Regarding the formation of ENARGAS-ENARGAS' Board, *see* explanation in previous note.

Chapter 2. Judicial Regime of the Argentinean Regulatory Agencies Institutional Variety

849. As it was afore-pointed out, Argentina does not have a general regulatory regime under which the roles and functions of the different actors of the regulatory process are regulated. The competences, powers, and organizational structure of the regulatory agencies are contemplated in a separated way in the respective regulatory frames of public services in the sector.

850. In Argentina, there is not such a thing a homogenous model or concept of the regulatory agency since there are relevant differences in different aspects in their configuration.

851. As follow, we will briefly mention the principal ones:

(a) *The opportunity of creating the regulatory agency.* In some case, the regulatory authority was created before the privatization of the service[269] and in other cases the other was about.[270]
(b) *The regulatory instrument creating the agency which confers the latter its powers.* In many cases this happened through decrees from the Executive Branch,[271] and in other cases means of a law.[272]
(c) *The procedures to appoint and remove authorities from the regulatory agencies.* At a national level, only in the cases of the electricity regulatory agency (ENRE[273]) and gas regulatory agency (ENARGAS)[274] it is established that the members of their respective Boards of Directors are to be elected by the Executive Branch, for the term of five years, with the Congress intervention, based upon open selection procedures. In turn, as regards the removal of the members

269. For example, Telephones.
270. For example, Gas and Electricity.
271. Under Decree 1.185/90 the National Commission of Telecommunications was created (CNT). After that, by means of 31 of the Decree 660/96, with amendments introduced by similar 952/96 and 1.260/96, National Commission of Telecommunications was created as from the merger of CNT and the National Commission of Post and Telegraph (CNCT). Then, under Law No 27.078 the Federal Agency of Information Technology was created (AFTIC), assuming the role of regulation and control of the Communication Secretariat of the Nation and the CNC. By means of Decree 267/2015 The National Agency of Telecommunications (ENACOM) was created a conferred the competencies of the AFTIC and the Federal Agency of Audiovisual Communication (AFSCA), with basis on the need of a unique agency in the context of technological concurrence. In turn, by means of s. 40 of Decree 660/96 the National Regulation Commission of Transport was created (CNRT), as from the merger of the National Commission of Automobile Transport (CONTA), created by Decree 104/93 and its amendments and the National Commission of Railways Transport (CNTF) created by Decree 1836/93 and its amendments; the CNRT will act as a decentralized agency in the scope of Work and Public Services Secretariat of the Ministry of Economy, Works and Public Services.
272. This way happened with the electric energy regulatory agency (s. 54, Law No 24.065), gas regulatory agency (s. 50, Law No 24.076) and water regulatory agency (Law No 23.696, Annex I, ap. III and Decree 999/92; nowadays s. 4, Law No 26.221).
273. Section 57, Law No 24.065.
274. Section 53, Law No 24.076.

of the board of said agencies, the regulatory frame establishes this can be based upon a justified decision from the Executive Power, prior communication of the reasons of the decision to the National Congress Commissions, the one that *must* in the case of ENARGAS and *may* in the case of ENRE answer within the term of thirty running days.[275]

In the rest of the regulatory frameworks of public services, appointment procedures ensuring the professional judgment and independence of the members of the board have not been stipulated, so the appointments remain at the Executive Branch's discretion.[276]

(d) *The nature and the scope of the powers conferred to the agencies.* All the regulatory frameworks confer executive, normative powers and those of control and sanction, those for dispute resolutions under the sector of their supervision to the agencies; however, there are deep-rooted differences regarding their extension and content.

As an example it is worth mentioning the big differences in the powers conferred to solve disputes. In some case, it is obligatory to submit the individuals' controversies to the resolutely competences of the agency (ENARGAS,[277] ENRE[278] and the Regulatory Agency of the Airports National System (ORSNA)[279]) before submitting the dispute to judicial courts, where in other cases this is optional (e.g., former Telecommunications National Commission (CNC)[280] and Health and Water Regulatory Agency (ERAS)[281]).

---

275. Sections 55, second paragraph, Law No 24.076; and 59, second paragraph, Law No 24.065.
276. Despite the appointment procedure of the agencies' authorities – with prior merit bid and the participation of the legislative power – that does not guarantee per se that political criteria will be applied or not on them, – it is clear that it is potentially superior than the one of a mere discretional selections. Obviously, it is useless to have bid procedures of selection if, afterwards, they are not followed or are biased. This is the reason for the relevance of decisions such the one passed 10 September 2009 by Room V of the National Federal Court of Appeals on Contentious and Administrative Matters by which a complaint lodged by an NGO's users and consumers was sustained and they ordered the Department of Energy to arbitrate the necessary means to perform a public bid and to comply with the rules established in The Procedures to appoint the members of the ENRE's Board of Directors (file 'A.C.I.J. and other v. E.N.', LL, 2009-F, 500). Such judgment was Rex Judicata after the Supreme Court overruled the appealed file submitted.
277. Section 66, para. 1, Law No 24.076:'Any and all controversy arising between subjects under this law, as well as all kinds of interested third parties, whether physical or legal person, due to capitation, treatment, transport, storage, distribution and commercialization services of gas, shall be previously and obligatory submitted to the agency's jurisdiction'.
278. Section 72, Law No 24.065 'Any and all controversy arising between generators, carriers, distributors, large users, due to the supply or the public service of transport and distributions of electricity, shall be previously and obligatory submitted to the agency's jurisdiction. It is optional for the users or all kinds of interested third parties, whether physical or legal person, due to the same reasons as the ones elaborated in this section, to submit themselves to the prior and obligatory agency's jurisdiction'.
279. Section 29 of Decree 375/97 establishes: 'Any and all controversy arising between physical or legal person due to reasons derived from the administrative and/or exploitation of the airport National System of Airports shall be previously and obligatory submitted to the Regulatory agency's jurisdiction of the National System of Airports which is the only one administrative body with jurisdictional powers on this matter'.
280. Section 6, subs. q), Decree 1185/90.
281. Section 42, subs. k), Annex 2, Law No 26.261.

(e) *The means of challenge in administrative and judicial courts of the acts issued by the agency.* There are several differences in this regards and no uniform criteria, so it is necessary to analyse the regulations in each sector to know the ways of challenge in administrative and judicial courts of the acts issued by the regulatory agencies and by the controller agencies, according to the case.[282]

Beyond those cases in which there is specific regulation, in the national order, the judicial and administrative challenge of the decisions of all regulatory agencies are subject the provisions in the legislation of administrative procedures, contained in the Decree Law No 19.549, and its regulations (Decree 1759/72, T.O. 1991).

852. By virtue of the laws or pursuant to provisions in some regulatory frameworks (e.g., gas and electricity regulatory frameworks) and with the exception of some specific cases, as a general rule, the decisions of the regulatory agencies, as autonomous entities, are susceptible of being challenged by means of an administrative remedy before agencies of the central administration. This has received harsh criticism from the part of the doctrine as this produce a clear vulnerability in the independence of the agencies.[283]

---

282. As an example it is worth mentioning the regulatory framework of gas which clearly expresses that the jurisdictional punishable actions are challengeable in judicial courts by means of direct judicial remedies before the National Federal Contentious Administrative Court of Appeals and there is term of fifteen days for the first of the cases and thirty days for the rest. In turn, for other challenges of other types of decisions made by ENARGASENARGAS it is possible to lodge an appeal with an intermediate Appellate Court for review of the decision of a public body, if rejected it gives the right of the judicial revision by means of lodging a direct remedy before the Court aforementioned.

    On the other hand, the regulatory framework for electricity, the same as the gas regime, lays down that: 'the applicable sanctions by the agency can be challenged before the National Federal Contentious Administrative Court of Appeals by means of a direct remedy within thirty working judicial days after its notification (s. 81, second paragraph, Law No 24.065)' and it is stated that 'The resolutions of the agency may be challenged by means of an appeal lodged with an intermediate appellate court for review of the decision under the Terms laid down in the National Law of Administrative Procedures and its regulatory provisions. After that the appeal will proceed in the judicial court before the National Federal Contentious Administrative Court of Appeals (s. 76, Law No 24.065). However, different from the regulatory framework of the gas, a judicial direct remedy regarding the agency's jurisdictional decisions is not contemplated. The same as in the Law No 24.076, in the Decree 375/97, regulating the operation of the Regulatory Agency of the National System of Transport it is set forth *that* the decision of a jurisdictional nature of the agency '*will use up the administrative way*' (s. 30, Decree 375/97). As there is no specific judicial way the challenge of the cited act shall be submitted before the federal administrative contentious bodies of original jurisdiction federal capital, pursuant to provisions under Title IV of the Decree Law 19.549.

283. Conf. Gordillo, Agustín, *Tratado de derecho administrativo y obras selectas*, FDA, 1st ed. Bs As, 2013, Chapter XV, pp. 7/8 and Uslenghi, Alejandro, 'Reforma de organismos de control de los servicios públicos', AA.VV *Derecho Administrativo y aportes para el rediseño institucional de la República*, Revista Jurídica de Buenos Aires, Abeledo-Perrot, Bs. As., 2004, pp. 150/151.

Chapter 3. The National Regulatory Agency of Gas (ENARGAS) and the National Regulatory Agency of Electricity (ENRE)

Creation

853. The regulatory frameworks of transport services, and electricity and natural gas distribution were the first, in the process of privatization carried during the 1990s that were instrumented by means of a law from the National Congress.

854. There is great consensus about the importance of this circumstance, and also a greater consistence in terms of the regulation contained therein. It is worth highlighting, notwithstanding the intrinsic differences of the industries regulated by laws 24.076 and 24.065, that the regulatory frameworks are structured on the basis of similar designs; especially in relation to institutional, procedural, aspects as well as regarding the functions and attributions of the regulatory agencies – except for minor differences – they are almost identical.

855. As regards the gas industry, Law No 24.076 created the National Regulatory Agency of Gas (ENARGAS),[284] an administrative authority of an autonomous nature, which basically has the competences of regulation and control of the transport and distribution of natural gas.[285,286]

At the same time, in the electric energy sector, by means of Law No 24.065 the National Regulatory Agency of Electricity was created (ENRE),[287] also as an administrative authority of antonymous nature,[288] with power to regulate and control the transport and distribution of electricity.[289]

856. Both the ENARGAS and the ENRE have a Board of Directors with five members, who have to be chosen among people with professional and technical background in the field. The members are appointed by the National Executive Branch for a five-year period, which can be renewed indefinitely. Moreover, the mandates will expire at one-year intervals.[290]

284. Section 50, Law No 24.076.
285. Section 51, Law No 24.076.
286. Section 50, Law No 24.076 The cited rule provides that this agency must have in each distribution area a minimum sufficient structure to deal with the relationship between the distributors and users in each area.
287. Section 54, Law No 25.065.
288. Section 55, Law No 25.065.
289. Sections 50 and 52 subs. a), Law No 24.076.
290. Sections 53 and 54, Law No 24.076 and 57 and 58, Law No 24.065.

857. So as to allows such intervals both regulatory frameworks provide that the Executive Branch must establish different duration terms in the board members' mandates, that is to say, when appointing the first member of ENARGAS y el ENRE.[291]

Powers

858. Regarding the powers granted to the regulatory agencies under the law of creation, the doctrine has proposed different classifications.

859. As far as Nallar is concerned he points out that 'the regulatory agencies' powers and duties are, truth be told, numerous and unlimited'[292] and he classifies them upon the basis of 'four essential functions': to control, to rule, to apply the sanctions and to settle disputes as an arbitrator.[293]

860. We, not having the intention of classifying them, will describe the most important powers conferred to the natural gas and electricity agencies pursuant to their regulatory frames.

861. It is worth saying that all the powers of the regulatory agencies are to be exercised under the principle of speciality, by virtue of which Cassagne elaborates: 'the scope of action of the administrative body is previously limited by rule (especially due to its aim) and cannot be extended by the public agent's mere will. This principle covers explicit and implicit powers (e.g., derivation or extension of expressed provision), as well as the inherent powers arising directly from the objectives in regulatory frameworks of creation of the agency, with the exception of the powers to establish tax provisions or those covered by zone of legal reserve (creation of taxes, duties or other sanctions) where a law from the Congress is required'.[294]

Regulatory Competences

862. Regarding ENARGAS and ENRE's regulatory powers, and notwithstanding the nature and basis of the regulatory legislation implied in the powers,[295] the following can be pointed out:

---

291. Sections 54, Law No 24.076 and 58, Law No 24.065. Identical solution must be used in the hypothesis of the intervention of such regulatory agencies, for the integration of the first board as from its normalization, that is, after the end of the intervention.
292. Nallar, *La regulación* económica, cit., p. 382.
293. Nallar, cit., pp. 383 and the following.
294. Cassagne, *Curso de derecho administrativo,* cit., t.I, p. 237.
295. On this item further elaboration on, Perrino, Pablo E., *Naturaleza y Fundamento de la potestad normativa de los entes reguladores de servicios públicos*, Revista de Derecho Administrativo No 75, Bs. As., 2011 pp. 186 and the following.; Comadira, Julio Pablo, *La potestad normativa de los entes reguladores*, Revista Argentina del Régimen de la Administración Pública No 405, Bs. As., 2015.

(1) To lay down rules of procedure to which the so-called *subject to the law n 24.076,*[296] that is: carriers, distributors, marketers, storage agencies and consumers who directly contract with the natural gas producer, and the producers, carriers, distributors and users of electricity in the frame in the provisions under Law No 24.065, in relation to: (i) security, (ii) technical standards and procedures, (iii) consumption billing and measurement, (iv) control and use of meters, (v) interruption and reconnection of the supplies, (vi) access to property by third parties, (vii) quality.[297]
(2) To establish the basis for the calculation of tariffs for carriers and distributors.[298]
(3) To approve the tariffs applied by the renderers (ENARGAS).[299]
(4) ENARGAS in conferred the power of laying down rules of procedures so as to guarantee that the carriers and distributors establish plans and procedures for the maintenance in good condition of the goods affected by the service for the period of the respective commissions.[300] The attribution of such power may have its basis on the fact that the model of privatization implied – different from the electric sector that resorted to the modality of concession[301] – the transfer of the assets from the National State.[302]

Control Powers

863. Regarding the powers related to the activity of control, the regulatory frameworks confer powers to both ENARGAS and ENRE:

(1) To intervene in the assignment, extension, expiration or replacement of the concessions.[303]
(2) To solicit the renderers the necessary documents and information to check the compliance of the regulatory framework and the rest of the laws, as well as the terms of the contracts (certifications, contracts of concession, whether that is in the sector of gas or electricity) and to carry out inspections.[304] This generic attribution is the matrix where a countless number of administrative acts are based upon, tending to materialize the role of control of the public services granted to the agencies.

---

296. Section 9 of the Law No 24.076.
297. Section 52 subs. b), Law No 24.076 and 56 subs. b), Law No 24.065. it is worth mentioning that in relation to security, quality and odorization ENARGASENARGAS competence also covers compressed natural gas (s. 52, subsection), Law No 24.076).
298. Section 52 subs. e), Law 24.076 y 56, subs. d) Law No 24.065.
299. Sections 42 and 52 subs. f), Law No 24.076 and 42 subs. c) and 43, Law No 24.065.
300. Section 52, subs. c), Law No 24.076.
301. Section 3, Law No 24.065.
302. In the model design of privatization of natural gas transport and distribution services, the transfer of the goods conforming the equipment of the public services has taken place.
303. It is the ENARGASENARGAS and ENRE's role to favour before the Executive Power, when it applies, the assignment, extension, expiration, or replacement of the concessions (s. 52 subs. j), Law No 24.076 and 56 subs. h) Law No 24.065).
304. Section 52, subs. o), Law No 24.076 and s. 56, subs. n), Law No 24.065.

(3) To apply sanctions,[305] with the prior development of the administrative procedure, in which the constitutional right of the effective administrative stewardship should be respected[306] (section 18 of the National Constitution).

Other powers of administrative nature

864. Both ENARGAS and ENRE, apart from their role of regulation and control, have other powers directly related or derived from them:

(1) To set the terms and conditions of the public tender for the natural gas transport and distribution certifications award[307] or the electricity transport and distribution concessions.[308]
(2) To authorize easement of the pipeline passage, transit, use and occupation of installation in favour of transport and distribution licensees of natural gas[309] and electro ducts.[310]
(3) To organize and apply the public hearing regimes,[311] to publish report and to give counsel to the natural gas and electricity industries' actors.[312]

865. Moreover, both regulatory frameworks establish an expressed and identical general clause of power of attorney, by means of which ENARGAS and ENRE are granted the power to '*to perform any and all further acts necessary for the best performance of their duties and the provisions of this law*'.[313]

Powers for the settlement of controversies

866. Apart from the control and regulation powers, the gas and electricity frameworks confer ENARGAS and ENRE the special role of settling certain controversies in the administrative stage prior and obligatory to the judicial one.

---

305. Sections 52, subs. o), Law No 24.076 and 56, subs. o), Law No 24.065.
306. Perrino, Pablo E. 'El derecho a la tutela administrativa efectiva', AA.VV. El Derecho Administrativo hoy. 16 años después', Jornadas organizadas por la Universidad Austral, Facultad de Derecho, RAP, Bs. As., 2013, pp. 75 and the following.
307. Section 52, subss h), i), Law No 24.076.
308. Section 52, subs. f), Law No 24.065.
309. Section 52, subs. k and concordant 22 and 23, Law No 24.076 and s. 56 subs. i) and 81, Law No 24.065.
310. Sections 52, subs. i) and 18, Law No 24.065.
311. Sections 52, subs. l), Law No 24.076 and 56 subs. j), Law No 24.065.
312. Section 52, subss p) and s), Law No 24.076 and 56 subs. ñ), Law No 24.065 – By virtue of provisions under Decree 1738/92, the annual reports with the news produced during the year, the performance in the industry in aspects such as claims from the clients, compliance with the service standards, infraction to the security standards, etc. and even a suppliers' merit order for their performance in these matters shall be published.
313. Section 52 subss x), Law No 24.076 and 56 subs. s), Law No 24.065. *See*: Vázquez, Claudio, 'Algunas reflexiones sobre la naturaleza jurídica de las potestades de los entes reguladores de servicios públicos privatizados', Revista Argentina de Derecho de la Energía, Hidrocarburos y Minería (RADEHM), No 4, pp. 1 and the following.

867. Thus, section 66 of the Law No 24.076 sets forth: 'Any and all controversy arising between the subjects of this law, the same as from any interested third party, whether physical or judicial persons, due to collection, treatment, storage, distribution and commercialization services of gas, shall have to be prior and obligatory submitted to the agency's jurisdiction.'

The agency's decisions of a jurisdictional nature can be appealed in the Federal National Contentious Administrative Court of Appeal of the Federal Capital:

> The remedy shall be filed founded before the Agency within fifteen (15) days of the notification of the resolution. The appeal shall be submitted before the Court within five (5) days counting as from the lodge of the remedy and a copy shall serve to the other party for fifteen (15) days.[314]

868. The subjects to the law – referred to in the first paragraph of the transcribed provision are the ones referred to in the second paragraph of section 9 of the same legal body that is: the carriers, distributors, marketers, storage companies and consumers directly hiring with producer. However, an ample interpretation on section 66 of the Law No 24.076, has allowed to construe all users – instead of those hiring directly with the producer – are submitted in its scope of application.[315]

869. Furthermore, regarding the residential users, there are alternative procedures before the administrative authorities of the consumers' advocacy, pursuant to the Consumer's Advocacy Law No 24.240, amended by Law No 26.361.[316] However, when the controversy refers specifically to the tariffs ENARGAS has exclusive competence.[317]

870. In turn, from the objective or material view, the dispute of the cited section must refer to collection, treatment, transport, storage, distribution and commercialization of gas.

871. As far as the ENRE is concerned, section 72, paragraph 1 of the Law No 24.065 establishes: 'Any and all dispute arising between generators, carriers, distributors, large users, due to the supply or public service of transport and distribution of electricity shall be submitted prior and obligatory to the agency's jurisdiction.'

However, the second paragraph of such section establishes the non-binding character of such intervention in certain cases: the prior and obligatory submission to

314. About the type of procedure and scope of the decisions taken under one or another regime, further consultation in Boullade, Gustavo and Massimino, Leonardo, 'Marco Regulatorio del Gas en Argentina', en *Derecho Administrativo, Legislación Usual Comentada*, Karina Cicero, directora, La Ley, B. A., 2015, Book IV, pp. 522 and the following.
315. Boullade and Massimino, *supra*, Book IV, p. 521.
316. *See*: Perrino, Pablo E. 'Algunos comentarios acerca del régimen jurídico de protección de los usuarios de servicios públicos', AA.VV. *Derechos, garantías y potestades en los contratos públicos,* Ediciones RAP, B. A., 2014, 75.
317. Boullade and Massimino, *supra*, Book IV, p. 524.

the agency is optional for the users, as well as for interested third parties, *whether physical or legal, due to the same reasons under this section.*

872. It is worth further saying that the issue of the jurisdictional roles of the regulating agencies of public services for the settlement of disputes and its scope has been a controversial issue in the whole country.[318]

873. The Supreme Court of the Nation in *'Angel Estrada' case*, in which the constitutionality of ENRE's powers to settle disputes of net worth content arisen between users and public service renderers were examined, established that, the constitutional principle of trial by defence and due process under section 18 of the National Constitution and the prohibition for the Executive Branch to exercise judicial functions (section 109), are safeguarded as long as: *(i) 'The bodies of the administration with conferred powers to settle disputes between private persons have been created by law', (ii) 'their independence and impartiality are guaranteed',*[319] *(iii) 'the economic and political objective considered by the legislator to create them (and to restrict the jurisdiction the national Constitution confers to the ordinary justice) has been reasonable' and (iv) 'it decisions are subject to the ample and sufficient judicial control'.*[320]

874. About this, in the afore-cited case 'Ángel Estrada', the high tribunal pristinely and emphatically established that 'no any controversy shall be validly deferred to the administrative body knowledge with the mere condition that its decisions shall be subject to an ulterior sufficient judicial control. The reasons considered by the legislator *to take the matter out of the jurisdiction of the ordinary judges*

---

318. *See*, among others: Cassagne, Juan Carlos, 'Las facultades jurisdiccionales de los entes reguladores (regarding "Ángel Estradas case)", LL, 2005-C, 736; Bianchi, Alberto B., 'Algunas precisiones sobre el alcance de las facultades jurisdiccionales de los entes reguladores', El Derecho Administrativo (EDA) 00/01–449 and 'Qué son los entes reguladores (Notes on the internal coherence of its judicial regime), ED 186–675; Coviello, Pedro J.J., '¿Qué es la jurisdicción primaria? Su aplicación a nuestro ordenamiento (as it was mentioned in Estrada's case)' El Derecho Administrativo (EDA) 2005–429; Mata, Ismael, 'Panorama del control sobre los entes reguladores', El Derecho Administrativo (EDA) 00/01–610; Comadira, Julio Rodolfo, *Derecho Administrativo. Acto administrativo. Procedimiento administrativo. Otros estudios*, Lexis Nexis Abeledo-Perrot, 2nd ed., B. A., 2003, p. 662; Aguilar Valdez, Oscar R., 'Reflexiones sobre las funciones jurisdiccionales de los entes reguladores de servicios públicos a la luz del control judicial de la Administración -con especial referencia al Ente Regulador del Gas y de la Energía Eléctrica-', Anuario de Derecho de la Universidad Austral, Vol. I, Abeledo-Perrot, 1994, pp. 181 and the following; Huici, Héctor, 'La actividad jurisdiccional de los entes reguladores', LL, 1996-B, 843.
319. In the case 'Litoral Gas S.A.', in which the legal status of ENARGASENARGAS was examined, The Court considered that 'the formal guarantees of independence and neutrality set forth for its actuation in the Law No 24.076 – Cf. ss 53, 54 and 55 of that legal body on appointment and removal of the agency's directors – are not enough to categorize it as an administrative court' (Rulings: 321:776).
320. Rulings: 328:651. Cassagne when examining the judgment passed by the National Supreme Court in the case 'Estrada 'it reads: ' … as long as the jurisdiction is maintained, the way has been closed to those who pretend open it to create administrative courts hearing, with established competence as a general clause, in the administrative disputes (in the same way the possibility of commissioning those courts of controversies between private parties has been closed, regulated by Civil Law)' (Cassagne: *Curso de Derecho Administrativo*, cit. t. I, p. 47).

has to be reasonably founded since, the administrative jurisdiction so created would otherwise lack constitutional support, and would entail a wrong interpretation of powers granted under section 116 of the National Constitution which defines them as exclusive of the Judicial Branch of the Nation. To admit that the Congress could delegate judicial administration powers to the agencies without material limitation whatsoever it would as unconceivable as to let the legislator delegate the substance of his own legislative functions which is absolutely prohibited under section 76 on the National Constitution, unless it is expressly provided'.[321]

875. To further elaborate on the matter, the Court has also laid down that to grant jurisdictional powers to an administrative body, the '*principle of speciality*' should be taken into account according to which such endowment is only possible 'in topics related to the reasons considered by the legislator to create the agency in question' and that would entail the application of a specific statutory or regulatory regime.[322]

876. Based on those arguments, the High Court concluded that ENRE did not have competence to fix compensation for damages.[323]

877. After six years of the judgment delivered in the case 'Ángel Estrada', on 13 July 2011,[324] the National Federal Contentious Administrative Court of Appeals passed a plenary decision in which it examined the constitutional validity of the powers of ENRE to condemn the electric energy distributors to compensate the users for the value of replacement of the objects damaged due to deficiency in the technical quality of the energy supply (section 72 of the Law No 24.065).

878. Most of the judges in such Court affirmed that in such case, different from 'Ángel Estrada', in which a compensation for loss of earning had been claimed, in this case the payment of the emerging damage was claimed (repair of the damaged object) with the basis on section 3 subsection e) from the Electric Energy Supply regulations,[325] which typifies a type of claim that the regulatory agency has been solving since its inception in 1993 in defence of the users' rights of electricity as a public service and with no judicial appeal from the part of the distributor. After that, it was highlighted that the power of ENRE to fix the compensation set forth under provisions cited is an aspect that the Court considered not necessary to analyse, in

321. Whereas 14.
322. Whereas 15 and 16 *in fine*.
323. It has been construed that an exception to such guideline is in s. 22 of the 24.076 which grants ENERGAS the power to fix a temporary compensation in the cases of controversies produced in facilities or licensees of natural gas distribution or transport services as a consequence of the Constitution of easement (Boullade and Massimino, *supra*, pp. 521 and the following).
324. Case '*Edesur S.A. v. Resolution 361/05 ENRE-RS 568/08 SE*', sentence from 13/7/2011, LL 011-E, 360 -DJ 23/11/2011, 74. *See*: note of the ruling Rejtman Farah, Mario, 'La competencia de los entes reguladores para determinar el daño directo a la luz del plenario 'EDESUR'', Quote Online: AP/DOC/472/2012 and 'Sobre la incompetencia de los entes reguladores para resolver reclamos por daños y perjuicios' Regarding CNACAF's plenary decision, in the case '*Edesur S.A. v. resolutoin ENRE 568/08*', Buenader, Eduardo, El Derecho Administrativo 2012–190 [2012].
325. Resolution ENRE No 82/2002.

the light of the factual context posed in 'Ángel Estrada'.[326] After that it was explained that: if the ruling were not construed applying the reasonability criteria, it would be considered that that decision would be *suitable for each person whose electric devise were affected due to the insufficient supply by the energy company – at first not protected from the liability for unforeseeable event or* force majeure – *to file a complaint to obtain compensation for the value of replacement of such damaged object. The lack of reasonability of that effect would be so evident that it is unnecessary to further elaborate on that to prove it. (Cf. in the same sense PTN, Rulings: 256:358).*

879. Based upon the aforesaid and expressing that 'each individual has the right to protect their own economic interests and to have efficient procedures for the prevention and settlement of disputes (section 42 NC) and the State's duty is to provide such protection and that includes the legislative, administrative and jurisdictional functions', the Court concluded that National Regulatory Agency of Electricity (ENRE) was competent to repair the emerging damage – repair value of replacement of the damaged object – when the users thus solicit it (cf. section 72, Law No 24.065).[327]

Powers regarding the defence of the competition

880. As follows Special reference of the powers ENARGAS are ENRE are endowed with under section 52, subsection d) of the Law No 24.076 and 56 subsection c) of the Law No 24.065, respectively, with reference to defence of the competition.

881. Pursuant to such regulations – of the same kind – as regulatory agencies they are endowed with powers in relation to anticompetitive, monopolist and unduly

326. From this ruling it was argued that: '*once the contractual failure to compliance was proved from the part of the distributor from the part of the ENRE, the fixing of the value of the damage of a determined object it does not mean the ENRE is invading the Judicial Branch role, as it is just the mere act of knowing a simple piece of information: how much the device is in the market according to the quality and the brand. The cycle if exercise of such competence and jurisdiction is completed when giving the user a certificate recognizing his right, and freeing him from the process for the judicial co-validation in the case the distributor does not pay in the administrative court*' and that '*the distributors of electricity had previously agreed for the ENRE to have the jurisdictional power, any time the Regulations of Supply are part of the Terms and Conditions of the Concession Contract*'.

327. In the dissident vote of the judges Jorge Eduardo Morán and Pablo Gallegos Fedriani it was sustained that: '*not only is the ENRE incompetent to fix any compensation derived from damages, but also it is not their task to deal with and submit to its jurisdiction the Distributor's responsibility in these cases*'. It was further said: '*In the case of granting itself a power which belongs to the judicial branch, the ENRE would be incurring in subjugation and it would be consequently deriving in the resolution of cases not of its competences affecting among others the principle of divisions of powers.' It was further asserted: 'in the case of "Angel Estrada" has been set clear that in our highest court's criteria, the intervention of the ENRE was irrelevant – criteria extendible to other cases with the same goal – in issues that exceed the strictly regulatory competence which has been conferred by law of its creation and thus it has no power to decide about compensation for damages to a user who considered himself damaged for the interruption of the service*'.

discriminatory behaviours among the participants of each of the stages in the industry, producers and consumers included.[328] It is worth pointing out, in furtherance, that in relation to defence of the competition, provisions of the Law No 25.156 are also applicable to the industry under analysis regulating all concerns about research and sanctions of the actions considered restrictive of the free competition, that is to say, the analysis of actions or behaviours that may affect the competition in a relevant market as well as all concerns about structural politics or control of economic concentrations, which implies a prospective analysis on how the relevant market would operate if the concentration operation was completed, whose aim is to prevent situations of concentration that would incite or ease conducts prohibited by law.

882. Pursuant to that, it is important to say that the articulation of such competences ins structured on the basis of the regulator's pre-emptive intervention, by means of the creation and incentive of conditions for the competition through the regulatory practice, whereas the authority of the defence of competition has an *ex post intervention* whether facing the hypothesis of a possible anticompetitive behaviour[329] or the intervention in operations that can be cases of economic concentration affecting the relevant market.

---

328. This power has relationship with the prohibition of the natural gas and electricity carriers and distributors and the electric energy generators to perform acts implying disloyal competition or abuse of their domineering position in the market under ss 23 of Law No 24.076 and 19 of the Law No 24.065.

329. Section 2 of the Law No 25.156 establishes that: 'the following behaviours, among others, as long as they constitute the hypothesis of s. 1, are restrictive practices of the competitions: a) To fix, agree, or manipulate in a direct or indirect way the sales or purchase price of goods and services offered to or demanded from the market, as well as to exchange information with the very same object or effect) To establish obligations to produce, process, distribute, buy or commercialize just a restricted or limited quantity of goods, or to render a service restricted or limited in number, volume or frequency; c) To distribute horizontally zones, market, clients and sources of supply; d) To coordinate or agree positions in bids or tenders; e) To arrange the limitation or control of the technical development or the investments destined to the production of commercialization of goods and services; f) To block, or make it difficult to third parties the entrance or stay in a market or simple to exclude them; g) To fix, impose or practice directly or indirectly, in agreement with competitors or individually, in any way whatsoever, prices and conditions of sales or purchase of goods, rendering of services or of production; h) To regulate markets of goods or services, by means of agreements to limit or control the technological research and development, the production of goods, or the rendering of services or to hinder investment destined to the production of goods or services or the distribution thereof; i) To subordinate the sale of an item to the acquisition of another or the rendering of a service to the use of another or to the acquisition of an item; j) To subject the sale or purchase to the condition of not using, acquiring, selling, or supplying goods or services produced, processed, distributed or commercialized by third parties; k) To impose discriminatory conditions for the acquisition or purchase of goods and services without a founded reason in commercial customs and uses; l) To refuse with no founded reason to meet concrete orders for the purchase or sale of goods or services, done under the current conditions of the respective market; m) To postpone the supply of a monopolist domineering service in the market for the beneficiary of a public service or that of public interest; n) To transfer goods or render services lower than the cost, without founded reasons in the commercial customs and uses with the aim of displacing the competition or causing damage to the image or net worth or the value of the brands of their suppliers of goods or services'.

883. In relation to the last case, section 16 of the Law No 25.156 establishes that 'when an economic concentration involves a company or person whose economic activity is regulated by the national State through a regulatory agency, the national Court of Defence of the Competition, before the adoption of a resolution, shall solicit to that state agency a report with founded opinion on the proposal of economic concentration in relation to the impact of such competition on the market or regarding the compliance with the respective regulatory frame. This state agency shall inform in that respect within the term of a maximum of 90 days, after the term has expired it shall be deemed that it has no objection thereof'.

884. Law No 25.156 does not exclude from its scope of material or subjective application the sectors regulated in general, or public services, in particular; it further provides under section 59 the derogation of any power of competition related to the object or aim of such legal body given to other State agencies or institutions. So, under the provisions in Law No 25.156, before its bodies and pursuant to The Procedures provided therein, issues related to anticompetitive conducts or behaviours, as well as those concerning economic concentrations involving regulated sectors are resolved, in this case, with the intervention of the regulating agency in the scope of the provisions of the precited section 16.[330]

330. Prior to the enactment of Law No 25.156, ENARGAS construed and applied provisions under Law No 22262 and the National Commission of Defence of Competition had the opportunity of explaining the scope of its competence and that of the regulatory agencies in the sense that the latter ones are in condition to perform the follow-up of the conducts of the companies licensees of public services. Furthermore, during the validity term of the Law No 22.262, since it did not contemplate the economic concentrations, the role of prevention in situations or conducts of anticompetitiveness and the control in the maintenance of the requirements of vertical and horizontal segmentation regarding gas natural transport and distribution were carried out by the regulatory agency. For further elaboration on the issue *see*: Aguilar Valdez, Oscar, 'Entes reguladores de servicios públicos. Apuntes sobre su funcionamiento y perspectiva en argentina', *Revista Ibero-Americana de Direito Público*, year 4, 2nd three-month period 2003, Volume X, América Jurídica, Brazil, pp. 203 and the following.

Part VI. Energy: Investment & Dispute Settlement

Chapter 1. Social Development and Energy Investment

885. The importance of having cheap and abundant energy to accompany economic growth and population's standard of living improvement is constantly pointed out. However, and especially in countries with a lower rate of relative development, as in the case of Argentina, it is observed that, even though they are rich in resources, great quantities of population lacked access to gas and electricity services; and so the official budgets are forced to incur very expensive costs and import energy products to meet the population and productive system's basic needs. According to the Inter-American Development Bank (BID), in Latin America and the Caribbean, about 34 million people lack access to modern electricity services and fuel imports increase the smallest countries' public expenditure.[331]

886. Argentina has unbeatable conditions to carry out energy investment projects if we consider the resources it has in terms of quality and quantity; favourable conditions for hydro-electrical projects, abundant hydrocarbon reserves, from conventional and non-conventional oil fields, as well as ideal conditions for wind, solar, and biomass energy generation projects and for biofuel production. Nevertheless, the Argentinean case of recent years is illustrative of the complex scenario with a fall in the production, deficit in the energy scale and the deep decay in the infrastructure conditions and consequently in the quality of the service by public services concessioners and permit holders. Due to countless reasons, this context evidences the limitations in the public and private investments flow destined to this sector which is vital for the economy and that reveals the lack of attention to a suitable energy infrastructure development and maintenance to meet the needs for the demand in energy products.

887. The BID has pointed out that the countries in the region need to double the investment in infrastructure in general to reach a GDP growth of 5%.[332] The challenge to recompose our energy infrastructure is of great magnitude.

331. http://www.iadb.org/es/sectores/energy/overview,18338.html.
332. Financing infrastructure in Latin America and the Caribbean: How much and by whom? Tomas Sebresky and others https://publications.iadb.org/bitstream/handle/11319/7315/Financiamiento_de_la_Infraestructura_en_LAC.pdf?sequence=4&isAllowed=y.

888. The present work boards relevant aspects, conceptual as well as empirical, for the decision-making of investment in this vital sector of the economy to be addressed; aspects which are applied to private investment prospects in public infrastructure as well as to those projects involving exclusive decisions of the private sector which are common to both areas. Without intending to develop an exhaustive study of each aspect of this comprehensive issue, the main contribution will be to recommend a set of practical tools to influence in the decision-making of investing in energy infrastructure projects, such as the rules regarding risk analysis, actors and instruments identification for the structuring, financing and execution of infrastructure in the energy sector. In that sense, some recognized instruments for the energy infrastructure development management will be reviewed, which reveal in their background our public works concession contract, the public-private partnership and the mechanism internationally known as *Project Finance*. In all the cases, institutional, legal, environmental and social aspects considered by the private as well as the public sponsors of the contracts are to be considered to deal with their financing and development. A case in point, and so as to focus on the analysis of specific cases, some of the risks which are common to energy investment projects in Argentina are to be dealt with, risks such as those derived from the lack of integration in the legal framework with influence in the decision-making process of a determined sector.

889. The objective of this contribution is to focus on the main issues of this topic in view of this opportunity that Argentina now has to convene the investing effort to support the urgent developments in the energy infrastructure sector as a necessary condition for the economic growth and the population's standard of living improvement.

§1. The Development of Energy Infrastructure Projects in Argentina

890. In his work 'Private Investment in the Public Sector', Dr Julio Cesar Crivelli carries out a very interesting analysis of the private capital participation by means of the concession contract of public work in the investment of infrastructure, in the stage of national organization motivated by the farming and exportation development.[333] After that, Argentina followed the historic evolution of most emerging countries regarding the development profile of energy infrastructure projects, focusing on the state support for the infrastructure developments with financing mainly from governmental sources, credit multilateral institutions and export credit agencies, channelled through the big state-owned companies leading important megaprojects such big hydroelectrical works, transmission lines and

333. The author puts it this way: '*Argentina planned the infrastructures that it needed and accepted the financing, construction, and operation of the private sector. The State did not consider that its mission could be beyond that of control and planning. The right financial flows of the Argentine economy attracted capitals from every corner of the world which developed one of the ever highest investment ratios up to that moment.*' Editorial Astrea Ediciones RAP.

nuclear generation projects, among others.[334] However, in more recent decades, the countries in the region experimented with restrictions on the public funds' availability for the financing of the works. The Administrations lost their financial leadership to support – through direct financing or credit – the volume of infrastructure projects required by the economies. At the same time, a global change on the vision of many Administrations, multilateral institutions and public entities in the development of infrastructure was produced. These changes revealed the lack of capital to export in the developing countries, the growth in energy demand and the need for foreign investment to meet the infrastructure increasing needs. In this new context, the private sector turned out to be more reliable, since the states accepted that this sector was able to develop, build and operate large-scale infrastructure projects, and in a more efficient way, when the regulatory frames showed the suitable signals to consider reasonable earnings for the investment in a certain context.

891. Dr Crivelli, in the cited work, asserted with reference to the new process of incorporation of the private sector to the infrastructure and the public services in the nineties that *'the leading role recovered by the private sector through the concession contract in the infrastructure and the public services, resulted in a significant increase in the investment which updated the argentine infrastructure to levels that had not been seen in the last fifty years.'* The new rules of the energy in the model of private management in those years consecrated the argentine hydrocarbon industry deregulation with concession contracts with free supply of the resources exploited for its commercialization in the domestic or international market indiscriminately with free prices. At the same time, the natural gas transport and distribution, with the passage of Law No 24076, meant that the licensee companies were subject to a regulatory regime due to their condition of natural monopoly and public services with rules, for its development, in accordance with the international trends. The tariffs, which should be fair and reasonable, were regulated and subject a general review every five years and included the recognition of an investment factor.

892. Likewise, the electrical industry with Law No 24065 went through a structural change. The wholesale electrical market (WEM) was created with the presence of generators, distributors, carriers and large users and the Dispatch Agency (DA) was implemented to administer the transactions among the agents. In the regulatory framework, the generation as an activity of 'general interest' was considered with free access to the WEM, except in the case of hydro-generation, which required a concession, and the transport and the distribution considered 'public service'

334. About the apparition of the 'philanthropic ogre' and the advent of the state paradigm and its influence in the infrastructure, Dr Julio Cesar Crivelli asserts: *'as far as we are concerned in this point, it was considered strategic for the infrastructure, and hence, subject to the State, which abandoned the promoter, planner and controller role, to turn into the financer, constructor and operator of the most varied infrastructures. From the hydrocarbons to the railroads, from the ways to the ports and housing, all transports, mining, and energy, the telecommunications and the sanitary Works. ... the State reserves all the "Strategic Activities" setting up public and private companies and turning them into "public services", "state monopolies", with an exorbitant legal regime, for the private sector, filled with irrational privileges'* Editorial Astrea. Ediciones RAP.

under the condition of natural monopoly. The regulatory framework comprised as well in this case, the recognition in the tariffs of the incidence of the investment projects, called K factor.

893. According to what Dr Daniel Montamat says 'with the private investment, which almost totally replaced the public one, the natural gas industry was sustainable again, and the gas development was boosted; ... natural gas production was doubled (from 23,000 m3 million per year to 45,000 million), that of the transport's almost doubled (from 67 m3 million daily to 114 million daily), and the distribution networks were incremented by 52.7%. This allowed to widen the consumers' spectrum by 33%. Six million new clients and 250 new locations were incorporated'.[335] However, due to the 2001 crisis, the Law of Public Emergency No 25561 established the conversion into pesos of all the tariffs and the imposition of export duties on the crude oil and its derivatives, among other measures with a price for the energy industry. According to the experts, the conversion into pesos of the gas, used as an anti-inflationary tool and a redistributive mechanism, caused very serious problems in the sector, among which there was the important disinvestment that turned the energy into an obstacle for the growth of the economy.[336] The same happened with the electrical industry that could not get away with the critical moment either. As from the economic emergency, the new seasonal prices as well as the variable production costs, and the price of the power and that of the non-supplied energy were converted into pesos. A new procedure was implemented for the variable production costs statement and the value of water for the production of electrical energy and a maximum spot value and so a clear limit for the differential rate which the generators could access was established.

894. With the mechanisms established for the discretional recognition of the costs, all signals and incentives contained in the principle of marginalist organization of the electrical dispatch were destroyed. Consequently, the generation sector lacked the necessary investments to prevent its depletion and its dependence on more expensive machines.[337] In this way, there was a clear distinction of the old structure in Argentina with stranded costs impossible to recover and the new infrastructure with rules to recover the investment and obtain reasonable profitability. For the latter, the Argentinean Administration resorted, in this context, to the fiduciary fund mechanism coming from beneficiaries' contribution, and with future increases in the tariffs, and above all, public resources.[338] It is therefore not surprising that long-term project investors and lenders, such as those of energy infrastructure, did not find a favourable scenario to invest their resources, which at the same time recoiled in an unavoidable setback of the system. Whatever the management model, when the economic costs were not recovered through the prices anymore,

---

335. Daniel Montamat. Energía. 'De Rehén del Corto Plazo a Estrategia de Desarrollo'. Editorial El Ateneo. p. 137.
336. *Ibid.*, p. 252.
337. *Ibid.*, p. 264.
338. The National Energy Plan (2004–2008) consisted in – based on this modality – the increase of the Yaciretá fee, the Federal Transportation Plan, the termination of the Power Plant Atucha II, The Northwest Gas pipeline and the Gas-Transport system extension in the south.

the energy industry missed the chance to refinance itself.[339] Thus, the increase of the state intervention due to political more than economic reasons resulted in a reduction in the investment flow that ended up affecting the capability of the sector to produce energy resources, creating a need for importation and generating a dramatic deficit in the energy balance of trade.[340]

895. As it will be observed in the present study, the decision to develop and finance an energy project, under several modalities, should be made in a context in which the underlying economic premises, such as the security of the income generated from the investment, the level of taxes payable, the possibility of repatriation of the profits, among others, are not affected by the political decisions of the context.

§2. The New Rules to Face the Infrastructure Emergency in the Energy Sector

896. With the advent of the new government, Argentina has been considering its significant deficit in energy infrastructure and has commenced an adjustment plan in its legal framework to get closer to the basic rules of investment and financing at an international level. This is also true for the economic and institutional policies generation which defines a minimum trust, since these rules are not to be changed overnight and without sufficient compensation.

897. In December 2015, by means of Decree No 134/2015[341] the emergency in the National Electrical Sector was declared rescuing the principles of the Law No 24065 which fostered private investments in production, transport and distribution to guarantee the long-term supply. By means of the set of rules, it has been recognized that the systems of remunerations established in the WEM *'have not given enough economic signals to force the private actors to make the investments required'* to allow the necessary growth of electrical energy sector and that the delay in infrastructure investment levels in the electrical energy distribution nets resulted in an increase in the number of supply interruptions and their duration, evidencing a progressive decrease in the quality of the service with lack of renewal in the transmission systems and their extensions.

339. Dr Daniel Montamat in that sense affirms: *'The only way to revert this scenario is with new investments. However, today the sector offers the worst scenario for investments. The energy markets are not a good option anymore; and at the same time there is no central plan. The private investment is forced and the public one is delayed. The energy resources are not allocated due to signals of prices, and the public intervention just plugs holes, manages cuts and flows of gas according to the emergency, buys and distributes fuel to very expensive plants, creates fiduciary funds that no one pays and administers the prices of the fuel in the domestic market with differentiated retentions over the crude and products which can derive into supply issues.' Supra.*

340. The energy importations have ascended over USD 12,000 million per year.

341. Official Bulletin of 17 Dec. 2015.

898. The technical diagnosis for the justification in declaring the emergency covered, among others, the following factors:

- Average power failure incidence indicator by the user progressively increasing.[342]
- Level of reliability of the conventional thermal generation park installed well below the industry's international standards.
- Scarce levels of operative reserve in days and hours of high demand with the consequent restriction risk in the supply in the case of unexpected events.
- Lack of enough certainty regarding the installation of new generation equipment and the firm and foreseeable availability of primary resources, specially imported gas and gas oil.
- Risks related to the characteristics of the generation installed in certain nodes of the distribution system due to the obsolescence of the equipment.
- Risks related to the liquid fuel transport logistics and the high dependence on imported gal supply.

The need for the currency was also considered for the payment for imported fuels and the continuity of the supply; and the concrete need for more efficient generation projects to diversify the energy matrix and to reduce the dependence on fossil fuels use. To that end, the declaration of emergency suggested the implementation of a necessary action plan in relation to the electrical energy generation, transport and distribution segments of national jurisdiction, *'so as to adequate the quality and security of the electrical supply and to guarantee the electricity public services rendering under suitable technical and economic conditions'.*

899. Lack of efficiency and reasonability criteria when setting the WEM prices had increased the cost of satisfying the demand of electric energy in a suitable way, distorting the economic signals and thus discouraging private risk investment in the generation of electrical energy to meet the national demand. In this context, as regards electrical energy generation, Resolution No 21/2016 of the Electrical Energy Secretariat was adopted[343] to summon investors ready to act as WEM's generator, co-generator and self-generator agents for the introduction of a new generation offer related to the AIS. This system contemplated the execution of 'Contracts for the Demand of Distributors and Large Users' considering prices in US Dollars for the availability of the power to be offered and the electrical energy to be produced. Moreover, by means Resolution No 287-E/2017, an open announcement to sell electrical energy coming from the installation of new generation capacity

342. Until 2003 for EDENOR S.A. there had been was a 4.73 interruptions per year; and for the year 2014, there were 9.33 interruptions per year, while the same indicator for EDESUR S.A. was 3.56 interruptions per year and 5.44 interruptions per year.
343. Official Bulletin of 23 Mar. 2016.

through the use of technology of: (a) combined cycle or (b) co-generation. All of this by signing of Contracts of the Wholesale Demand (CdD) with the demanding parties of the WEM.[344]

900. The announcement was made under the premise that the whole construction and installation of new combined-cycle centrals would require the integration with new solutions of electrical transport and alternate fuel supply in significant volumes that would imply much more time and regulatory issues solution.

901. Under the very same understanding, the new administration decided to promote the renewable sources electrical energy generation, by means of the Program of Renewable Sources RenovAr, which could give a quick answer to the need of new generation with the suitable support so that the investments could be materialized. At that moment, the renewable sources represented as little as 2% of the Argentinean energy mix; thus to meet the objective of the Law No 27191 of having 8% of the electricity consumed at a national level generated by renewable resources by 2018, strong investments would be needed.

902. Law No 27191 considered the mechanisms for the boosting of the activity such as the creation of a Renewable Energies Trust Fund (FODER); the Electrical Energy Users' contribution to meeting the objectives of the Foster Regime, the treatment of the fiscal increments, the implementation of the importations regime, among other sensitive issues for the investor. With the Decree 531/2016, the 'Regime of National Fostering for the Use of Renewable Energy destined to the Production of Electrical Energy' was approved.

903. This Program RenovAr, undoubtedly, drew the investors' attention, local as well as international, from the very first moment as they contributed in the process of drafting The Terms and Conditions had mechanisms to cover the risk analyses, such as the prevision of long-term contracts in dollars and the resolution of technical issues in relation to this method of generation, among other measures to give guarantees to the investment further depicted in this article.[345]

---

344. The criteria defined by the Ministry to assess the offers was based on calculating the savings of gas and liquid fuels of each Project and their repayment was planned through long-term contracts with the electricity final demand. The Ministry of Energy received thirty-three offers from eleven companies in the event of opening the envelopes and reading the economic offers in the open bid for the interested parties to incorporate new generation of electrical energy by means of Open Cycles and Co-generation closing. The Co-generation Projects – located in seven provinces – are related to the oil, petrochemical, distillery, chemical and gas industry; and the net power offered is 3,129 MW. The projects will be financed with private investment estimated in no less than USD 3,000 million and its repayment will be done through long-term contracts with the demand.

345. In accordance with a PWC report as part of the commitment, the first auction – sponsored by the World Bank – with several important participants and encouraging results: offers for more than 6,200 MW were made, and fifty-nine projects for more than 2,400 MW were awarded (1,473 MW of wind energy and 916 MW of solar energy), with an estimated investments of USD 1,800 millions. The biddings awarded in this first stage were 2.3 GW of renewable sources of the energy matrix, which together with the installed capacity and other additional factors let meet the objective of 8% set for 2018. It is projected that at the end of this plan, Argentina will have an installed

904. All this evolution related to regulations, to go back to the traditional fostering schemes in infrastructure investment based on modern rules, finally had transcendent tools with the passage of Law No 27328[346] of the Public-Private Participation Contracts (PPP Law) whose fundamental objective is to open a new stage in Argentina in which the private sector can have a leading investment role owing to the international experience. Due to its relevance in this work, a detailed analysis of this Law has been included.

905. This programme was regulated in August 2017 through Resolution No 281/2017 and stipulates the contracting mechanism between private companies as an alternative to joint purchases. The MaTer reaches Large Users who have an average annual demand greater than 300 kW (Large User Enabled – GUH) and offers them the possibility of contracting directly for convenience. In this way, GUHs can choose their renewable electricity provider and negotiate the purchase conditions with it. Additionally, the National Registry of Renewable Energy Projects (RENPER) was created, leaving CAMMESA in charge of managing the dispatch priority (ordering the dispatch between different renewable generation plants).

906. The registered projects can request the Certificate of Inclusion in the Regime of Promotion of the Renewable Energies to obtain the fiscal benefits of Article 9 of Law No 27191, from the inscription in the MaTer.

907. At the moment, 49 projects received dispatch priority from CAMMESA. This means guaranteeing access to the electricity transmission grid that allows generators to commercialize renewable energy in the long term with the GUH. These projects add 1,164.4 MW of power and are of wind and solar photovoltaic technology.

§3. Conditions for the Development of Energy Infrastructure Projects

908. This section will analyse some conditions to consider in structure and development of investment projects in energy infrastructure. Consequently, with the recognition of the emergency in the sector, it was clear in Argentina that our macroeconomic situation was crucial to the evolution and boosting of the investment projects. Thus, it was obvious that the economic context had to be stable enough so as to motivate long-term investment and the giving of loans to make it possible. In fact, the economic stability was recognized as a crucial aspect of the project. And,

capacity of 1–2 GWH of solar energy and of 5–6 GWH of wind energy, which will make possible that the renewable energies represent almost 20% of the country's electrical consumption.

346. Published in the Official Bulletin of 30 Nov. 2016.

of course, it is widely recognized, among the experts in project financing, that countries having stable exchange rates and inflation and a predictable political environment are more likely to successfully develop projects.[347] Based on that, the macroeconomic adjustments performed in Argentina with the change of administration at the end of 2015, through the exchange restrictions removal, the recovery from *default* and the return to the financial markets and of international capital and a new international immersion proposal constituted necessary conditions for an energy infrastructure investment process. Moreover, this condition had to be accompanied by a consensus to promote stability and foreign investment required for the structuring and the financing of the projects. Hence, the analysis of several conditions limiting the decision of investment in energy projects is required; conditions which are related to regulation of energy markets, as well as to the condition of the legislation in key aspects such as the participation of the private sector in the public infrastructure, the care of the environment, the social impact of the projects, the access to the information, the people's and community's participation in the area of the projects, original communities included, among other important aspects identified as *'above ground risks'*.[348] Herein under, an analysis of the most relevant aspects to be considered in the decision-making process in energy sector infrastructure investment will be developed.

I. Stability of the Legislative and Regulatory Systems

909. The legislative and regulatory systems in relatively less developed countries are not generally defined than in developed countries and this leads to an intense analysis of the rules applicable to any given Project. The question is that, beyond the predictable political or economic stability, the projects require an understandable and stable legal framework for the operation of the businesses. The projects require the laws effective enough to ensure that the investment will not be subject to significant changes during the development and operativity stage; or in case those changes occur, to have a certainty that some mechanisms will be exercised to obtain due compensation and to be able to face the commitments assumed for their financing. At least, this framework must include basic legal provisions in relation to contracts compliance, permits efficient deliveries, as well as an effective disputes resolution through arbitration. It is pointed out in that sense that the developing countries might not have suitable regulations regarding infrastructure projects ownerships, tax collection, and profits distribution. The regulations being normally revised by the sponsors are the following, among others:

- The government agencies' role and responsibility in the sector.
- Procedure about permits, franchises and licenses issuance.

347. Scott L. Hoffman. *The law and business of International Project Finance* (3rd ed., Cambridge University Press), p. 101.
348. This concept is generally used in the energy industry to refer to the non-technical risks such as regulatory and environmental issues. In more general terms, it refers to a wide range such as the political risk, the cooperative risk, security and corporative government whose impact is difficult to quantify, but could be significant if one or more of those risks turn into a real threat.

- Prices regulation and control.
- General Business regulation.
- Intervention and control over the companies having foreign investors.
- Payment restrictions for the owners.
- Rights related to easement and other real estate rights such that of the surface.
- Labour laws and social security.
- Laws and regulations relating to Environment, health and industrial security, widely known as HSE standards.
- Regulations related to the execution of contracts.
- Tax duties.

For that to be effective, the legislative and regulatory system must be well defined so that the operations are transparent. The aims of the current legal body must be well developed and articulated, with clear procedures and permits and licences processes that should be as objective as possible.

910. On the other hand, as we will see in specific cases, unless a country's laws and regulations are well developed to support the projects, the stability will have to be given – from the part of the government – by means of agreements, such as Investment Guarantee Agreements.

911. A prototypal case in Argentina regarding stability in the regulatory framework is the legislative regime applicable to the non-conventional hydrocarbon fields, a topic in which Argentina intends to be a role model. With the amendment of Law No 17318 by Law No 27007 it has been observed that several attempts to have a unified regulatory regime at a national level have been left halfway.

912. Argentina has a vast number of national and provincial regulations of application for the hydrocarbon activity; consequently, the drafting of an integral regime for the non-conventional hydrocarbon fields at a national level would be a good starting point for its realization. The enactment of Law No 27007 meant:

- The standardization of initial process at a national level of the awarding conditions for hydrocarbons exploration and exploitation contracts for conventional as well as non-conventional fields.
- The adaptation of the permit's terms and the concessions to the peculiarities of the investments in the non-conventional field projects, which required more realization time in the pre-development as well as the development stage.
- The giving of predictability signals in some rules in the provinces' participation in sensitive topics such as the limit in the royalties, the definition in the extension bonds and others due to the social corporate responsibility; and also new rules of participation of state provincial entities to replace the former haulage regulations.
- Legislative recognition of the Investment Promotion Regime for the Hydrocarbons Exploitation created by Decree 929/13 and innovation in relation to the access conditions so that it can be used by a larger number of investments.

However, in some aspects, this law seems to have stagnated in improving the positioning of those already present in the Argentinean market, to the detriment of the generalization of competitive selection processes as a way to improve, attract investments and to further allow a more efficient capture of the hydrocarbons profit from those asserting domain. This law, just partially modifying Law No 17319, does not suggest an integral regime for the new realities of the hydrocarbon activity in Argentina, especially in the area of non-conventional. On the contrary, it has limited itself to the crucial pending topics on fiscal matters and on the setting of environmental minimum contents and all matters related to the Model Terms and Conditions approval.

913. In the case of the fiscal regime, they could have given shape to it, and it is advisable to do this in the future, for the adoption of homogeneous and stable treatments in the hydrocarbon activities at a provincial and municipal level, such as the limits in the gross income aliquot and restrictions to the imposition of new taxes.

914. In relation to the environment, although the regulatory framework is well developed at a federal as well as provincial level, the drafting of a unified environment law to facilitate its construction and application in the whole territory, is still pending in this sensitive matter in the sector.[349]

915. It is expected that the measures arising from the Federal Energy Council, recently created in the frame of Federal Energy Agreement,[350] meet the objectives of counselling on amendments required by the legislation regarding energy, the public service regulatory frames included. In the meantime, an individual policy agreement with benefits of the context will continue, which proves the importance of working on our legislative system solidity in this so important sector. However, as it was aforementioned, Argentina has been progressively advancing with the legislative requirements regarding energy regulation, recovering the regulatory frames and contracts compliance, as well as regarding the general legislation to create suitable environment for investments in this and other sectors.

II. Political Risks

916. In all the analyses related to projects, especially in the case of energy projects, considered as 'strategic' for the national economies, involving international actors, the so-called political risks are certainly relevant. The topic of political risks is identified as an area of uncertainty for projects, above all, in developing countries. In fact, it is a sensitive aspect that may result in higher prices so as to

349. Law 27007 s. 23 – the National State and the Provincial States, pursuant to provision under s. 41 of the National Constitution, shall tend towards the establishment of a uniform environmental legislation which will be basically intended to apply the best practices in environmental management for the hydrocarbons exploration, exploitation and/or transport so as to develop the activity with a suitable care of the environment.
350. Decree 854/2017 Official Bulletin of 26 Oct. 2017.

give the structure a complex programme of insurance, contractual adjustments and governmental guarantees. In general, it is believed that the political risk can arise from several sources:

- The political instability, which implies that the development of investment projects may suffer due to the political changes that could affect the business and institutional environment initially considered.
- The government's attitude in relation to foreign investments, which leads to the analysis of the country's history regarding the investment rules. Unfortunately, in this sense Argentina, with a long history of non-compliance with contracts related to investments, holds the record of having the highest number of complaints before the CIADI, having forced concessionary companies to the *peso* convertibility and tariffs freeze, among other things.[351,352]
- The government's degree of participation in the country's economy, which implies the will to give participation to the private sector in the exploration, exploitation, of natural resources and the production of energy. Our history in hydrocarbons is full of ups and downs in the relationship with the private sector and this has obviously affected our energy infrastructure investments.[353] Just look at the recent privatization, 'nationalization' and expropriation of the main Argentinean energy company, YPF SA; our reputation regarding our credibility about the State's role in the sector cannot be more tarnished.
- The country's economic projections, which implies the analysis the growth perspectives of its product and the behaviour of the main variables such as the Exchange rate, inflation, balance of trade and of payment, among others, and the possibility of translating this into scenarios of stability or social and political unrest.[354]

In conclusion, the investors, sponsors, and financial institutions need to rely upon the stability of the country's political environment before making financial commitments to a specific project.

351. Dr Julio Cesar Crivelli has pointed out: 'the Country's Administration condemned the concessioners to live on subsidies, "benefitting" the consumers with very low tariffs being financed with the sudden increase of the tax pressure in general and in the farming and other special sectors, and with inflation when the expenditure was more than expected. It is impossible for the private sector to invest in such a context of uncertainty, depending upon the subsidy that the State can or cannot give in the future.' 'Private Investment in the Public Sector' p. 22.
352. Source: Pérez-Aznar, F. *'In 2003, the executive branch informed the Congress that there were more than 50 lawsuits involving BITs (Bilateral Investment Treaties). Half of them were filed in accordance with the ICSID Arbitration Rules or the United Nations Commission on International Trade Law (CNUDMI), whereas the other half never reached the stage of arbitration, which means there were settlements. Events after 2003 are well-known, with a total of 59 cases presented against Argentina, most of which involved government measures to face the economic crisis'*. https://www.iisd.org/itn/es/2017/06/12/recent-argentina-qatar-bit-challenges-investment-negotiations-facundo-perez-aznar/#_edn6.
353. 'Historia del petróleo en la Argentina' by author Nicolás Gadano. Ed. Edhasa. 2012.
354. Scott L. Hoffman. *The Law and Business of International Project Finance* (3rd ed., Cambridge University Press), p. 99.

917. Political predictability is valuable when analysing long-term investments such as the ones required for the energy sector, which arises from the consensus and the suitable functioning of the institutions. In Argentina, we have countless examples of when a happy medium cannot be reached, whether it is due to electoral or institutional barriers, the predictability is less probable and this will directly affect the decisions of making the investment.

918. On the contrary, it is observed in the recent interest in the energy sector that when certain stability conditions are established in the regulatory framework, in a suitable political context, there exists less fear from the part of the companies to make certain decisions than in other contexts.

919. These political conditions may give place to events affecting the success, the capital flow, and the operating costs of the project; hence, mechanisms to mitigate them need to be developed. As follows, some of the most representative political risks are analysed below.

A. *Expropriation and Nationalization Risk*

920. In this case, the owner of the assets of an investment project is deprived of its ownership or of exercising the rights of the contract or of the use or control of the investment. Expropriation, in the broad sense of the word, may include any other type of governmental restrictions with a similar effect, such as (i) the prohibition of exercising a right regarding an asset, (ii) the impossibility of keeping control over investment, or (iii) the unilateral non-compliance with a determined fiscal benefit implying a confiscatory measure or behaviour for the investment, among others.

921. In Argentina, the main mechanism to mitigate this risk is the protection standard given under section 17 of the National Constitution which guarantees that the property is inviolable and that no inhabitant can be deprived thereof, but for, sentence based on Law pursuant to that, the expropriation can be effective only due to a public use, based on law and must be previously compensated.

922. Similarly, in the Treaties of Reciprocal Promotion and Protection of Investment subscribed by Argentina, mechanisms letting the investor claim for the State's Responsibility in the case of expropriation are considered by means of a double-scale system of controversy settlement: one applicable to the relation between the Member States and the other, a commercial one between the foreign investor and the Receptive State of the investment.[355]

---

355. According to Javier Guiridlian Laroza in 'Contratación Pública y Desarrollo de Infraestructuras (nuevas formas de gestión y financiación) Lexis Nexis Abeledo-Perrot. p. 153.

923. In some treaties, it is guaranteed that the compensation in these cases must be promptly recognized, suitable, at market value, and possible to be transferred to the investor's country.[356]

924. Anyway, beyond all legal protection, in the relevant contracts of investment projects the management of this risk is contemplated considering the impact of the costs and the perspective of the investment plan term. This protection, at a contractual level, considers the principles as follows: (i) it must cover the direct expropriation as well as any indirect way to perform it; (ii) it can only be permitted in the cases where the public interest is involved and respecting the legal procedures; (iii) it must be subject to fair and not discriminatory treatment; (iv) it must guarantee a compensation that has to be effective in the shortest time possible in convertible currency and in a price set by independent appraisers.

B. Armed Conflicts and Civil Turmoil

925. This risk includes acts of public enemies, declared or not declared war, civil war, guerrillas' or terrorists' activities, hostilities, sabotage, revolution, insurrection, among other similar events. Also in this category, civil turmoil, direct actions included carried out by political, environmentalist, included social groups, or owners hindering access to the buildings, or to the material or necessary equipment for the Project, or direct actions such as labour strike.

926. The first protection in case of those events is the civil and commercial laws applicable to the contracts in which force majeure or acts of God are considered.[357]

927. In the Treaties of Reciprocal Protection and Promotion of Investment, the standard treatment for these events considers mechanisms to compensate for the losses related to armed conflicts or domestic turmoil as well as the guarantee to have the same treatment given to the nationals of the receptive country of the investment.[358]

356. In the Agreement for the reciprocal protection and promotion of investment between Argentina and Spain, subscribed on the 3 Oct. 1991 and passed under Law 24118, in s. V, it establishes that: '*Nationalization, expropriation or any other kind of similar effective measure that can be adopted by the authorities of one Party against the other Party's investor's investment in its territory, should exclusively be applied due to public use pursuant to legal provisions and in no case whatsoever shall this be discriminatory. The Party adopting any of these measures shall pay the investor or its rightful claimant, with no unjustified delay, a suitable compensation, in convertible currency.*' On the one hand, s. VI establishes the possibility of *'freely transferring the rents or profits or any other payment related to the investment, specially, but not exclusively, the following: ... – the compensations set forth under Section V'*.

357. Section 1730 of the Civil and Commercial Code in Argentina *'Acts of God or Force Majeure is considered when the act cannot be foreseen, or in the case it can have been foreseen, it could not have been avoided. The case of Acts or God or Force Majeure, exempt from liability unless otherwise provided. This Code uses the phrases "Act of God" and "force majeure" as synonyms.'*

358. Law No 24124 Treaty subscribed with the United States of America about the Reciprocal Protection and Promotion of Investment. '*The Nationals or Partnerships of one Party whose investments*

928. On the other hand, the contracts related to investments give a suitable definition to these events as part of the Force Majeure and establish a clear procedure to claim and recognize them. It is usual to recognize in the relevant contracts with the States, that the term as well as the investment plan will be extended, when the execution or the possibility to generate profits are affected. In some cases, the mitigation mechanisms of this risk consider compensations due to stoppage costs, mobilization or repair or replacement time.

C. Restrictions on Capital and Dividends Repatriation

929. This risk is materialized when the owner of the investment is subject to restrictions related to the transfer of the investment or of the capital invested as well as the earnings corresponding to total or partial liquidation of the investment which can at the same time entail restrictions over *management fees* or any other type of compensation due to the investment. These restrictions can also operate by means of measures affecting the repatriation terms or the Exchange rate affecting the value of such flows.

930. In legislation related to foreign investments,[359] mechanism of recognition of capital repatriation rights is established. In the Treaties of Reciprocal Promotion and Protection of the Investment, the protection has changed from the establishment of safeguards recognizing the right of the Receptive State of imposing exchange restrictions due to the occurrence of certain exceptional financial circumstances equally valued and in good faith to agreements in which the capital and dividend transfers must be carried out without delay in fully convertible currency at a conversion rate applicable to the date of the draft and in accordance with the procedures already laid down in the receptive country.[360] On a contract level, it is important to highlight in favour of the investor, as a mitigating mechanism of this risk, the right to receive, control, use, convert and transfer overseas any resulting funds from the investment or in relation thereto. This covers the possibility to transfer: (i) any type of net earnings or benefit, (ii) the amount derived from the sale of

---

shall be affected by losses in the territory of the other Party due to war, or any other armed conflict, revolution, national emergency condition, insurrection, civil turmoil or any similar event whatsoever, shall be granted a not less favourable treatment that the most favourable one given to their own nationals or partnerships or those national or partnerships of other third countries in relation to the measures taken due to such losses'.

359. Section 5 of Law 21382 (text in order, Decree No 1853/1993), which established a legal regime tending to promote foreign investments in the country, states that the foreign investors may transfer overseas the net income coming from their investments as well as repatriate their investments.

360. Law No 24124 – Treaty subscribed with the United States of America about the Reciprocal Protection and Promotion of Investment s. V 2: '*Transfers shall be made in the currency of free convertibility, at the current Exchange rate in the market on the date of the transfer regarding the operations in cash realized in the currency to be transferred. The free transfer will take place in accordance with the procedures established by each part; these procedures shall not hinder the right laid down in this Treaty*'.

assets related to the investment, (iii) any and all type of fiscal benefit or compensation, (iv) amounts related to payments of properties or services rendered (loans included), as well as the renewal of those payments, or any other type of repayment of rewards, fees or commissions.

931. As a derivative of this recognition of rights, the following rights are as well covered: (a) to receive due payments, (b) to keep the control and use of bank accounts in and outside the country and to dispose of the funds thereof, (c) to buy and sell currency without restrictions on the market, and in the event this was removed, the chance to buy currency in any other market replacing it, without discrimination in relation to the other transactions.

D. *Risk of 'Instability' of Regulations*

932. The constant changes in the political and economic conditions in which the investment was performed have its sequel in the changes in the regulatory framework in force at the time of the realization of the Project. The legal regulation of general application lack stability and, thus, no investor has acquired rights in reliance solely on the legal system of general application.

933. As a consequence, the so-called stability clauses are aimed to guarantee that when a regulation is changed, those in force on the date of the investment shall continue to be applicable.

934. At a legislative level, the protection regimes of investment and fiscal stability[361] for determined sectors are aimed at guaranteeing that, in case of regulatory modifications that may impact the project, the investor shall have suitable compensation mechanisms at his disposal. In the investment protection Treaties, the States are obliged not to take measures to modify or derogate the local laws that may have a negative impact on the foreign investment in their territory.

935. Likewise, in the contracts related to investments there exist terms and conditions regarding the stability of the legal framework in force, authorized permits and supplementary contracts included, establishing no unilateral modification or the recognition of the adjustment mechanisms in the investment plans or in the compensations derived from changes in the regulations or in the judicial or administrative interpretation with an effect in the investment.

361. Section 8 of Law 24196 of Mining Investment establishes that: *'The mining start-ups contained the regime herein shall be guaranteed fiscal stability by the term of thirty (30) counting as from the date of presentation of their feasibility study'.*

E. Risk of Denial of Justice

936. This risk has been identified as the lack of willingness of an independent jurisdictional instance being able to solve controversies duly and diligently in any and all matters affecting the execution plans compromised, and in turn to guarantee the property rights whose recognition has been the essence of the decision of investing.

937. It is generally understood that the local courts, notwithstanding their professional or moral capacity, have much less experience in the resolution of controversies related to investments; without even considering that they may be influenced by the Receptive State of the investment in detriment to the foreign investor.

938. Thus, at a constitutional as well as a legislative level, the guarantee of due process and the arbitration remedy are recognized so as to mitigate this risk. In the same way, the investment protection treaties have improved in the removal of requirements prior to the arbitration stage.

939. The correlation in the contracts regarding investment is given by submitting controversies to the foreign tribunals, and applying alternative mechanism to solve disputes as the arbitration of third countries, without the requirement of the local resource depletion and under the rules of specialized institutions.

940. As it has been previously mentioned, the nature of the projects determines the political risk. The energy projects are sensitive and strategic and the most affected by the risks identified. In fact, they are the ones that have historically been affected by a change in the regulatory frameworks, expropriations, and restrictions to the availability of funds and the convertibility of the currency, among other materialized risks.

941. In this new stage in Argentina, demanding a new vision in the face of the substantial investments required to rescue and re-launch our energy infrastructure, it is recommendable to work on strengthening the mitigation mechanisms of the political risks. These measures should include the analysis of all the sponsors' support set of mechanisms in the legislation considering guarantees for the investor in the face of political risks, the use of the reserve funds in the case of events like this, as well as the application of additional guarantees of multilateral credit institutions and a renewed model of protection at a contractual level.

III. Economic Instability

942. Regarding the economic instability, a trait of the developing countries, it is crucial to point out that this instability profoundly affects the necessary financing structure for an energy project. Thus, this situation directly affects the consumers', users', and/or beneficiaries' capacity to make use of the facilities and to face, with their financial capacity, at least the production costs of the energy products.

943. In fact, in a gloomy picture of an economy, the energy infrastructure projects can provide a necessary service; yet at a price that the government authorities are not willing to transfer to the community or, at a cost the great majority of the population and its companies are not able to pay.

944. It has already been mentioned in this article that the decisions made in times of crisis in Argentina have hindered the recognition of tariffs, of the energy generation costs or of the increases in the public service concessionaire companies' operations.

945. From the experts' point of view, however, well-adapted to the current reality in Argentina, it has been said that: 'The decisions of promoting energy generation projects from the part of the private sector can be a regrettable solution for the consumers of such subsidized energy. On the other hand, it is sometimes necessary that the subsidies be removed to grease the wheels in the private sector's development. Unless there is a political consensus in the development of infrastructure with the participation of the private sector, the opposition could hinder the reformist efforts'.[362]

946. On the other hand, to understand the macroeconomic context of a country is crucial to structuring a long-term investment project and obtaining competitive financing. The economic stability is crucial for a project. The fundamental indicators of the economy such as stable inflation and Exchange rates, the existence of an internal capital market, the credit ratings and the interest rates, and also the 'country risk' have a direct effect upon the financing cost of the projects and consequently on the internal rate of return. In that sense, if the financial cost ends up being too high, the income required by the project to amortize the investment can be socially not profitable and can affect its feasibility and this is what has happened in Argentina in recent years.[363]

IV. Centralized Systems of Infrastructure

947. It has been pointed out that other structural weaknesses of the developing countries to project development and financing is related to centralized systems of infrastructure.[364] In fact, whether it is due to political positions or lack of private capital, most of the infrastructure projects have been boosted and/or have been owned by the State in the developing countries and this can have a negative impact on the competition, increasing the probabilities of the market efficiencies. A clear

---

362. Scott L. Hoffman. *The Law and Business of International Project Finance* (3rd ed., Cambridge University Press), p. 99.
363. Dr Crivelli in the work cited supra affirms that: 'No one would be willing to pay the resulting tariffs, if the marginal benefit of the use of the infrastructure were less than the cost of the tariff charged to be used. Argentina-risk rate, and thus our financial cost reached, in the last ten years, values of infrastructure that could be developed in places other than in Argentina'.
364. Scott L. Hoffman. *The Law and Business of International Project Finance* (3rd ed., Cambridge University Press), p. 102.

effect of that, in the case of Argentina, is the participation of the provincial energy companies in the hydrocarbon exploration and exploitation of the so-called areas of reserves.

948. In fact, due to the amendment of the Hydrocarbons Law No 17319 with Law No 27007, the provincial governments promoted that, in relation to the areas of reserves, the awarded parties of the concession contracts would sign joint venture contracts which scheduled the concept of *carry*, by means of which the provincial company – controlled by the owner of the resource – participated in the distribution of the production but without financing the investment in the activities for its extraction.

949. Law No 27007 incorporated section 91 in the text of the Hydrocarbons Law that sets forth, in relation to the hydrocarbons exploration and exploitation of the respective provincial domains, that no new reserves whatsoever shall be established in the future in favour of its public companies or with majority state stake, under any legal way. It was further laid down that for those areas that had been reserved in favour of the public companies or agencies for the exploration and development before the amendment of the Hydrocarbons Law but that at the moment of the enforcement date of the amendment did not have contracts with third parties, associative schemes would be performed; however the participation during the development stage would be proportional to the committed investments and provided that they had effectively been done by the state-participation companies. In this way, the possibility of conditioning the adjudication of those partnership contracts to the private partners facing the percentage of the development investment corresponding to the public company or entity, and sharing the production afterwards, was removed. In this example, it is clear how the developers of the infrastructure projects have to consider the real effect of the presence of the public sector in the decision-making process, especially in the case of energy projects which, due to their commercial risk, have a significant profit. Other possible effects may include having to compete with projects belonging to the State, which may tend to reduce the charges or tariffs in their products or service due to the circumstances considering short-term political gains. Similarly, the change of paradigm in the ownership of the natural resource and/or of the infrastructure, with privatization or nationalization processes changing the market conditions as well as the entrance of new actors benefited by the context can have an impact; all of these are risks which are part of the recent history of the energy sector in Argentina.

§4. Key Actors and Agreements for the Structuring of Infrastructure Investment Projects

950. As it previously elaborated, the development of any complex energy or infrastructure project requires the interaction of a complex set of contractual relationships with the involvement of several actors in the public as well as the private sector so as to ensure the ability to finance and all the risks identified for each of the stages need to be mitigated.

I. The State's Role in the Decision-Making Process of Investing

951. Beyond any shadow of a doubt, the State has the main role in any project since it controls the legal and regulatory framework in which the projects are carried out. Moreover, it is important to highlight that the State, whether national or provincial, is the owner of the natural resources in its territories and based on that, it controls the way in which the profit of those resources is captured, by means of the energy policies setting or the management of permits or concession for exploration and exploitation of natural resources.

952. In Argentina, in accordance with section 124 of the National Constitution, the provincial States consider the original domain of the natural resources as their exclusive competence. The concept '*original domain*', contained in section 124 of the National Constitution, is understood as an autonomous concept coming from the Mining Law which assumes the power of the '*eminent domain*'.[365,366] The eminent domain is a supreme power connected to the notion of internal sovereignty which is exercised over the property placed in the state, whether it is private or public domain thereof, or that of the individuals' property. It refers to *powers* and, in this sense, it is a power of legislation over the people and the property, not recognizing other limitations than those laid down in the Constitution as an expression of internal sovereignty. In accordance with the doctrines, the powers and rights coming from the original domain that section 124 of the National Constitution recognizes in favour of the provinces in relation to the existing natural resources in its territory, the powers to: (i) give permits, concessions or licenses destined to transform the abstract domain of the recumbent natural substances in the underground of effective domain,[367] and to dictate execution acts in relation to the use of such resources, as

365. Part of the doctrine divides the property into eminent domain and civil domain. Hence, while the State has the right to rule the conditions and the public charges of the private property, it does not hold a true ownership right regarding the properties placed in its territory, but it keeps a power of legislation, jurisdiction and contribution. Cf. Marienhoff, Miguel, Tratado de Derecho Administrativo, Abeledo-Perrot, 4th ed. updated, Buenos Aires, 1998, book V, p. 38. Cited at Cassagne *supra*.

366. 'Last paragraph of section 124 N.C. gives constitutional status to the eminent domain each province possesses regarding its natural resources, notion already considered by most of the doctrine which does not allow the National State – through laws such as 17319 and 17500 – to give itself the ownership of the resources placed in provincial jurisdiction. Thus, the concept of original domain consecrated in the Constitution and the civil domain regime coexist, without overlapping. This concept of eminent domain is cited in the note to section 2507 of the Civil Code*, where the codifier explains that 'the Nation has the right to rule the conditions and the public charges of the private property. The collective being called the State, has in relation to the property which is in its territory, a power, a right to legislation, jurisdiction and contribution, that when applied to real property, is one part of the domestic territorial sovereignty. About this right of the State's, which is not a real domain or property right, the proprietors are only to submit their rights to the necessary restrictions of the general interest … '. Acerca Del Dominio Originario De Los Recursos Naturales *by Federico J. Iribarren.* http://farn.org.ar/archives/libros/acerca-del-dominio-originario-de-los-recursos-naturales *(Argentinean Civil Code: Today derogated).

367. Effective or useful domain of the real right which has neither the perpetual nor non-prescribing nature and which is in the power of the legitimated individual to exploit and explore a portion of the original domain and to place hydrocarbons in the surface at the service of men for its evacuation, industrialization or commercialization. Cf. Eduardo Zapata 'Hidrocarburos en Argentina Generalidades – Antecedentes. Régimen Actual'. Presentation Class CEARE 2011.

well as to dispose of its revocation or expiry in case of non-compliance with the terms and conditions; (ii) collect the payment of the benefits established in the law such as royalties, etc.; (iii) exercise the local, exclusive, or concurrent regulatory power of state, according to the cases.[368]

953. Based on that, rules or acts destined to protect the health, the security or the environment are to be passed to protect against possible threats coming from exploitation project of the natural resources. The hydrocarbon fields original domain consists of a set of powers and rights which are to be applied pursuant to the principles of special laws, prescriptions from the Mining Code and the principle of the administrative law in accordance with the substantial legislation laid down by the Congress on the matter pursuant to section 75 subsection 12 of the National Constitution.

954. Regarding the jurisdiction over natural resources, in terms of the scope, it has been agreed about its scope as one of the complex issues of concurrent jurisdiction between them.[369] In Doctrine, jurisdiction is defined as the power to pass legal norms, the possibility of applying them by means of the organs of the administrative power, as well as the possibility of solving the disputes through the judicial power. Hence, the power of passing regulatory norms in the activities related to the natural resources is coming from the demarcation of boundaries of the jurisdictional powers between the National and the Provincial States laid down in the National Constitution.

955. The National Constitution recognizes the federal powers to rule the use and benefit of the natural resources and thus to fix the national policy on the matter pursuant to sections 41 and 75, subsections 12, 18 and 19. Thus, the jurisdictional powers corresponding to the federal scope in relation to the natural resources regime has been progressively received by the national legislation and had been treated and recognized by the Case law and Doctrine of our Supreme Court. In the case 'Chevron San Jorge S.R.L. against/ Neuquén Province about/ unconstitutionally action (C 2126 XLI Original)', the Supreme Court stated that: *'it is important to point out that section 124, in fine, of the National Constitution only recognizes to the provinces the original domain of the natural resources placed in its territory; however they do not keep the jurisdiction over them. Such conclusion is not modified by the passage of Law 26197, since section 2°, in fine, establishes the responsibility on the design of the energy policy in the hands of the National Executive Power (conf. case P.1749.XL 'Pan-American Energy LLC branch Argentina about/ inhibition in the case titled "Neuquén province about/ Pan-American Energy LLC about/ ordinary", ruling of August 10 th 2010)'.*

---

368. Juan Carlos Cassagne. The property of the hydrocarbon fields and their relationship with the National and provincial powers (Issues arising after the Constitutional Reform of 1994)http://www.cassagne.com.ar/publicaciones/_La_propiedad_de_los_yacimientos_de_hidrocarburos_su_relacion_con_las_potestades_nacionales_y_provinciales,_pdf.
369. The Supreme Court decided that *'domain and jurisdiction are neither equivalent nor correlative concepts and they can exist independently'*, Rulings 154:312.

956. It is crucial, at this stage of assessment of the investment project, to analyse our legal system in detail so as to establish the competent state intermediaries as well as the their respective powers.

957. As it is analysed further in this article, that the State has a leading role not only to grant the concession contracts for the natural resources exploration and exploitation but also to channel the investing capacity of the individuals by means of public works concession mechanisms of the Law No 17520 and of public-private partnerships of the Decree 1299/00 and more recently of the Public-Private Participation Contracts of the Law No 27328. In fact, without the granting of certain rights to the investors for a specific period of time by the State, the investor will not have the legal possibility of developing an energy project in the country.

958. In that sense, it is important to highlight the leading role of the State in fostering projects related to energy and its infrastructure, as well as the risk entailed when revoking those rights in any of its development stages.

II. The Private Investor as the Sponsor in the Investment and the Relevant Contracts

959. The development of an investment project in energy infrastructure requires, especially when equipment, materials and services in different countries are involved, a complex contractual structure to cope with any and all risks identified by the private investor as its sponsor. In fact, each aspect of the project resulting in higher expenses or lower income derived from unexpected events can lead to a failure of the private investor's business plan. The projects, structured under diverse modalities, are designed to mitigate the effects of any adverse consequences for the sponsor through underlying contracts by allocating and mitigating to those risks.

A. *Investment Agreements*

960. In complex projects, any significant investment has, as a fundamental basis, an implementation agreement or investment agreement with the State. By means of this agreement, the political and financial elements which are doubtful or non-existent in the legislation and which are at the same time, are necessary for the financing of the project, are to be defined.

961. These agreements are to be construed as an effort of the State to reduce the private investor's risks and so to boost the development of an eligible Project in a context of uncertainty.

962. This type of agreement deals with some or all of the uncertainties related to projects such as: (i) sovereign guarantee, (ii) expropriation risk, (iii) permits and other governmental authorizations, (iv) fiscal benefits and other incentives, (v) exchange and political risks, (vi) authorization for the commercial activity in determined sectors, such as the authorization of the partnership of the investment to be the producer of an electrical energy project, (vii) exclusivity right, and (viii) general cooperation with the investor by the state agencies.[370]

963. In the structuring of one of the relevant Projects in Latin America, the construction of the heavy crude pipeline in Ecuador, it was considered that the changes in the Government or in its policies could entail political or financial events that could affect the completion or operation of the installations. To that end, the project was structured on the basis of an Authorization Contract and an Investment Guarantee Agreement.

964. By means of the contracts, some protections were guaranteed for the investment, for example, legal and tax stability, the right of free conversion of the funds generated by the operations, as well as the right to repatriate the funds, to make payments in a foreign currency, and to keep accounts overseas. Likewise, protections in case of expropriation or nationalization or non-discriminatory treatment were considered. As regards financing, the lenders' involvement was contemplated in the Investment Guarantee Agreement. Moreover, the State promised its assistance in getting the permits and the easement rights for the right of way.

B. Input Contracts

965. The availability of the company vehicle of the investment (*Special Purpose Vehicle* –SPV) to make earnings as from the operations of the Project is the basis of any and all financed projects; hence, the contracts guaranteeing the supply of the raw materials for each business are fundamental for the feasibility of the Project and the management of the commercial risks. The contracts defining the cost of the fuel and other inputs are very important as any change in the cost or the availability under those contracts will affect the capital flow. For example, in a project to finance the construction of a refinery, the risks related to the raw material are as important as the price of the final product.[371]

966. The so-called *input contracts* shall not interfere with the payment expectation of the debt nor with the earnings of the project. Consequently, if the risks in these contracts are unacceptably assigned from the Project lender's point of view, it will be necessary to improve the structure of financing with other elements such as letters of credit, capital contribution commitments, guarantees and insurances.

370. Scott L. Hoffman. *The Law and Business of International Project Finance* (3rd ed., Cambridge University Press), p. 147.

371. Yang Chu and Tony Medina, *Quantitative Evaluation of the Relationship Between Supply and Off Take Contracts in Petroleum Refinery Projects Utilizing Project Finance*, 17(1) The Journal of Structured Finance (2011) 76–79.

967. If the inputs predictability is not well managed in terms of the contract, or the reliability risks are not assigned in a reasonable manner, it will be necessary to improve the structure of the project to protect it from contingencies, such as their availability and their transport, the lack of depth of the market where they are taken from, and the changes in the law. The financed Projects, in general, require a long-term contract, such as *supply-or-pay* for basic inputs such as fuel, whereas in other projects, this type of long-term contracts are not necessary as the supplies and the transports are available at all times.

C. Construction Contract

968. Another essential contract in the structuring of an infrastructure Project is the Construction contract, which gives the sponsor an installation to meet the demands of the Project such as the generation, the storage, the transport or the distribution of the energy products to the consumers.

969. From the financing structure's point of view of the Project, the Construction contract must be a tool to guarantee that the terms established are respected and that the installations meet the specific performance criteria, generally by a fixed or truly fixable Price. To that end, the contracts most widely used cover the development of the engineering as well as the management of the inputs and equipment purchases, and the construction itself, internationally known as by the acronym in English 'EPC' contract (Engineering, Procurement and Construction Contract), being the 'Turnkey' the most frequently used.[372] The EPC contracts 'turnkey' are the most suitable when structuring a *project finance,* in which it is considered that the main risk is the completion of the construction (*completion risk*), that can happen because: (i) the work cannot be completed at the agreed price, (ii) the term is not met, (iii) the performance quality (production) required is not achieved. Under this type of contract, the contracting party is committed to delivering the project fully completed according to the applicable specifications and on the agreed date. Hence, this is convenient for the investors as it is possible for them to identify the contracting party as the risk taker and responsible for the construction. This contract depicts, among other things, the project performance metrics, the completion dates, the price and the circumstances in which the contracting party can solicit a

372. The term 'Turnkey' is a characteristic of the construction contracts, especially in industrial installations, under which a sole contractor is in charge of all the installations is the single point of responsibility. With full technical and administrative capacity, he is responsible for the design executed and delivered to the customer, with certain economic benefits related to that scope of independence in the decision-making process. The Legal Guide of the UNCITRAL (United Nations Commission on International Trade Law) on Drawing up International Contracts with the Construction of Industrial Works establishes that: '... *in a turnkey contract, the contractor himself is the one that supplies the equipment and makes the construction following the design contained in his offer; it is possible that such design reflects technical, constructing and manufacturing economies in the hands of the contractor, that will result in an more economical and efficient construction'. Page 17 United Nations, Nueva York, 1988.*

time extension and additional compensations. The contract also defines the contracting party's scope of responsibility for the low performance or delay in the execution of the project or in relation to other participants in the project. The aim of this model is that the contracting party, who has the completion risks under control, takes responsibility for them whatever the causes, whether they are due to errors in the design, underground conditions, construction interfaces, interferences, and further issues of the context, among others. As a general rule for this model of contract, it is considered that most risks should be transferred to the contracting party, who in the frame of its technical and administrative autonomy must achieve the expected result. In that sense, it is assumed that all the necessary activities to meet the objective of the contract, apart from the description of specific tasks given by the scope of the work, are deemed as exclusive responsibility of the contracting party. Due to this critical stage of the Project and to mitigate the risk of delays in the completion, many contracts consider compensations for completion on a date earlier than the deadline and penalties on a date later than the deadline. The risk of the construction costs exceeding the funds available to complete the project is the subject of discussion between the parties involved.

970. The execution committee's participation is, at first sight, more limited in comparison with other contractual modalities. However, it is also considered that the transfer of risks to the contracting party in certain issues is convenient since the committing party may be in better conditions to deal with topics such as changes in law, third parties' interference or force majeure events. In conclusion, this modality is chosen by the large-scale project developers so that the complex projects can be completed according to the times, budgets and qualities agreed even if that means losing areas of control and paying a higher price.

971. The management of risks is considered by means of contracting the necessary insurances to cover those events that are beyond the guarantee inherent in the construction contract. On the other hand, the sponsors assume the contingencies for events not covered by the insurance policy so as to offer a complete guarantee of completion of the work. This widespread preoccupation with the 'construction risk' has forced international specialized institutions to deal with the issue. For instance, the International Federation of Consulting Engineers (FIDIC)[373] has developed a set of model contracts widely recognized in the industry, among which is the Silver Book for '*Turn Key Projects* aimed at delivering the installations that was realized by the contracting party as from its engineering to the performance tests.

972. Finally, it is important to highlight that the financing party does not take risks related to the construction. Thus, the party will check that the set of construction contracts, the insurance policies and completion guarantees fully mitigate the '*completion risk*'. To that end, a detailed '*due diligence*' of the building company's technical background and of the project will be performed by an independent engineer who will review the construction schedule, costs, and specifications, among other aspects, to clearly identify potential deviations and their magnitude.

---

373. http://fidic.org.

D. Operation and Maintenance Contracts

973. The sponsor of a project has two options for the project operation and maintenance. He can operate the Project directly, without an operation agreement, or by means of a third party assuming the responsibility for the activity. The contracts for operation and maintenance of infrastructure projects should be useful to give the sponsor an installation operating throughout the life of the contract, according to the performance specifications and at a cost previously agreed.

974. The risk identified for this stage is that the operation and maintenance costs may exceed the estimated budget. If this occurs, the additional money needed should come from the reserves, if there are any, or from funds that can be used to pay debts, or from the owners' profits. The basic concept is that since the operation and maintenance costs are 'controllable' by the sponsors, they should be the ones in charge of optimizing this management and of any further potential surcharge, by means of additional capital contributions or subordinated debt.

975. The financer assumes the risk in this stage since if the earnings are significantly lower than the projected ones. Possibly, there are no sufficient resources in the project to cover the debt. To that end, the financer will exhaustively revise the project income projections with the help of independent specialists and will demand a series of supplement security measures to be able to face adverse scenarios.

976. The operation and maintenance agreements generally have provisions detailing the scope of the job, the Price, which can be fixed or variable, performance guarantees and penalties for non-compliance, among others. In at least one aspect, the operation contract does not have the importance of the construction contract: the operator can be replaced without serious consequences depending on the technical difficulty of the operation of the project and the availability to replace the workers.

E. Energy Sale Contracts with an Off-Taker

977. Another important contact, to give way to an energy infrastructure investment, is the long-term sale contract connecting the sponsor with the energy to be produced by the project installations. This counterpart is known as the *off-taker* in the terminology of project financing. The sale contract has a two-folded role: it is an operative document, but in turn it is the main revenue contract and the primary source of debt repayment. Generally, when a project is developed and boosted by the State, the buyer of the energy is a state-owned company or another institution connected to the State authorized to buy and sell the energy produced under a mid or long-term contract.[374]

---

374. Marc Z. Michael and Juan C. Garcia, *Balance of Power Between Local and International Partners in Infrastructure and Energy Projects in Latin America,* Page 8 – The Guide to Infrastructure and Energy Investment Latin Lawyer 2017.

978. In the analyses carried out for the case of the new projects of electric energy generation of renewable sources in Argentina, this contract has been deemed relevant as a cash-flow source generation contract for its performance. To prove the importance of this instrument, for the specific case, those analyses have pointed out some relevant aspects worth mentioning in this article, which can be of *mutatis mutandis* application for the rest of the energy projects. Thus, it has been observed that:

(a) The *off-taker* must be assessed as a subject of credit so as to analyse the financing of the project. In that case, it has been considered that the concept of Compañía Admninistradora del Mercado Eléctrico Mayorista (CAMMESA) (Wholesale Electrical Market Company) and the electricity distributors such as the *off-taker* in the Argentinean System are evaluated as a possible weakness based on credit history.
(b) The term of the contract must be consistent with the term of investment amortization and should not be affected by early termination clauses without a cause or adequate compensation.
(c) The cash flows certainty generated in the contract must be kept even in situations such as tax charges changes, technology costs changes, Exchange rate modifications, and other possible well-identified risks.
(d) The compensation conditions in the case of termination due to non-compliance and the associated guarantees must be specifically covered so that the cash flows involved can be replaced by the compensation.
(e) There must be a clear scenario for the case of 'force majeure' which can otherwise lead to non-compliance by the generator.
(f) There must be a clear scenario for unexecuted lack of dispatch, as well as for the suitable treatment in the cases of impossibility of dispatch due to reasons beyond the generator's control; especially in a context of transmission capacity restrictions.[375]

It is important to point out that unless these conditions are suitably treated, especially the *off-taker* credit rating in relation to its past, present and future financial performance, some improvement in the project's credit profile will be necessary by means of State's guarantees or multilateral credit agencies' support.

F. *Financial Contracts*

1. General Observations

979. Mainly due to reasons of scale, the financing scheme is a key aspect in most projects for the natural resources exploration and the exploitation as well as for the

375. Siboldi Agustín. Necessary aspects for the massive incorporation of non-conventional renewable energy sources Revista Argentina de Derecho de la Energía, Hidrocarburos y Minería. RADHEM Number 12 Feb. 2017–April 2017.

necessary infrastructure construction to generate, store, transport and trade the energy. Owing to that, the best financing strategy during the early stages of the project is feasibility analysis.

980. As the project is being structured, the sponsors and the State analyse the contributors' availability of debt or capital based on the objectives or risks set, any and all time the lenders' or investors' profiles change due to these risks and objectives. For example, it is considered that the commercial lenders aim at financing projects which are developed in a stable political and economic context, whereas the multilateral credit institutions, less worried about these conditions of the scenario, are more willing to analyse other types of projects where external social and environmental conditions are involved.[376]

981. Under concessions scheme, the sponsor of the project should be solely responsible for the installation's construction financing with the financial institutions or capital markets' support. The financing structure varies whether it is to finance the future flow of the income coming from the users or possible contributions derived from the State's participation or of a combination of both. Furthermore, there is a deep analysis of the factors influencing the definition of potential sources of debt and capital. For example, a concrete risk in a project, in the same country in which it is analysed, may postpone the whole financial scheme, such as a serious event of pollution in energy matters biasing the public opinion against certain productive processes. A clear example of this is the case of non-conventional field exploration and exploitation in some countries. Thus, it has been recommended that the sponsors and the State, as the promoters in certain sectors, simultaneously explore different financial options for the same project, such as the financing of commercial banking or rated bonds.[377]

982. The financing sources are also affected by the States' and the sponsors' circumstances. In fact, the States and the State-owned companies have been unable to participate in projects due to public indebtedness *ratios'* limit many times.[378] Likewise, the sponsors and their financers may want to limit their exposition to certain business or countries.

---

376. The BID group considers financing lines for projects related to the climate change so as to support the investment decisions for the public as well as the private sector considering that *'the business models and technologies that can finance this transition face risks and barriers regarding costs that very often hinder its initial development, its further expansion, integration or institutionalization'* Source: http://www.iadb.org.
377. Scott L. Hoffman. *The Law and Business of International Project Finance* (3rd ed., Cambridge University Press) p. 277.
378. Section 16 of the Law 27328 establishes that: 'In the case that the public-private participation contract compromises the public budget resources, prior to the public bid there must be the authorization to commit future exercises pursuant to section 15 of the law 24156 and its amendments, which can be given in the respective general budget law or in special law, as long as the accumulated stock for the firm quantifiable contingent commitments, net of income, assumed by the non-financial public sector in the public-private participation contracts calculated at current value, does not exceed the seven per cent (7%) of the gross domestic product at current prices of the previous

983. Due to that, the experts recommend that all financing options should be considered, those coming from equipment suppliers, multilateral agencies, bilateral agencies, local development banks, specialized funds, loan institutions, capital investors, local and international commercial banks included.

984. The incorporation of the private sector to the public infrastructure context necessarily requires long-term financing in terms of the debt as well as the shareholders' equity's contributions.

985. From the financial point of view, the profit for a private company participating in a project is determined by the income earned in the exploitation or operation stage.

986. The international experience shows that the level of leverage in infrastructure projects is on average75–25, that is to say 25% is contribution of their own capital and 75% is financing with debt. The level of remuneration or return of each portion of capital structure is closely related to the project's underlying risk and the market's conditions.

987. Generally, the capital's portion financing comes from the company concessioner's partners' contributions or from a special purpose (SPV) created to that effect. On the other hand, at an international level, financing parties are international companies, deferring from the Project's country of origin, participating with less than 50%, in association with a local company. The short-term profit for the partners of the concessioner company comes from the earnings of the construction. A percentage of those earnings, not more than 35% are left aside as an initial contribution of the *equity*, the rest of the capital generally comes from a credit from the headquarters and/or with income from tolls as from the APP's inception.

988. For the long-term debt financing, the private companies participating in the APP agreements, generally have at their disposal, two financing options with totally different characteristics: the banking credit (local or international) and bond issuances (local or International).

2. Contracts with Commercial Banks

989. The commercial banks are an option for the financial needs of local as well as international entities. The local banks due to restrictions from their headquarters or to their scale have less capacity to offer financial support for big projects especially in certain countries that, as in the case of Argentina, do not have a strong financial reputation. Moreover, the local banking industry does not have specialized teams in project financing to understand and structure the risks so that they can be

year. This limit can be annually revised, together with the treatment of the budget law, considering the infrastructure and public services requirements in the country and the impact of the commitments on the public finances sustainability.

suitably presented and evaluated by their credit committees. Anyway, it is observed that the local banks may have a key role in certain stages in the financing due to their knowledge of the context, and with their *due diligence,* they may allow the participation of their headquarters or of international banks getting involved in the financing.

990. The selection of local versus international options also has to do with the future flow currency denomination of the project. Hence, it has been observed that if the project has revenues in local currency, the first alternative, with the lowest risk, normally consists of getting financing in the local market in the currency of the profit to avoid the risk of currency 'mismatch'. On the contrary, the energy infrastructure projects whether they are of natural resources generation or exploitation whose income is in a foreign currency, and specifically in US dollars, do not have the local market as their first option of financing source.[379]

991. Additionally, due to reasons of scales, in projects requiring longer terms, this financing is given by a set of institutions under the syndicated loan mode. In large-scale projects, with investments of around USD 500 million, it is impossible to fulfil their financing requirements through local banking, even if acting in syndicate, and so they have to resort to the international lenders. However, it has been observed that the banking is not a natural long-term lender, but an intermediary between the depositors and institutional investors who provide the resources, and the financing borrowers, who seek a profit for the intermediary role and in the shortest term possible.[380]

992. From the point of view of the project's risk analysis in a typical transaction, the funds are given with different risk rating for the stage of: (i) construction, in which the risk of non-delivery or delayed delivery of the facilities is higher and (ii) operation in which the risk is significantly reduced. As a consequence, it is clear that the financing can be structured with one source of funds for the construction and another for the operation.

---

379. The aforesaid has occurred in several markets, possibly being Chile one of the most emblematic cases. In the 1990s, the country had an ambitious project portfolio to finance for more than USD 8,000 million, all of them in local currency and re-adjustable according to the local inflation. However, the local banking did not have experience in Project finance, since, up to that moment, all experience had been gained in the mining sector, which required financing in USD and thus had been dominated by the international banking. Source Dr Sergio Alejandro Hinojosa Main Advisor PIAPPEM August 2015 http://www.piappem.org/file.php?id=485.

380. *'Regarding the projects, the competitive pressure among the specialized banks forced them to give financing terms never seen before, not so common in the banking, letting them compete even with the international investors, that is to say, with the bonds emissions financing, giving more flexibility and simplicity in the execution, in comparison with the bonds emissions. With the financial crisis, however, the banking excesses were penalized by the market with a clear lack of solidity and funding, especially in the long term; hence, the international bonds virtually closed their offer to finance concession projects. Nowadays, due to the crisis, everything has gone back to normal setting aside the long-term requirements, and the local and international Banks focus on the short and medium term, where they can have a, in turn, a more liquid funding essential for the efficient financing of concession projects.'* Source Dr Sergio Alejandro Hinojosa Main Advisor PIAPPEM August 2015 http://www.piappem.org/file.php?id=485.

993. Among the disadvantages of financing APP Project with the banking there are the following: (i) the local banking's relative lack of experience, the natural financing supplier in local currency, which forces to resort to international banking; (ii) the failure to get long-term financing high amounts, being it necessary to syndicate or to mix several financing sources; (iii) restriction in long-term loans in times of crisis; (iv) in the case of loans at a variable rate, the need to enter into interest safe swaps which entails an additional cost and financing rigidness

994. The advantages of the bank financing vis-à-vis the bond financing are the following (i) there is more certainty of closing, as the negotiation is with the lender in the whole process, whereas in a financing with bonds there is uncertainty until the debt is tendered, which is the final stage of the process; (ii) the banking is more flexible to negotiate the conditions and to assume certain risks, whereas the financing with bonds is less flexible and is subject to the external criteria of the credit rating agencies; (iii) higher flexibility and availability to make adjustments after the financial closing, for example, to make modifications or extensions to the initial project or to refinance the debt.[381]

3. Financing by Institutional Investors

995. The bond-financing structure is similar to that of commercial loans; however, the lenders are investors who buy bonds from the borrower in a private placement or debt market. The stock or via-bonds financing has become a widely used tool as a consequence of the international crises imposing limitations on the banking financing in the international market and restrictions in the local banking not deeply familiarized with the financing of the project. Together with the growth and development of the institutional investors' portfolios, such as the pension funds, a significant knowledge base about the risks of the projects and the structure for the mitigation of such risks have been developed, through the risk rating agencies, which allow these investors – not having risk-analysis department for the projects – to access to specialized and independent risk-analyses views.

996. The institutional investors are not intermediaries like the banks, but they are natural long-term paper holders who normally keep them at term. This characteristic turns them into the natural market to get financing for long-term projects, which in turn are looking for investors seeking to obtain the least return and the mitigation of the intermediation risks.

997. In recent years, several products with credit enhancement such as total or partial financial guarantees have been developed, letting the projects reach high credit ratings even during the construction stage, when the risks of the projects are higher. With this type of products, supplied by third parties such as insurance companies and multilateral agencies, a project is able to issue securitization debt and to

381. *Ibid.*

obtain the highest credit ratings (AAA), making them attractive for all the institutional investors, since they have a risk level equivalent to those of the governmental papers but with higher profit.

998. The institutional investors are better understanding the financing discipline in the projects, since they are not only considering credit ratings, but they are as well developing their own capacity to evaluate risks in the projects, having some of them already specialized teams in projects and structured financing that allow them to actively participate in the search for this type of investments.

999. Bond financing has a series of advantages for the private sponsor who intends to finance a project. These advantages are natural elements providing solutions for the great numbers of issues of the banking finance: (i) they practically do not have limitation in time, since they are investments recognizing the long term, and can pay a 'premium' for long-term instruments; (ii) different from the baking finance where the loan size is a disadvantage and they are forced to syndicate with several Banks, a high amount may result in an advantage, since the bonds are only limited to the fact that a sole investor can have a certain percentage of the total issuance; (iii) the fixed rate is a requirement from the investors, that is to say, the pensions, life annuities and insurances, which frequently impose a fixed rate, at the same time forced the investors to invest part of their resources in fixed-rate instruments, allowing them to articulate their commitments with the assets returns; (iv) since the pension, insurances, and life annuities are normally obligations in local currency, these investors in turn favour the investment in local currency.[382]

1000. Based on these advantages, the cited studies consider that the institutional investors represent the 'natural' market to finance the public infrastructure projects of public-private participation. However, their use has not been widespread due to several reasons ranging from the lack of knowledge of implicit costs in the transaction due to a strict revision of the Project's background and the great bulk of necessary legal documents being necessary to give the financing an external credit improvement generally in the form of a financial guarantee issued in favour of the investors, to reasons of uncertainty to reach a finance closing with the bonds issuance at the end of the process.[383]

---

382. *Ibid.*
383. In relation to the report cited: *'In Latin America, for example – region that has witnessed the proliferation of APP schemes in the last two decades and that has had the participation of the APP's international groups of big promoter (Ferrovial, Dragados, ACS, Skanska, Hochtief, Bouygues, Vinci, Impregilo, FCC, SacyrVallehermoso, Acciona, etc.) – it was in 1997 that the first financing for an APP Project was carried out through debt emission in the stock exchange, for the highway Talca – Chillán in Chile, which was not product of a deliberate decision due to the access to this market, but the result of a lack of capacity and experience in the local banking system (Gutierrez De Gregori, 2010). This experience, the first one in the region, opened the stock Exchange financing to the concession projects, and encouraged the other international sponsors to examine and seriously consider this option ... The financing of bonds, has been specially important in the United Kingdom and in Chile, which has been a pioneer in infrastructure bond emission in Latin America'.*

4. Credit Financing to the Exportation

1001. The import-export finance agencies, known as *Export Credit Agencies* (ECAS), are institutions supported by the States to promote a country's trade or other interests in the world trade. These Agencies' finance generally comes from funds belonging to the States themselves and is aimed at promoting the operations of the infrastructure projects equipment, ranging from the mains to the spare parts and process unit components, equipment, and any other type of supplies that can be added to this scheme. The methods generally used for financing are:

(a) Direct loans: the loan to the borrower, conditioned on the purchase of property or services subject matter of the operation, and the lender is the exporting and importing bank.
(b) Loan with a financing intermediary: the exporting and importing bank lends funds to the financing intermediary, as a commercial bank, which in turn lends funds to the importing entity.
(c) Interest rates equality: It is the structure of interest compensation between the loan obtained by the importation company at an interest rate below the market and the rate the lender will be able to obtain in the market where the difference is contributed by the intervening exporting and importing bank.

1002. It is important to point out that construction contracts, which are part of an infrastructure project, include provisions recognizing the possibility of intervention from the part of these agencies in the stage of supply management of the project.

5. Co-financing

1003. This modality refers to mechanisms under which the multilateral credit agencies, such as International Finance Corporation (IFC), the World Bank, or the Inter-American Investment Corporation (IIC)[384] of the Inter-American Development Bank, provide credit lines as guarantee to the borrower that the State will continue supporting the project which obviously predisposes the commercial banking in a better way to take part in the operations. This structure comprises parts of loans where the commercial banking takes part as the 'co-lender', not in a direct contractual relationship with the borrower, but through a multilateral agency that controls of the fulfilment of the obligations and the acceleration of the debt. The commercial lenders participate by means of deposit agreements with the multilateral agencies.

384. *'The CII (Inter-American Investment Corporation) offers financing by means of loans, guarantees and capital investments, to foster the creation, enlargement and modernization of private and state-owned companies. In close collaboration with the private sector, the CII seeks to meet the challenges of growth, to improve the business strategies, and to adopt new technologies to improve productivity. The CII also acts as a catalyst to attract additional financing resources, new technologies and know-how through co-financing and syndication, so as to maximize the impact of the development.'* http://www.iic.org/es/qué-ofrecemos#.WgHFSsZDR-U.

6. *Project Finance*: Concept Applied to the Energy Infrastructure Projects

1004. The examined relationships so far let us identify the relevant issues which are taken into account for the infrastructure Project structuring to be able to be financed by the financial institutions and the rating agencies regarding the infrastructure bonds and so the necessary funds can be raised for investment. In this context, the scheme under which the financial agents do not directly demand real guarantees, represented in physical assets or monetary resources backing the main source of payment of the Project is known as *Project Finance*.

1005. *Project Finance* is the financing whose main source of repayment is the cash flow generated by the project structured with no or with recourse resources against the private sponsor of the Project. The debt taken by the project is not considered the sponsor's corporate debt, which allows him to implement several projects without affecting his creditworthiness. That means it is an 'off-balance sheet' debt. Due to this advantage, the project investors are willing to get involved in a longer, more complex and costly financing process, such as that of, for example, the Public-Private Partnership (PPP). In fact, in this scenario, the debt's financers are given the maximum guarantees for the project to generate the creditworthiness to repay the debt by means of the contracts whether the earnings come from the State or the users. The financing structure seeks to guarantee that the project has a suitable financial fortress for the risk level sought to be reached and which will be mainly able to honour the debt; even in contexts of financial stress. Based on that, the non-revocable and non-conditional character of the funds involved must be a condition guaranteeing the long-term financing, and there is a set of relevant clauses aiming to mitigate the risk regarding: (i) the end of direct payment mechanisms to financial institutions; (ii) remediation and termination in favour of the financial institutions or the bonds holders, to as to cover any lack of compliance by the sponsor and thus prevent the early termination of the contract; (iii) limitations of sanctions and penalties; (iv) definition of force majeure events and their consequences;(v) economic-finance restoring in the event of changes in the regulations in force; (vi) compensation for non-compliance; (vii) assignment; and (viii) mechanisms to solve technical and contractual disputes by means of the modern technical boards (Dispute Boards) and arbitration, among others.

The techniques of the *Project Finance* are used as financing techniques for the construction of a new energy infrastructure both in industrialized countries such as the United States of America and emerging countries such as Eastern Europe and the Pacific.

Chapter 2. The Legal Instruments Contemplated in Our Legislation

1006. In this section, the most recognized legal instruments in the relationship between the so-called public sector and the private investors for the development investment Project in relation to production, transport, distribution and commercialization of energy products will be analysed.

1007. It is important initially to highlight that when talking about the energy infrastructure, a universe of physical installations and equipment as well as the rights related to goods and services rendering to produce, transport, distribute and commercialize such energy products are mentioned.

1008. In this concept, a universality of means is understood to achieve not only the capture of 'primary energies' directly obtained by the nature such as the solar, hydraulic, wind, biomass, geothermal oil, natural gas or carbon ones; but also the production of 'secondary energies' coming from the transformation of primary energy for direct consumption and other uses such as fuels, electricity, gas oil, and other derivatives.

1009. These infrastructures cover installations for the exploration and exploitation of resources (water, hydrocarbon, coal, air, radiation solar, biomass), the process of *in situ* treatment, the transport and storage, its transformation, distribution, and commercialization (with activities ranging from the importation to the exportation).

1010. In these universalities, there coexist private free initiative projects at their own risk with low control from the part of the State's, and other considered public infrastructures under the State's control with the private sector's collaboration.

1011. Anyway, since in most cases of infrastructures there must be significant collaboration from both the private and public sectors, most projects and activities are internationally known in general as 'PPP' projects according to its acronym in English *Public-Private Partnership.*[385]

1012. With its origin in Great Britain, the policy known as Private Finance Initiative (PFI), which encouraged the private sector's participation in the infrastructure contracts, gave birth to this denomination PPP worldwide recognized with several comprehensive modalities.

1013. In the legal system in Argentina, the private sector has the legal power to initiate the projects which are deemed convenient subject to the applicable regulations. The infrastructure energy projects can be implemented under different legal

385. José V. Lopes Enei and Mauro Bardawil Penteado. *Brazilian Public – Private Partnerships: Retrospect of Past Decades and New Trends Ahead*, p. 14 – *The Guide to Infrastructure and Energy Investment* Latin Lawyer 2017.

regimes depending on their nature and classification as an activity of general interest, such as the electric energy generation, or as a public service such as the case of transport and distribution.[386]

1014. In our context, the contribution of the private sector with the public sector has been classified under different criteria by the doctrine. One of them, considering the nature of the funds given to the infrastructure management divides the infrastructures into:(i) out of budget covering those Works being performed with funds not coming from the public funds, for instance, the concession contract and (ii) in budget, supposing the use of public funds.[387]

1015. Another classification has been made based on the risks allocation, considering 'pure' schemes, those in which the risks are taken fundamentally by the public or the private sector. Under this classification, there are as well the 'mix' modalities such as those concessions with shared risks in which the use of public funds for the payment of the work does not imply that the private sector does not take any risk in relation to the construction and exploitation or the financing. In this group, also to be considered are those innovative modalities introducing rules of the private law to give more guarantees to the contractor investor and those contributing funds for its financing such as those allowing PPP modalities.[388]

1016. In another classification, Dr Crivelli considers, as part of the analysis of the public-private collaboration contracts for the public infrastructure development, concessions and public-private partnerships (PPP) as modalities of the same contract since they share the same general principles, objectives, parties and difficulties and the very same paradigms even when they are concepts with different legislative treatment.[389]

1017. By means of this modality of contract, a new legal regime is established under which the private sector is able to 'design, finance, construct, operate and maintain public infrastructures destined to render public services, in exchange of a compensation coming from the users, from the State or from both', which makes it possible to overcome the current fiscal resources restriction and to finance them with an inter-generational criteria.[390]

386. Section 1 Law 24065. *'The transport and distribution of electricity shall be deemed as public service. However, its monopolistic nature shall be exempted, the transport extension regime when it does not have as its main purpose the improvement or maintenance of the reliability which, as long as it shares the rules of the market, will be a free initiative at the risk of the one executing it. The activity of generation, whichever its way, totally or partially destined to supply energy to a public service, will be considered of public interest, affected to such service and framed in the legal regulations guaranteeing its normal operation'.*
387. In accordance with Javier Guiridlian Laroza at 'Contratación Pública y Desarrollo de Infraestructuras (nuevas formas de gestión y financiación) Lexis Nexis Abeledo-Perrot, p. 28.
388. *Ibid.*, pp. 29-30.
389. Crivelli, Julio C. *supra*, p. 39.
390. *Ibid.*, p. 44.

1018. According to this author's opinion, it is important to relate the concession and the public-private partnerships with the PPP modality, which is identified at an international level with the following topologies:

(1) DBFO Contract (Design, Build, Finance, Operate), which similar to the concession contract considers the infrastructure to be (i) designed, with the collaboration of its basic detailed engineering; (ii) constructed, up to its mechanical completion and tests; (iii) operated and maintained to be commercially exploited; and (iv) financed, by the sponsor whether that be with its own funds or those of third parties; all of this in a term in which the sponsor receives a compensation which allows him to give back the loan and to obtain a profit and finally to revert the asset to the State.
(2) BOT Contract (Built, Operate, Transfer). This typical modality for the development of infrastructure in developing countries is similar to the DBFO contract; however, in this case, the State gives a definite design, with different stages of engineering development so that the contractor completes the engineering and proceeds to the construction.
(3) BOOT Contract (Built, Own, Operate, Transfer), establishes that the contractor holds the property of the asset until its reversion to the State at the end of the concession contract, which means a higher guarantee for the investors and a better financing profile. Based on this differential characteristic, some have considered it similar to a temporary privatization of the project.
(4) BOO Contract (Built, Own, Operate). In this case, in opposition to the other modalities, the contractor designs, finances and builds his infrastructure for the rendering of the public service.
(5) Contract of leasing (Built, Lease, Transfer). In this type of contract, the developer builds the facilities which during the operation stage are leased by the State who exercises the control of the operation as the lessee. This contract, which distinguishes the property from the right to use of the parties in the project, is utilized due to fiscal planning reasons and to give more protection to the lender.[391] For the foreign investors who take into account the country risk, this modality BLT offers good conditions as the company of the project keeps the property rights and avoid the operational risk at the same time. The loan is refunded by the lessor of the rents received by virtue of this contract that is given to the lender as a guarantee; this is why in some cases, it gives cheaper financing than the one a bank can offer. The property of the asset stays with the sponsor, but the operation is in the hands of the lessee. After the termination of the leasing, the property of the asset and the operational responsibility is transferred to the States at a Price arranged beforehand. It is frequent to see this type of contract for facilities that may operate independently from a more complex Project, such as water treatment or oxygen supply plants for industrial use. The main companies in this industry offer their services preferably under this modality.

---

391. Scott L. Hoffman. *The Law and Business of International Project Finance* (3rd ed., Cambridge University Press) p. 80.

A common characteristic of these contractual modalities is given by the fact that the States see them as beneficial to offer the community a Project without affecting their indebtedness *ratios*, and at the same time still having the control on the management of the project by means of the regulation of the tariffs, of the established deadlines to finish certain stages of the project and the possibility of ending the concession if any issue with the company arises. Likewise, it is useful for the State to train to the local labour and suppliers, taking the private sector's experience in more complex operations developed in an efficient and modern way.

1019. Then, the sponsors of the projects and their lenders – under this contractual modality – require certain guarantees from the State for the making of income, such as the access to supplies, working visas for the management, real property rights, among other supplements of risk management. Also, the requirements regarding financing may include the possibility of the lender to intervene in case of non-compliance and to give consent in the case of concession transfer.

§1. References of the Argentinean Positive Law

1020. In accordance with the classification made by the cited Dr Crivelli, the Public-Private Partnership (APP) term corresponds to the private participation promotion regime of the Decree 1299/00, ratified by Law No 2414 which excludes projects in which the income comes from third parties' payments such as a fee, toll or instrument of similar nature higher than 60% of the investment, being thus important the differed payment of the contracting agency. Under this modality, the compensation has no connection with that of the public, but with the payments of the State's contribution in time regardless of the installations use or a fee combined with a trust in guarantee for the protection of differed payments of some type of tax or charge or any other type of payment whatsoever.

1021. On the other hand, the concept of public work concession is related, according to the author's criteria, to the contracts ruled by Law No 17520 amended by Law No 23696, in which the compensation comes from the users closely dependent from the performance of the service.

1022. So, in the author's view which I share due to legal practical reasons, in both cases, the differences are minor when referring to the treatment of the private investment in public infrastructure, as they have the same elements, the same role and the same objective and are subject to identical principles.[392]

1023. The common thread is that the private sector assumes the realization of the work at his own risk and expense with the expectation of recovering the total of

392. As it was aforementioned, both modalities refer to the contracts by means of which the State '*gives an individual the infrastructure development which comprises the design, finance, construction, and operation and maintenance for a fixed or fixable term, during which the private contractor receives a benefit from the State, the users or from both*'.

the investments, expenses, financial costs and a profit through the collection of a compensation differed in time, that is to say after its finalization, under different modalities that, internationally speaking, are in constant evolution.

1024. In fact, as it is further analysed, the Law No 27328 on Public-Private Participation Contracts introduces the innovation over the basis of these pre-existing modalities to give a better treatment to issues that, such as the commutability and the strengthening of the rendering balance, will favour the generalized use of these tools and their most convenient financing.

§2. Law No 27328 about Public-Private Participation Contracts

1025. Among the recent legal instruments in Argentina to boost investments in infrastructure, the regime on Public-Private Participation Contracts – hereinunder PPP Contracts – established by Law No 27328, has been the most relevant so as to bridge a gap in the national legal system making infrastructure projects possible with the state contribution and the private sector's entrepreneur and financing effort.

1026. As it has been pointed out, the size of the challenge to face in term of infrastructure investment exceeds the possibilities of just the state boosting and the existing legal mechanisms.

1027. The process to enact this Law No 27328 means it has been important to consider recent experiences in Latin American countries such as Brazil, Colombia and Peru. This law, recently established by Decree118/2017, places Argentina in the course of the world trend, letting the private sector contribute not only its projects development and management capacity but also, and especially for the developing countries, the access to new financing techniques and to capital markets.

1028. Due to their relevance in consideration of the coming energy infrastructure projects, as follows the analysis of some of the main aspects.

I. Risk Assignment in the PPP Contracts

1029. One of the most relevant aspects introducing this new regime is how to treat the risk management of the infrastructure projects, and also to assign those risks to the one who is in the best position to manage them.

1030. In that sense, the PPP Contracts must necessarily contain provisions on 'the equitable and efficient divisions of contributions and risks between the parties to the contract, considering, to that effect, the best conditions to prevent, assume or mitigate them, in such a way that the project cost is minimized and the operation conditions are eased'.[393]

1031. In this way, the relationship between the public and the private sector shall be submitted to the same logic of efficiency in the allocation of risks as the rest of the projects requiring an eligibility status for the financers.

1032. The State shall be compelled to avoid transferring certain risks that may put the development of the project in danger, for instance, the political risks; on the other hand, the private counterparts will contribute their experience in the risks management and operation of the facilities.

II. PPP Regime Application

1033. From the text of the law, it is important to highlight those crucial aspects that may contribute to the development of future investment projects in the energy sector. In this aspect, the first thing to consider is that the PPP contract is established as a contractual modality to link the public sector with private subjects which have the necessary flexibility to adapt the structure to the special demands of each Project, and especially, those of the financing, pursuant to the best international practices in the subject. Thus, proved contractual formulae internationally recognized such as the ones aforementioned 'DBFO', 'BOT', 'BOOT', 'BOMT', 'BLT' are under this scope of this modality, among others of similar characteristics

1034. This flexibility is considered one of the most notable traits of the PPP contracts which consider that 'it is a contract containing, as a definite characteristic, to give course precisely to a contract ab initio modality absolutely indefinite and uniform' and which has been defined by the Spanish doctrine as a 'model to assemble'.[394]

1035. Regarding the scope, this regime is to be applied to the projects aimed at activities of design, construction, extension, improvement, equipment and goods supply, exploitation or operation, and financing applied to installations involving energy projects allowing to meet public interest objectives.

1036. However, by means of the regulation, and consistent with the general principles of the law, it has been declared that are excluded from this regime the projects *'whose unique objective is to supply labour, goods and the construction and execution of works substantially financed with funds from the National Treasure'*.[395]

393. Section 9 Law 27238 literal b.
394. Ignacio M. De la Riva *'¿Es la 'participación público-privada' (PPP) un nuevo contrato administrativo?* El Derecho Año LV EDA 2017 p. 4.
395. *See* s. 1 from Decree 118/2017.

III. PPP Contracts Involving Public Services

1037. In the cases in which the PPP contracts involve the rendering of the public service ruled by specific regulatory frameworks, such regulatory frameworks shall be applied to the rendering of such services.

1038. This is the case of the electricity and gas networks extension projects given by concessioners and permit holders in the condition of natural monopoly under the respective regimes of the Laws 24065 and 24072.

1039. In fact, the construction of these facilities must consider, as a repayment source, all provisions in the respective rules applicable in terms of identification of the new infrastructures' respective beneficiaries and the technical and commercial conditions for the connection between the existing concessioners and permit holders, for the operation and maintenance. To that end, it is important that both the Energy and Mining Ministry and the Public-Private Participation Unit assess regarding applications for each sector and what the respective terms and conditions establish.

IV. Principles of Law No 27328

1040. Law No 27328 has provided under its section 4 some guiding principles applicable not only to the promotion of the activity but also to the suitable protection of its control, and integration with the rest of the regulations in force in the field.

1041. As far as measures to boost the development of projects are concerned, the provisions regarding the terms of the PPP contracts are to be fixed considering the investments made, the financing applicable to the Project and the possibility to obtain a reasonable profit, taking into account the maximum of 35 years' time, occasional extensions included. Likewise, boosting the application of intra-generational, inter-generational or inter-regional mechanisms in the financing of the projects is recognized as a principle by Law No 27328.

1042. These promotion rules are considered with others to favour the conditions for the financing. Hence, the law establishes in its section 10 the guarantee in favour of the contractor that in all the cases of early termination of the PPP contract by the contracting party, the contractor is eligible to receive the total amount of the compensation pursuant to the valuation and procedure methodology of determination contained in the regulation, which shall not be lower than the investment non-amortized.

1043. It is important to point out that, according to the famous cases law of our recent history, the legislator emphasized that such compensation is to be paid prior to taking possession of the assets. In the same sense, Law No 27328 establishes that *'in any and all cases, the re-payment of the financing applied to the development of the project shall be guaranteed'* which constitutes a fundamental provision for structuring thereof.

1044. Regarding the contracting parties' patrimonial responsibility, it is established that it shall be subject to provisions under Law No 27328, its regulations, terms and conditions and the PPP contract and supplementary all the rules contained in the Civil and Commercial Code of the Nations. This provision is considered by the doctrine as an exception to the provisions in the Civil and Commercial Code which – under sections. 1764–1765 – establishes that the provisions on civil liability are not applicable to the State's responsibility in a direct or subsidiary way, and that such a responsibility is ruled by regulations and principles of the administrative law. As well, provisions under section 10 of the Law No 26944 establishing that *'the States contractual liability is ruled by specific standards. In case of absence of regulations, the law is applied as a supplement'* are to be considered. Thus, it has been considered that the innovation of Law No 27328 is relevant regarding the public party's liability in the PPP Contract in case of non-compliance whether as a partner or as sovereign in the exercise of public prerogatives pursuant to section 25 of the Law No 27328 about settlement of controversies through arbitration.[396]

1045. Regarding the principles of control of the PPP projects, the setting of control and supervision mechanisms to meet the terms and objectives in each stage is thoroughly pondered.

1046. Finally, the principles of the law establish that the contractor must consider the positive external issues generated by the PPP project by means of:

- the identification of public interest objects;
- the weighing of economic and/or social profitability of the projects;
- the promotion of the social inclusion, in the area of projects development, so as to optimize the access to infrastructure and basic services;
- the generation of new labour sources and vacancies in the country;
- the small- and medium-size companies' direct and indirect participation, the companies capacity development in the private sector, the added value generation in the national territory and the new and more efficient technologies and services supply;
- the local capitals market development and the access to international capitals market;
- the environment conservation and the economic, social and environmental sustainability in the area where they are executed.

396. *Diana Nicolás. Cuestiones generales sobre el Contrato de Participación Público Privada (PPP) LA LEY 2017 – B*, p. 3.

As from those principles, arises the need to integrate those mechanisms with the compliance of the laws in force applicable to those investment projects in environmental, buy local, community participation matters, among others analysed in this work.

V. Environmental Issue in the PPP Contracts

1047. Law No 27328 and its regulations well establish the adjustment that has to exist between the PPP contracts regime and the applicable legislation in environmental matters. And it cannot be otherwise, as the Projects realized by means of this modality, especially those involving natural resources and energy products, necessarily entail a significant environmental and social impact that has to be carefully analysed so that they are socially and legally viable.

1048. Thus, it is established that before assigning the convening authority and calling for bids, the Ministry of Environment and Sustainable Development has to intervene. In the flow-chart of the PPP process[397] published by the Public-Private Participation Unit, the intervention of the Ministry of Environment and Sustainable Development is observed, prior to the report set forth under section 13 of the Law No 27328.

1049. In the process of the projects selection, as in the case of the private counter-party, the legislation establishes that there must be an environmental care and protection mechanism and the implementation of prevention, mitigation, sanction or compensation measures of the negative or adverse impacts eventually caused to the environment, pursuant to the legislation in force and applicable to each project.

1050. Pursuant to Law No 27328 and its regulations,[398] in the PPP Contracts terms and conditions, each party's responsibilities and obligations about the environment as well as the environmental management mechanisms provided under the applicable legislation on the matter, must be clearly laid down.

VI. Buy Local in the PPP Contracts

1051. So as to maximize the benefits of the projects in the national economy, under this modality, and considering the state's contribution in its development, Law No 27328 establishes that the PPP Contract must cover the minimum national standard component of 33% of the goods and services therein. In the specific projects, the scope of 'national component' shall be determined contemplating the kind of goods and services involved in the project.

397. https://www.minfinanzas.gob.ar/uppp/docs/Flujograma_UPPP.pdf.
398. *See* s. 5 of the Law 27328 and its regulation.

1052. For the completion of the Buy Local maximization system, the preferences system established under Law No 25551 has also been considered in favour of the local goods in the contracts performed for PPP projects. This regulation establishes – under section 1 – that in the hire of public services, supplies and goods, the centralized administration as well as decentralized and independent agencies, the state-owned companies and the private companies, licensees, concessionaires and permit holders of public works and services, and their respective direct subcontractors, shall give priority to the acquisition or contract of goods of national origin. In accordance with this regulation, a product is of national origin, when it has been produced or extracted in Argentina, as long as the cost of the raw material, nationalized imported products or materials does not exceed 40% of its gross production cost. As a general rule, the referred preference should happen when, for identical or similar products, payment in cash, the Price is the same or lower than that of the products offered not of national origin, increased by 7%, when such offers are realized for companies regarded as SME's, and by 5% for those performed for other companies.

1053. The PPP regulations establish that, in special cases, the national Executive Power may except or limit the demands and preferences mentioned in the previous paragraph by means of a funded decision and prior intervention of the Production Ministry of the Nation[399] in accordance with the special needs and conditions of the project.

1054. In the screening processes, eligibility criteria establishing comparative advantages in favour of the national companies over the foreign ones and in favour of those considered micro-, small- and medium-sized pursuant to Law No 25300 about the promotion of micro-, small- and medium-sized companies are to be encouraged unless their exclusion is justified by a funded decision for a specific project.

VII. Basic Terms and Conditions of the PPP Contracts

1055. Law No 27328 deals with determining fundamental terms and conditions to be considered in the PPP contracts so that basic guidelines are contained in order to meet the objectives of the regimes.

1056. Among other, the provision to clearly consider *'the equal and efficient division of the contributions and risks between the parties to the contract'* This regulation contains the principle of allocation of risks to the one in the best conditions to manage them (*'prevent, assume or mitigate them'*), what is positive so as to facilitate its financing conditions.

1057. Thus, the following terms and conditions are considered in general for the PPP contracts:

---

399. *See* Flowchart at https://www.minfinanzas.gob.ar/uppp/docs/Flujograma_UPPP.pdf.

- Definition of the obligation in relation to the distribution of risks and contributions.
- Compliance Control mechanisms of the obligations assumed and the sanctions for breaches of contract.
- Minimum technical requirements applicable to the infrastructure to be developed; quality control standards and mechanisms.
- Ways, modalities and opportunities of remuneration payment, whether it is from users/beneficiaries, third parties or the contracting entity, being the latter contributions of Money, transfer of funds of public credit operations, of the ownership of property, of fiscal, contractual and budgetary credits, or of any other kind whatsoever whose assignment shall be admitted by the applicable regulation, the assignment of rights, the constitutions of land rights over the property of public and/or domain, the awards of debt instruments, tax benefits, subsidies, franchises, and/or the assignment of rights of use and/or exploitation of public and/or domain property, and any other kind of concession or other contributions susceptible to be realized by the National State.
- Revision mechanisms of the Price of the contracts so as to preserve the contract's financial-economic equation.
- Variations' compensation suggested by the contractor of up to 20%. In the regulations, it is established that the calculation of these compensations, must always be done in such a way that the present net value of the variations shall be cero, considering the discount rate applicable pursuant to the Terms and Conditions and/or the PPP Contract and the economic effect that the variations may cause to the Project.
- Minimum income Compliance guarantees of the contract in favour of the contractor and of Payment in favour of the contracting party, when due to the nature of the project and its financing, shall be necessary to establish.
- The ownerships and the exploitation, affectation and destination regime, after the termination of the contract, of the property or real estate being used and/or constructed during its term.
- The causes to terminate the contract; basically considering that in the event of contract termination due to reasons of public interest, rules about limitation of liability contained in Laws 21499 and 26944 and in the Decree 1023/2001 shall not be applicable, and establishing that the suspension or nullity of the contract due to reasons of illegitimacy shall be requested to and declared by the competent court.
- The possibility of assignment or guarantee of the credit rights emerging from the contract, the right to perceive the contributions committed by the contracting party, the remuneration, and the pertinent compensations as well as the cash flows ownership included.[400]

---

400. Decree 118/2017 regulatory of the Law 27328 establishes that the PPP contractor may assign the PPP contact in guarantee and, in its case, the guarantees and that the assignment of the emerging credit rights of the PPP contract shall be modified before the Contracting Agency under the terms of s. 1620 of the Civil and Commercial Code of the Nation. In case of benefits for the use, the requirement set forth under s. 1620 of the Civil and Commercial Code of the Nation the rights assignment to the collection of benefits from the part of the users for third parties to be effective,

– Transfer of the stock control of the partnership with a specific purpose, and the control of the certificates of participation in the case of Trust, in favour of third parties, considering the previous acceptance of the financers, guarantors, warrantors, and endorsers.
– The specification of the property and real estate that will revert or be transferred to the National State when the contract is terminated, granting the possibility of agreeing that the ownership of the work or the infrastructure built will be transferred to the State after the termination of the contract.
– The procedures and methods to settle the technical controversies, as well as a technical board internationally known in the infrastructure contracts industry as *Dispute Boards*.
– The settlement of the controversies by means of arbitration.
– The due compensation to the contractor in the cases of early termination of the PPP Contract by the Contracting party and previous to taking possession of the assets, which in no case whatsoever can be inferior to the investment not amortized, further granting the repayment of the financing.

Supplement to that is the provision about the Contracting party's power to be able to collaborate to obtain the necessary finance for the execution of the Project. It is clear the bias of the regulation in giving the PPP Contract minimum contents to facilitate its use in the frame of *Project Finance* mechanisms and to be able to involve a wide range of investors and financers in these prospects.

1058. In accordance with these guidelines, and so as to structure the financing of the Project, the regulations in the law establish that the PPP contractor can *'take out loan, issue debt securities placed or not in the market, set up trust – financial or not-, issuing debt securities or certificates of investment, create mutual investment funds and any and all financial structure susceptible to be granted through the assignment of the PPP contracts and/or credit lines rights arising from the PPP contracts and their corresponding guarantees'*.

1059. Furthermore, the intervention of the Ministries of Economy and Finance is considered to decide on the terms and conditions of the PPP contract regarding economic and financial matters on the assumption of risk and obligations from the part of the National Public Sector related to the proposed financial structure, the financial cost included and as long as the public debt is involved.[401]

1060. The Public-Private Participation Unit has the role of assisting the Executive Power in preparing contractual guides and models of general application for the different modalities of financing established in the legislation.[402]

---

shall be considered fulfilled with the publication of the assignment for the term of three days in the official Bulletin and its case in a newspaper of the jurisdiction of the project's placement.

401. *See* s. 6 of the regulations.
402. *See* s. 28 literal.

VIII. The Real Surface Right of the PPP Law

1061. One of the new instruments making reference to Law No 27328 as part of the possible contributions that the contracting party can make as a financing assistant is found in the constitution of the real right of surface over public and private-domain goods.

1062. Section 2114 of the Civil and Commercial Code defines this right with the scope as follows:

> The surface right is a temporary real right that is granted over other people's property, giving the holder the power to use, enjoy and materially and legally dispose of the right of planting, foresting, or building, or the right over the planted, forested or built on the surface, the air or subsurface, according to its exercise modalities and term established in the deed sufficient for the construction, and pursuant to the provisions of this Title and the Special Laws.

In accordance to the doctrine,[403] this right defines the legal relationship between the landowner, the one who owns the land or real property, and the land user which has the power to exercise the use, enjoyment and legal and material disposition to build and to whatever is built upon the land. This right may be granted over the subsurface, the surface and the air of the affected real property. Thus, when the right is granted there is a distinction between the owner of the property having an imperfect domain or bare legal title and the one exercising the surface right for a period of time.

1063. It is also important to observe that this right may be granted as a right over one's own goods, over part of the land or excluding the existing constructions, which allows a better adaptation thereof regarding the flexibility objectives sought with its constitution. At the moment of the extinction of the surface right, the bare legal title owner makes use of the constructed or planted areas free of real or personal rights imposed by the land user.[404] On the other hand, the land user has ample powers to establish personal rights such as rent or bailment, etc. for the term of his rights.

1064. In the regulations under Law No 27328, it is provided that the surface rights granted over public or private goods shall have the same legal effect as the PPP contract that is has been affected. They can only be extinguished – under any legal title and without the PPP contracting party's consent – as a consequence of the respective PPP contract extinction and the effects provided for that matter in the law, the regulations, and the terms and conditions and the PPP contract. Unless otherwise provided in the PPP contract, the following rules are to be applied: (a) In all

403. Manuel C. Gómez de la Lastra The real right of surface. A landmark in the financing of the productive activity LL Year LXXXI No 166 p. 1.

404. Mariani de Vidal Marina, Abella Adriana 'Derecho Real de superficie en el Código y Comercial' La Ley 2016-A 117 AR/DOC/507/2016 cited by Manuel C. Gómez de la Lastra, *supra*.

the cases, the surface right shall only be transferable to third parties as a consequence of the assignment, duly authorized, of the PPP contract; (b) in the case of early extinction of the PPP contract, the compensation provided under section 2126 of the Commercial and Civil Code of the Nation, will be understood replaced by the payment supposed to be done by the contractor to the contracting party of the PPP in such a case; (c) In the event of extinction of the PPP Contract owing to the due term, the PPP contracting party shall be entitled to no compensation whatsoever for the accompanying extinction of the surface right of such PPP contract.

IX. Selection Procedures of the PPP Contracting Parties

1065. Regarding the selection procedures established in sections 12 to 17 of the Law No 27328, the intention is to give them the guarantees of essential competences in order to provide investors with a reliable mechanism.

1066. In accordance with the principles, the public tender bid procedure is established and can be national or international according to the project's technical complexity, the local companies' capacity of participation, among other economic and/or financial reason related to the characteristics of the project, such as the available contracting capacity and/or the origin of the funds when referring to projects that need or have external financing.

1067. Likewise, section 14 of the Law No 27328 establishes a transparent consultation procedure between the contracting party and pre-qualified interested parties, known as the competitive dialogue,[405] with the Public-Private Participation Unit's intervention, so as to improve the terms of the bid to be consistent with the objectives thereof. The Law delegates in the aforementioned unit the establishment of the procedures for the consultation to be carried out.

1068. With the objective clearly establishing the public interest engaged in the adjudication and further celebration of the PPP contract subject of the call for public bid, under section 13 of the Law No 27328 a report from the part of the authority is to be drafted with the items as follows: (a) the feasibility and justification of the contract vis-à-vis other available contracting alternatives; (b) the budget impact of the contract; (c) the estimate of the financial effect and the budget of the contract during which the contract will be executed; (d) estimate of the sufficient public sources flow during the terms of the contract; (e) the positive externalities, including the estimate of probable future income flow in favour of the pertinent jurisdictions; (f) the impact in terms of employment generation and the foster of SME's and the national industry participation; (g) the socio-environmental impact; (h) a cost-benefit valuation of the PPP contract, considering the risk in case of the contract

405. *Supra* in which s. 179.1 of the Law of Contracts of the Public Sector in Spain is cited as a source of this procedure.

extinction; (i) the evaluation of the risks equal division between the parties in accordance with the PPP law principles established in the contract; (j) other useful data to evaluate the convenience of the project by means of the PPP contract.

1069. Our Law No 27328, different from other legislations, does not expressly consider the PPP process of private initiative; however, it establishes under section 17 that the selection procedures regarding any PPP contract are compatible with that of private initiative procedures considered in our system.

X. The Contracting Party's Payment Obligations and Guarantees

1070. In line with the rules under Law No 27328, in Chapter III, provisions related to the contractor's payment obligation and the guarantees thereof, supporting the financing structure designed under this scheme, are established. Thus, the following mechanisms are taken into account:

(a) Specific affectation and/or transfer of the tax resources, property, funds and any other kind of credit and/or public earnings.
(b) Trusts created or to be created to which the fiduciary property of the tax resources, credits, property, funds or any other type of public income can be exclusively and irrevocably transferred, and under provisions of section 1666 and following of the Commercial and Civil Code of the Nation so as to support and/or guarantee the payment of the pecuniary obligations assumed in the contract.
(c) Grant of surety, guarantee, warranty from recognized and solvent entities in the national and international market and/or the constitution of any other instruments used as a guarantee.
(d) Guarantees on the exploitation rights of the public or privatedomain goods being given to the contracting party to guarantee the repayment of the financing.

These provisions, together with the PPP contracting party's powers to take loans, issue securities with or without public bid, set up a trust, financial or not, create mutual investment funds, among others, that may be the guarantee through the assignment of the PPP contracts and/or of the emerging credit rights of the PPP contract and its corresponding guarantees, are the scheme core of these projects' financing structuring.

XI. Controversy Settlement Mechanisms under Law No 27328

1071. The possibility to timely solve controversies arising between the parties during the life of the PPP Contracts, the need for long periods of execution, and of mechanisms for their settlement that suppose the intervention of specialized experts, are elements of high consideration in the projects structuring assessment.

1072. On the other hand, the controversies settlement in national tribunals is not a favourable option for the project developers in the sense that they can be influenced by the local parties and in a PPP project by the State's interests. These considerations are to be taken into account for the practice of resorting to alternative mechanisms in the controversies resolutions such as national as well as international conciliation, mediation or arbitration. Then, as it is a consolidated practice in the international contracts involving energy infrastructure projects, to submit disputes to the decision of specialized arbitrators instead of resorting to national tribunals is the best option.

1073. The arbitration mechanism has several advantages and it is more acceptable for the parties due to the considerations as follows, among others: (i) it is private way to solve disputes allowing a more efficient time management in the specific decision-making process; (ii) the arbitrators decide the disputes in a definite way and their decisions can be recognized and executed in most countries; (iii) the execution of the awards is generally easier than the execution of local tribunal decisions; (iv) the procedures suppose certain advantages regarding proceeding rules in which the parties' autonomy is the norm.

1074. The use of recognized rules by all the actors such as the rules of International Commerce Chamber (ICC)[406] or those of the United Nations Commission of International Trade Law (UNICTRAL),[407] are frequently used in international contracts involving investments in infrastructure contracts.

1075. Furthermore, pursuant to provisions under section V paragraph 1 'e' of the1958 New York Convention about recognition and execution of arbitration awards that establishes that the award can be annulled or suspended by the competent authority of the country, where the decision has been entered into, it is important to evaluate the possibility that the country chosen as a seat to settle the dispute in the frame of the PPP contract has a modern arbitration legislation which has been ratified so as to facilitate the formality of implementing the award in the country of origin of the parties to a dispute.

1076. Other aspects that can be summarily identified as relevant when considering the use of arbitration in the PPP Contracts are: (i) the number of arbitrators solving the dispute and their background (ii) the arbitrators' nationality, (iii) the language of arbitration, (iv) the issuance of injunctions, (v) the date to issue the award (vi) waiver of sovereign immunity, (vii) the recognition and execution of the arbitration awards against the sovereign assets, among others that are to be specially considered in the context of the project assessment.

1077. Law No 27328 introduces an international acceptance standard for disputes resolution for the execution, application, and/or interpretation of this type of

---

406. https://iccwbo.org.
407. http://www.uncitral.org.

contracts that has to be considered in the terms and conditions and in the corresponding contractual documentation.[408] In that sense, Law No 27328 establishes that in the case of opting to arbitration to solve disputes, the arbitration clause is to be included.

1078. In the PPP law, some important rules for the use of arbitration are included:

- Institutional Arbitration. The administration of the arbitration and the arbitrators' appointment can be commended to recognized civil associations or other national or international institutions, and the regulations are to be added to the arbitration contract.
- Arbitration Tribunal Integration. It is provided that the tribunal is formed by one or three de jure arbitrators.
- Arbitrators' Nationality. It is established that the tribunal's president's nationality shall not coincide with that of the Parties' or the shareholder's having more than 10% of the PPP contracting party's shares.
- Autonomy of the arbitration clause. The PPP contract's eventual inefficacy does not hinder the arbitration clause or agreement validity, and the arbitrators shall keep their competence to issue the award.
- Seat outside the territory. In the case of opting for an arbitration seat outside Argentina's territory, the approval of the Executive Power is to be obtained and the National Congress is to be informed about it.

Finally, it is important to point out that if the tribunal seat were Argentina, Law No 27328 establishes as a solution in terms of award remedies that a motion to vacate or explanatory remedy can only be filed under section 760 of the Nation Commercial and Civil Code in the terms and conditions therein established; and those remedies will, in no case whatsoever, give place to the review of the appreciation or application of the case's facts and, of the applicable law, respectively.

XII. Panels of Experts

1079. The appointment of an Experts' panel, international known as *Dispute Board* (DB), which is created ad hoc for the settlement of technical disputes, is an instrument increasingly widely used in contracts of energy projects. The DB is aimed at efficiently and quickly solving disputes, proposing a reasoned and well-funded decision of the dispute based on the contract, and it can be established when a difference comes up, even though the trend is to settle it at the onset of the Project.

---

408. Section 25 – Arbitration and/or settlement mechanisms are likely to be established for all disputes that may arise due to the execution, application, and/or interpretation of the contracts entered into under the regime imposed by the current law, the terms and conditions, and the corresponding contractual documentation.

Hence, the parties have a way to solve the disputes without having to resort to the arbitrations cost and time, contributing at the same time to the continuance of the project.

1080. Generally the decision made by the technical panel is binding for the parties, unless one of the parties puts forward a note of not being satisfied and requests its revision by means of the amicable dispute resolution mechanisms or arbitration.

1081. In many contract models of international use, such as the so-called Silver Book for Turnkey contracts of FIDIC it is established in its Clause 20.4 that the DB can be applied to any type of controversy between the parties, or that may arise from the contract, or in relation to the execution of the works, any dispute regarding certification, determination, instruction, opinion or valuation of the Board included. The experts on the subject consider the modalities as follows: (i) *Dispute Adjudication Board* ('DAB') issuing a decision which is binding until there is a termination of the contract or arbitration award about underlying controversies; (ii) *Dispute Review Board* ('DRB') issuing a non-binding recommendation (but that can be binding in the future if the non-satisfaction notice is not given on time); (iii) *Combined Dispute Board* ('CDB') issuing a binding decision as well as non-binding recommendation.

1082. In the international practice, even though it has been a significant contribution in the quick and specific settlement of technical disputes, it has at the same time evidenced certain issues in the practice related to the calculation of terms to initiate the dispute and accept the decision, Board members' differences, and conflicts of interests or the interpretation of the DB's final and binding decision and its connection with the arbitration way.[409] As from all this exposed by the experts in the field, it is observed that in numerous cases these issues can generate unnecessary delays and expenses hindering the DBs' initial idea.

1083. Nevertheless, regarding the international trend, Law No 27328 establishes in its section 9 the use of technical boards to settle the *'technical, interpretative or patrimonial disputes that may arise during the execution and termination of the contract'*.

409. In the case of submission to decision to the Singapore Supreme Court, the parties proposed to resort to arbitration under ICC to make effective a DAB decision considered binding but not definite. In a first ruling, the Court decided that the Arbitration Tribunal was not legitimated to make the DAB decision executive without going into the merits of the matter (two disputes). However, the Court in a further ruling in relation to a second ICC arbitration regarding a binding and definite decision from the DAB, decided to pay the amount ordered by the DAB without the need of the second dispute regarding the merits of the matter (only one dispute) considering arbitration as the direct way to solve the controversy. PT Perusahaan Gas Negara (Perseo) TBK v. CRW Joint Operation (Indonesia) 2014 SGH146.

1084. To that effect, it is considered that the technical board should be formed by professionals and/or representatives of foreign and national universities proving Independence, impartiality, aptitude, and national and international background in the field.

1085. In the regulations of the law, the following important aspects are to be considered for this institution:

- The parties are allowed to use in subsidy the operations regulations of international institutions or organizations specialized in the subject.
- It is established that the PPP Unit will prepare a list of professionals with their background before the public bid to be shortlisted by the parties. It shall be further analysed if its utilization is an unnecessary limitation for the parties' autonomy, and if it is not compatible with the system's flexibility, especially in the case of foreign parties' intervention.
- It is established that in the controversies to be submitted to the Technical Board, whether they are technical, interpretative or patrimonial arising from the execution to termination of the PPP contracts, the revision of the sanctions imposed to the PPP contracting party as well as any other act or measure established by the contractor, having effect over the PPP contract, is included.
- The previous submittal of administrative claims or impugnation of any kind whatsoever is not required; however, having they have been submitted, the use of the Technical Board to settle the dispute implies the waiver of such claims or impugnation.
- The technical Board's recommendations shall only be binding for the parties as long as none of them has posed their disagreement within the term established in the Terms and Conditions or in the PPP contract. The party posing the disagreement is then authorized to submit the controversy to the competent judicial or arbitration tribunal. This possibility of the parties being entitled to put forward discrepancies have caused issues of practicality in relation to this institution, any and all times that the parties have used time and resources to submit the matter to a Board and then due to an inconvenient decision bring the matter back to square one, that is to say to the initial stage of the disputes.
- The Parties are entitled to submit the dispute to the competent judicial or arbitration tribunal if the technical Board does not make a decision in the term agreed.
- In the case of a biased opinion to foster the use of this type of mechanism, it is established that if the PPP contract considers a Technical Board, no technical, interpretative or patrimonial controversy can be submitted to competent judicial or arbitration tribunals without being previously submitted to such Board unless the PPP contract is terminated due to reasons of public interest.
- According to the international practice, the competent judicial or arbitration tribunal cannot be asked to review the Technical Board recommendations which are definite when there are no discrepancies submitted by the parties within the term fixed to that effect in the PPP Contract. On the contrary, in the case of non-compliance with a definite recommendation by the Technical Board, the other party may solicit its compliance through the judicial or arbitration way.

Finally, it is important to point out that in the case a Technical Board has not been formed and the arbitration has been agreed, the impugnation ways provided under Law No 19549 and its regulations will be optional for the PPP contracting party who shall be entitled to submit the dispute directly to the Arbitration Tribunal.

It is important to highlight that for a contracting party to be able to finish a controversy submitted to the Technical Board o to consent a recommendation issued by the Board, the prior authorization given by the competent Ministry or higher authority will be necessary in the case of des-centralized agencies.

XIII. The Economic-Financial Equation of the PPP Contracts

1086. Among the new instruments introduced by Law No 27328, the rules related to the preservation PPP contract financial-economic equation are the most relevant ones since they are aimed at guaranteeing contracting party, who decides to connect with the public sector under this modality, that financial-economic premises to enter into the contract are to be established when due to reasons impossible to foreseen have been significantly changed.

1087. This is a strong signal for the investors since by means of this mechanism not only are important risks mitigated, but also is a more efficient equation with greater possibilities of success likely to occur. In fact, this principle related to the commutability of the benefits, which should exist in the PPP contracts, is more important in the administrative contracts which acquire relevance as a correction mechanism for the functional and positional inequalities between the parties, privilege funded in the pursuit of the public interest.[410] The principle faithfully reflects the need for striking a balance between the public prerogatives and the private party's guarantees.

1088. As the doctrine so reads, 'the PPP Law architecture was built under certain basis tending to the protection of the contractual bilateral aspect and was inspired in the premise of ensuring the public infrastructures financing and construction taken from the traditional models and concession of public Works.'[411]

1089. Thus, the aim is to keep a balance between the advantages and disadvantages for the co-contracting party in the execution of the contract.[412]

1090. The preservation of the economic-financial equation of the PPP contract was introduced in the legislation as an independent principle, not limited to concrete cases, but in general to recognize certain guarantees regarding prices to obtain enough income[413] and a reasonable rent,[414] as well as to revise the prices in the PPP

410. Milagros Ibarzábal, El principio del equilibrio económico – financiero en los contratos de participación público – privada. El Derecho Year LV EDA 2017, p. 4.
411. *Ibid.*, Quote 23.
412. *Ibid.*, Quote 39.
413. *See* s. 9 subs. k of the Law 27328.

contract. Provisions, which are relevant in the case of structured financing, since they make it possible to suitably define, and to keep stable throughout time, the income flow to ensure the payment of the financing and the return on investment.

1091. Law No 27328 clearly establishes that in the contractual documents the procedures for the revisions are considered *'so as to preserve the contract's economic-financial equation'*[415] such as prices readjustments, terms extension, investment plan modifications, supplementary activities enabling extraordinary income or direct economic compensations

1092. On the one hand, and in relation to the power of the contracting entity to establish variations unilaterally, they are limited to 20% of the value of the PPP contract. Law No 27328 is clear to establish that the alleged compensation for the contracting party should keep the original financial-economic balance, and, above all, considering *'the possibilities and conditions of the financing'*. Hence, the modifications which are consequences of the variations shall be offset to the contracting party by means of the modification of some factor of the PPP contract economic regime letting the present net value of the variations be equal to cero considering the discount rate established by the contracting party.[416]

1093. The procedure to make this instrument effective is defined in the regulations that set that: 'The PPP contract shall contain mechanisms to re-establish, within a maximum term set in the Terms and Conditions, its original economic-financial equation whenever it is significantly altered due to unforeseeable reason at the moment of the award and not known by the party declaring the imbalance, all this, in the conditions covered by the Terms. When that term is due without any satisfactory solution for the damaged Party, the latter may resort to the Technical Board, if there was any, or to the arbitration or the competent judicial tribunal. According to the provisions under the Terms and Conditions, an alteration shall be considered significant when the parameters, established to that effect in the Terms and Conditions or the PPP contract, have been reached'[417]

1094. It is interesting to observed that the regulation considers that the term is to be fixed so that the financial-economic equation of the PPP contract is restored at the contracting party's satisfaction, so as to give a rapid solution to the dispute and thus to foster the continuity of the project.

1095. To sum up, according to the elements contemplated in the Law No 27328 and in its regulations, it is clear that this principle consecration of restoring the PPP contract's financial-economic balance, is a guaranty of stability that will not only entail fewer risks for the contracting party but also more competitive prices for the public interest's sake.

---

414. *See* s. 4 subs. d of the Law 27328.
415. *See* s. 9 subs. f of the Law 27328.
416. *See* s. 9° subs. i of the Law 27.328 and s. 9 item 8 of Decree 118/17.
417. *See* s. 9 of Decree 118/17.

Chapter 3. Risk Analysis Regarding the Social-Environmental Impact of the Infrastructure Projects

1096. Recently, the topic of the environmental and social impact of the investment projects in infrastructure have been put into consideration not only by the States and the sponsors but also by the public opinion in general.

1097. The protagonist role of the society in relation to this topic, based on the global awareness about the industrial activities and climate change and the populations' quality of life, is becoming bigger and bigger and this has been noticed by the decisions-making parties chain to define an investment project in infrastructure.

1098. The environmental and social impact issues are becoming more and more important in every stage of the Project and even after their development. The companies, nowadays, deal with issue related to the finalization of the Project and the departure of the companies from the communities.

1099. The increasing operational and construction costs related to the equipment to meet the new environmental standards, the insurance costs and the contingencies due to civil and criminal sanctions for cases of pollution, among other contingencies, have their effect on the projects and their sponsors.

1100. The States are more and more protective of the environment are and very conscious of the greater participation the society must have for the projects to be viable. Both the centralized administration and the state-owned agencies accompany this orientation with their policies and actions. Likewise, the law-makers are more and more involved in the regulation updates by means of the consecration of environmental-wise rules regarding infrastructure in accordance with the international trend. High courts, as well, with their rulings have laid down doctrine about sensitive topics regarding the compliance of the administrative environmental procedures, the spreading of the information about the projects, as well as the political participation in the impact-assessment stage.

1101. Likewise, internationally speaking, the multilateral credit agencies consider the environment protection a central component of their activity. As a result of that, the different regulatory frameworks for energy projects, as well as multilateral institution policies taking part in the financing, need that the impact of a project in the environment be taken into account before the construction approval or the financing disbursement occur. Hence, the projects with the intervention of the agencies anticipate that the specifications in the contracts for the execution stage meet the standards.

1102. In accordance to these standards, the processes consider the drafting of a declaration regarding the environmental impact, in which the environmental effects are described, the mitigation plans are developed, and the agencies having jurisdiction on the project are identified. The information and the analysis included in such statement vary according to the type of Project and the different applicable legislations, but in general they cover the topics as follows:

- The description of the place where the Project will be developed. The basic elements of the analysis are the topography, the type of soil, the changes in the topography and the possibilities of erosion.
- The emissions to the air during the construction and operation.
- The use of water. The analysis of groundwater availability, the quantity necessary for its use, as well as its further treatment and availability; apart from the impacts on superficial waters such as streams, rivers and lakes.
- The effect on the flora and fauna is of the utmost importance if the Project is affecting endangered species.
- The potential danger for the health related to the project's construction and operation due to the air pollution, electromagnetic camps and other potential dangers as, for instance, risk of explosion or more direct chemical effects.
- Ear impact, the management of the noise levels in the most silent hours.
- The aesthetic and landscape impact, a relevant factor in areas in which the energy project competes with other industries such as tourism.
- The effects over the historical or cultural heritage.
- The analysis of the impact on the existing transport and on the public services, as well as the use of other ways or systems used by the community.

The environmental feasibility study and the environmental impact declaration include the study of the permits required by the government to construct and operate the project. If the permits are not obtained, this may result in civil claims. However, the worst effect of not obtaining the permits is the prohibition to construct and operate until authorized what may entail delays and overcharges in the projects.

1103. In a recent case, an appeal was lodged for protection of constitutional rights against the National State and Santa Cruz province respectively, to cancel the Works of the Project of 'Hydro-electrical Use of the River Santa Cruz Presidente Dr Néstor Carlos Kirchner – Gobernador Jorge Cepernic', placed in that province, as environmental impact studies requirements prior to the beginning of the Works were not met and neither was the call for public bids made, to determine the impact on the ecosystem, especially on the Lago Argentino, to the Perito Moreno, Upsala, Spegazzini Galciars and to the National Park Los Glaciares.[418]

1104. In the context of the environmental protection of rights, the lawyers' association plaintiff filed a precautionary measure to request reports to the defendants to check if the formation and environmental impact study and the public bids had been carried out, in compliance with the environmental rules in the frame of the project,

418. 'Asociación de abogados ambientalistas de la Patagonia against/ Santa Cruz province and other about environmental protection'. 21 Dec. 2016 CSJN 5258/2014.

with the request to immediately cancel the works until the requirements of law had been met, that is to say, the environmental impact study and the call for public bids.[419]

1105. The Court ordered reports to the National State to confirm if the environmental impact study had been carried out before the initiation of the Works and if the call for public bids had been made effective in accordance with the Law of Hydraulic Works 23879. Once the report submitted by the National State was analysed, it was unanimously decided that there was a legal context to concede the precautionary measure. The Court assessed that such circumstances '*constitute reasons to impose the preventive cancellation of the Works until the environmental impact study process and the public bids are initiated pursuant to Law 23879, or until the final judgment is passed, whatever happens first*'.[420]

1106. The doctrine derived from this judgment about the critical nature gives strict compliance to the applicable environmental regulations. However, the case evidences the high operative impact that these issues can have in the development of the projects, with the waste in time and costs that can obviously be inferred.

§1. The Environmental Standard in the Legal System in Argentina

1107. Due to the relevance of this risk regarding environmental regulations compliance, the environmental regulations fundamental basis in our country to be taken into account in the infrastructure projects assessment will be analysed.

1108. First, it is worth pointing out that the Argentinean environmental doctrine is clear when considering that the environmental protection regime in our country is wide and has a significant regulation development in different levels.

1109. For The State's federal organization according to our National Constitution, the public environmental management is shared by the National State, the provinces and the municipalities.[421] Pursuant to section 41 of the National Constitution, the Nation must lay down the rules containing the minimum protection environment estimates and the provinces are to pass the supplementary regulations provided that the latter do not alter the local jurisdictions.

1110. Furthermore, by constitutional mandate the Provinces are empowered with the attributions as follows: (i) To lay down rules for the management and use of the natural resources under their jurisdictions, as they are given original domain over

419. Specially they seek to prove if for the Project they have complied with the provisions under Law 23879 (Hydraulic Works) in its ss 1, 2 and 3, under the Law 25675 (General Environment Law) in its ss 11, 12 and 13 (Environmental Impact Appraisal), and 19, 20 and 21 (Public Hearings), as well as s. 7 of the Law 26639 (Law on Minimum Budgets for Glaciers).
420. Ruling CSJN 5258/2014 Whereas No 8.
421. Nestor Cafferatta. Perspectivas del Derecho Ambiental en Argentina http://www.planetaverde.org/arquivos/biblioteca/arquivo_20131101100031_4499.pdf.

them (section 124 of the National Constitution); (ii) to pass the necessary rules to foster the protection of the environmental rights, the rational use of the natural resources, the preservation of the natural and cultural heritage, and the environment formation, and to supplement the rules with the minimum protection estimates in environmental matters (section 41 of the National Constitution), (iii) to establish the administrative organization regulations and (iv) to exert the power not delegated to the federal Government by the National Constitution.

1111. The regulations about minimum environmental estimates, established under section 41 of the National Constitution afore-cited are those laid down by the National Congress so as to guarantee the basis for the minimum protection at a national level. In order to achieve a sustainable development, these rules consecrate a set principle of public order which will be a fundamental guide for the suitable development of the productive activities, in such a way that they meet the environmental protection parameters.[422]

1112. In this analysis, it is worth further mentioning that the National Constitution consecrated as from its last reform of 1994 that the natural resources are original domain of the provinces. As it is not a power delegated by the national administration, the management of the resources belongs to the Provinces and they are the one regulating their use, respecting the parameters fixed by the National Constitution and the federal rules.

1113. In this section, the environmental regulations of minimum contents currently in force and applicable to the impacts generated by the infrastructure projects are succinctly analysed, any and all times that the suitable identification of the regulatory framework in force is fundamental for the right use of the environmental management plans of the projects.

I. Law No 24051 on Hazardous Waste

1114. This is a law of minimum[423] contents which regulates the generation, manipulation, transport, treatment and final availability of dangerous waste generated or placed (i) in places submitted to national jurisdiction, (ii) in territory of one province when they were destined to the transport out of it, or when, in the competent authority's opinion, such waste could affect the people or the environment outside the territory in which it has been generated.

---

422. '*The National Constitution in its Section 41, incorporates a new right: the right to a balanced and healthy environment. It also defines a philosophical position regarding the use of the environment that most authors think it is about the inclusion of the sustainable development principle. This section also contemplates the protection of the environment from the part of the population in general, and with more concrete mandates from the part of the State.*' Pastorino Leonardo F. El Daño al ambiente. First Edition – Lexis Nexis, Argentina.

423. This law is regulated by Decree 831 dated on 23/4/93.

1115. It is as well applicable when the relevant hygiene or security measures have such a sensitive economic impact that it is advisable to inform them in the whole territory of the Nation.

1116. Pursuant to section 2, hazardous waste is defined as the one that can cause damage, direct or indirectly, to living organisms or can pollute the soil, the water, the atmosphere or the environment in general; thus it is applicable to several elements handled in the construction and operation of energy projects specially the hydrocarbon ones.

1117. The definition of generator is found in section 14, which establishes that it refers to any and all individual or legal person who, as a result of his acts or of any other process, operation or activity, produces waste qualified as hazardous. They have to request their registration in the National Registry of Generators and Operators of Hazardous Waste.

1118. Furthermore, there are other concepts about treatment and final disposition plants. The treatment plants are those in which the waste is modified, in such a way that their harmful properties are removed or their material resources and/or energy is recovered, or else a less dangerous waste is obtained, or it is susceptible to be recoverable, or more secure for transportation or final disposition. The final disposition plants are places especially conditioned for the permanent deposit of hazardous waste in environmental security conditions.

1119. The Law establishes the principle of the generator's liability for the damage caused due to the hazardous waste, which entails the obligation of reparation. Moreover, it does contain regulations for the application of sanctions.

1120. All the regulations establish standards of binding compliance for most of the activities handling hydrocarbons and especially for those related to the use of chemicals applicable to non-conventional fields.

II. General Act on Environment nª 25675

1121. This law from 2002 establishes minimum estimates for the suitable and sustainable management of the environment, for the protection and preservation of biological diversity and the implementation of sustainable development, and also defines objectives for the environmental policy at a national level.

1122. In its section 6, it defines the rule of minimum environmental estimates as the one 'that gives a uniform or common protection for the whole national territory and is aimed at imposing the necessary conditions to guarantee the environmental protection. The necessary conditions to guarantee the dynamics of the ecological systems, to maintain its load capacity and in general, to ensure the environmental preservation and the sustainable development are to be covered in its contents'.

1123. As from 2002, the National State has been exercising its power to pass regulations on minimum estimates of environmental protection through the enactment of laws such as:

- Law No 25612 of Industrial Waste.
- Law No 25670 of the regulation of the PCBs use in electrical installations.
- Law No 25688 of Environment Management of the Water.
- Law No 25831 about Public Environmental Information.
- Law No 25916 of Domestic Waste.
- Law No 26331 of Native Forests.

The General Law of Environment 25675, contains principles of environmental policy (sections 4 and 5), introduces the category of collective environmental damage[424] (section 27) and incorporates in the Argentinean legislation the collective environmental process among other important provisions, establishing to that respect protection application at a national level.

1124. Among other instruments on environmental policy and management defined by the Law No 25675 there is the environmental legal system of the territory defined in sections 9 with the following scope: *'The environmental legal* system *will develop the Nation's global operating structure of the and this will be generated by the inter-jurisdictional coordination between the town halls and the provinces, and the latter and Buenos Aires City with the Nations through the Federal Environmental Council (COFEMA) which shall consider the interests reconciliation among the different sector in the Society with one another, and between them and the public administration'.*

1125. This instrument tends to an essential coordination among the different sectors of competences in relation to activities with environmental impact covering several jurisdictions at a territorial level.

1126. In such a frame, in all the jurisdictions the estimates regarding environmental management established by this law such as the following are to be considered:

- Assessment of Environmental Impact: It is establishes that *'Any and all activity that, in the territory of the Nation, be susceptible of degrading the environment, any of its components, or affecting the quality of life of its population in a significant way, shall be subject to an assessment procedure of environmental impact before its execution'.*

---

424. 'The collective environmental damage is the one affecting the community's heritage or one of its sectors, of a supra-individual, non-differentiated collective nature, according to the harmonic interpretation of the General Argentinean Environmental Law about this negative relevant alteration or modification of the environment, the ecosystem's equilibrium, its resources, goods or collective values'. Nestor Cafferatta. Perspectivas del Derecho Ambiental en Argentina, http://www.planetaverde.org/arquivos/biblioteca/arquivo_20131101100031_4499.pdf.

Pursuant to that, the requirements of the environmental impact assessment are depicted in the special laws and the respective competent authorities determine the approval or not of the studies put forward.

- Environment Information: In accordance with this instrument, those developing activities that can degrade the environment must present the information and all inhabitants shall be entitled to obtain from the authorities the environmental information not legally kept as confidential. On the other hand, the authorities have the responsibility of informing about the condition of the environment and the possible effects that the current and future anthropic activities may cause to it.
- The Community Participation: Regarding this topic, so sensitive in activities having a potential impact over the surrounding communities, it is establishes that any and all individual is entitled to be consulted and to give their voice about administrative procedures related to the environment conservation and protection.

To that effect, the authorities have the legal burden of institutionalize consulting procedures and public bids as an obligatory stage for the authorization of those activities that may generate significant negative impacts over the environment. Although the participants' opinions or objections are not binding for the competent authorities, their contribution is anyway important since, in the case of not considering them the authorities have the obligation of indicating the publicly well-founded reasons for their decisions.

III. Law No 25688 on Environmental Management of Water

1127. This law establishes the minimum environmental estimates for the conservation, use and rational utilization of the water.[425]

1128. This law also sets forth the competent authority to give permits of water use, especially in the case of inter-jurisdictional basins. It also established that the national competent authority must set the pollution maximum limits acceptable for the waters pursuant to the different uses and draft a National Plan for the conservation, use, and rational use of the waters to be enacted as a law by the Congress of the Nation.[426]

425. Passed: 28 Nov. 2002. Enacted: 30 Dec. 2002.

426. This law, which was not regulated, was harshly criticized by the specialists as they do not consider it strictly a rule defining environmental protection minimum contents, and since it assumes powers for the Nation which have not been delegated by the Argentinean provinces and that should be subject to the coordination of the concurrent topics which the provinces and the Nations possess, such as for example the regulation of the non-sailable uses of the interprovincial rivers. *See* regarding that 'El agua, principal elemento del medio ambiente una polémica ley argentina la ley 25688 de gestión ambiental del agua y su posible incidencia sobre el acuerdo del colorado y el COIRCO (Río Colorado inter-jurisdictional Committee) Aldo GUARINO ARIAS http://www.acaderc.org.ar/doctrina/articulos/el-agua-principal-elemento-del-medio-ambiente.-una/at_download/file.

IV. Law No 25831 on the Regime of Free Access to Public Environmental Information

1129. The principles about environmental information and the community participation contained in the General Law of Environment are supplemented by Law No 25831 passed in 2003,[427] which establishes the minimum estimates to guarantee the right to environmental information access[428] which are in the hands of the State, in the national, provincial and municipal jurisdictions and that of the Buenos Aires City, as well as those of independent agencies and companies rendering public services whether they are public, private or mixed.

1130. As it was previously mentioned, all matters related to investment in natural resources and energy, deemed as strategic for the society in general having great social and environmental impact at the same time, force the projects regarding their development to be under the public scrutiny, even more than other sectors of the economy.

1131. In this context, it is important – because it represents a current affair – to point out that the Supreme Court of Argentina in the case '*Giustiniani, Rubén Hector against/ Y.P.F. S.A. about/amparo due to arrears*', in relation to the delivery of a copy of the YPF Project investment agreement with the Company *Chevron Corporation*, has highlighted that even though section 7 subsection c of the Law No 25831 establishes that the information requested can be denied whenever the commercial or industrial secret or the intellectual property could be affected, such restrictions *'must be truly exceptional'* and that the reservation shall only be admissible to guarantee others' rights or reputation, or the national security protection or the public order or the health or public moral.[429]

1132. The case was about the access of private individuals to the agreement entered into regarding non-conventional hydrocarbons field exploitation activities in the area of 'Vaca Muerta', Neuquén Province. The plaintiff, protected by the law regarding access to public information, wanted to obtained information derived from the agreements between the companies involved, since they considered YPF S.A was a company with a majority state stake, thus it was obliged to reveal the agreement due to law. In this case, it was considered that the right to seek and receive information had been expressly consecrated by the American Declaration of the Human Rights and Duties of the Man (section IV) and by section 13.1 of the American Convention of Human Rights (CADH).[430]

---

427. Law 25831 was enacted on 6th of January 2004.
428. Environmental information is deemed as any and all information in any way of expression or support whatsoever related to the environment, the natural or cultural resources and the sustainable development. (Section 2 Law 25831).
429. Giustiniani, Rubén Héctor against/ Y.P.F. S.A. about/ Protection of right due to default, 10 Nov. 2015. 338:1258.
430. The Inter-American Commission of Human Rights has interpreted to that respect that s. 13 of the Convention (CADH) includes the right to Access to information in the hands of the State and has resulted in that *'the people have the right to request … documentation and information kept in the*

1133. The Supreme Court decided that YPF S.A was under the spectrum of the law covering the access to public information for various reasons; among others, it considered that the law regulating the activity exercised by YPF S.A, (section 1° Law No 26741) declared it of national public interest. The very same law expressed the fundamental role YPF S.A has in the activity to meet objectives of public interest (Title III Law No 26741). Thus, the Supreme Court ruled that '*so, and as the very same law recognizes it, the company develops important and transcendent activities in which the public interest is involved; hence, in the frame of the principles of a democratic society and based on the cited case law and doctrine, it can't deny information of undoubtedly public interest, regarding the transparency and publicity of its management*'.[431]

§2. Risks Related to Social-Environmental Impact

1134. Many energy infrastructure projects, due to their characteristics of a wide territorial extension, great logistics, and mobilization of provision of goods and services produce significant impacts in the surrounding communities.

1135. In the case of infrastructure projects related to hydrocarbons exploitation, and even the stage of Wells operation, several impacts are observed, among others those related to for example the logistics in handling the waters. At an international level, there have been impacts by the hydrocarbons movements produced when the capacity of the oil and gas pipeline exceeds, which has brought about as a consequence impacts in the communities and important deteriorations in the ways, apart from the several serious accidents with spill of oil and its derivatives. Another clear example of this risk is identified in the construction stage with the high use of the routes by the contracting companies in the transfer of their workers, equipment and supplies.

1136. Moreover, from the social point of view, the impacts caused by the arrival of new inhabitants in the area of the projects has been analysed since with a difference in salaries they distort the local prices, especially those of the real estate. Moreover, with the increase in the quantity of workers, there are alcoholism and prostitution issues, and lack of labour opportunities among the internal migrants.[432]

1137. An improper handling of these risks may cause overcharges due to the delay in the project in the event of demonstrations among the inhabitants. Consequently, the study of the public opposition should be considered as an important factor to measure the success of the Project. The mitigation of these risks has derived in the need for (i) a greater social participation to deal with these impact issues over

---

public archives or processed by the State' and, in general any and all type of 'information deemed as of public source or … as official governmental documentation' Ruling CSJN 338:1258. Whereas No 6.

431. Ruling CSJN 338:1258 Whereas No 17.

432. This topic is masterly depicted in the work of Bianchi, Alejandro. 'La Argentina Saudita'. Ed. Suramericana, 2015.

the community, (ii) an improvement in the spreading of essential information of the projects and (iii) the companies' commitment to have high standards in their policies in relation to corporate social responsibility (CSR) and other compensation actions regarding the negative impacts on the populations.

1138. In this aspect, the companies have assumed certain commitments at a legal level with the social environment in which they operate, including laws about the hiring of local workers, goods and services.

1139. Likewise, the companies themselves have tried to obtain a social license identified in the mining-energy projects industry with the term *Social Licence to Operate* (SLO) drafted with the support of the affected parties (*stakeholders*).[433,434]

1140. Hence, the aspects of the social impact handling of the projects can be summarized as follows:

- Rules about Social Corporate Responsibility (RSE).
- Rules about hiring labour and of 'buy local'.
- Rules about free access to information and community's participation in the public hearings.
- Rules about the community's participation and information about sensitive matters of the impact during the operation such as the joint environmental control and the operations closing processes.
- Rules about alternative productive promotion projects alternative to the hydrocarbon exploitation lasting beyond the projects.
- Rules about specific commitments on the local infrastructure improvements, for instance, on water supply sources and ways.
- Rule to intervene jointly with the communities with anticipation in the negative social impacts, such as the increase in the real estate prices in the areas of influence of the projects or social issues such as alcoholism, prostitution and the abandonment of the Project.

These social and environmental aspects are a clear benefit for the smooth development of the activity since a proper treatment brings about the right environment between the industry and the community.

---

433. The NGO 'Business for Social Responsibility (BSR)', in its report considers that 'to meet the social expectations entails obtaining the Social License to Operate. This means that company has gained the support of the interested parties (stakeholders) for the execution of the project, over the legal requirements for its exploitation. '*The Social License to Operate*' '*Minera El Desquite Report Esquel, Argentina*' Annex 4 www.bsr.org.

434. This SLO topic has been critical in the evaluation of the high social impact projects and has caused debates in the industry about the real scope of the commitment in this sense well beyond the legislation in force. This with respect to the licensing which supposes a permit, however the truth is that the projects may reach a level of tolerance, even if regulatory standards are obeyed and the companies do their best to gain social acceptance. To that respect, *see* the article *'Rethinking Social License to Operate – A Concept in Search of Definition and Boundaries'* 7(2) Business Council of British Columbia – Environmental and Energy Bulletin May 2015, http://www.bcbc.com/content/1708/EEBv7n2.pdf.

I. The World Bank's Environmental Standard

1141. The advancement of the international corporation in relation to the environment protection has had its relationship with the rules developed by the multilateral credit agencies so as to establish a compliance standard applicable to the infrastructure projects financed by such agencies.

1142. Mainly, the World Bank has designed environmental standards that have also been applied to other institutions such as the International Financial Corporation (IFC) and the Overseas Private Investment Corporation (OPIC) whose compliance is incorporated in the relevant contracts of the investment projects in the energy sector.

1143. The '*World Bank Social and Environmental Standards*' have been defined as those rules, practices and safeguards defined by the World Bank and applicable to the projects financed and/or guaranteed by the Bank.[435] For example, in our country, in the renewable energy generation projects of the Renovar Program[436] the compliance of this standard is an essential condition for the validity and enforceability of the guaranteed given by the World Bank.[437]

1144. The following Performance Rules about Social and Environmental Sustainability of the IFC have been incorporated to the Terms and Conditions of the Renewable Energy International Bids of:

- Performance Rule 1: Assessment and Management of the Social and Environmental Impacts and Risks.
- Performance Rule 2: Labour Conditions and Work.
- Performance Rule 3: Efficiency in the use of Resources and pollution prevention.
- Performance Rule 4: Community's health and security.
- Performance Rule 5: Land acquisition and involuntary resettlement.
- Performance Rule 6: Biodiversity Conservation and Sustainable management of live natural resources.
- Performance Rule 7: Indigenous Communities.
- Performance 8: Cultural Heritage.

1145. The Performance Rule no1 establishes the importance of: (i) an integral assessment to identify the project's social and environmental opportunities, impacts,

435. http://go.worldbank.org/USUSUJSRL0.
436. https://www.minem.gob.ar/www/833/25413/renovar-programa-de-energias-renovables.
437. In the Treaty of Adhesion and Incorporation to the Fund for Renewable Energy Development of the Renovar Program it is established under s. 5.3: '*World Bank Regulations. The Validity and Enforceability of the World Bank Guarantee subject to the compliance from the part of the Seller of the Rules about Forbidden Practices of the World Bank and the Social and Environmental Rules of the World Bank. The seller recognizes and accepts that the non-compliance of the Rules about Forbidden Practices of the World Bank and the Social and Environmental Rules of the World Bank can bring about, in the cases provided in the World Bank Guarantee, to the temporary suspension or cancellation of such World Bank Guarantee*'.

risks; (ii) an effective participation from the part of the community, based on the spreading of the project's information and the consultation to the local communities about the topics they are directly affected by; and (iii) the client's management of the social and environmental performance during the course of the project. In the cases in which social or environmental risks or impacts are identified, they shall be managed by means of a social and environmental management system.

1146. Similarly, it is considered that the guides about environment, health and security of the World Bank Group are technical documents of reference with general and specific examples of good international practices in the sector. The IFC uses these guides as a technical source of information during the assessment of the projects. In the IFC rules it is established that when the rules of a host country defer in levels and measures included in the guidelines, it is expected that the projects comply with the most demanding of the two options.

1147. Even though all the risks and possible pertinent social and environmental impacts are to be considered in the context of the assessment, some Performance Rules, such as Rule No 7 about the indigenous Peoples, demand special attention.

II. Analysis of Regulations in Argentina Regarding Original Communities in the Frame of Energy Infrastructure Projects

1148. As part of the social impact analyses of the projects, the special affectation cases of indigenous peoples living in the area near the settlements have been repeatedly dealt with. The indigenous peoples are those whose lands and natural resources are part of their culture and identity.

1149. The National Law No 23302 about indigenous politics and support to the indigenous communities recognizes the support, attention, development, protection and full participation of the original communities living in the country as of national interest respecting their values and customs. section 2 of this legal body establishes that '*Indigenous communities are those sets of families recognized as such for the mere fact that they descend from population that lived in the national territory at the time of the conquest or colonization and indigenous to those belonging to such community. The legal identity shall be obtained by means of the registry in the Indigenous Communities Registry Office and shall be extinguished by means of its cancellation.*'

1150. The differential treatment of the so-called original peoples' rights that the national law has, especially for the transcendence the topic has acquired in the Constitutional Reform of 1994, makes it necessary to analyse the legal implication in the management of the projects related to the energy infrastructure development.

1151. Thc prevailing principle in the topic, incorporated into the National Constitution, has been the recognition of the pre-existence of the original communities to the State. This has forced to change the whole legal system to adapt it so as to guarantee the recognition of the original communities and the protection of their cultural heritage.

1152. The constitutional reform of 1994 incorporated into the National Constitution under section 75, its subsection 17 the powers of the National Congress in this topic with the scope as follows: '… *to recognize the ethnic and cultural pre-existence of the Argentinean indigenous peoples. To guarantee the respect to their identity and the right to a bilingual and intercultural education; to recognize the legal identity of its communities, and the communal ownership and possession of the lands they traditionally occupy; and to regulate the delivery of others apt and sufficient for human development; none of them shall be either alienable or transferrable or susceptible to attachment or embargo. To guarantee their participation in the referred management of the natural resources and other interests affecting them. The provinces can concurrently exercise these powers.*'

1153. As it can be seen, there are numerous implications about the constitutional recognition expressed in this rule, above all regarding the energy infrastructure projects development, since it is related to guarantee their participation in the management referred to 'their' natural resources and other 'interests' affecting them.

1154. This expression is fundamental in the environmental management plan development of the projects, since to effectively comply with the constitutional mandate, the original communities recognized as such pursuant to the regulations in force, are called to participate in any way in the management of the natural resources involved.

1155. Furthermore, it is important to consider that in 2000, Argentina ratified the Convention169 of the World Labour Organization (WLO) about Indigenous and Tribal Peoples, which started to be in force and was incorporated to the national legislation in 2001. In this international Treaty, Argentina's position in terms of consecrating the rights of the indigenous communities was reaffirmed. Consequently, obligatory rules concerning possession and ownership of land as well as the indigenous peoples' participation in the administration of natural resources were strengthened as well.

1156. The WLO Convention 169 imposes a fundamental obligation for the Signing States regarding the indigenous communities' rights recognition. In its section 14 it is laid down that '*The interested peoples are to be recognized the right of ownership and possession over the land they traditionally occupy …* ' thus imposing that the States being part of the Convention give the ownership of the land to the indigenous communities and so adjust their legal bodies for the compliance in that sense.

Section 15 of the WLO Convention 169, clearly sets forth the way to regulate the indigenous communities' participation in relation to the natural resources. The section reads: '*1. The rights of the peoples' concerning the natural resources in their lands shall be specially safeguarded. Those rights include the right of these peoples to participate in the use, management and conservation of such resources. 2. In the case in which the State retains the ownerships of minerals or sub-surface resources or have rights over other resources pertaining to the land, the governments shall establish or keep procedures through which they shall consult these peoples, so as to determine if the interests of those peoples' could be prejudiced, and to what extent, before undertaking or permitting any exploitation or exploration program of the resources pertaining to the land. The people concerned shall participate as long as it is possible in the benefits of those activities, and to receive a fair compensation for any damages they may suffer as a result of those activities.'*

1157. This section 15 re-affirms what is set forth in subsection 17 of section 75 of the NC, when explicitly establishing the obligation of the State to guarantee the effective participation of the indigenous peoples in the use, management and conservation of the natural resources according to their interests. It further establishes the scope of this right recognizing the possibility (i) to participate in the benefits and (ii) to receive a compensation for damages derived from the exploitation of the resources.

1158. Likewise, in the Civil and Commercial Code of the Nation, some substantial amendments were introduced regarding indigenous peoples in comparison with the derogated Civil Code. This legal body regulates all issues related to the indigenous property in the title 'Law and Goods'. Section 18 of the Civil and Commercial Code establishes that '*the indigenous communities have the right to the ownership and possession of the lands that they traditionally occupy and of those apt and sufficient for the human development pursuant to the law, in accordance with provisions under section 75 subsection 17 of the National Constitution.*'

1159. Moreover, the Civil and Commercial Code establishes in its section 240 the limits to exercise the individual rights over the goods. In this legal body, it is laid down that the individual rights have a limit over the rights of collective incidence, such as those of the indigenous communities. The concerned section establishes that the exercise of the individual rights must be '*compatible*' with the rights of collective incidence and must conform to the local and rules of national and local administrative law, as well as to those public interest inside which we can find those of the original communities. So much so that the same section expressly consecrate as a limitation that '*cultural values*' are not to be affected either'[438]

1160. In compliance with the international Treaties in the subject, Law No 23302 consecrates in its title 'IV' the regime of land adjudication. Section 7 of the same law establishes '*Proceed to adjudicate lands apt and sufficient for farming,*

438. According to the specialized doctrine '*the concepts of property and possession of the indigenous communities lands, since they have a collective meaning, that is to say, not belonging to a single individual, but to the group, has no correlation with the individual property, which is the one legislated in the the civil codes*' criteria that, according to this opinion is coherent to the interpretation made by the Inter-American Court of Human Rights. Vázquez, 2012:949. Cited in La Propiedad Comunitaria Indígena en el CCYC. Revistas Electrónica del Instituto de Investigaciones Ambrosio L. Gioja, 2016, Year X Number 16, PP 79-9, Buenos Aires.

forestry, mining, industrial or craft exploitation to the indigenous communities duly registered and existing in the country according to every community's modality. The lands are to be situated in the place where the community lives, or in the most proximate area for their development. The adjudication shall be carried out choosing the communities having insufficient or no land at all; this can also be done in favour of indigenous non-integrated to communities favouring those who are part of a family. The competent authority shall as well be in charge of giving the definitive deeds who those having temporary or precarious ones'.

1161. Furthermore, this law establishes the differential modalities and characteristics regarding the ownership rights. The adjudication of the lands to the indigenous communities shall be done by gratuitous title and the beneficiaries shall be exempt from national taxes, and free from administrative rates and fees (section 9), the lands they will possess shall be non-sizeable or unenforceable (section 11). The competent authority shall draft the adjudication and exploitation plans of the lands. It is fundamental to consider that the lands shall be awarded to the communities without taking into account the property domain ownership.[439]

1162. In this context, Law No 26160 declared the emergency regarding the possession and the ownership of the lands which were traditionally occupied by the indigenous communities. Under its section 2, it is established the suspension, for the term of the emergency, of the execution of sentences, procedural or administrative acts aiming at the eviction of the lands in possession of the original communities which are registered in the National Registry of Indigenous Communities pursuant to the national or provincial legislation.

1163. In the same sense, the Supreme Court of the Nation has confirmed the application of this law revoking sentences which disposed an eviction injunction over the indigenous lands. In the case 'Martínes Pérez, José Luis c. Palma, América and others about/ injunction about/ cassation',[440] the Supreme Court revoked the injunction ordering the eviction from lands being occupied by the community applying Law No 26160; and it was clear that the communities did not occupy the lands on a date around that of injunction's but that '*they had been exercising that traditional indigenous possession from years gone*'; thus the suspension of the evictions consecrated by law, is applicable for the ancestral connection exiting between

439. Section 8 of the Law 23302 establishes that '*The competent authority shall draft, to that effect, adjudication and exploitation plans for the lands pursuant to the provisions of the law in force and of the specific provisions of the regulations in force about this, so as to promptly perform the adjudication of the fiscal lands owned by the Nation to the corresponding beneficiaries. The Executive Power shall dispose the transfer of the lands affected to that end to the competent authority for the granting of the possession and further respective deeds. If, in the place where the community was settled, there were no fiscal lands owned by the Nation, apt and available, the transfer of provincial or communal fiscal lands shall be disposed for the purposes indicated herein, or its direct adjudication by the provincial government or the municipal one. If necessary, the competent authority shall dispose the expropriation of the lands privately-owned to the Executive Power that will promote the necessary laws before the National Congress'.*

440. Martínes Pérez, José Luis c. Palma, América and others about/ injunction about/ Cassation' Supreme Court of the Nation 10/11/2015.

the communities and their land even though the community has actually been occupying the land for a short period of time.

1164. To sum up, from the regulations previously analysed, we can observe the way in which the Argentinean legal body as from the Constitutional Reform of 1994 has tended to give more protection to the original communities. Such protection is broadly speaking developed by means of three main factors: the recognition of their legal status, the adjudication of the land that they traditionally occupy and their participation regarding the natural resources management.

1165. In addition to that, it is important to highlight that in 2005, the World Bank approved a policy for the indigenous peoples. Such policy was designed to offer them participation and access to the information of the projects. As it was aforementioned, one of Performance Rules about Social and Environmental Sustainability of the IFC specifically refers to the issue of the indigenous peoples.[441]

1166. Hence, when evaluating the risks of the projects in general, and especially in relation to investment in energy infrastructure, it is crucial to know the rules operating in the law to protect the indigenous communities' rights. Regarding the relevant factors about original communities, when planning energy infrastructure projects, first it is important to spot the communities settled in the territory in which the Project is to be developed so as to establish the existence of registered communities or that could potentially enjoy that recognition. This is due to the fact that those communities registered and with legal status recognized by law, shall have all the protection of the laws analysed in this work given to indigenous communities, including those regarding the participation in the benefits based on their interests. Second, if registered communities are identified, it should be considered that the lands that they traditionally occupy could be adjudicated to them and any and all procedural or administrative act ordering an eviction from those lands shall be suspended.

---

441. Performance Rule No 7 recognizes the Indigenous Peoples as social groups with different identities from those of the dominant groups in the national communities, generally in more marginal and vulnerable sectors of the population. In many cases, their financial, social and legal situation limits their capacity to defend their rights and interests regarding lands and cultural and natural resources, and can limit as well their capacity to participate in the development and enjoyment of their benefits. They are especially vulnerable if their lands and resources are significantly modified, occupied or deteriorated. Their languages, cultures, religions, institutional and spiritual beliefs can also be affected. Thus, the Indigenous Peoples can be more vulnerable to the adverse impacts associated to the development of the project than the non-indigenous communities. This vulnerability may entail the loss of identity, culture and means of subsistence dependent on natural resources, as well as the exposition to diseases and impoverishment. The projects of the private sector can create opportunities for the Indigenous Peoples to participate and be benefited from the activities connected to those projects, and at the same time can help them to meet their social and economic development expectations. Besides, the Indigenous Peoples can perform roles in sustainable development, promoting and carrying out activities and companies, as partners in the development. In general, governments play a key role in the management of issues related to the Indigenous Peoples and the clients should contribute with the authorities responsible for the management of the risk and impact of their activities.

1167. So, a fundamental factor to assess in the development of energy infrastructure projects is the one related to the participation modalities that the original communities must necessarily have in the management of the natural resources in the territories they traditionally occupy, since the lack of participation could bring about legal and disvalued operative consequences in the execution thereof.

Selected Bibliography

Aguilar Valdez, Oscar R., 'Reflexiones sobre las funciones jurisdiccionales de los entes reguladores de servicios públicos a la luz del control judicial de la Administración – con especial referencia al Ente Regulador del Gas y de la Energía Eléctrica', Anuario de Derecho de la Universidad Austral, Vol. I, Abeledo-Perrot, 1994.

Aguilar Valdez, Oscar, 'Entes reguladores de servicios públicos. Apuntes sobre su funcionamiento y perspectiva en argentina', Revista Ibero-Americana de Direito Público, Año 4, 2o Trimestre de 2003, Volumen X, América Jurídica, Brazil.

Alsina, Mario Á. et al., Código Aduanero comentado, Abeledo-Perrot, Buenos Aires, 2011.

Altamirano, Alejandro C., Derecho tributario: teoría general, Marcial Pons, Buenos Aires, 2012.

Althabe, Mario Enrique, El impuesto sobre los ingresos brutos, La ley, Buenos Aires, 2010.

Álvarez Echaguöe, Juan Manuel (dir.), Derecho constitucional financiero y tributario local, Ad-Hoc, Buenos Aires, 2015.

Álvarez Echaguöe, Juan Manuel (dir.), Tributación local: provincial y municipal, Ad-Hoc, Buenos Aires, 2010.

Arthur, B., 'Competing technologies, increasing returns and lock-in', Economic Journal 99, 1989.

Artigues (dir.) A., 'Le financement d'une électricité verte: le cas de la souscription volontaire des consommateurs', Working Paper, CREDEN-LASER (Cahier de Recherche), 2004.

Assoumou, E., 'Modélisation MARKAL pour la planification énergétique a long terme dans le contexte français', thèse Ecole de Mines de Paris, 2006.

Atkeson, A. & Kehoe, P.J., 'Models of Energy Use: Putty-Putty Versus Putty-Clay' American Economic Review, 89(4), 1999.

Averch H. & Johnson, L., Behavior of the Firm under Regulatory Constraint, AERW, 1962.

'Balance de gestión en energïa 2016 – 2019,' Secretaria de Gobierno de Energia, Buenos Aires, 2019.

Balassa, Bela, The Theory of Economic Integration, Homewood, Richard D. Irwin, 1961.

Banco Interamericano de Desarrollo (BID), Integración Energética en el Mercosur Ampliado, estudio realizado por Mercados Energéticos S.A., Washington, 2001.

Selected Bibliography

Barlet, M. & Crusson, L. 'Quel impact des variations du prix de pétrole sur lacroissance française?', Economie et Prévision, No 188, 2009.

Barreiro, Rubén A., Derecho de la energía eléctrica, Ábaco, Buenos Aires, 2002.

Barreiro, Rubén A., Derecho de la energía eléctrica. Dinámica legal, derechos y obligaciones del usuario. Tratamiento exegético del Marco Regulatorio Eléctrico. Texto ordenado de las leyes 15.336 y 24.065 y normas reglamentarias. Comentado, concordado y anotadocon jurisprudencia administrativa y judicial, Buenos Aires, Ábaco, 2002.

Barrera, Mariano A., La entrega de YPF: análisis del proceso de privatización de laempresa, Buenos Aires, Atuel, 2014.

Bastos, Carlos M. & Abdala, Manuel A., Transformación del sector eléctrico argentino, Pugliese Siena, Córdoba, 1995.

Benabou, R. & Tirole, J., 'Individual and Corporate Social Responsibility', Economica, 77, London School of Economics, 2010.

Berndt, E.R. & Woodt, D.O., 'Engineering and Econometric Approaches to Industrial Energy Conservation and Capital Formation: a Reconciliation', MT.

Energy Laboratory, Working Paper no MIT-EL77 040 WP, noviembre, 1977.

Berndt, E.R. & Woodt, D.O., 'Engineering and Econometric: Interpretations of Energy Capital Complementarities', the American Economic Review, junio 1979.

Berndt, E.R. & Woodt, D.O., 'Technology, Prices and the Derived Demand for Energy' Review of Economics and Statistics, agosto, 1975.

Berthelemy, J.C. & Devezeaux de Lavergne, J.G., 'L'impact des chocs pétroliers.Una simulation rétrospective 1973-1982', Revue Economique No 3, mayo, 1987.

Boehringer, C., 'The Synthesis of Bottom-Up and Top-Down in Energy Police Modeling', Energy Economics, 20(3), 1998.

Bertero, Raúl, 'Integración Regional Gasífera – Ciento ochenta años de proyectos de integración', Revista Petrotecnia, junio 2007.

Besando, Dranove & Shanley, Economics of Strategy, Wiley & Sons, 1996, 135.

Bielsa, Rafael, La locución justo y razonable en el derecho y la jurisprudencia, La Universidad, Rosario, 1942.

Blake, G., Pratt, M., Schofield, C., & Brown, A.A. (eds), Boundaries and Energy: Problems and Prospects, Kluwer Law International, London, 1998.

Blaug, M., History of economic thought, 1990.

Bodemer, Klaus, 'Integración energética en América del Sur: ¿eje de integración o fragmentación?', Una región en construcción. UNASUR y la integración en América del Sur, Manuel Cienfuegos y José Antonio Sanahuja (eds), Barcelona, Fundación CIDOB, 2010.

Boiteux, M., Sur la gestion des monopoles publics astreints a l'équilibre budgétaire, Econometrica, 1956.

Bosch, Juan, 'El método de cálculo tarifario en el sector eléctrico nacional', en ReDA, Lexis Nexis Depalma, Buenos Aires, 2004, No 49.

Boullade, Gustavo & Massimino, Leonardo, 'Marco Regulatorio del Gas en Argentina', en Karina Cicero (dir.), Derecho Administrativo, Legislación Usual Comentada, La Ley, Buenos Aires, 2015.

Bouvet, L'unité de gisement: Hydrocarbures et autres matières mineraux, L'Harmattan, 2004.

Bravo, Víctor, '¿Por qué privatizar YPF?', Realidad Económica, No 110, agosto-septiembre, 1992.
Bulit Goñi, Enrique G. (coord.), Derecho tributario provincial y municipal, Ad-Hoc, Buenos Aires, 2002.
Bulit Goñi, Enrique G., Constitución Nacional y tributación local, Ad-Hoc, Buenos Aires, 2009.
Bulit Goñi, Enrique G., Impuesto sobre los ingresos brutos, Depalma, Buenos Aires, 1997.
Bull, Hedley, La sociedad anárquica: un estudio sobre el orden en la política mundial, Madrid, Los Libros de la Catarata, 2005.
Caballero Santos, 'Tres hitos del proceso de integración sudamericana a la luz de las teorías de las Relaciones Internacionales', presentación ante el Seminario de Investigadores en Formación, Miraflores de la Sierra, noviembre de 2008.
Caballero Santos, Sergio, El MERCOSUR ideacional: un enfoque complementario para la integración regional sudamericana, Rosario, Centro de Estudios de Relaciones Internacionales de Rosario, octubre-diciembre, 2009.
CAMMESA, Informe Anual 2014. Disponible en http://www.cammesa.com/linfoanu.nsf/MINFOANU? Open FrameSet.
Cassagne, Ezequiel, 'Análisis contractual y normativo del desarrollo de la generación de energías renovables en la Argentina', RADEHM, No 3, 2014.
Cassagne, Juan Carlos Curso de derecho administrativo, 11a ed., Thomson Reuter La Ley, Buenos Aires, 2016.
Cassagne, Juan Carlos, 'La crisis de los servicios públicos en Argentina', Servicio Público y Policía, Juan Carlos Cassagne (dir.), El Derecho, Universitas, Buenos Aires, 2006, p. 386.
Cassagne, Juan Carlos, Cursode Derechoadministrativo, LaLey, Buenos Aires, 2011.
Cassagne, Juan Carlos, Derecho Administrativo, Abeledo-Perrot, Buenos Aires, 2009.
Cassagne, Juan Carlos, El Contrato Administrativo, Abeledo-Perrot, Buenos Aires, 1999.
Caubet, Amanda B., Trabajo y seguridad social, La ley, Buenos Aires, 2013.
CEPAL, El regionalismo abierto en América Latina y el Caribe, Santiago de Chile, CEPAL, 1994.
CEPAL, Integración Eléctrica en América Latina: antecedentes, realidades y caminospor recorrer, Beno Ruchansky (coord), febrero, 2013.
CEPAL, Recursos naturales en UNASUR. Situación y tendencias para una agenda de desarrollo regional, Serie Recursos Naturales e Infraestructura. Disponible en: www.eclac.org/cgi-bin/getProd.asp?xml=/publicaciones/xml/3/49893/ P49893 .xml&xsl=/tpl/p9f.xsl&base=/drni/tpl/top-bottom.xslt.
Ceppi, Natalia, Encuentros y desencuentros en la gestión bilateral de recursos naturales compartidos: Los casos de la Cuenca del Pilcomayo y la represa Yacyretá, Grupo de Estudios Sociales sobre Paraguay, Facultad de Ciencias Sociales de la Universidad de Buenos Aires – Asociación Paraguaya de Estudios de Población (ADEPO), 2009.
Chari, V.V. & Weber, R.J., 'How the U.S. Treasury should Auction its Debt', Federal Bank of Minneapolis Quarterly Review, fall, 1992.

Selected Bibliography

Cherp and Jewell, 'The Three Perspectives on Energy Security: Intellectual History, Disciplinary Roots and the Potential for Integration', Current Opinion in Environmental Sustainability, Elsevier, agosto, 2011.

Cicero, Nidia Karina (dir.), Legislación usual: derecho administrativo, Buenos Aires, La Ley, 2015.

Cicero, Nidia Karina, 'El procedimiento administrativo en los entes reguladores de los servicios públicos', en G. Tawil (dir.), Procedimiento Administrativo, Abeledo-Perrot, Buenos Aires, 2010.

Comadira, Julio Pablo, 'La potestad normativa de los entes reguladores', Revista Argentina del Régimen de la Administración Pública No 405, Buenos Aires, 2015.

Comadira, Julio Rodolfo, Derecho Administrativo. Acto administrativo. Procedimiento administrativo. Otros estudios, Lexis Nexis Abeledo-Perrot, Buenos Aires, 2003.

Consejo Mundial de Energía, Estudio sobre Integración Energética en América Latina, realizado por el Centro de Estudio de la Actividad Regulatoria Energética de la Universidad de Buenos Aires y el Instituto de Economía de la Universidad Federal de Río de Janeiro, 2006.

Coppers, F. & Vivet, D., The single European electricity market, Bruselas, WP, BNB, 2006.

Corden, V.M. & Neary, J.P. 'Booming sector and de-industrialization in a Small Open Economy', Economic Journal 92, diciembre 1982, pp. 823–848.

Cotter, Juan Patricio, Derecho aduanero, Abeledo-Perrot, Buenos Aires, 2014.

Coviello, Pedro J.J., '¿Qué es la jurisdicción primaria? Su aplicación a nuestro ordenamiento (a propósito de su invocación en el caso Estrada)', El Derecho Administrativo (EDA), 2005.

Criqui, P. & Percebois, J., 'Stratégies énergétiques: cigales et fournis', Economies et Sociétés, no4, série EN, 1988.

Crivelli, Julio César, 'La emergencia y la ruina de la República', elDial.com, 2015.

Crivelli, Julio César, La emergencia económica permanente, Buenos Aires, Ábaco, 2001.

Curien, N., Microéconomie, Ecole Polytechnique, 1997.

Dalla Via, Alberto R., Derecho Constitucional Económico, Lexis Nexis/Abeledo-Perrot, Buenos Aires, 2006.

Damarco, Jorge H (dir.), Derecho tributario: impuesto al valor agregado, La ley, Buenos Aires, 2010.

Damarco, Jorge H. (dir.), Derecho tributario: impuesto a las ganancias, La ley, Buenos Aires, 2010.

Dargay, J., Gately, D. y Huntington, H.G. 'Price and Income Responsiveness of Oil Demand, by Product', Energy Modeling Forum, Stanford University, USA, 61, agosto, 2007.

Dargay, J., Gately, D., 'The Imperfect Price Reversibility of Non-Transport Oilin the OCDE', Energy Economics, vol. 17, no1, 1995, pp. 59–71.

Darmstadter, J. Dunkerley, J. y Alterman J., 'International Variations in Energy Use', in Darmstadter, J. Dunkerley, J. y Alterman J., How Industrial Societies Use Energy, John Hopkins University Press, Baltimore, 1977.

Darmstadter, J., Energy in the World Economy, John Hopkins University Press, Baltimore, 1971.
De Espona, Rafael J., El moderno concepto integrado de seguridad energética, Instituto Español de Estudios Energéticos, 2013.
De Montbrial, Th., La science économique, PUF, 1988.
Deneix de Saint-Marc, R. 'Régulateurs et juges', Journaux Judiciaires Associes, No 17, 2003.
Diaz, A., Puch, L.A. y Guillo, M.D., 'Costly Capital Reallocation and Energy Use', The Review of Economic Dynamics, vol. 7, numero 2, 2004, pp. 494–518.
Díaz, Vicente Oscar, Impuesto de sellos, Errepar, Buenos Aires, 2009.
Dievert, W.E., Applications of Duality Theory, M.D. Intriligator y D.A. Kendrich(eds) Frontiers of Quantitative Economics, Amsterdam, North Holland Publishing Co., 1974.
Diez, Gustavo E., Impuesto a la ganancias, La ley, Buenos Aires, 2011.
Diez, Manuel M., Derecho Administrativo, Bibliográfica OMEBA, Buenos Aires, 1967.
Doucet, J., Percebois, J., 'Certificats noirs, verts et blancs: effets croises et impacts potentiels dans le marche de l'électricité', Cahiers du CABREE, Centre for Applied Business Research in Energy and the Environment, Universidad de Edmonton (Canada), diciembre 2006, p. 44.
'Environment Policies: Reconciling Bottom-Up and Top-Down', The Energy Journal, Numero Especial, 2009.
Esmaeili, H., The Legal Regime of Offshore Oil Rigs in International Law, Ashgate, London, 2001.
Etman, Gustavo E.L., 'Impuesto inmobiliario', en lvarez Echaguöe, Juan Manuel (director), Derecho constitucional financiero y tributario local, Buenos Aires, Ad-Hoc, 2015.
Fenochietto, Ricardo, El impuesto al valor agregado, La ley, Buenos Aires, 2007.
Fericelli, A.M., Principes de microéconomie, PUF, 1991.
Fernndández, Luis Omar, Impuesto a las ganancias: teoría, técnica y prÁctica, La ley, Buenos Aires, 2015.
Ferrara, P., Sovereignty Disputes and Offshore Oil & Gas, Nomos, 2016.
Ferrara P. (Ed.), Tratado de Regulación de la Energia, IAE Mosconi, Buenos Aires, 2017 (2 Vol).
Figueroa Pla, Uldaricio, Organismos Internacionales, Teorías y Sistemas Universales, RIL editores, Santiago de Chile, 2010.
Fonrouge, Máximo 'Cuestiones del procedimiento Administrativo ante los entes reguladores', AA.VV., Cuestiones de procedimiento administrativo, Ediciones RAP, Buenos Aires, 2006.
Fundación de Investigaciones Latinoamericanas (FIEL), La regulación de lacompetencia y de los servicios públicos. Teoría y práctica Argentina reciente, FIEL, Buenos Aires, 1999.
Gadano, NicolÁs, Historia del petróleo en la Argentina: 1907-1955: desde los inicioshasta la caída de Perón, Buenos Aires, Edhasa, 2006.
García Belsunce, Horacio A. (director), Tratado de tributación, Astrea, Buenos Aires, 2004.

Selected Bibliography

García Vizcaíno, Catalina, Tratado de derecho tributario, Abeledo-Perrot, Buenos Aires, 2014.

Gardini, Gian Luca, 'Proyectos de integración regional sudamericana: haciauna teoría de convergencia regional', Relaciones Internacionales, núm. 15, octubre 2010, Grupo de Estudios de Relaciones Internacionales (GERI) de la Universidad Autónoma de Madrid, España.

Gately, D. and Huntington, H.G., 'The Asymmetric Effects of Changes in price and Income on Energy and Oil Demand', in The Energy Journal 23(1), 2002.

Gebhardt, Jorge, 'Impuesto inmobiliario', en García Belsunce, Horacio A. (director), Tratado de tributación, Volumen II, Tomo 1, Astrea, Buenos Aires, 2004.

Geman, H., Commodities and commodity derivatives, Wiley & Sons, 2005.

Geman, H., Forward 'Curves, scarcity and price volatility in oil and natural gas markets', Energy Economics 31, 2009.

Gerchunoff, Pablo, Greco, Esteban y Bondorevsk, Diego, 'Comienzos diversos, distintas trayectorias y final abierto: más de una década de privatizaciones en Argentina, 1990-2002', Serie Gestión Pública No 34, Instituto Latinoamericano y del Caribe de Planificación Económica y Social (ILPES), CEPAL, Santiago de Chile, abril de 2003. Disponible en: http://cdi.mecon.gov.ar/biblio/doc/cepal/ gespub/3 4.pdf.

Ghiggino, Gonzalo, 'Las relaciones argentino-brasileñas: cómo se fue gestando el acercamiento que dio como resultado el MERCOSUR', Historia de las Relaciones Internacionales, Brumario No 1, Cuadernos de Pensamiento, noviembre-diciembre, 2009.

Ghiggino, Gonzalo, A sesenta años de la ALALC: problemática, inicios y fracaso de la primera integración latinoamericana, Grupo de Estudios Internacionales Contemporáneos, 2011.

Giraud, P.N., Economie industrielle des commodités, Paris IX, 2003.

Giuliani Fonrouge, Carlos M. (actualizado por Navarrine, Susana Camila y Asorey, Rubén O.), Derecho financiero, La ley, Buenos Aires, 2011.

Gonzales Arrieta, Gerardo M., 'Vinculación entre la integración bilateral y multilateral en América Latina: el caso argentino-brasileño en el sector de bienes de capital', Integración Latinoamericana, julio-agosto, 1988.

González Silva, Milko Luis, Nuevas perspectivas de la integración energética en América del Sur, Instituto Latinoamericano de Investigaciones Sociales-ILDIS, Caracas, 2008.

Gordillo, Agustín, Tratado de derecho administrativo y obras selectas, Buenos Aires, FDA, 2013.

Griffin, J.M. & Schulman, C.T., 'Price Asymmetry in Energy Demand Models, a Proxy for Energy-Saving Technical Change', The Energy Journal, 26(2), 2008.

Grisolía, Julio Armando, Tratado de derecho del trabajo y de la seguridad social, Abeledo-Perrot, Buenos Aires, 2013.

Grupo de Estudios del Sector Eléctrico, Integración eléctrica internacional deBrasil: Antecedentes, situación actual y perspectivas, UFRJ, 2015.

Guevara Labal, Carlos, La mística petrolera argentina y el espíritu de YPF, Buenos Aires, Imprenta del Atlántico S.A., 1964.

Guichon, Diego, 'Integración y Seguridad Energética en Países Exportadoresde Saldos', Aportes para el Debate, Asociación de Administradores Gubernamentales, No 22, agosto, 2009. Disponible en: http://www.asociacionag.org.ar/ pdfaportes /22/08.pdf.

Haas, Ernst B., The Uniting of Europe: Political, Social and Economic Forces, 1950-1957, Stanford University Press, Stanford, California, 1958.

Haas, R. & Schipper, L., 'Residential Energy Demand in OECD Countries and the Role of Irreversible Efficiency Improvements', Energy Economics, 20, 1998.

Hamilton, J.D., 'What Is an Oil shock', Journal of Econometrics, vol. 113(2), 2003.

Harvey, Brian W. & Parry, Deborah L., The Law of Consumer Protection and Fair.

Trading, 5ta. ed., Butterworths, Londres, Dublin y Edimburgo, 1998.

Henderson y Quandt, Microéconomie, Dunod, 2003.

Henry, C., Concurrence et services publics dans l'Union européenne, Paris, PUF, 2003.

Herrero, Luis René (dir.), Derecho del trabajo. Seguridad social, La ley, Buenos Aires, 2012.

Hirsh, Richard F., Technology and transformation in the American electric utility industry, Cambridge, Cambridge University Press, 1989.

Hotelling, H., 'The Economics of Exhaustible Resources', Journal of Political Economy, 2003.

Huber, C. & Haas, R., Action Plan for a Green European Electricity Market (EL Green), Energy Economics Group, IPSEE, WP, Universidad Tecnologica de Viena, 2001.

Hudson, E.A., & Jorgenson, D.W., 'The US Energy Policy and Economic Growth', Bell Journal of Economics and Management Science, vol. 5, 1974.

Humphrey, D. & Moroney, J., 'Substitutions among Capital, Labor and Natural Resource Products in American Manufacturing', Journal of Political Economy, febrero 1975.

Hunt, L.C., Judge, G., & Ninomiya, Y., 'Underlying Trends and Seasonality in UK Energy Demand a Sectorial Analysis', Energy Economics 25(1), 2003.

Hyman, Leonard S., America's Electric Utilities. Past, Present and Future, 6th ed., Public Utilities Reports, Arlington, Virginia, 1997.

Instituto Latinoamericano de Investigaciones Sociales (ILDIS), El factor energético y las perspectivas de integración en América del Sur, Caracas, ILDIS/Fundación Friedrich Ebert, 2008.

Janosie, E., & Grayson, L.S., 'Patterns of Energy Consumption and Economic Growth' in The Journal of Development Studies, 8(2) enero 1972.

Jarach, Dino, Curso de derecho tributario, Liceo Profesional Cima, Buenos Aires, 1980.

Jarach, Dino, El hecho imponible: teoría general del derecho tributario sustantivo, Abeledo-Perrot, Buenos Aires, 1971.

Jarach, Dino, Finanzas públicas y derecho tributario, Abeledo-Perrot, Buenos Aires, 1996.

Joskow, P., 'Vertical integration and long term contracts: the case of coal burning electric generating plants', Journal of law, economies and organization, 2003.

Khan, Kameel, 'Some Legal Considerations on the Role and Structure of State Oil Companies: A Comparative View', The International and Comparative Law Quarterly, Vol. 34, No. 3, 1985.

Lapeña, Jorge E., La energía en tiempos de Alfonsín: innovación, planificación estratégica, obras y autoabastecimiento, Buenos Aires, Eudeba, 2014.

Larthou, Juan & Eliaschev, Nicolás, 'La nueva Ley de Hidrocarburos y la competencia en los mercados de electricidad y gas natural', Revista Argentina de Derecho de la Energía, Hidrocarburos y Minería, No 5.

Leicach, Jorge, 'Impuesto sobre los ingresos brutos', en Volman, Mario (dir.),Régimen tributario, La ley, Buenos Aires, 2005.

Levy-Lambert & Dupuy, Les Choix économiques dans l'entreprise et l'administration, Dunod, 2003.

Lewington, Ilka, 'Experiences and Trends in Utility Regulation: Developing and Transforming Economies', Regulatory Review 1997, Centre for the study of Regulated Industries, Chartered Institute of Public Finance and Accountancy, London, 1997.

Lindberg, L. & Stuart, A. Scheingold (eds) Regional Integration: Theory and Research, Cambridge, MA, Harvard University Press, 1971.

Litvine, D., 'Révélation des préférences individuelles et choix de l'électricité verte: une analyse de la décision du consommateur', tesis CREDEN-LASER, Universidad de Montpellier I, 2008.

Livellara, Carlos Alberto (director), Derecho del trabajo y de la seguridad social, La ley, Buenos Aires, 2013.

Llambías, Jorge Joaquín & Alterini, Jorge H., Código Civil Anotado. Doctrina-Jurisprudencia, Tomo IV-A, Derechos Reales, Abeledo-Perrot, Buenos Aires, 1988.

Lorenti, Pedro M., 'Aproximación al régimen jurídico del sector eléctrico en la República Argentina y a sus fuentes en el Derecho comparado', en RAP, Buenos Aires, 1997, No 227.

Losman, Donald L., 'The Rentier State and National Oil Companies: An Economic And Political Perspective', Middle East Journal, Vol. 64, No 3, 2010.

Loulou, R., 'The Slow Convergence of Top-Down and Bottom-Up in Energy Models' Coloquio Internacional del 25 Aniversario GERARD, mayo 11, Montreal, 2005.

Mairal, Héctor A., 'La ideología del servicio público', ReDA, Depalma, Buenos Aires, septiembre-diciembre de 1989, No 14.

Mairet, N., 'Modélisation et déterminants de la demande d'énergie', Working Paper CREDEN-LASER, Universidad de Montpellier I, 2009.

Malamud, Andrés & Schmitter, Philippe, 'La experiencia de integración europea y el potencial de integración del Mercosur', Desarrollo Económico, Revista de Ciencias Sociales, Buenos Aires, Vol. 46, No 181, abril-junio, 2006.

Malinov, Guillermo V., 'Potencial y Desarrollo Hidroelectrico Argentino, Buenos Aires, 2013.

Mansilla, Diego, 'Integración Energética y Recursos Naturales en América Latina', Revista del Centro Cultural de Cooperación [en línea], No 11, enero-abril 2011, No 11. Disponible en: http://www.centrocultural.coop/revista/articulo/212/.

Marchevsky, Rubén Alberto, Impuesto al valor agregado: análisis integral, Errepar, Buenos Aires, 2006.
Marienhoff, Miguel Santiago, Tratado de Derecho Administrativo, Abeledo-Perrot, Buenos Aires, 1995.
Martin, J.M., 'L'intensité énergétique de l'activité économique dans les pays industrialises: les évolutions de très longue période livrentelles des enseignements utiles?', Economies et Sociétés, série EN, no4, abril 1988.
Martin, J.M., Economie et politique de l'énergie, Editions Armand Colin, Coleccion Cursus, 1992.
Martin, J.M., L'économie mondiale de l'énergie, Editions La Découverte, ColeccionRepères, Paris, 1990.
Martínez De Vedia, Rodolfo, Los servicios públicos nacionales (situación actual), RAP, Buenos Aires, 2010.
Martínez de Vedia, Rodolfo, La organización en la regulación de servicios públicos, Ábaco, Buenos Aires, 2003.
Mata, Ismael, 'Panorama del control sobre los entes reguladores', El Derecho Administrativo (EDA), 00/01.
Mata, Ismael, Ensayos de derecho administrativo, RAP, Buenos Aires, 2009.
Medina, E., 'Consommation d'Energie, essai de comparaisons internationals',Economie et Statistique, No 66, abril 1975.
Metcalf, G.E., 'An Empirical Analysis of Energy Intensity and its Determinants at the State Level', The Energy Journal, vol. 29 No 3, 2009.
Meunier y Defeuilley, Gestion du risque et intégration verticale dans l'électricité, Larsen, mayo 2008.
Meunier, F., 'La France et ses partenaires face au second choc pétrolier', Economie et Statistique, No 155, mayo 1983.
Meunier, F., 'Un deuxième choc pétrolier plus éprouvant pour l'économie française', Economie et Statistique, No 149, noviembre 1982.
Mittlestadt, A., 'Utilisation des elasticites de la demande dans l'estimation de la demanda', OCDE, documentos de trabajo No 1 (Dirección de Asuntos Económicos y Estadísticas), Paris, 1983.
Morishimia, M., 'A Few Suggestions on the Theory of Elasticity', Keizai Hyoron, 16, 1967.
Moreau Defarges, Philippe, 'Le multilatéralisme et la fin de l'histoire', Politique étrangère, 2004. Traducción disponible en: http://www.diplomatie. gouv.fr/es/IMG/pdf/0104-Moreau-espAVB-2.pdf.
Nallar Dera, Daniel M., Regulación y control de los servicios públicos, Marcial Pons, Buenos Aires, 2010.
Navarrine, Susana Camila (dir.), Derecho tributario, La ley, Buenos Aires, 2010.
Naveira de Casanova, Gustavo J. (coord.), Régimen Tributario Argentino, Abeledo-Perrot, Buenos Aires, 2011.
Ngoasong, M.Z., 'How international oil and gas companies respond to local content policies in petroleum-producing developing countries: A narrative enquiry', Energy Policy 73, 2014.
Nicchi, Fernando G., Ampliaciones en Infraestructura de transporte de energía eléctrica, Eudeba, Buenos Aires, 2013.

Oklander, Juan, Ley del impuesto al valor agregado: comentada, La ley, Buenos Aires, 2009.
Organización Latinoamericana de Energía (OLADE), Estudio para la identificación de alternativas de solución para las barreras a la integración energética en América Latina y el Caribe, Buenos Aires, CEARE/Universidad de Buenos Aires, 2012.
Ozlak, Oscar, 'Privatización y capacidad de regulación estatal: una aproximación teórico metodológica', Política y gestión pública, Buenos Aires, CLAD-Fondo de Cultura Económica, 2004.
Percebois, J., Economie de l'Energie, Editions Economica, 1989.
Percebois, J., Economie des finances publiques, Editions A. Colin, Coleccion Cursus, Paris, 1992.
Percebois, J., Prix internationaux du pétrole, du gaz naturel et du charbon, ConsejoFrancés de la Energía, 2008.
Perrino, P. 'Entes reguladores, calidad institucional y desarrollo de infraestructura pública', en AA.VV., Cuestiones de Intervención Estatal – Jornadas 2010 – Universidad Austral, RAP, Buenos Aires, 2012.
Perrino, Pablo E. 'Algunos comentarios acerca del régimen jurídico de protección de los usuarios de servicios públicos', Derechos, garantías y potestades enlos contratos públicos, Ediciones RAP, Buenos Aires.
Perrino, Pablo E. 'Elderechoalatutelaadministrativaefectiva', AA.VV.'ElDerechoAdministrativo hoy. 16 años después', Jornadas organizadas por la Universidad Austral, Facultad de Derecho, RAP, Buenos Aires, 2013.
Perthuis (de), C. & Boccon-Gibod, J.C., 'Le marche des quotas de CO2: leçonsd'un an de fonctionnement', Revue d'Economie Financière, 2° trimestre 2006.
Peyrelevade, J., Economie de l'entreprise, Fayard, 1989.
Picard, P., Eléments de microéconomie, Montchrestien, 1994.
Pisarello, María Teresa & Giménez, Susana Liliana, Obligaciones de la Seguridad Social: aspectos prácticos, La ley, Buenos Aires, 2010.
Putnam, P., Energy in the Future, Van Nostrand Pub., New York, 1953.
Pyndick, R.S., 'The optimal exploration and production of non renewablesources', Journal of Political Economy, 1978.
Raimondi, Carlos A. & Atchabahián, Adolfo, El impuesto a las ganancias, La ley, Buenos Aires, 2010.
Ramsay, Iain, Consumer Protection. Text and materials, Weidenfeld and Nicolson, London, 1989.
Ramsey, F., 'A contribution to the theory of taxation', EC Journal, 1927.
Reig, Enrique J., Gebhardt, Jorge & Malvitano, Rubén H., Impuesto a las ganancias: estudio teórico-práctico de la ley argentina a la luz de la teoría general del impuesto a la renta, Macchi, Buenos Aires, 2010.
Reiriz, María Graciela, 'Autoridades administrativas independientes para la regulación y control de los servicios públicos', Temas de Derecho Administrativo en honor al Prof. Doctor Agustín A. Gordillo, Editora Platense, La Plata, 2003.
Rejtman Farah, Mario, '¿Independencia de los entes reguladores?', AA.VV Cuestiones de intervención estatal. Servicios públicos, RAP, Buenos Aires, 2011.

Revilla, Pablo J. M., 'Impuesto de sellos', en Naveira de Casanova, Gustavo J. (coordinador), Régimen Tributario Argentino, Abeledo-Perrot, Buenos Aires, 2011.

Reynes, F. & Yeddir-Tamsamani, Y., 'Substituabilité des facteurs et rendement d'échelle sectoriels en France: une estimation par une fonction de cout flexible', OFCE, WP no2009-37, diciembre 2009.

Ricciardi, Darío A.,'Reflexiones sobre aspectos de la regulación tarifaria enlos servicios públicos del sector eléctrico', en ReDA, Lexis Nexis Depalma, Buenos Aires, 2004, No 48.

Rivera Banuet, José, 'Una visión sobre la integración energética regional'.Presentación en el Foro de OLADE sobre Integración Energética Regional, México, 7 de septiembre de 2006.

Rochet, J.C. yTirole, J., 'Two-sided markets: a progress report', Rand Journal of Economics, 2006.

Rodríguez Manzano, Irene, 'Funcionalismo, Neofuncionalismo y Relaciones Internacionales. Dos contribuciones doctrinales al estudio de la organización internacional', Revista Dereito, Vol. 5, No 1, 2006.

Rojas, Gustavo & Arce, Lucas, La renegociación de Itaipú: una nueva oportunidadpara el Paraguay, Observatorio Económico de la Red MERCOSUR, 2008. Disponible en: www.oered.org.

Romero, Luis Alberto, Breve historia contemporánea de la Argentina, Buenos Aires, Fondo de Cultura Económica, 1994.

Ruiz Caro, Ariela, 'La integración y la cooperación energética en América Latina y Caribe', Puente@Europa – Año VIII – No 1, abril, 2010.

Sabato, Jorge, Por una política nacional de la energía eléctrica, Nueva Vida, Buenos Aires, 1945.

Salanie, B., Les défaillances du marché, Economica, 1988.

Samuelson, P.A., 'Proof that properly anticipated prices fluctuate randomly', Industrial Management Review, 6:2, 1965.

Sanahuja, José Antonio, 'Regionalismo e integración en América Latina: balance y perspectivas', Revista Pensamiento Iberoamericano, 2007.

Sanahuja, José Antonio, La construcción de una región: Suramérica y el regionalism posliberal, Fundación CIDOF/Cienfuegos y Sanahuja editores, Barcelona, 2010.

Schindel, Ángel (dir.), Derecho tributario, La ley, Buenos Aires, 2015.

Schumpeter, Capitalism, Socialism and Democracy, 1942.

Shrestha, R.K., 'Uncertainty and the Choice of Policy Instruments, a Note on Baumol and Oates Propositions', Environmental and Resource Economics, 12, 1998.

Silva de Alfano, María Graciela Andina – Schneider, Rolando, 'La reestructuración del sector eléctrico argentino a través del actual marco regulatorio: Aspectos novedosos', en AAVV, Jornadas Jurídicas sobre Servicio Público de Electricidad, Ente Nacional Regulador de la Electricidad, 8 y 9 de junio de 1995.

Simesen de Bielke, Sergio A. & Eguöez, Hermosinda, 'El impuesto sobre los ingresos brutos', en Álvarez Echaguöe, Juan Manuel (director), Derecho constitucional financiero y tributario local, Ad-Hoc, Buenos Aires, 2015.

Smeers, Y., 'Regulation if the restructures electricity sector – Somme comments', WP, CORE-UC Louvaine, 2009.

Sobrecasas, Roberto P., Los contratos en el mercado eléctrico, Abaco, Buenos Aires, 2003.
Soler, Osvaldo H., El impuesto de sellos, La ley, Buenos Aires, 2001.
Soler, Osvaldo H., Tratado de derecho tributario: económico, constitucional, sustancial, administrativo, penal, La ley, Buenos Aires, 2014.
Solow, R., 'The Capital-Energy Complementarity Debate Revisited', The American Economy Review, vol. 77, 1987.
Stoffaes, C., Entre monopole et concurrence, Paris, PAU, 1994.
Taverne, B., Petroleum, Industries and Governments, Kluwer Law International, London, 1999.
Tawil,G.,EstudiosdeDerechoAdministrativo,Abeledo-Perrot, Buenos Aires, 2012.
Tawil, Guido S., 'El procedimiento administrativo ante los entes regulado-res', en AAVV. Procedimiento Administrativo, Ciencias de la Administración, Buenos Aires, 1998.
Thompson, P.y Taylor, T., 'The Capital-Energy Substitutability Debate: a New Look', in The Review of Economic and Statistics, vol. 77, 1995.
Tordo, Silvana. 'National Oil Companies and Value Creation', World Bank working paper no 218, 2011. Disponible en: http://siteresources.worldbank.org/INTOGMC/Resources/9780821388310.pdf.
Tosi, Jorge Luis, Código aduanero: comentado, anotado, actualizado con legislacióncomparada latinoamericana, Cathedra Jurídica, Buenos Aires, 2014.
Trillo Figueroa Martínez Conde, Jesús y de Borja López Jurado Escribano, Francisco, La regulación del sector eléctrico, Civitas, Madrid, 1996.
Uslenghi, Alejandro, 'Reforma de organismos de control de los servicios públicos', Derecho Administrativo y aportes para el rediseño institucional de la República, Revista Jurídica de Buenos Aires, Abeledo-Perrot, Buenos Aires, 2004.
Uzawa, H., 'Production Functions with Constant Elasticities of Substitution', Review of Economic Studies, octubre 1962.
Vergara Blanco, Alejandro, Derecho eléctrico, Jurídica de Chile, Chile, 2004.
Vidal Quera, Gastón F., 'Impuesto inmobiliario', en Naveira de Casanova, Gustavo J. (coordinador), Régimen Tributario Argentino, Abeledo-Perrot, Buenos Aires, 2011.
Vieira Posada, Edgar, 'Evolución de las Teorías sobre Integración en el contexto de las Teorías de Relaciones Internacionales', Papel Político No 18, Pontificia Universidad Javeriana, Colombia, 2005.
Villegas, Héctor B., Curso de finanzas, derecho financiero y tributario, Astrea, Buenos Aires, 2005.
Viña, Gonzalo Ariel, 'Hacia un control de YPF y la industria hidrocarburífera', Revista Argentina de Derecho de la Energía, Hidrocarburos y Minería, no 10 (agosto-octubre), 2016.
Volman, Mario (director), Régimen Tributario, La ley, Buenos Aires, 2005.
Voogt, M., Boots, S, & Martens, J.W., 'Renewable Electricity in a Liberalized Market: the Concept of Green Certificates', Energy and Environment 11, 2000.
Weitzman, M.L., 'Prices Versus Quantities', Review of Economic Studies, 41, 1974.
Wide Industry-Level Emission Trading to Reduce Greenhouse Gases – Results from PRIMES Model', Bruselas (EEC), 2000.

Yacimientos Petrolíferos Fiscales, YPF, una empresa al servicio del país 1922-1972, Buenos Aires, Departamento de Difusión y Ceremonial de YPF, 1972.
Zagame, P., 'Modeles de l'energie et nouvelles theories de progress technique', Working Paper, Conseil francais de l'energie, Paris, diciembre 2008.
Zardkoohi, Asghar, 'Competition in the Production of Electricity', en Moorhouse, John C. (ed.), Electric Power Deregulation and the Public Interest, Pacific Research Institute for Public Policy, San Francisco, California, 1986.

Selected Bibliography

Index

The numbers here refer to paragraph numbers.

Index

www.ingramcontent.com/pod-product-compliance
Ingram Content Group UK Ltd.
Pitfield, Milton Keynes, MK11 3LW, UK
UKHW020134290926
15471UKWH00003B/470

9 789403 527109